volume 2 Inner Heart

Alice 19th

story and art by **Yuu Watase**

Alice 19th
volume 2 Inner Heart

STORY & ART BY
Yuu Watase

English Adaptation/Lance Caselman
Translation/JN Productions
Touch-Up Art & Lettering/Walden Wong
Cover Design & Layout/Izumi Evers
Editor/Andy Nakatani

Editor in Chief, Books/Alvin Lu
Editor in Chief, Magazines/Marc Weidenbaum
VP of Publishing Licensing/Rika Inouye
VP of Sales/Gonzalo Ferreyra
Sr. VP of Marketing/Liza Coppola
Publisher/Hyoe Narita

Printed in Canada

Published by VIZ Media, LLC.
P.O. Box 77010 · San Francisco, CA 94107

10 9 8 7 6 5
First printing, December 2003
Fifth printing, February 2008

www.viz.com
store.viz.com

RATED T+ FOR OLDER TEEN

PARENTAL ADVISORY
ALICE 19th is rated T+ and is recommended for ages 16 and up. This volume contains violence, frightening situations, and partial nudity.

ratings.viz.com

The story thus far:
Alice Seno, a seemingly normal girl in high school, encounters a mysterious magical rabbit girl who introduces her to the sublime power of the Lotis Words. But power always comes with a price and Alice's sister, Mayura, accidentally gets sent into a world of darkness. Joined by hunky upperclassman, Kyô Wakamiya, Alice sets out to save her sister. From out of nowhere, a mysterious man named Frey appears to claim Alice as his fiancée and he also offers his support to save Mayura. But who is this man and can he really be trusted?

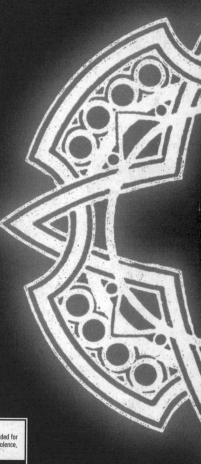

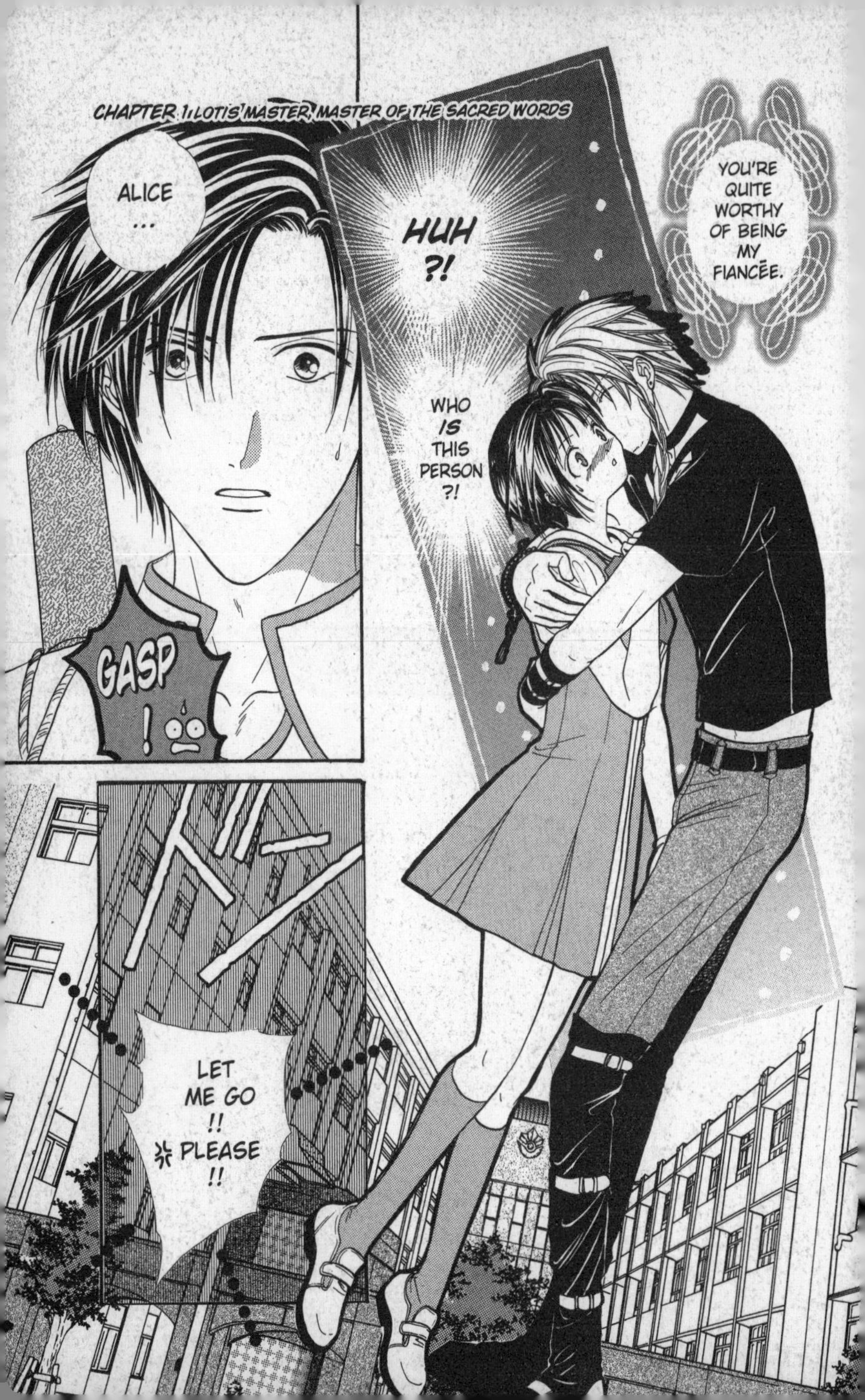
CHAPTER 1: LOTI'S MASTER, MASTER OF THE SACRED WORDS
YOU'RE QUITE WORTHY OF BEING MY FIANCÉE.
HUH?!
WHO IS THIS PERSON?!
ALICE...
GASP!
LET ME GO!! PLEASE!!

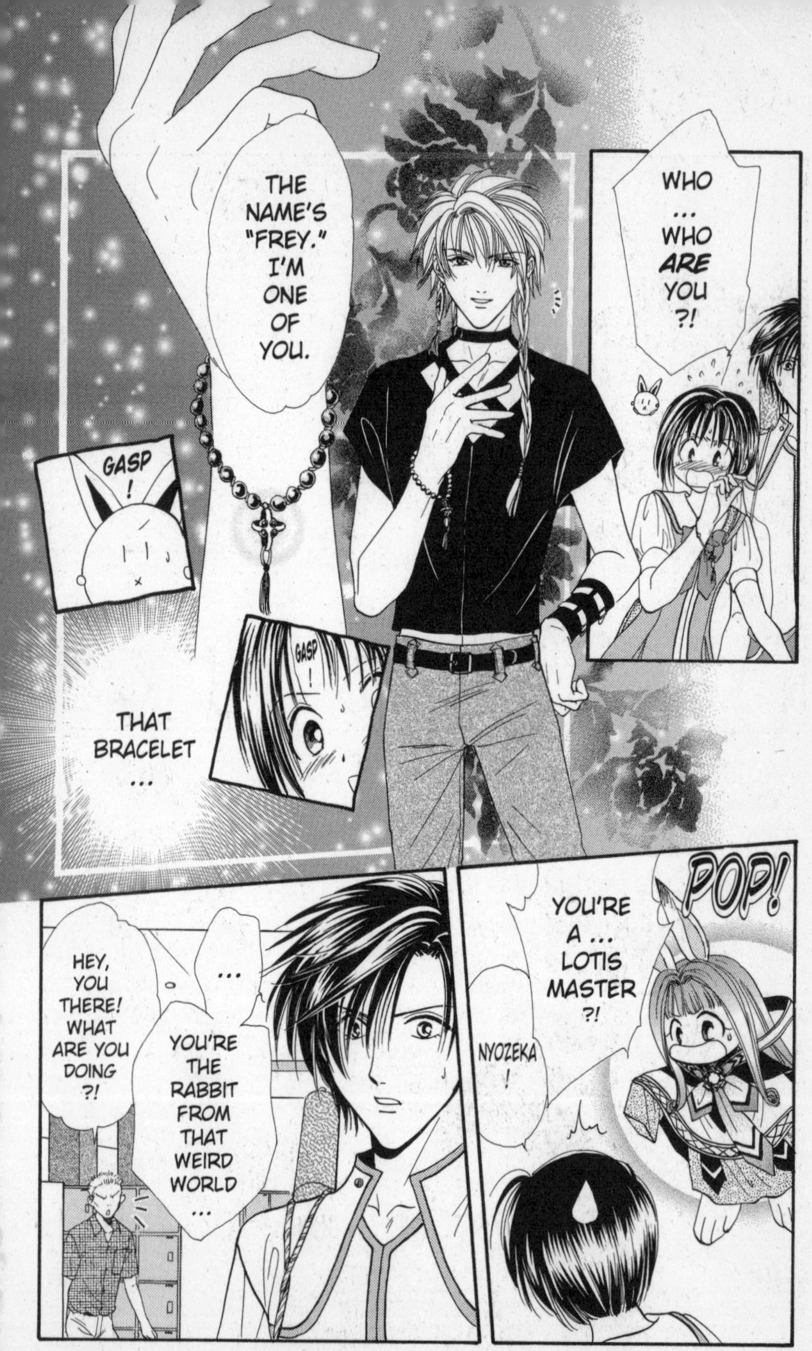

WHO ... WHO ARE YOU ?!
THE NAME'S "FREY." I'M ONE OF YOU.
GASP !
GASP !
THAT BRACELET ...
POP!
YOU'RE A ... LOTIS MASTER ?!
NYOZEKA !
...
YOU'RE THE RABBIT FROM THAT WEIRD WORLD ...
HEY, YOU THERE! WHAT ARE YOU DOING ?!

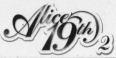

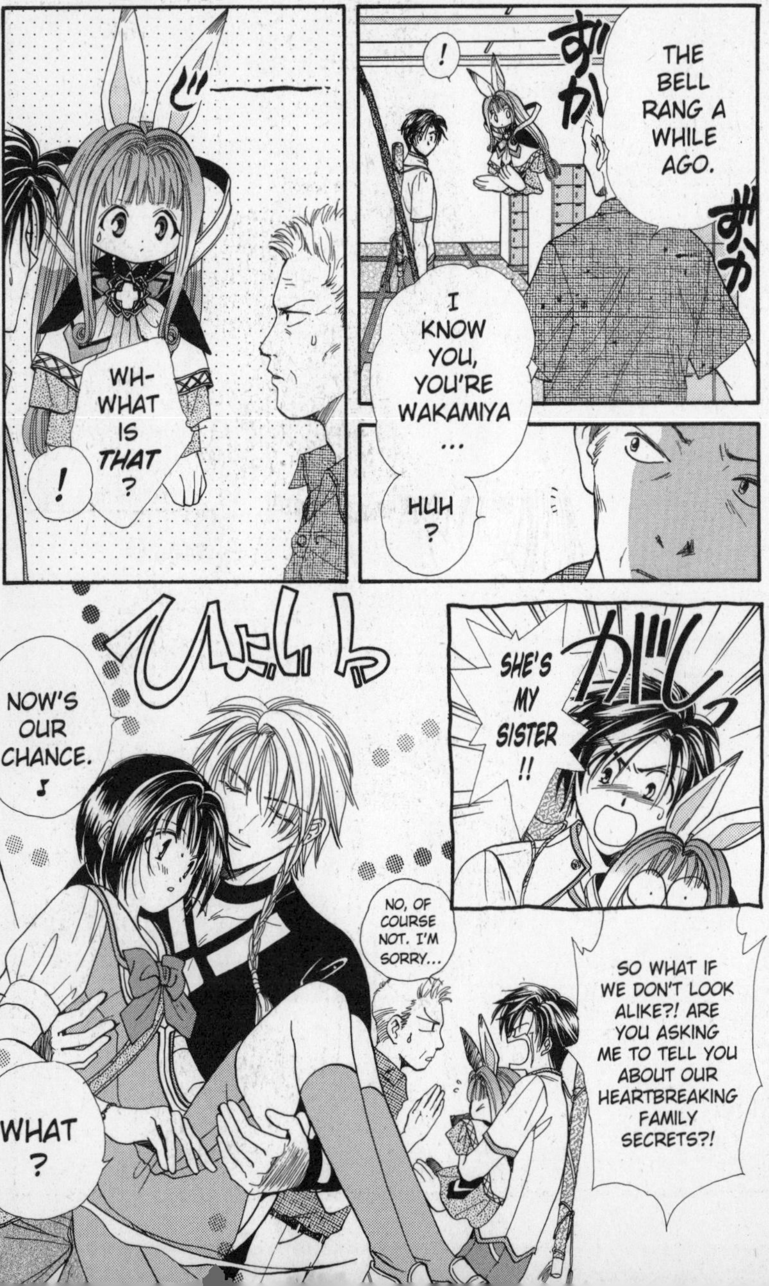
THE BELL RANG A WHILE AGO.
ずか
ずか
!
I KNOW YOU, YOU'RE WAKAMIYA ...
HUH ?
じー
WH-WHAT IS *THAT* ?
!
SHE'S MY SISTER !!
がしっ
SO WHAT IF WE DON'T LOOK ALIKE?! ARE YOU ASKING ME TO TELL YOU ABOUT OUR HEARTBREAKING FAMILY SECRETS?!
NO, OF COURSE NOT. I'M SORRY...
NOW'S OUR CHANCE. ♪
WHAT ?

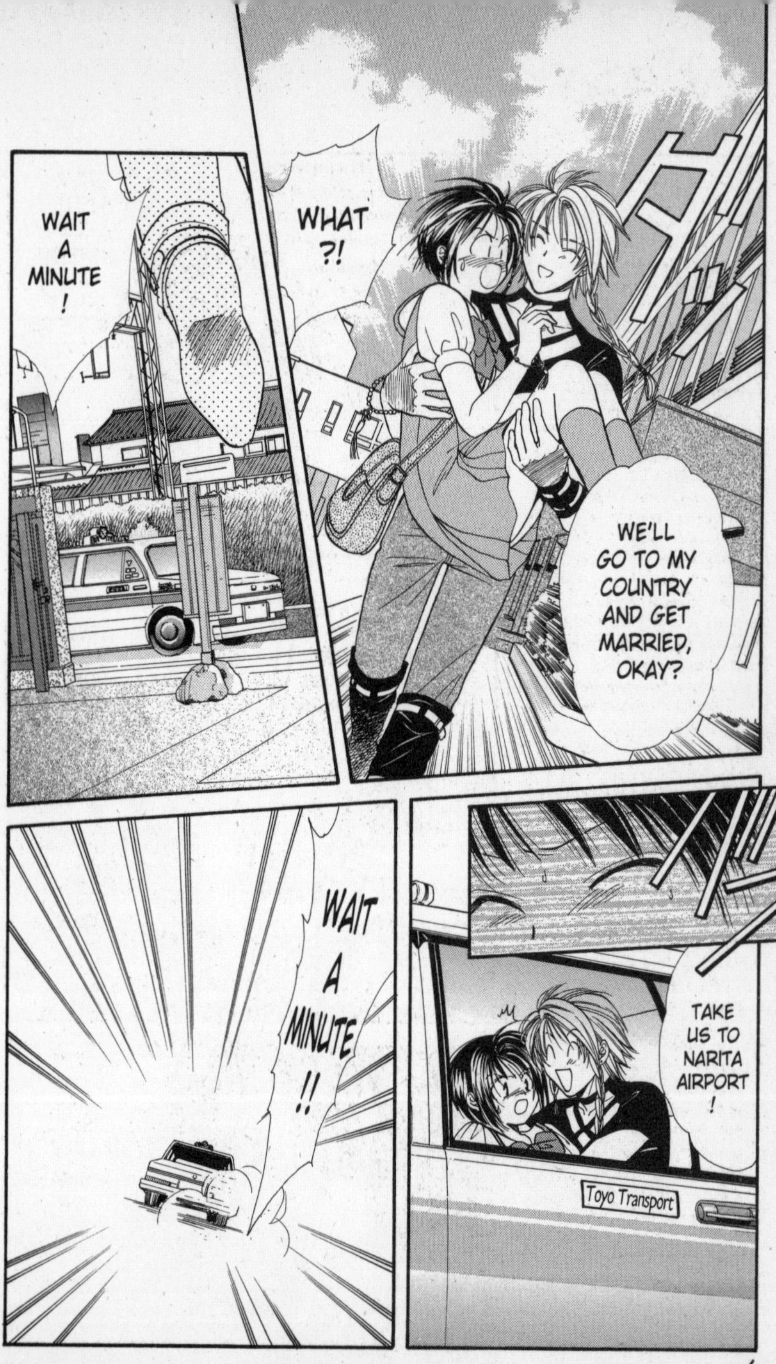
WHAT ?!
WE'LL GO TO MY COUNTRY AND GET MARRIED, OKAY?
WAIT A MINUTE !
TAKE US TO NARITA AIRPORT !
Toyo Transport
WAIT A MINUTE !!

AND THERE'S A GOOD REASON MY SISTER DRESSES THIS WAY!
It happened one cold, snowy morning. I was curled up at the kotatsu heater, stud
OKAY, OKAY !!
SEND YOUR SISTER HOME AND GET BACK TO CLASS!
YES, SIR!
WE'RE THE MOST UNLIKELY SIBLINGS IN THE WORLD!
IT WAS THE BEST I COULD COME UP WITH ON SHORT NOTICE.
SO WHAT EXACTLY IS GOING ON, ALICE?

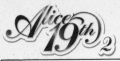

Thanks for reading this comic! We've got some special music in the background that my assistant always plays when things get hectic. The tape has only Final Fantasy battle music and up-tempo music. Oddly enough, when I hear fast songs, it seems like my hands move faster, too.
Well... Do any of you have recommendations for good background music to work to? I want more video game sound tracks. Alice 19th is a fantasy, so when I'm drawing a battle sequence, I want to listen to an appropriate battle song.
When I worked on Ceres, I always created battle scenes while listening to techno. But that doesn't fit the Alice 19th image. Depending on the world that you are creating, sometimes even the greatest piece of music won't be a good fit.
By the way, when I'm working on regular scenes I like to listen to the soundtrack for Earth Girl Arjuna. Maya Sakamoto is just a great singer! Sakamoto's Easy Listening is very beautiful. It's nice bittersweet music. It's great! Actually, singers like Enya are good, too. Are you getting a picture of what I like? I am very fond of music. I don't care much for Japanese pop, although I like some songs. Maybe I'm just strange!
Ever since I was a kid, I've never had much interest in regular mass market entertainment in Japan. Even now, most of my information comes from my assistants and cable radio programs.
And the rest comes from lunchtime variety shows. ☺
But if I ever do a manga about the world of show business, I'm sure I'll do some thorough research.

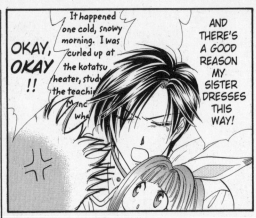

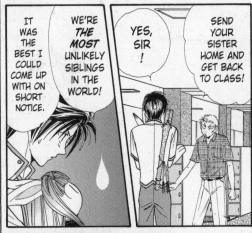

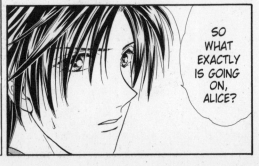

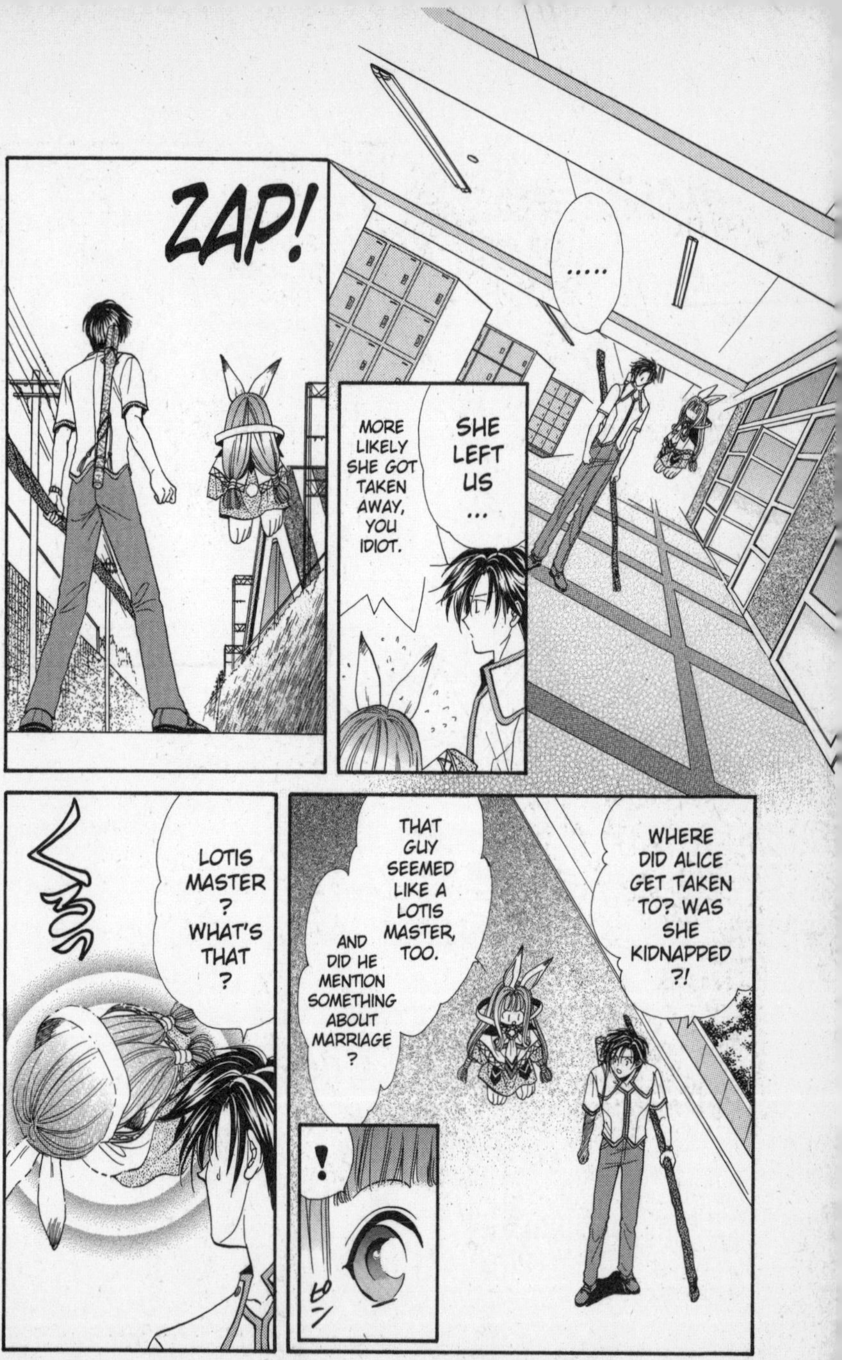
.....
SHE LEFT US ...
MORE LIKELY SHE GOT TAKEN AWAY, YOU IDIOT.
ZAP!
WHERE DID ALICE GET TAKEN TO? WAS SHE KIDNAPPED ?!
THAT GUY SEEMED LIKE A LOTIS MASTER, TOO.
AND DID HE MENTION SOMETHING ABOUT MARRIAGE ?
!
LOTIS MASTER ? WHAT'S THAT ?

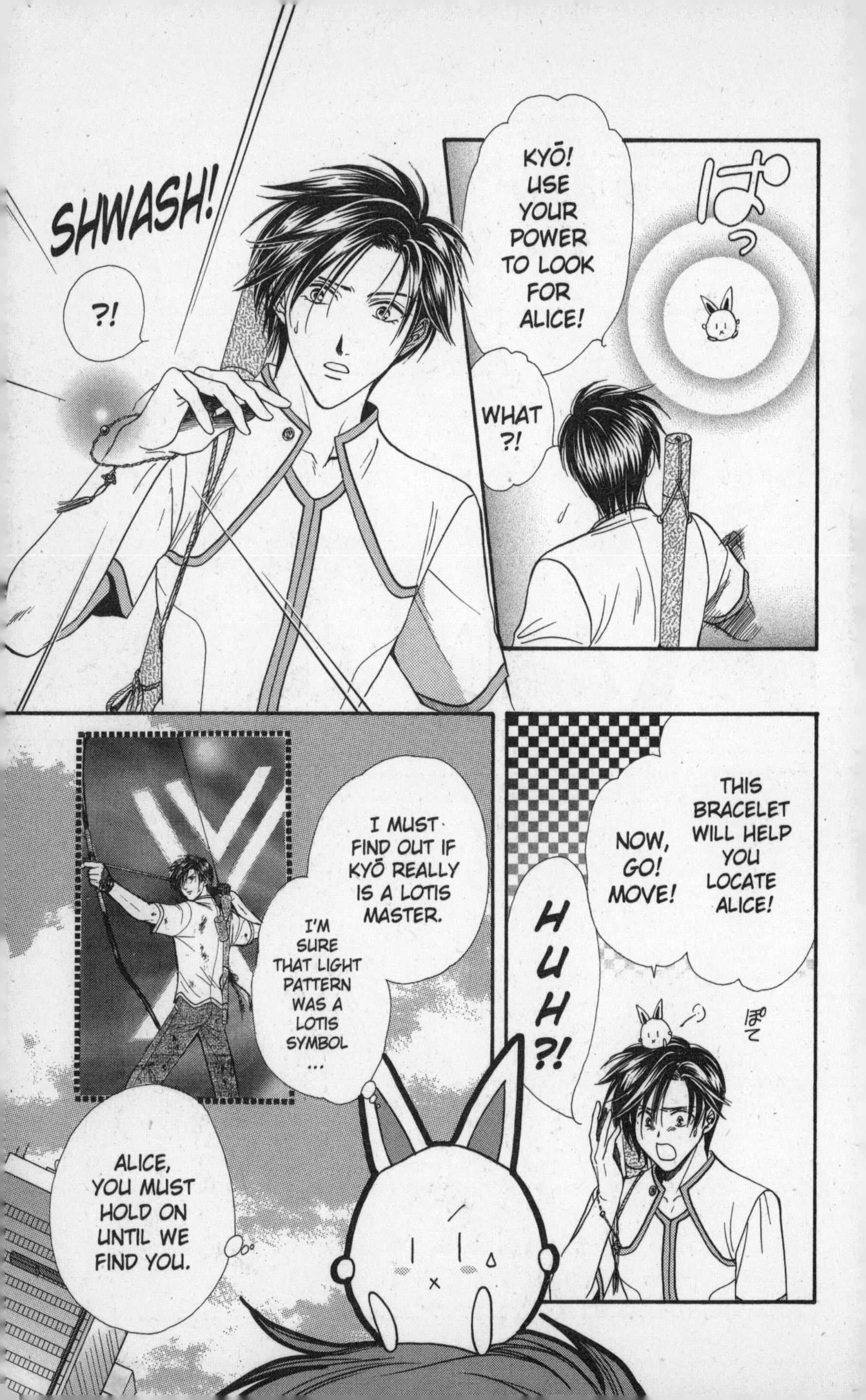
KYŌ! USE YOUR POWER TO LOOK FOR ALICE!
ぱっ
WHAT ?!
SHWASH!
?!
THIS BRACELET WILL HELP YOU LOCATE ALICE!
NOW, GO! MOVE!
HUH?!
ぽて
I MUST FIND OUT IF KYŌ REALLY IS A LOTIS MASTER.
I'M SURE THAT LIGHT PATTERN WAS A LOTIS SYMBOL ...
ALICE, YOU MUST HOLD ON UNTIL WE FIND YOU.

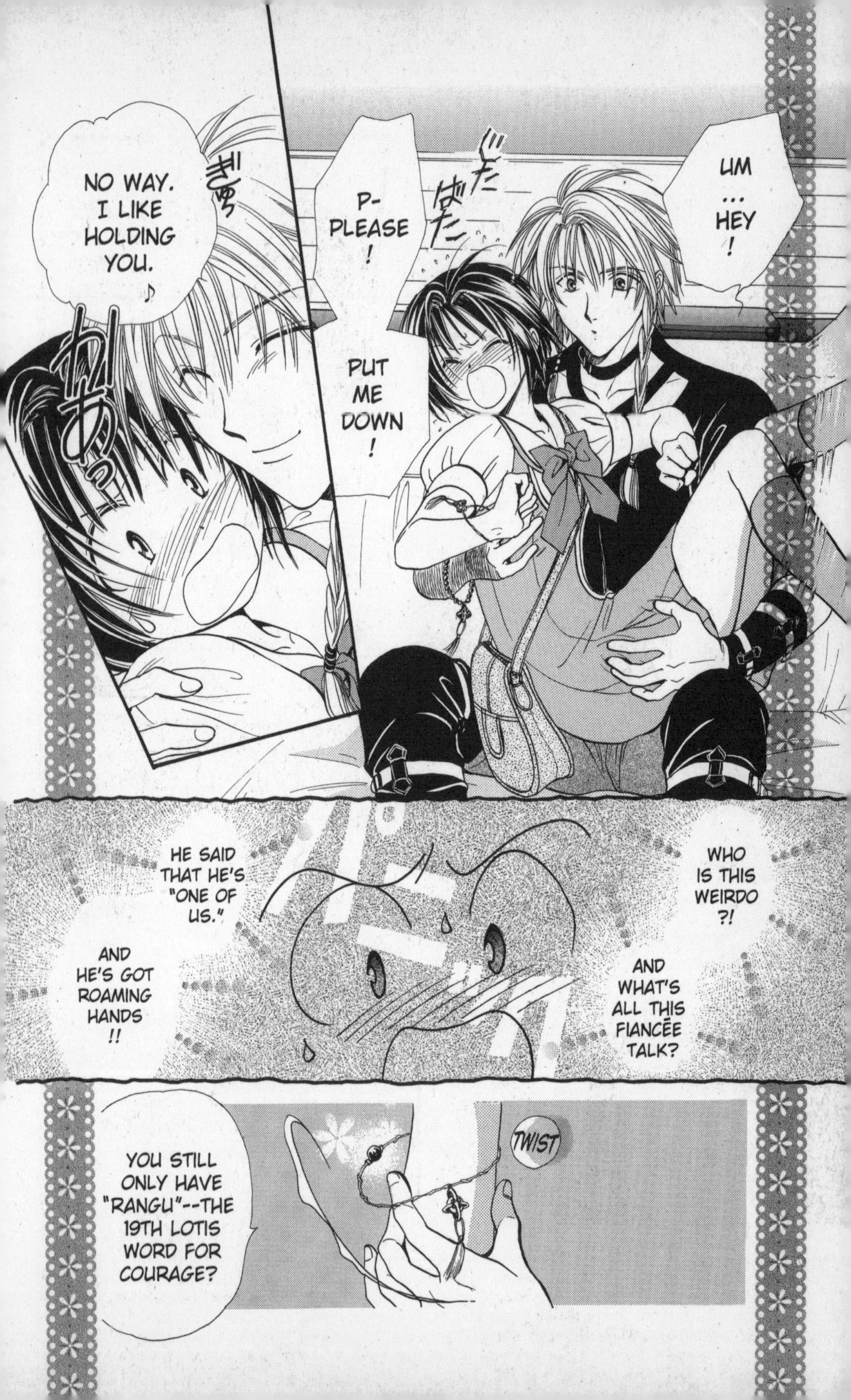
UM ... HEY!
P-PLEASE!
PUT ME DOWN!
NO WAY. I LIKE HOLDING YOU. ♪
WHO IS THIS WEIRDO?!
AND WHAT'S ALL THIS FIANCÉE TALK?
HE SAID THAT HE'S "ONE OF US."
AND HE'S GOT ROAMING HANDS!!
TWIST
YOU STILL ONLY HAVE "RANGU"--THE 19TH LOTIS WORD FOR COURAGE?

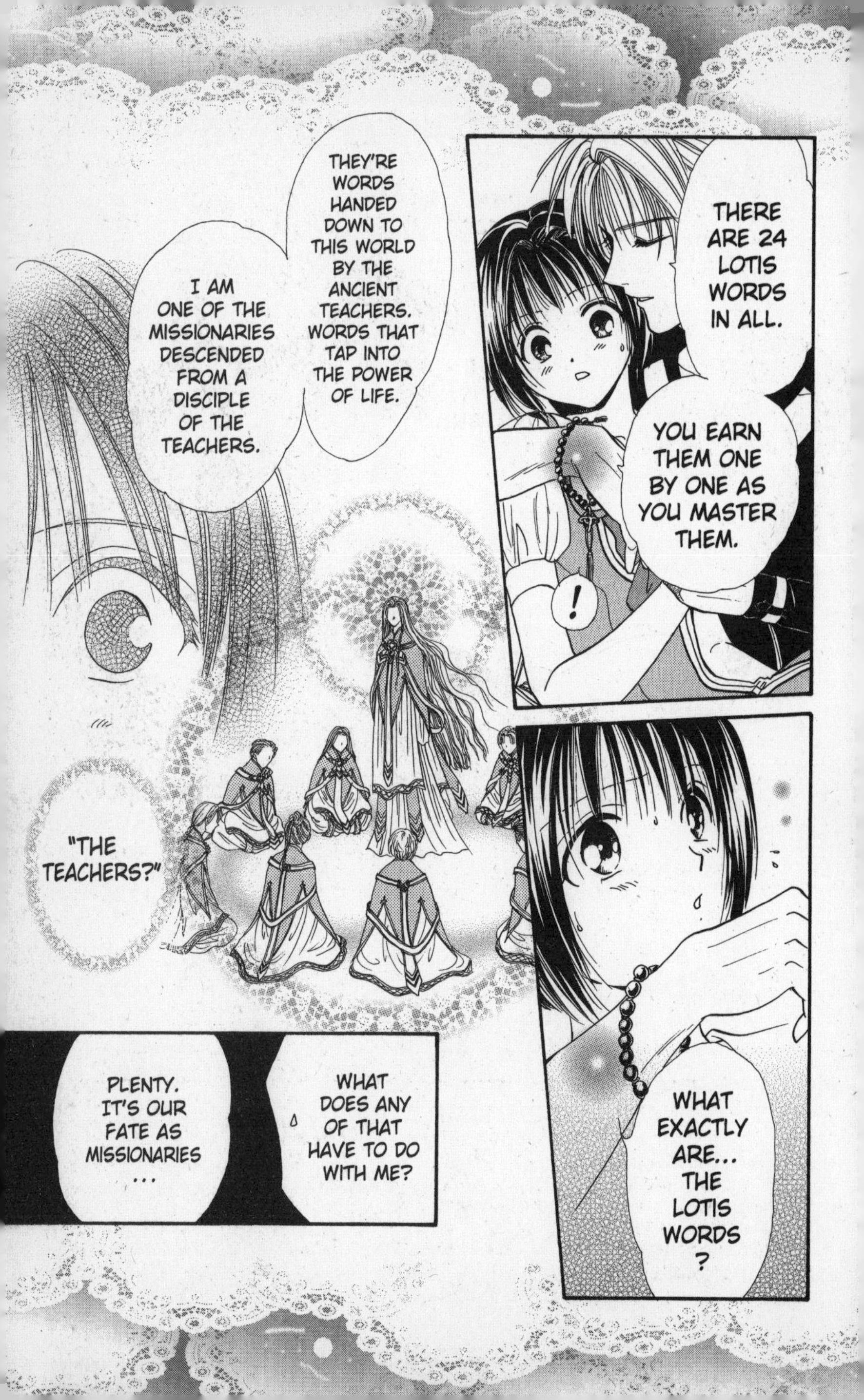
THERE ARE 24 LOTIS WORDS IN ALL.
YOU EARN THEM ONE BY ONE AS YOU MASTER THEM.
!
WHAT EXACTLY ARE... THE LOTIS WORDS ?
THEY'RE WORDS HANDED DOWN TO THIS WORLD BY THE ANCIENT TEACHERS. WORDS THAT TAP INTO THE POWER OF LIFE.
I AM ONE OF THE MISSIONARIES DESCENDED FROM A DISCIPLE OF THE TEACHERS.
"THE TEACHERS?"
WHAT DOES ANY OF THAT HAVE TO DO WITH ME?
PLENTY. IT'S OUR FATE AS MISSIONARIES ...

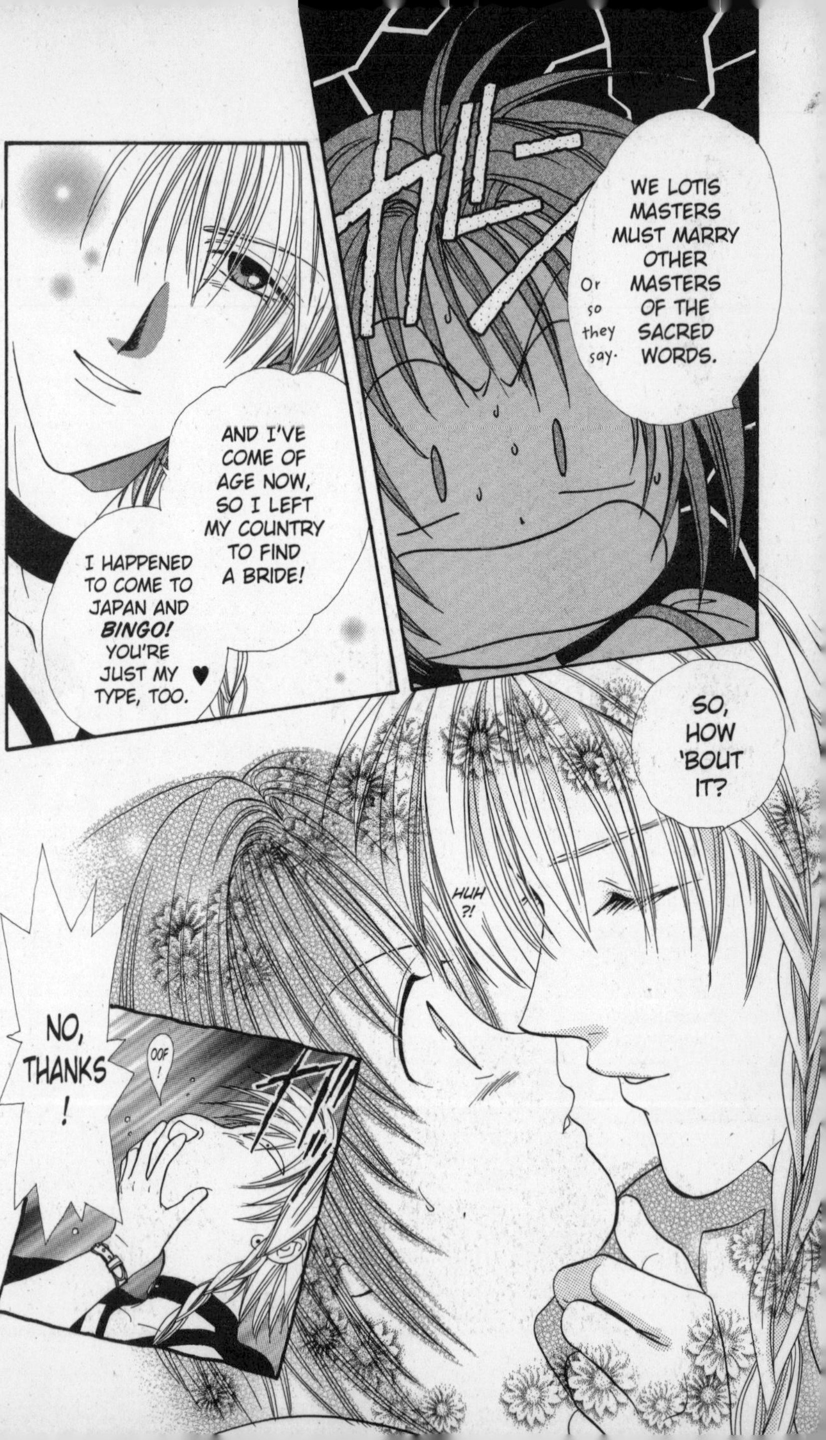
WE LOTIS MASTERS MUST MARRY OTHER MASTERS OF THE SACRED WORDS.
Or so they say.
AND I'VE COME OF AGE NOW, SO I LEFT MY COUNTRY TO FIND A BRIDE!
I HAPPENED TO COME TO JAPAN AND ***BINGO!*** YOU'RE JUST MY TYPE, TOO. ♥
SO, HOW 'BOUT IT?
HUH ?!
NO, THANKS !
OOF !

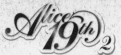

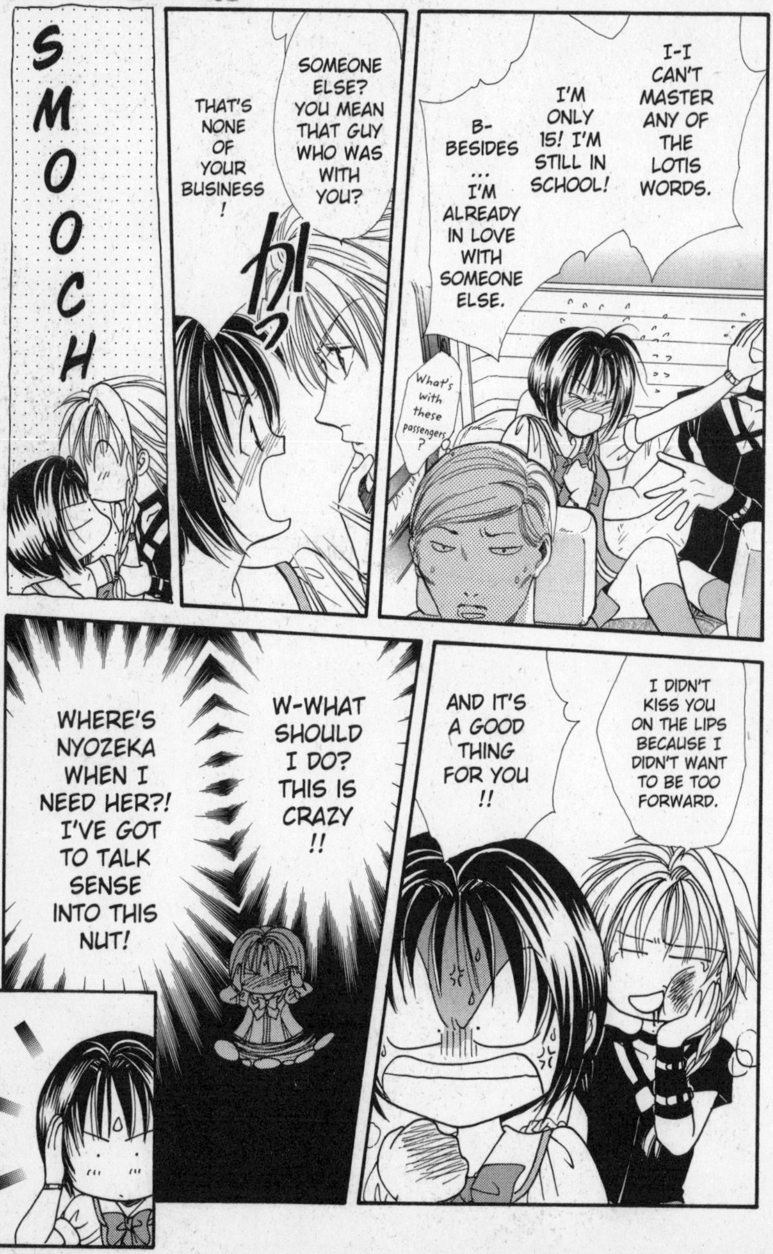
I-I CAN'T MASTER ANY OF THE LOTIS WORDS.
I'M ONLY 15! I'M STILL IN SCHOOL!
B-BESIDES ... I'M ALREADY IN LOVE WITH SOMEONE ELSE.
What's with these passengers?
SOMEONE ELSE? YOU MEAN THAT GUY WHO WAS WITH YOU?
THAT'S NONE OF YOUR BUSINESS!
SMOOCH
I DIDN'T KISS YOU ON THE LIPS BECAUSE I DIDN'T WANT TO BE TOO FORWARD.
AND IT'S A GOOD THING FOR YOU!!
W-WHAT SHOULD I DO? THIS IS CRAZY!!
WHERE'S NYOZEKA WHEN I NEED HER?! I'VE GOT TO TALK SENSE INTO THIS NUT!

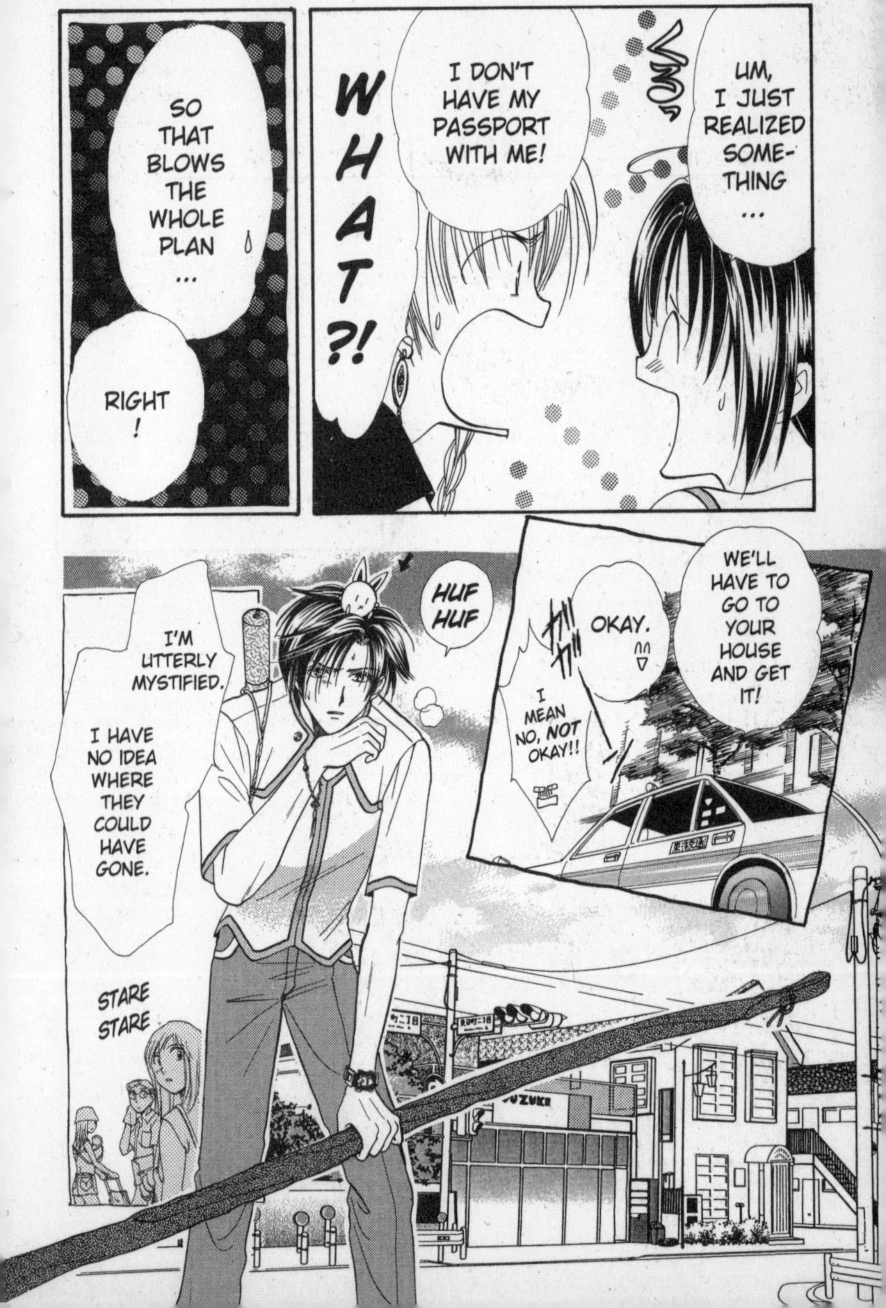
UM, I JUST REALIZED SOME-THING ...
I DON'T HAVE MY PASSPORT WITH ME!
WHAT?!
SO THAT BLOWS THE WHOLE PLAN ...
RIGHT!
WE'LL HAVE TO GO TO YOUR HOUSE AND GET IT!
OKAY.
I MEAN NO, NOT OKAY!!
HUF HUF
I'M UTTERLY MYSTIFIED.
I HAVE NO IDEA WHERE THEY COULD HAVE GONE.
STARE STARE

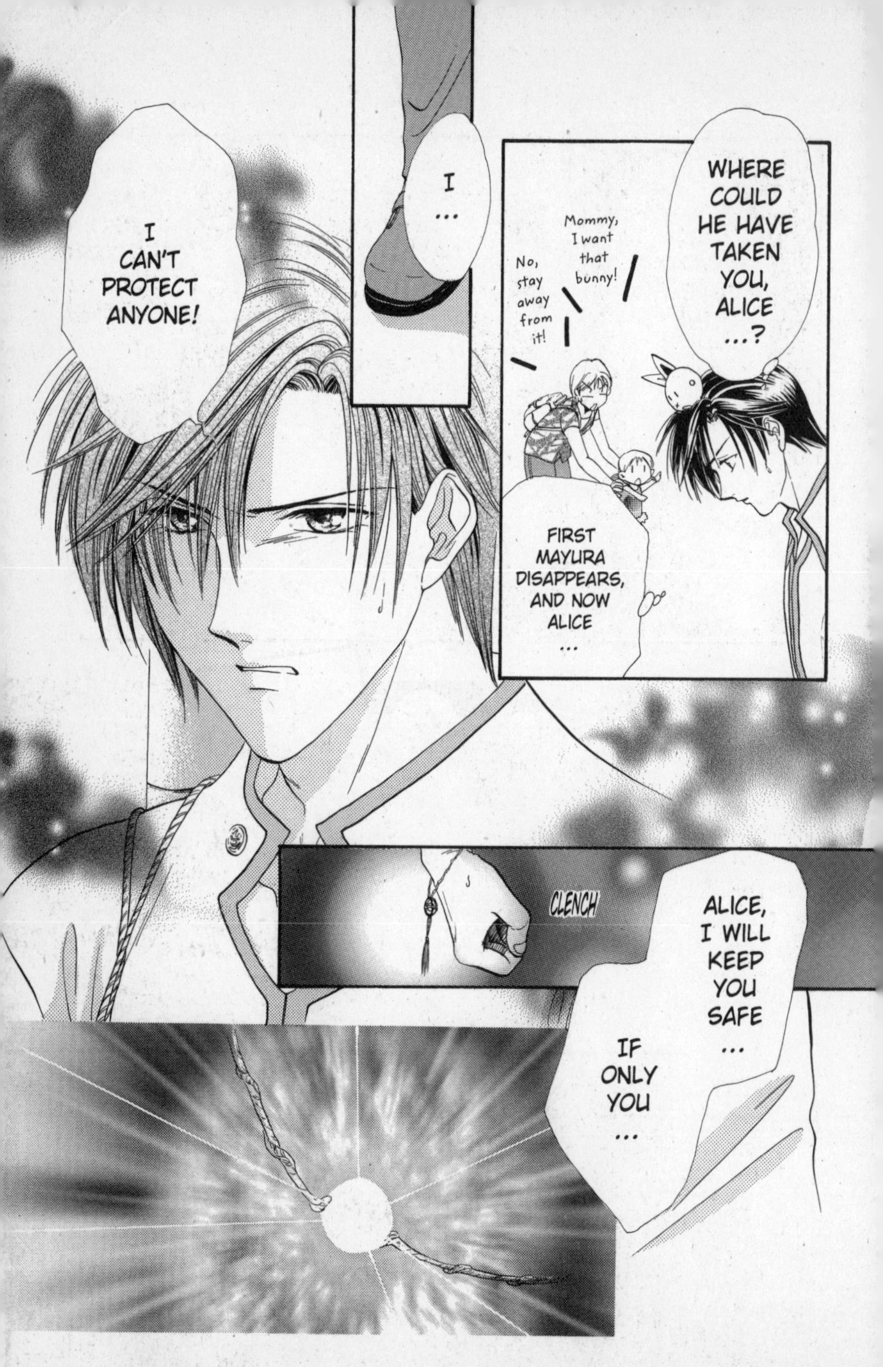
WHERE COULD HE HAVE TAKEN YOU, ALICE ...?
Mommy, I want that bunny!
No, stay away from it!
FIRST MAYURA DISAPPEARS, AND NOW ALICE ...
I ...
I CAN'T PROTECT ANYONE!
CLENCH
ALICE, I WILL KEEP YOU SAFE ...
IF ONLY YOU ...

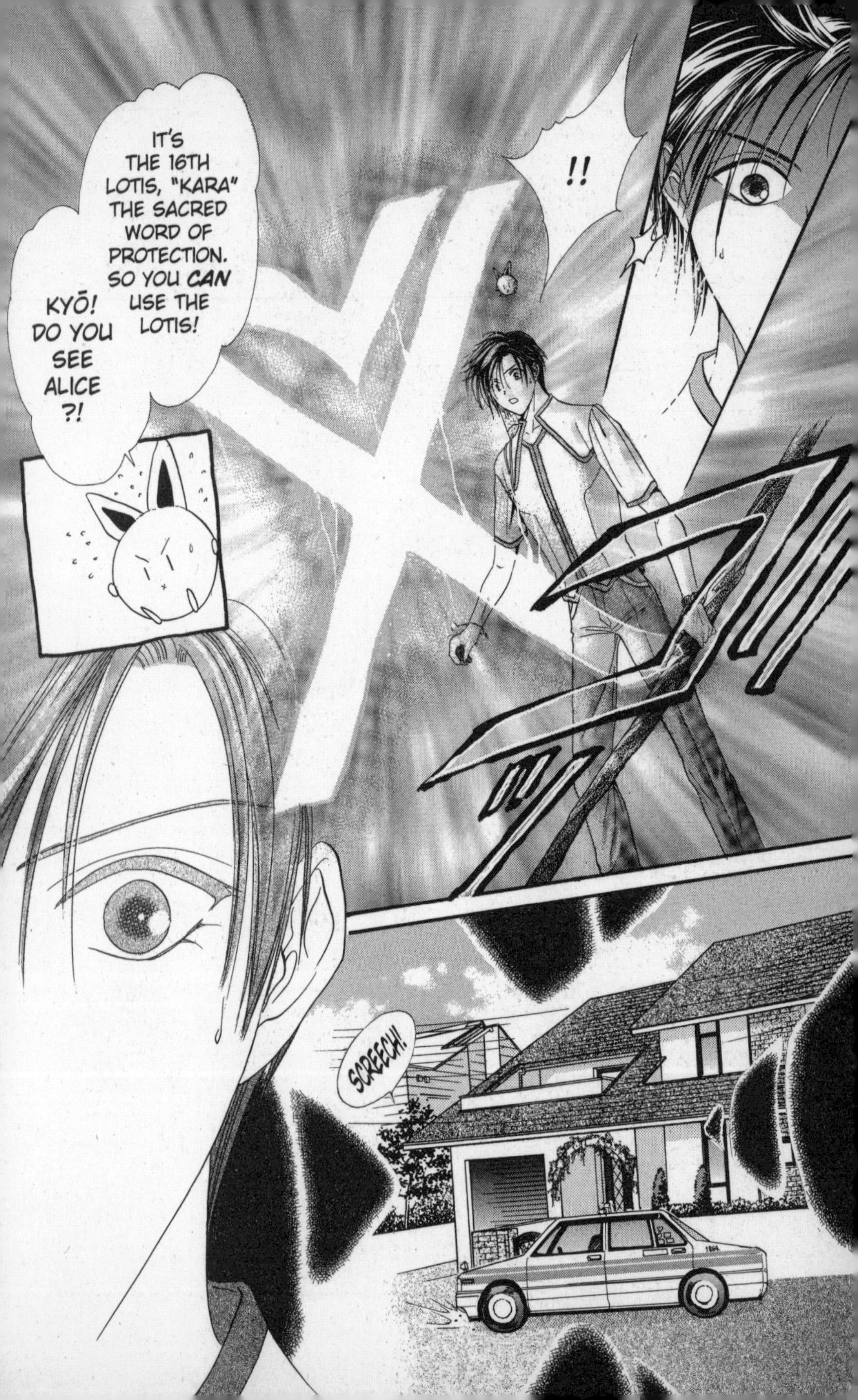
!!
IT'S THE 16TH LOTIS, "KARA" THE SACRED WORD OF PROTECTION. SO YOU CAN USE THE LOTIS!
KYŌ! DO YOU SEE ALICE ?!
SCREECH!

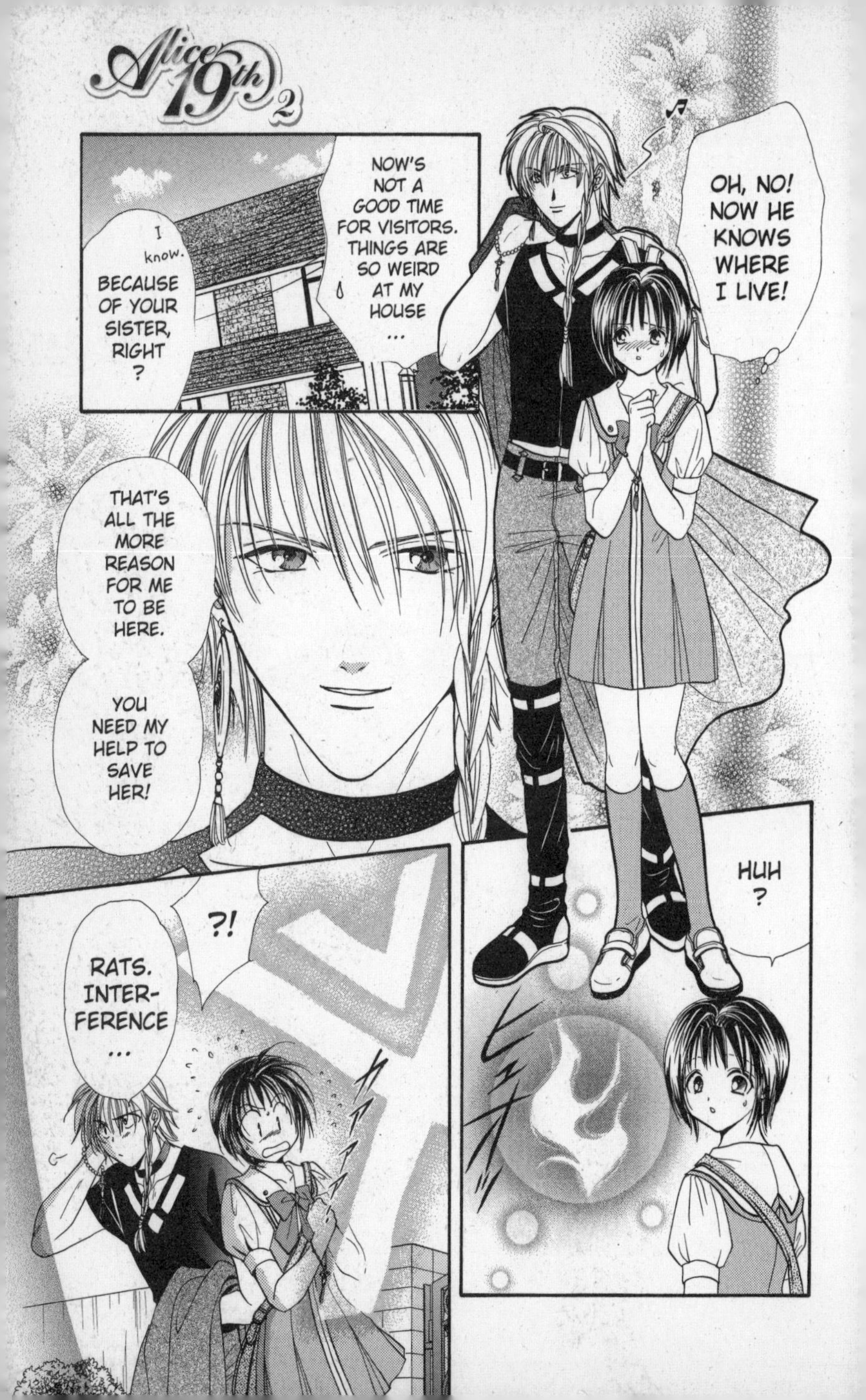
OH, NO! NOW HE KNOWS WHERE I LIVE!
NOW'S NOT A GOOD TIME FOR VISITORS. THINGS ARE SO WEIRD AT MY HOUSE ...
I know.
BECAUSE OF YOUR SISTER, RIGHT ?
THAT'S ALL THE MORE REASON FOR ME TO BE HERE.
YOU NEED MY HELP TO SAVE HER!
HUH ?
?!
RATS. INTERFERENCE ...

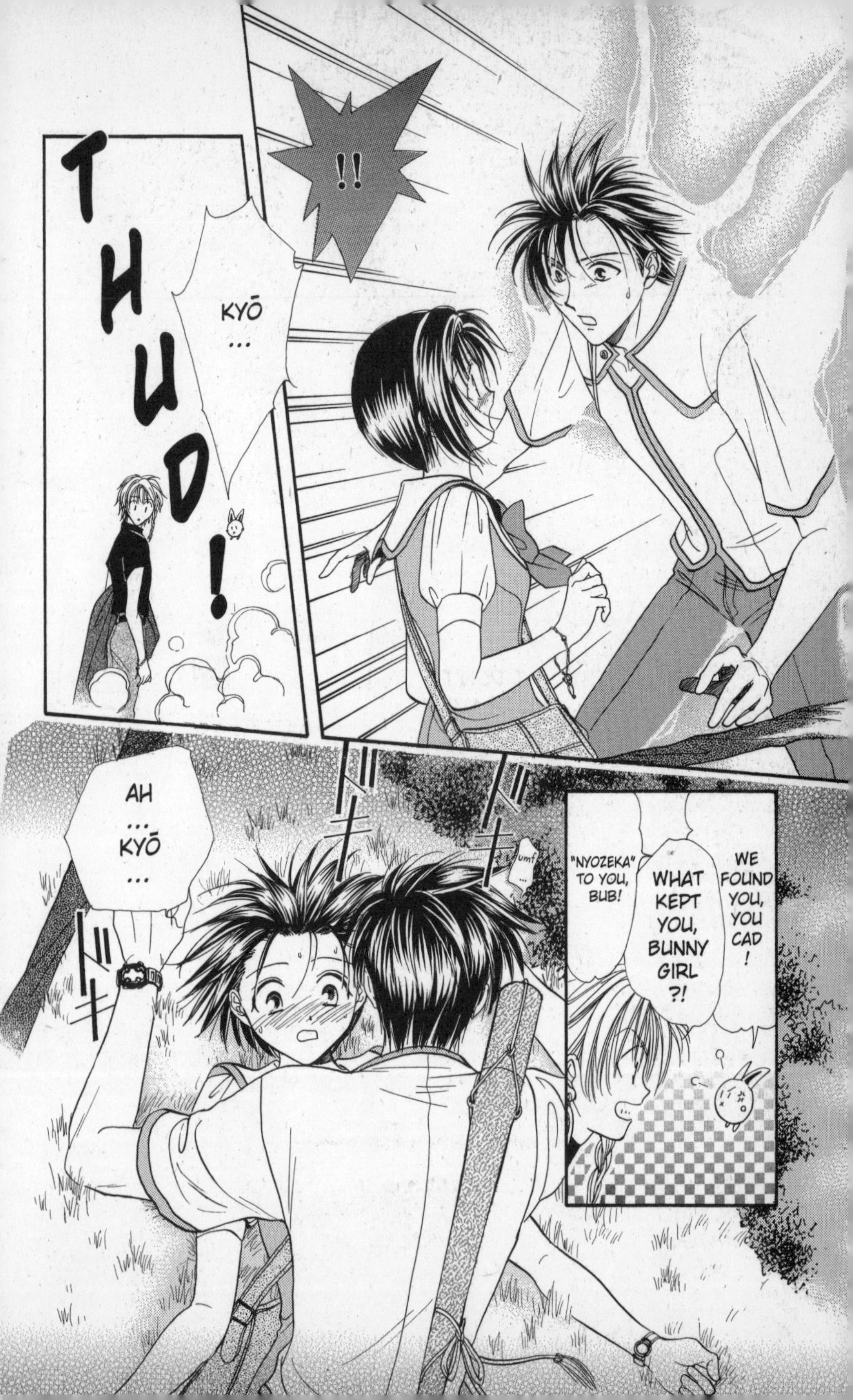
!!
KYŌ ...
THUD!
WE FOUND YOU, YOU CAD!
WHAT KEPT YOU, BUNNY GIRL?!
"NYOZEKA" TO YOU, BUB!
umf ...
AH ... KYŌ ...

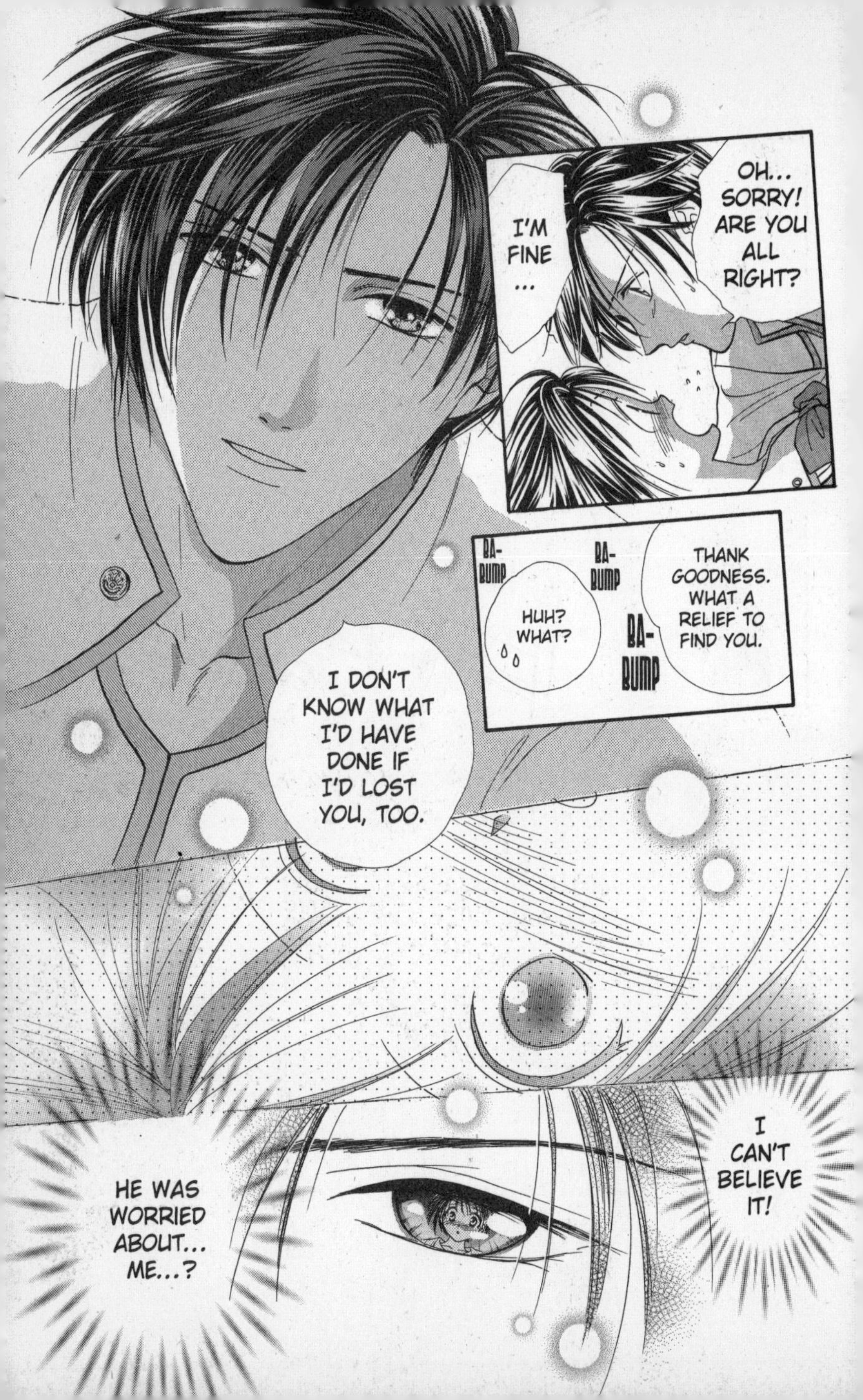
OH... SORRY! ARE YOU ALL RIGHT?
I'M FINE...
THANK GOODNESS. WHAT A RELIEF TO FIND YOU.
BA-BUMP
BA-BUMP
HUH? WHAT?
BA-BUMP
I DON'T KNOW WHAT I'D HAVE DONE IF I'D LOST YOU, TOO.
I CAN'T BELIEVE IT!
HE WAS WORRIED ABOUT... ME...?

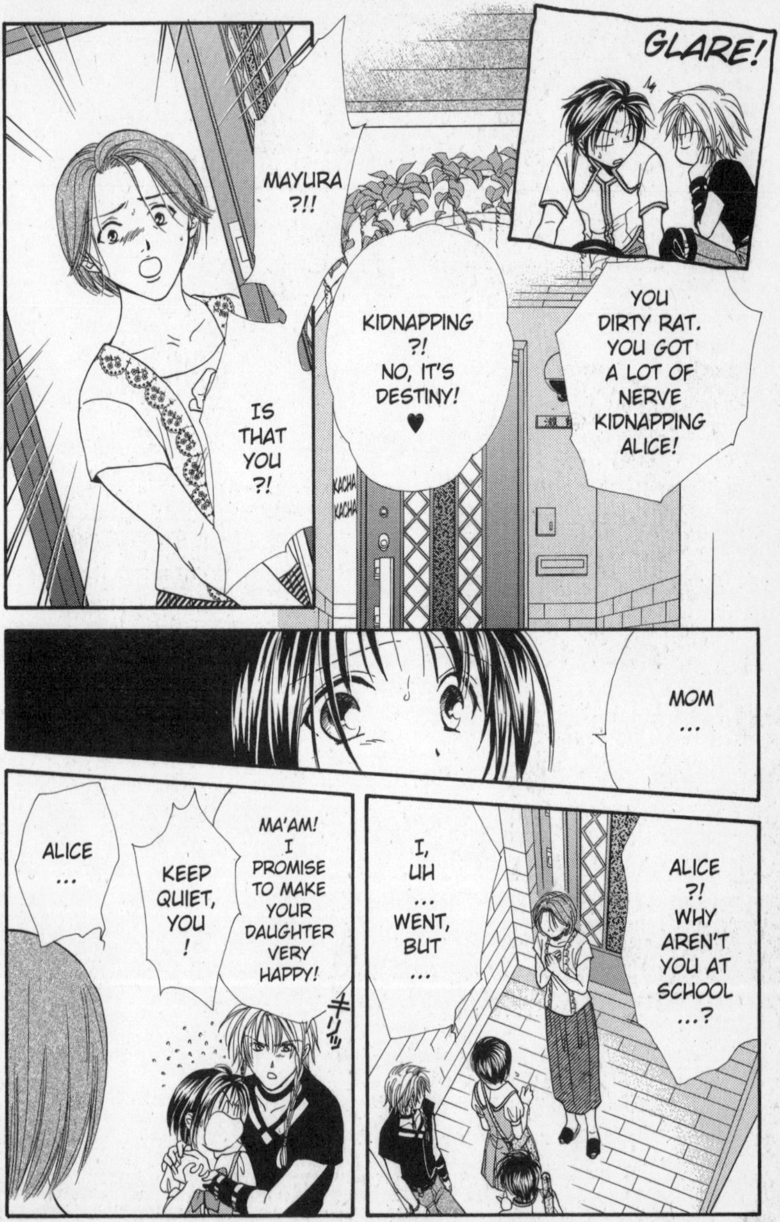
GLARE!
YOU DIRTY RAT. YOU GOT A LOT OF NERVE KIDNAPPING ALICE!
KIDNAPPING?! NO, IT'S DESTINY! ♥
KACHA KACHA
MAYURA?!!
IS THAT YOU?!
MOM...
ALICE?! WHY AREN'T YOU AT SCHOOL...?
I, UH... WENT, BUT...
MA'AM! I PROMISE TO MAKE YOUR DAUGHTER VERY HAPPY!
キリッ
KEEP QUIET, YOU!
ALICE...

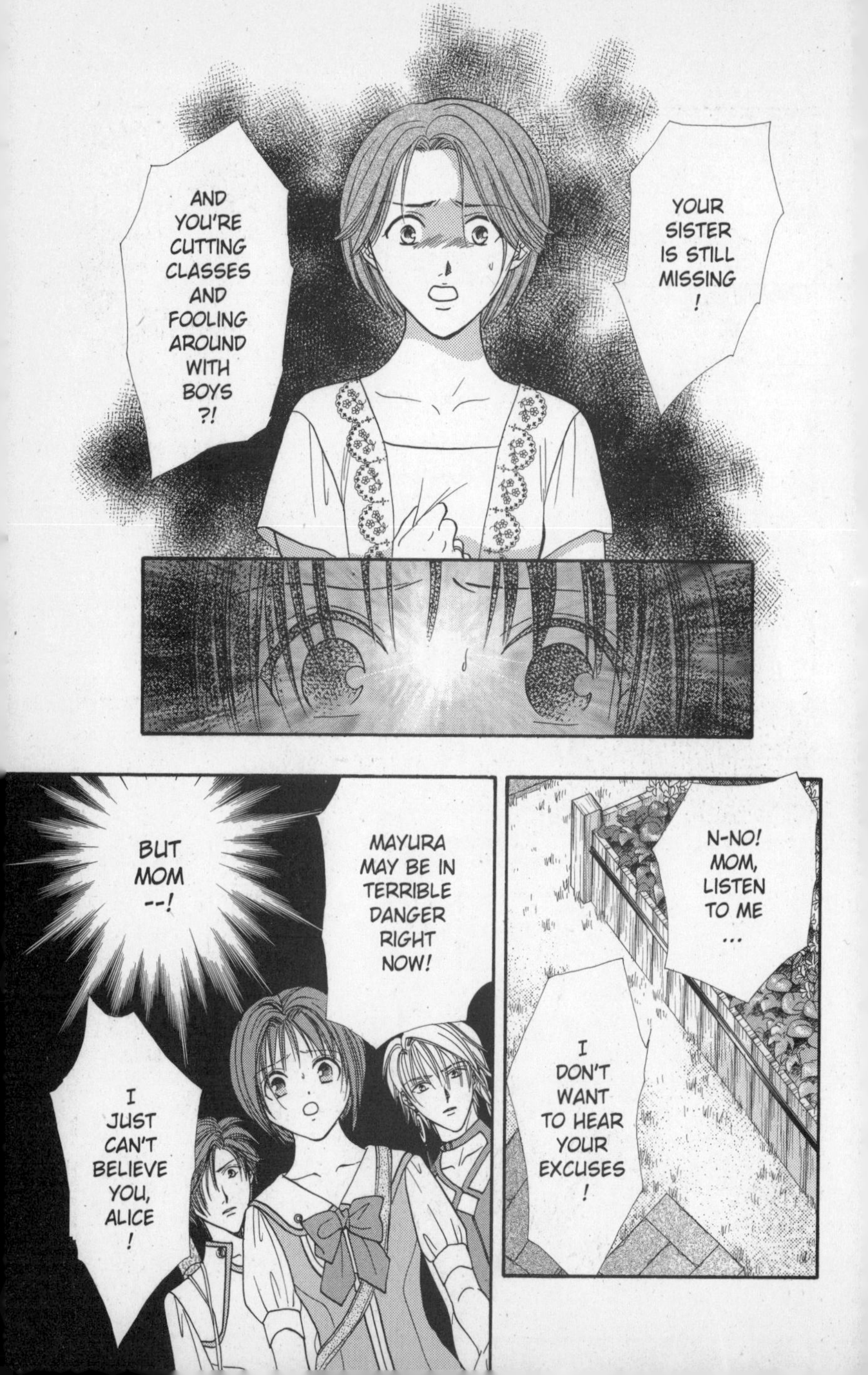
YOUR SISTER IS STILL MISSING!
AND YOU'RE CUTTING CLASSES AND FOOLING AROUND WITH BOYS?!
N-NO! MOM, LISTEN TO ME...
I DON'T WANT TO HEAR YOUR EXCUSES!
MAYURA MAY BE IN TERRIBLE DANGER RIGHT NOW!
BUT MOM--!
I JUST CAN'T BELIEVE YOU, ALICE!

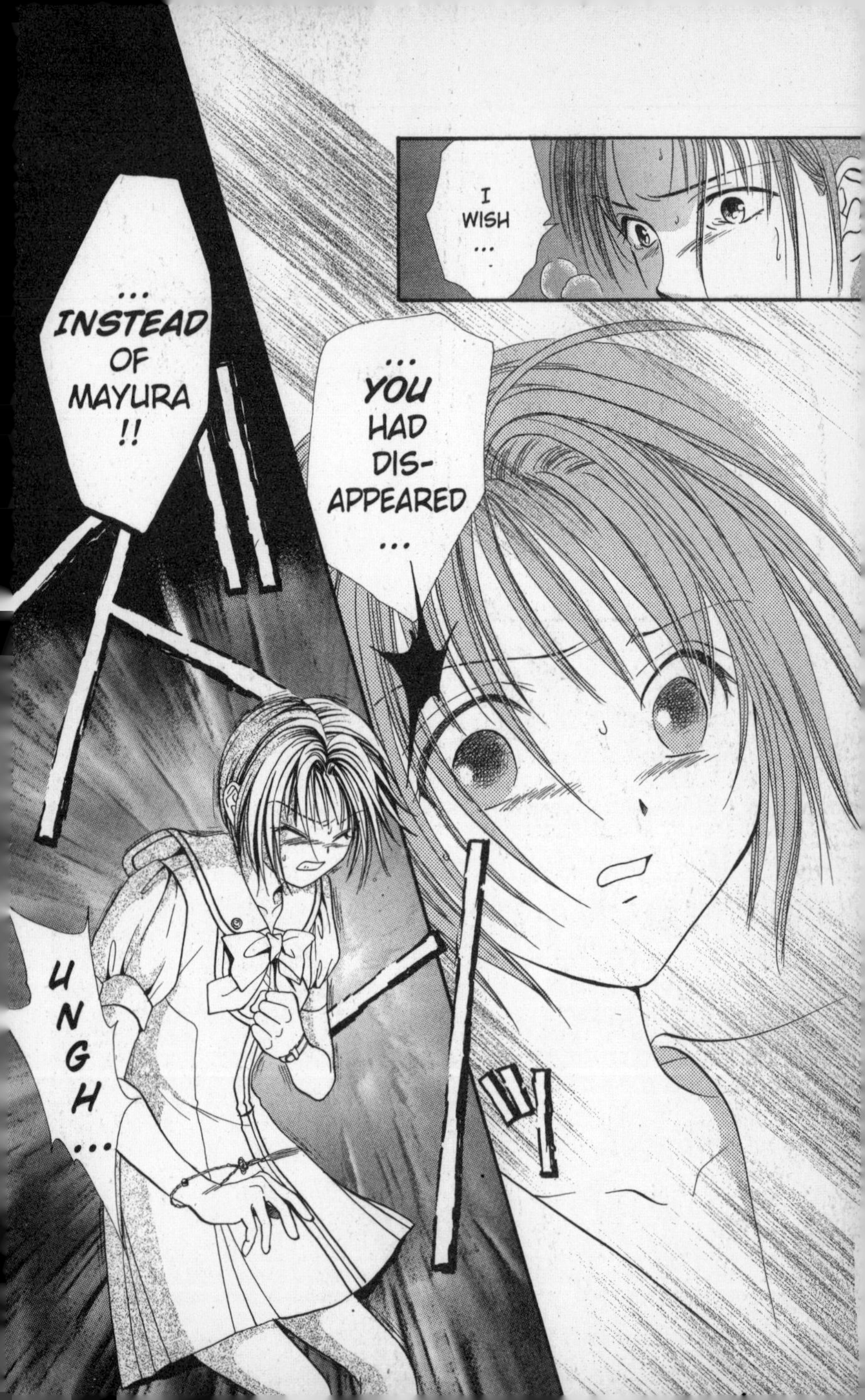
I WISH ...
... YOU HAD DIS-APPEARED ...
... INSTEAD OF MAYURA !!
UNGH ...

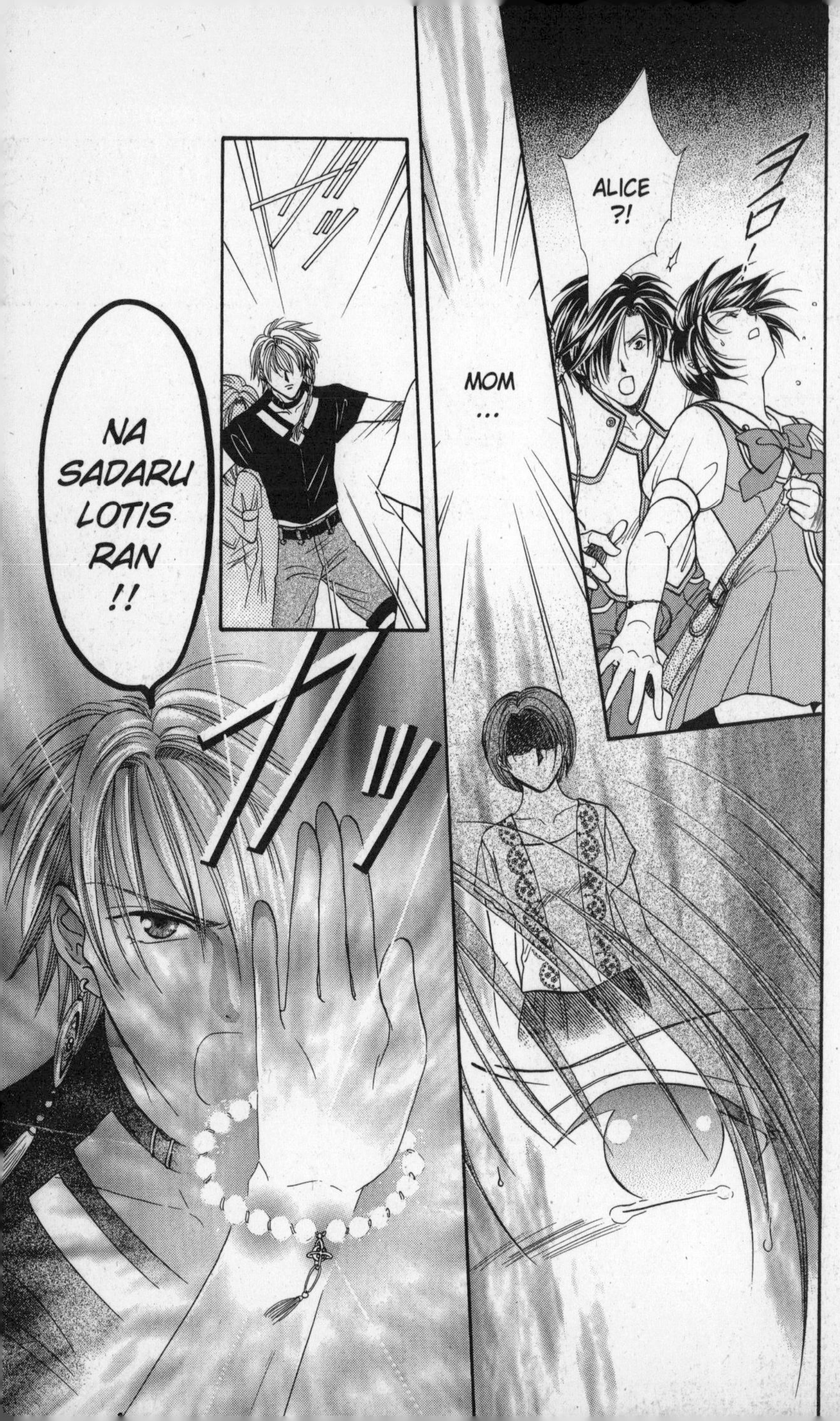
ALICE ?!
MOM ...
NA SADARU LOTIS RAN !!

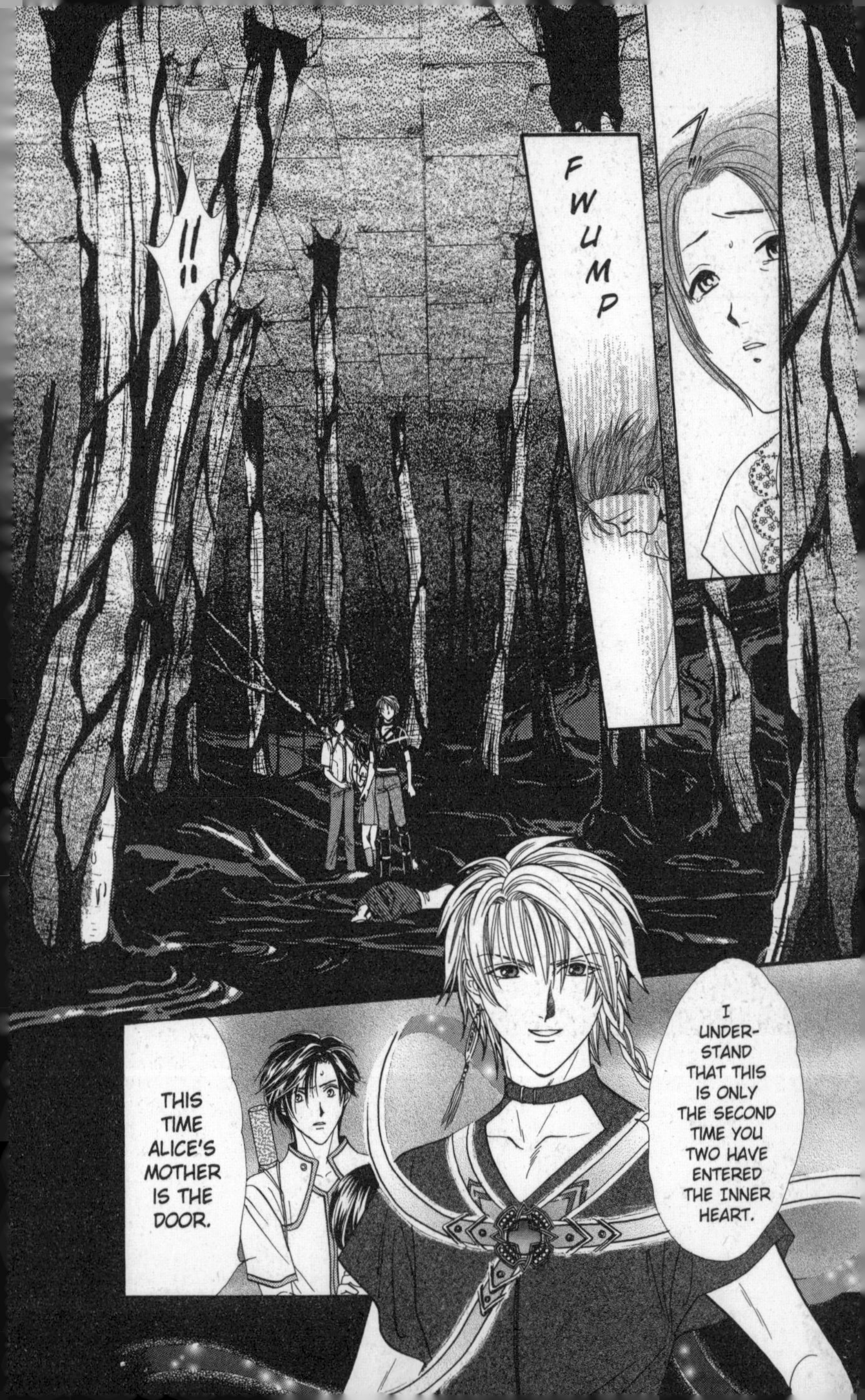
FWUMP
!!
I UNDER-STAND THAT THIS IS ONLY THE SECOND TIME YOU TWO HAVE ENTERED THE INNER HEART.
THIS TIME ALICE'S MOTHER IS THE DOOR.

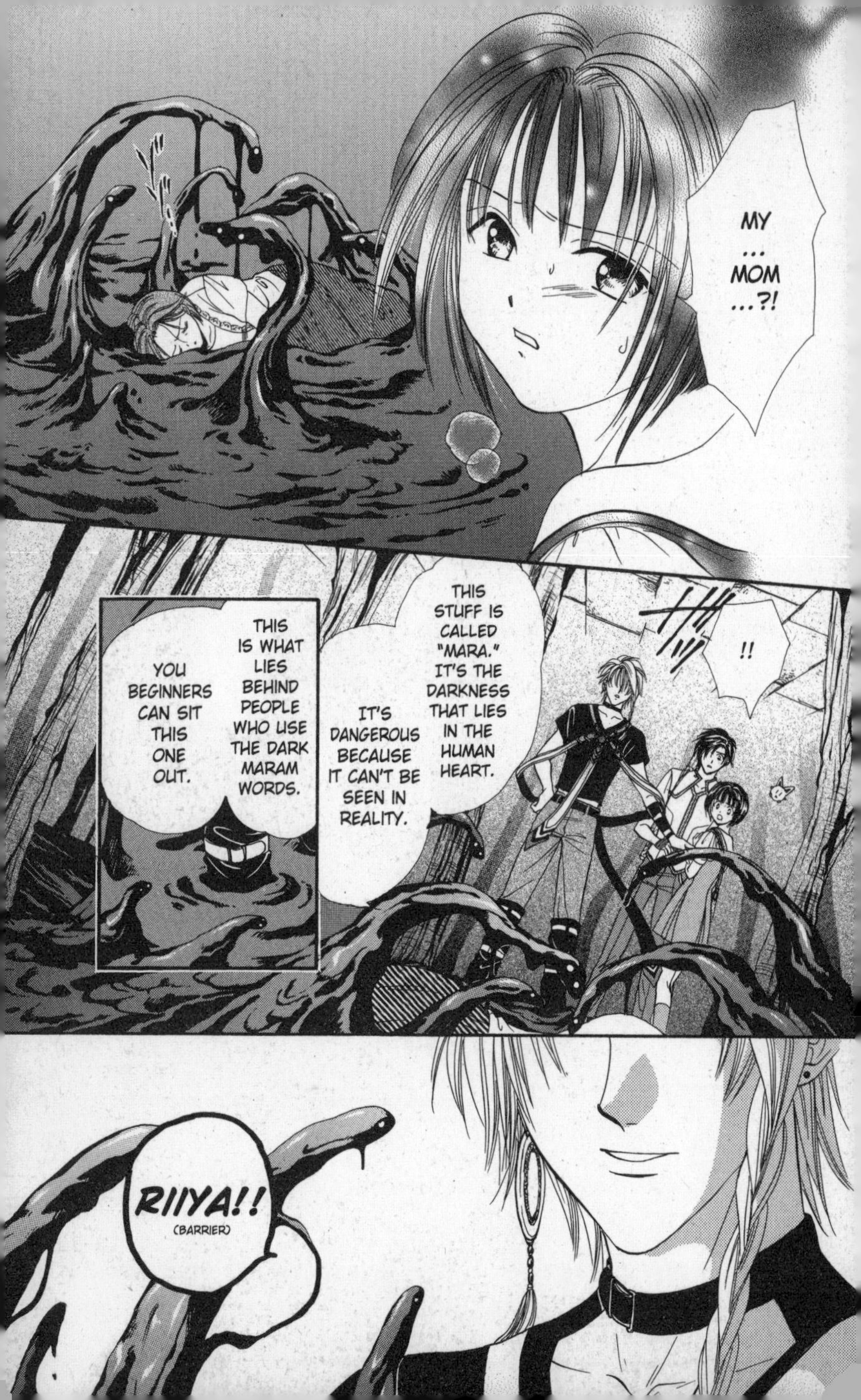
MY ... MOM ...?!
!!
THIS STUFF IS CALLED "MARA." IT'S THE DARKNESS THAT LIES IN THE HUMAN HEART.
IT'S DANGEROUS BECAUSE IT CAN'T BE SEEN IN REALITY.
THIS IS WHAT LIES BEHIND PEOPLE WHO USE THE DARK MARAM WORDS.
YOU BEGINNERS CAN SIT THIS ONE OUT.
RIIYA!!
(BARRIER)

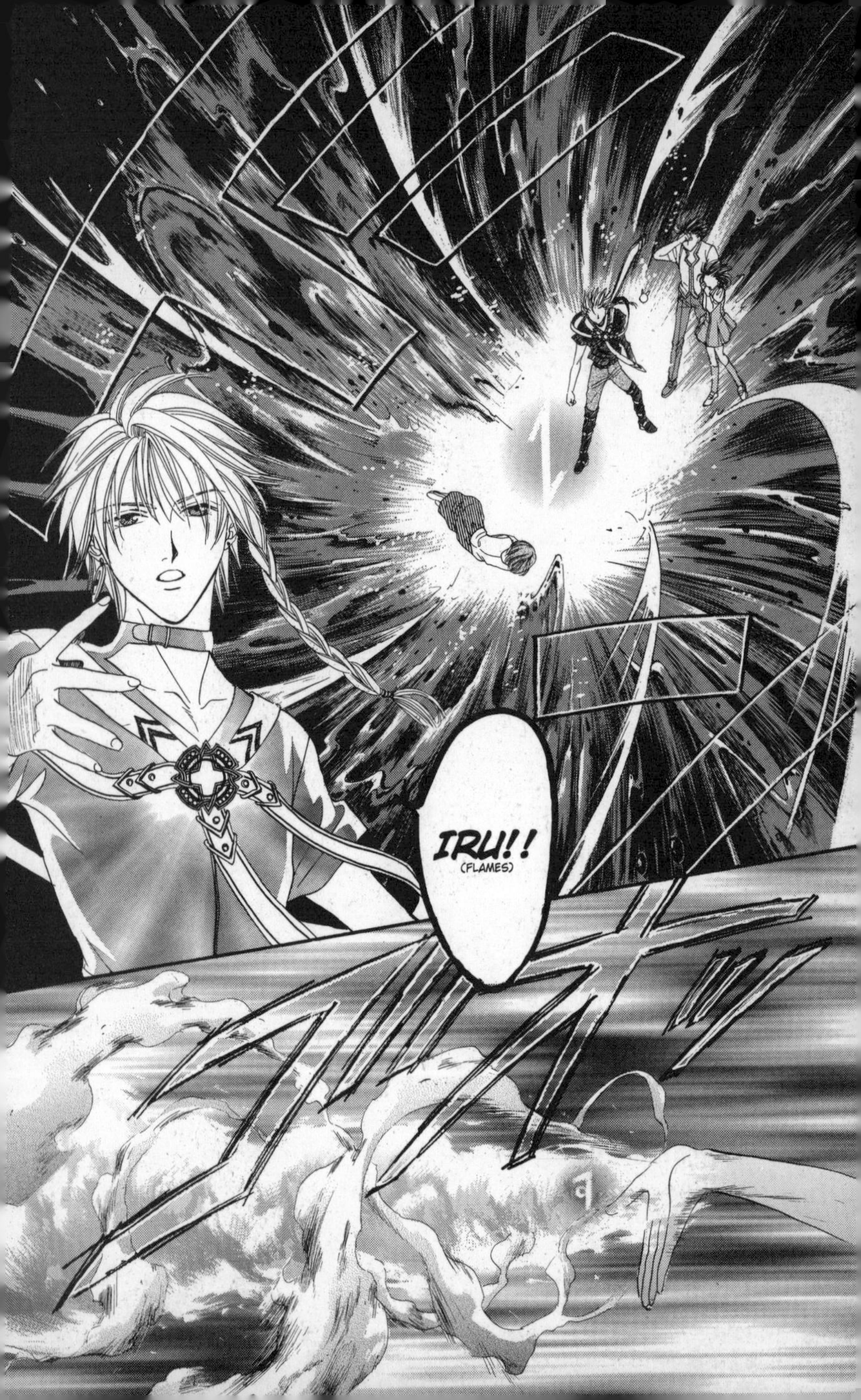
IRU!!
(FLAMES)

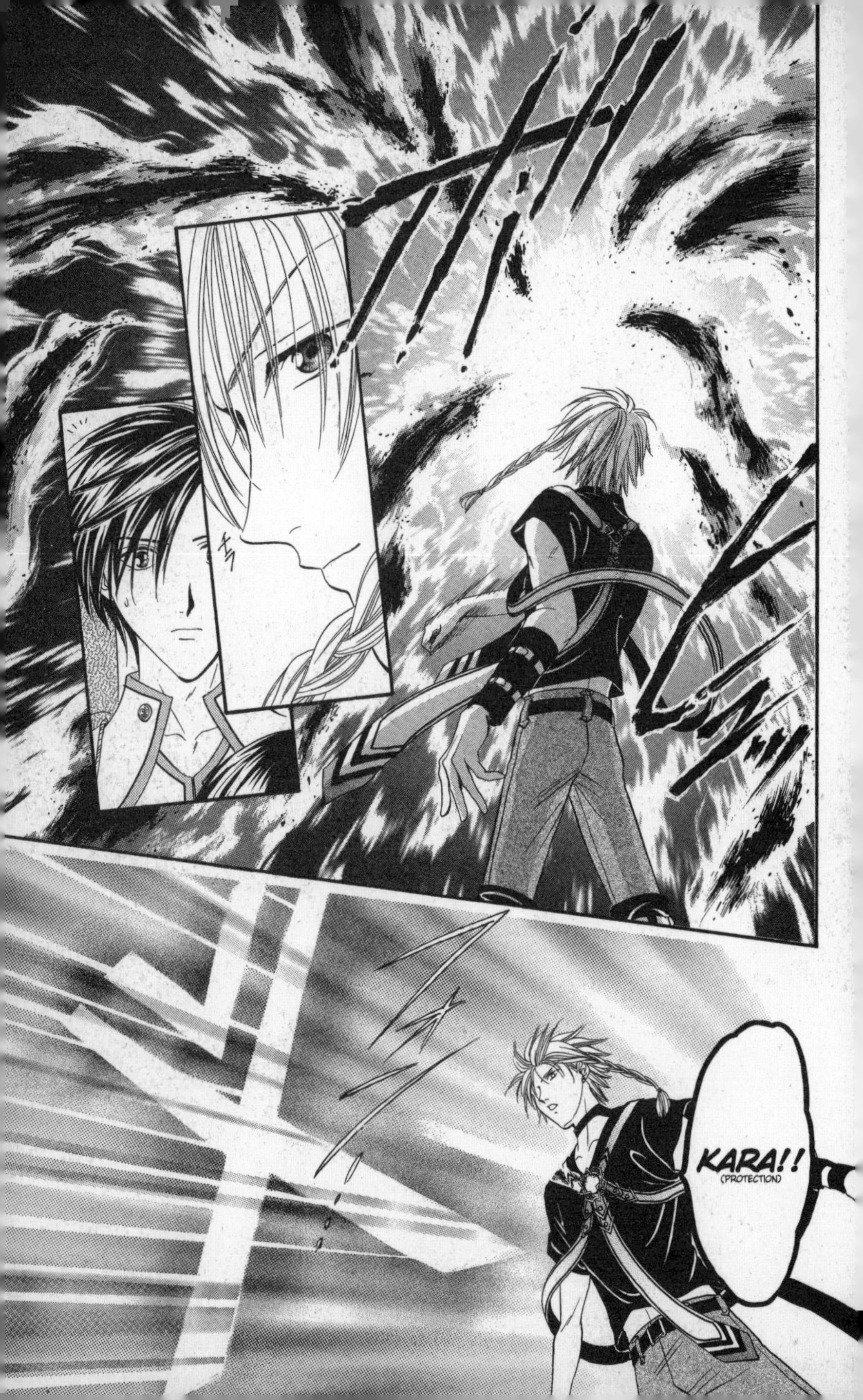
KARA!!
(PROTECTION)

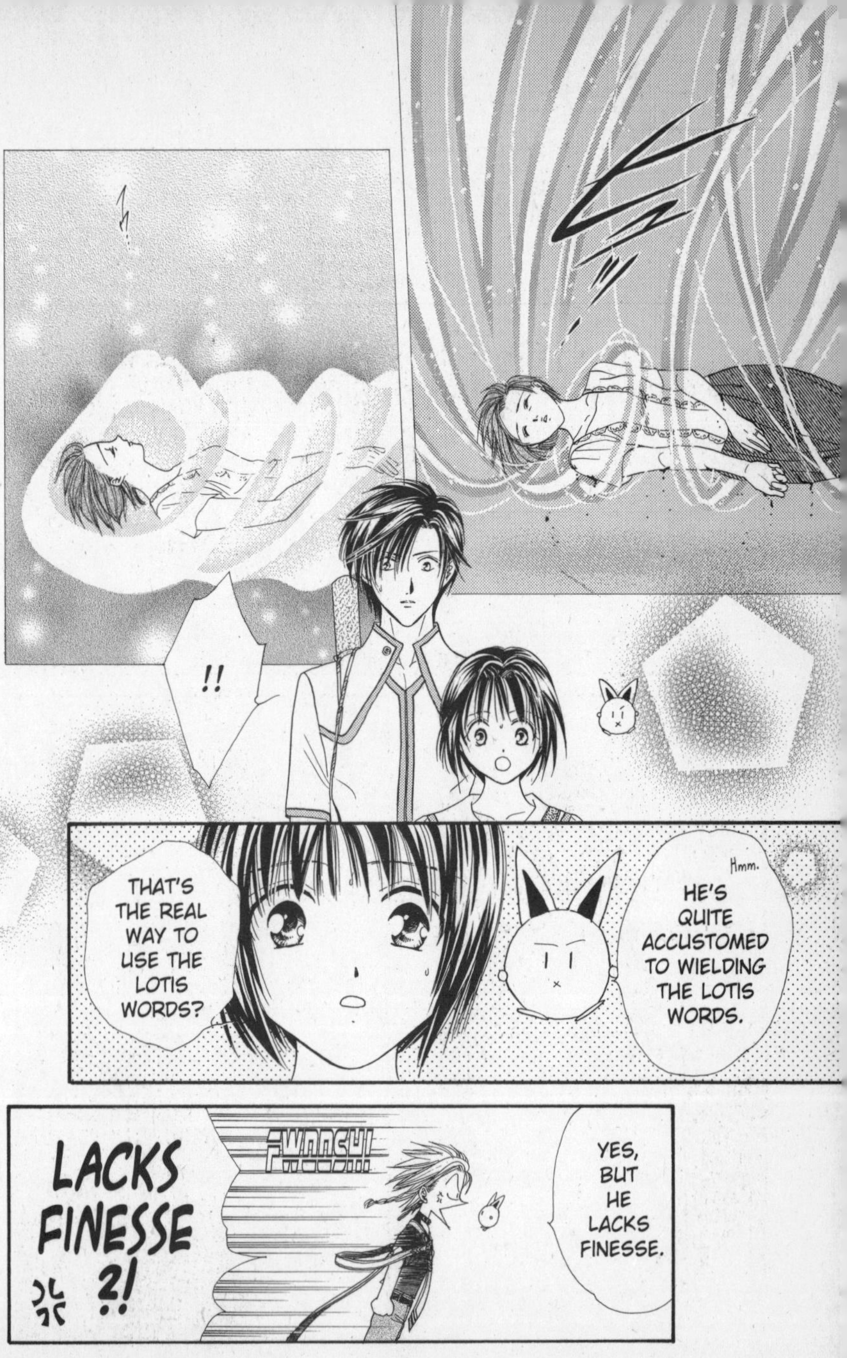

!!
Hmm.
HE'S QUITE ACCUSTOMED TO WIELDING THE LOTIS WORDS.
THAT'S THE REAL WAY TO USE THE LOTIS WORDS?
YES, BUT HE LACKS FINESSE.
FWOOSH!
LACKS FINESSE ?!

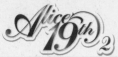

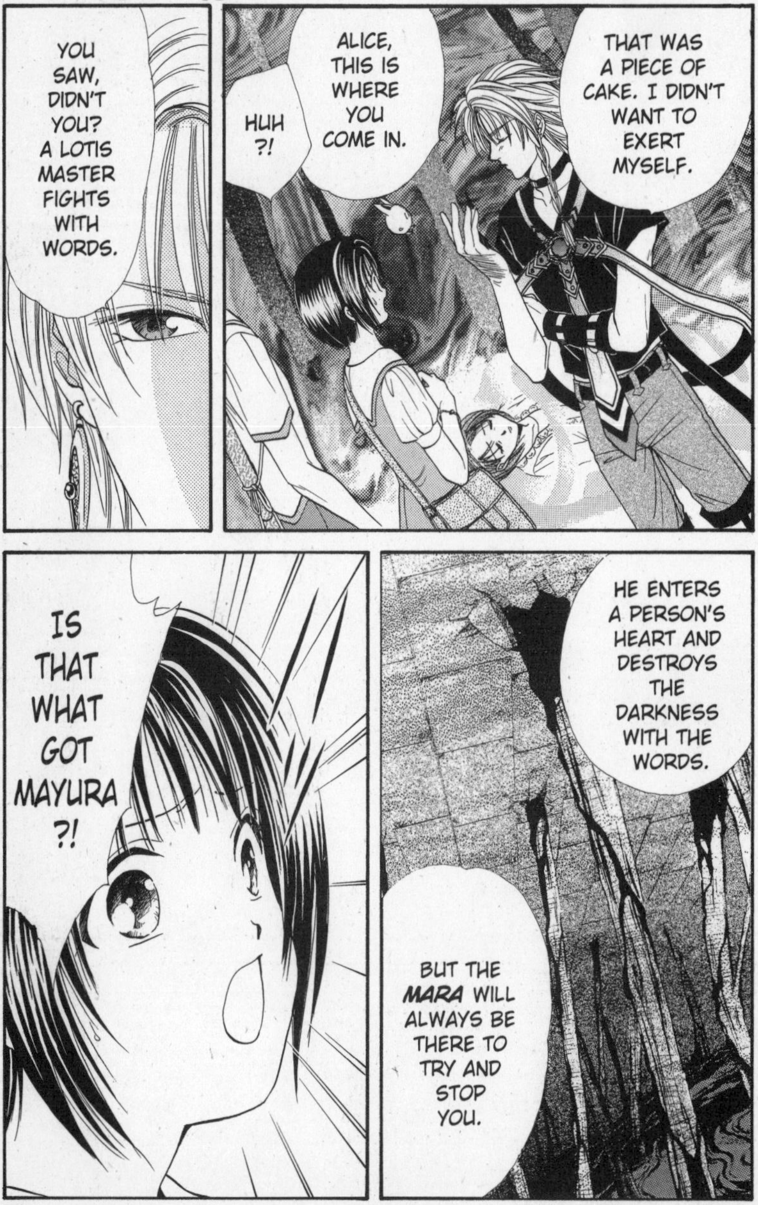
THAT WAS A PIECE OF CAKE. I DIDN'T WANT TO EXERT MYSELF.
ALICE, THIS IS WHERE YOU COME IN.
HUH ?!
YOU SAW, DIDN'T YOU? A LOTIS MASTER FIGHTS WITH WORDS.
HE ENTERS A PERSON'S HEART AND DESTROYS THE DARKNESS WITH THE WORDS.
BUT THE *MARA* WILL ALWAYS BE THERE TO TRY AND STOP YOU.
IS THAT WHAT GOT MAYURA ?!

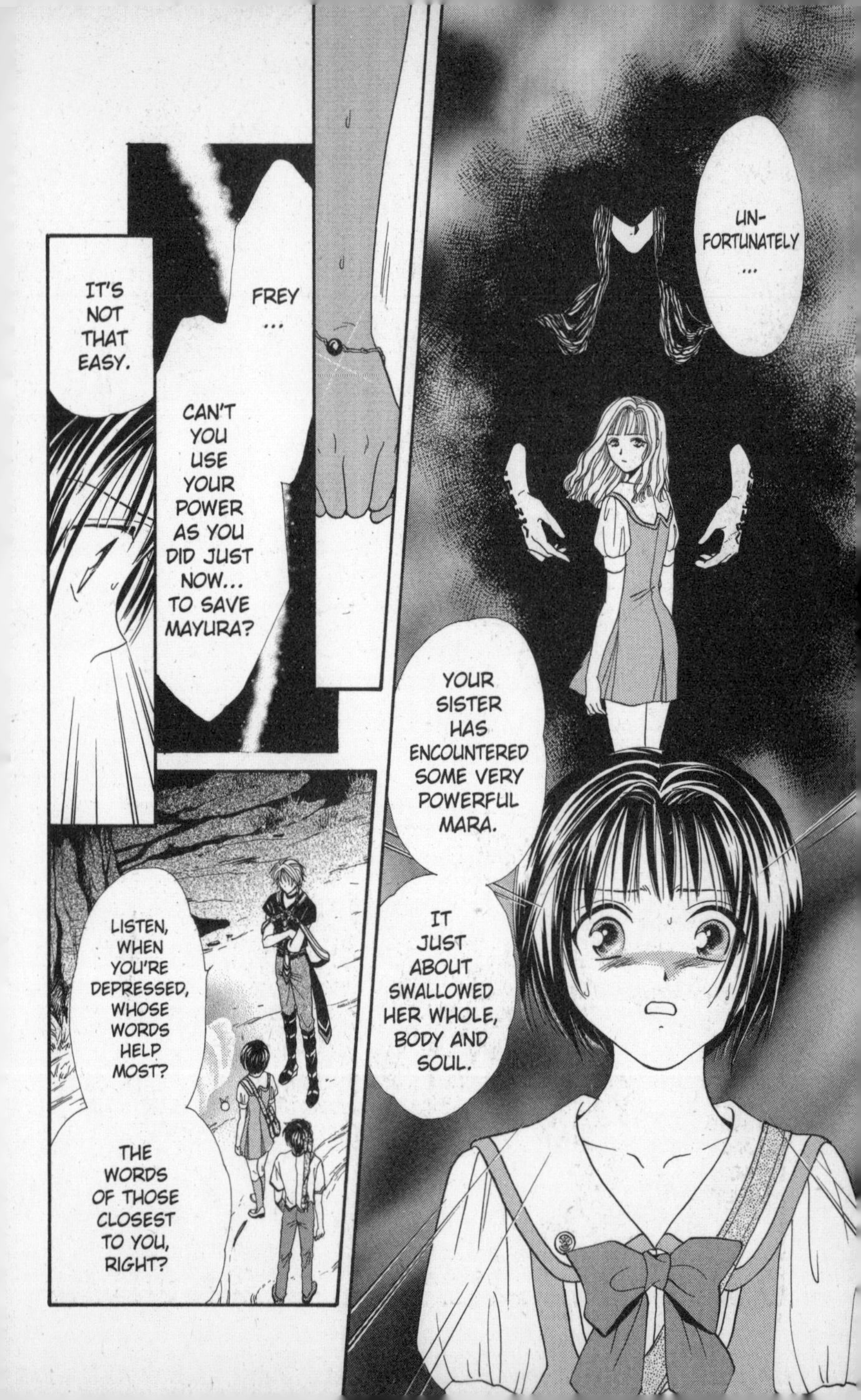
UN-FORTUNATELY ...
YOUR SISTER HAS ENCOUNTERED SOME VERY POWERFUL MARA.
IT JUST ABOUT SWALLOWED HER WHOLE, BODY AND SOUL.
FREY ...
CAN'T YOU USE YOUR POWER AS YOU DID JUST NOW... TO SAVE MAYURA?
IT'S NOT THAT EASY.
LISTEN, WHEN YOU'RE DEPRESSED, WHOSE WORDS HELP MOST?
THE WORDS OF THOSE CLOSEST TO YOU, RIGHT?

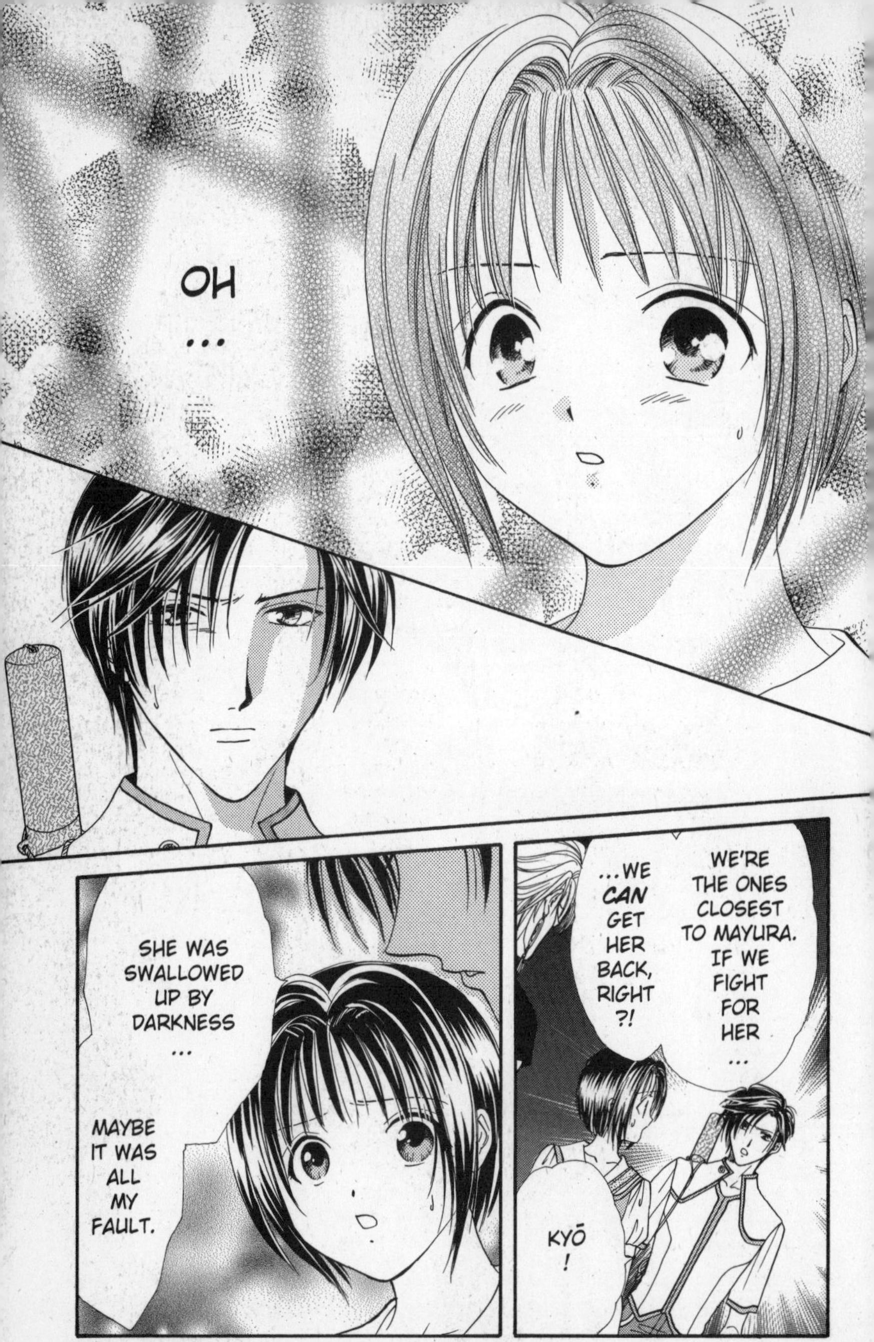
OH ...
WE'RE THE ONES CLOSEST TO MAYURA. IF WE FIGHT FOR HER ...
...WE CAN GET HER BACK, RIGHT?!
KYŌ!
SHE WAS SWALLOWED UP BY DARKNESS ...
MAYBE IT WAS ALL MY FAULT.

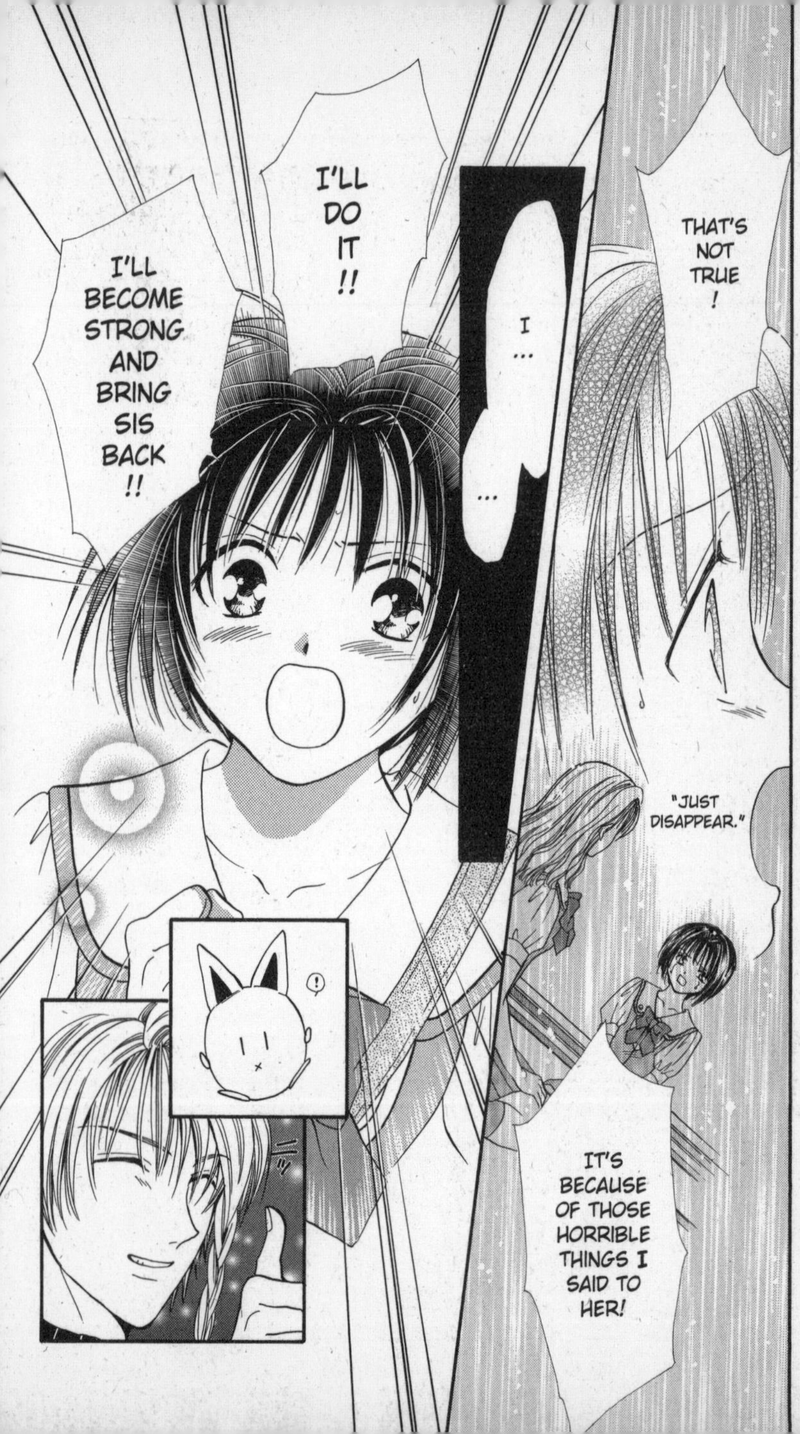
THAT'S NOT TRUE!
"JUST DISAPPEAR."
IT'S BECAUSE OF THOSE HORRIBLE THINGS I SAID TO HER!
I ... ...
I'LL DO IT!!
I'LL BECOME STRONG AND BRING SIS BACK!!

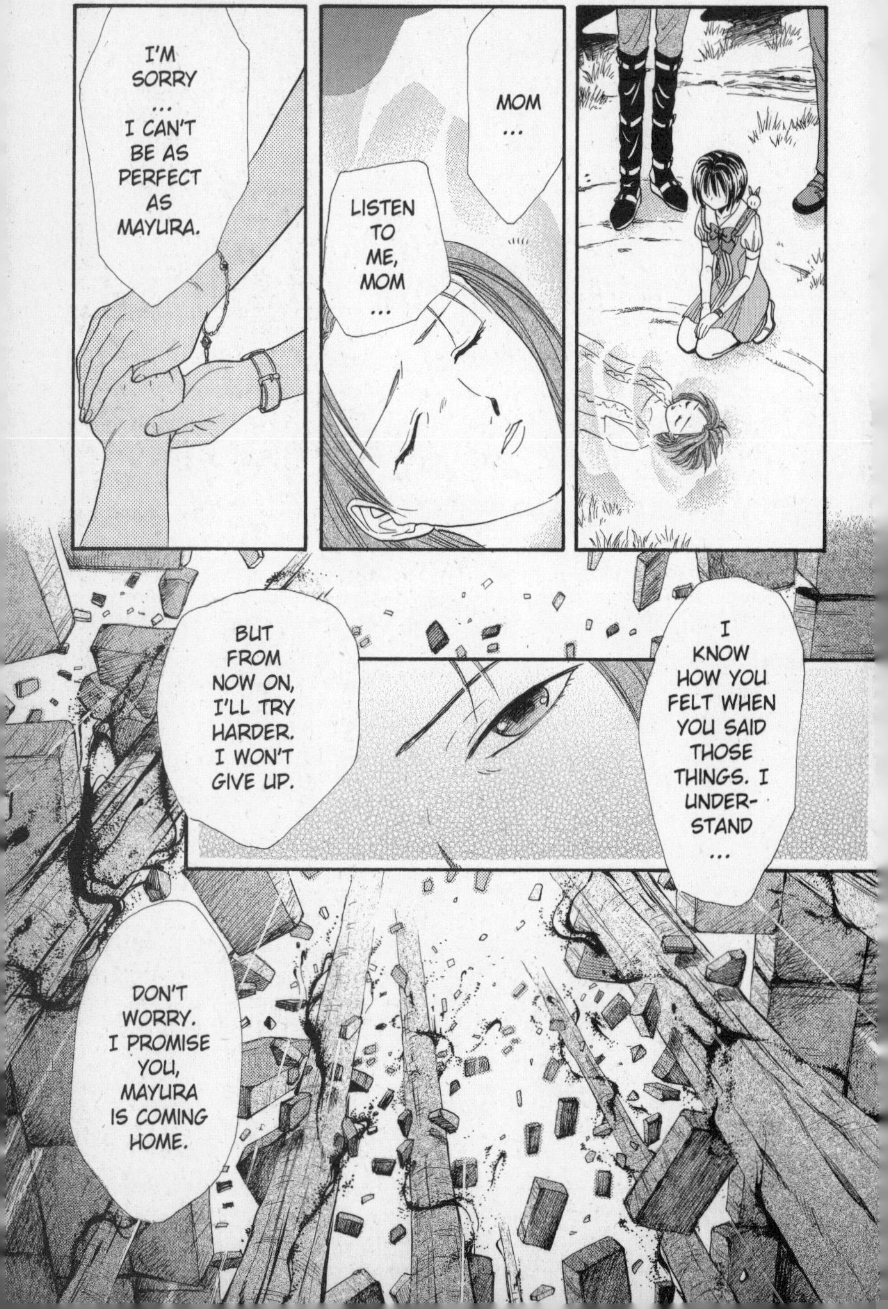
MOM ...
LISTEN TO ME, MOM ...
I'M SORRY ... I CAN'T BE AS PERFECT AS MAYURA.
I KNOW HOW YOU FELT WHEN YOU SAID THOSE THINGS. I UNDER-STAND ...
BUT FROM NOW ON, I'LL TRY HARDER. I WON'T GIVE UP.
DON'T WORRY. I PROMISE YOU, MAYURA IS COMING HOME.

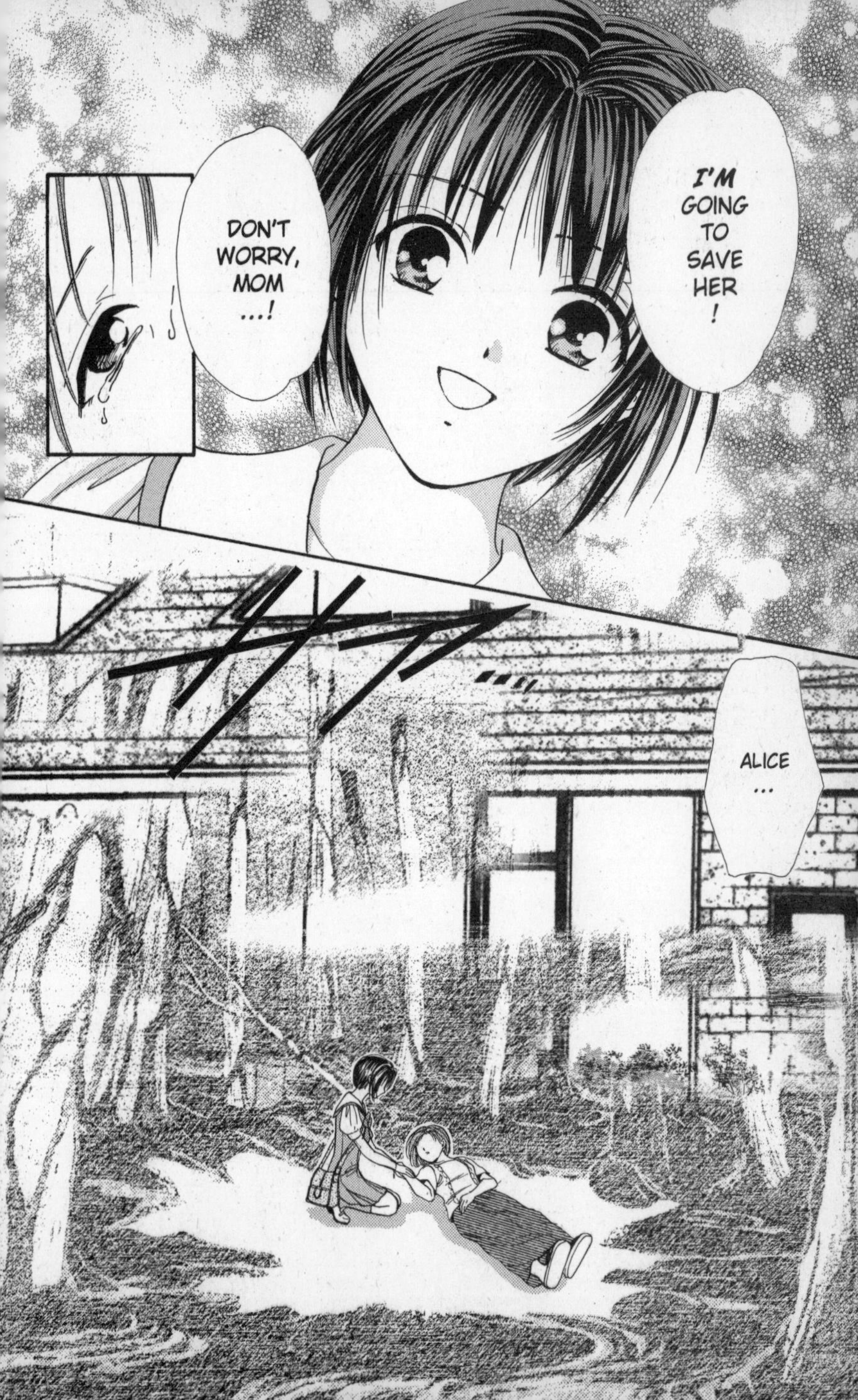
I'M GOING TO SAVE HER!
DON'T WORRY, MOM ...!
ALICE ...

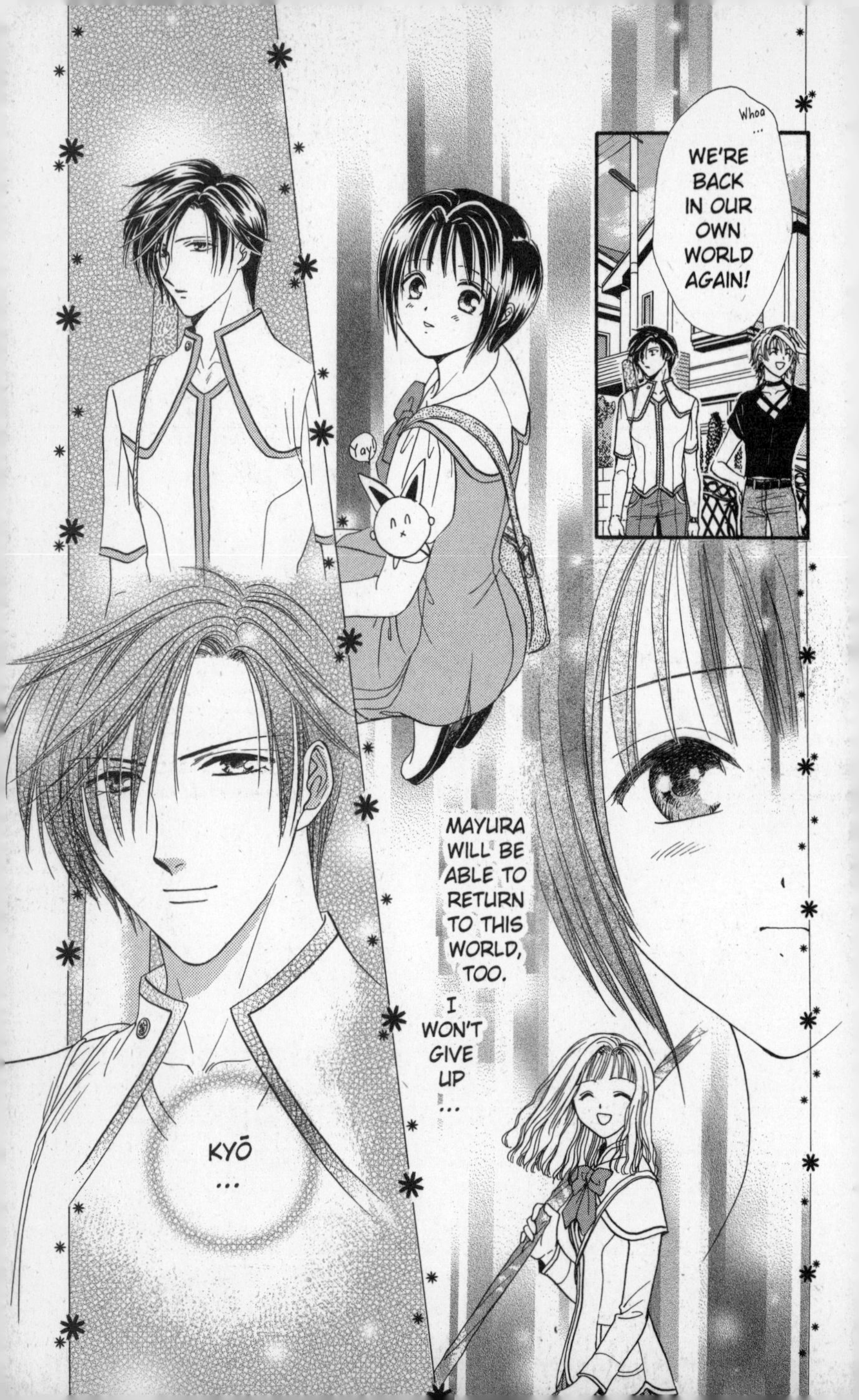
Whoa ...
WE'RE BACK IN OUR OWN WORLD AGAIN!
Yay!
MAYURA WILL BE ABLE TO RETURN TO THIS WORLD, TOO.
I WON'T GIVE UP ...
KYŌ ...

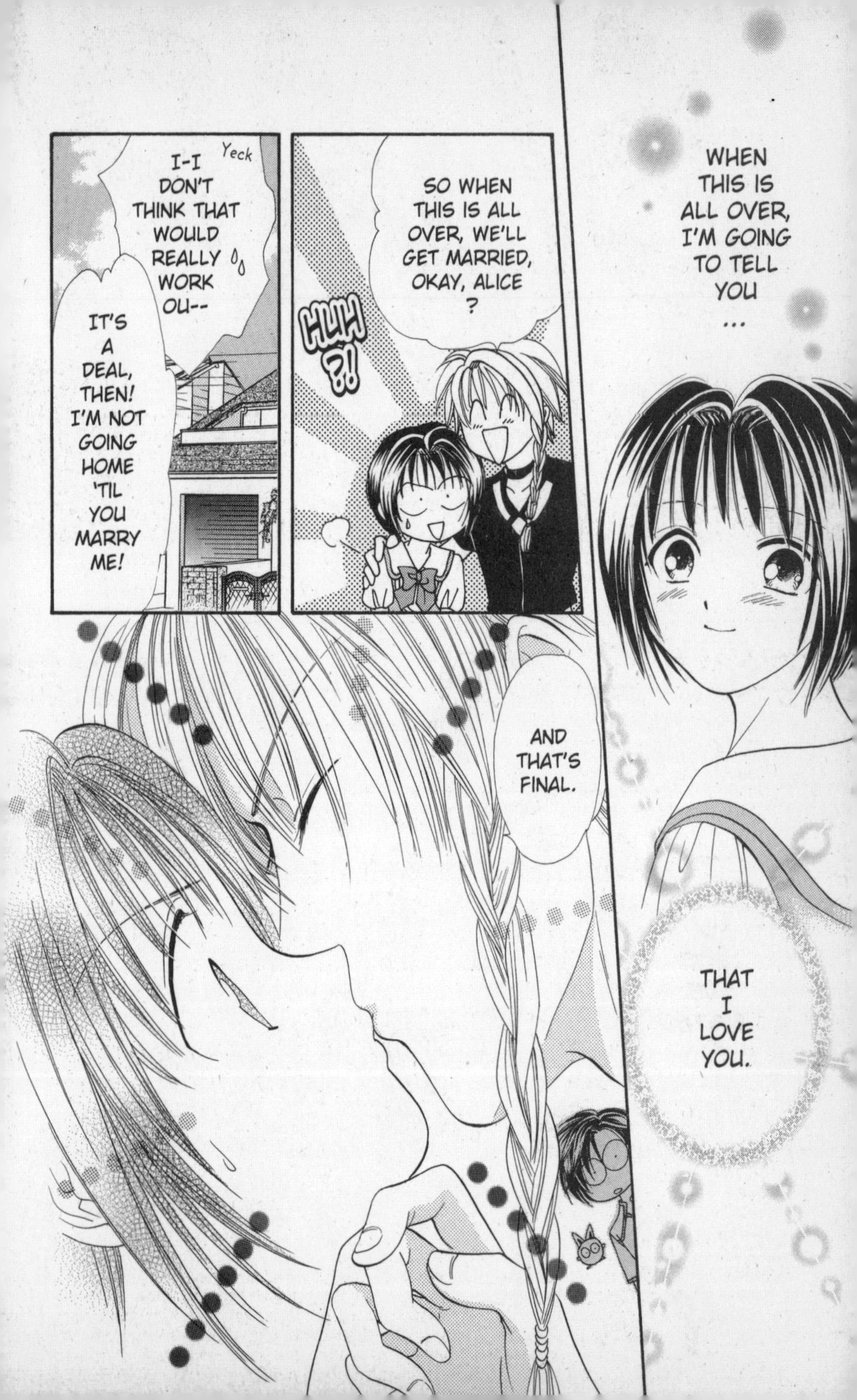
WHEN THIS IS ALL OVER, I'M GOING TO TELL YOU ...
THAT I LOVE YOU.
SO WHEN THIS IS ALL OVER, WE'LL GET MARRIED, OKAY, ALICE ?
HUH ?!
Yeck
I-I DON'T THINK THAT WOULD REALLY WORK OU--
IT'S A DEAL, THEN! I'M NOT GOING HOME 'TIL YOU MARRY ME!
AND THAT'S FINAL.

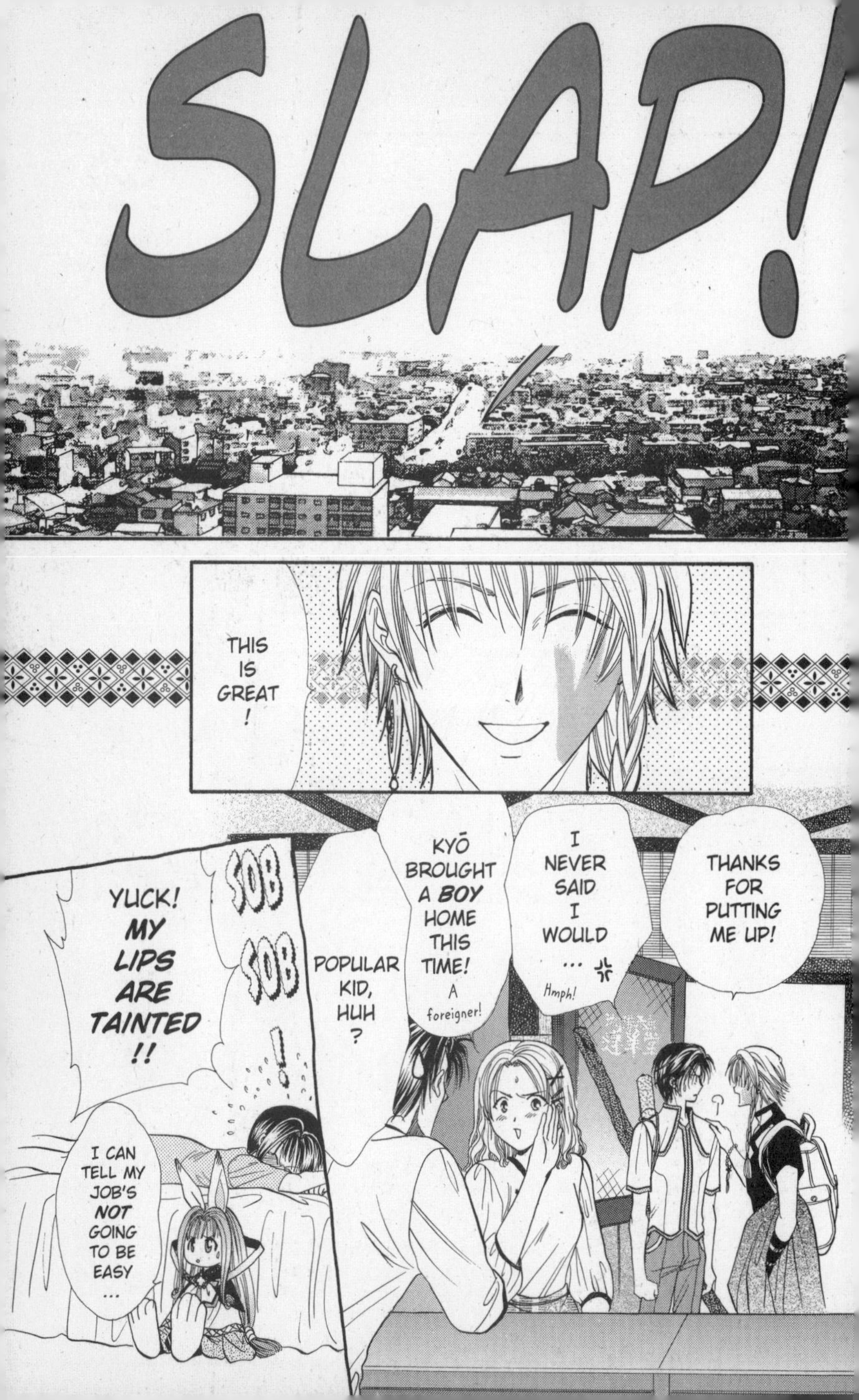
SLAP!
THIS IS GREAT!
THANKS FOR PUTTING ME UP!
I NEVER SAID I WOULD...
Hmph!
KYŌ BROUGHT A BOY HOME THIS TIME!
A foreigner!
POPULAR KID, HUH?
SOB SOB
!
YUCK! MY LIPS ARE TAINTED!!
I CAN TELL MY JOB'S NOT GOING TO BE EASY...

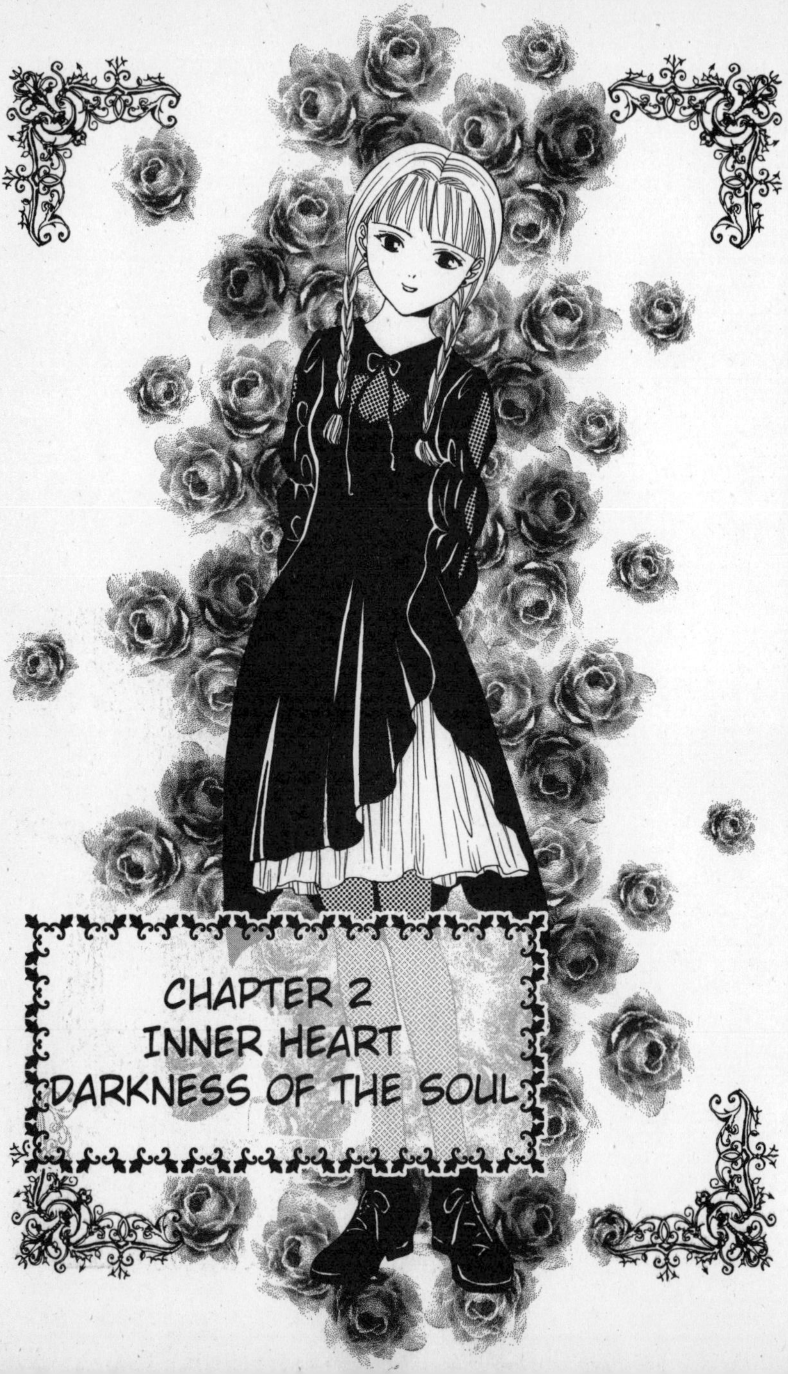
CHAPTER 2
INNER HEART
DARKNESS OF THE SOUL

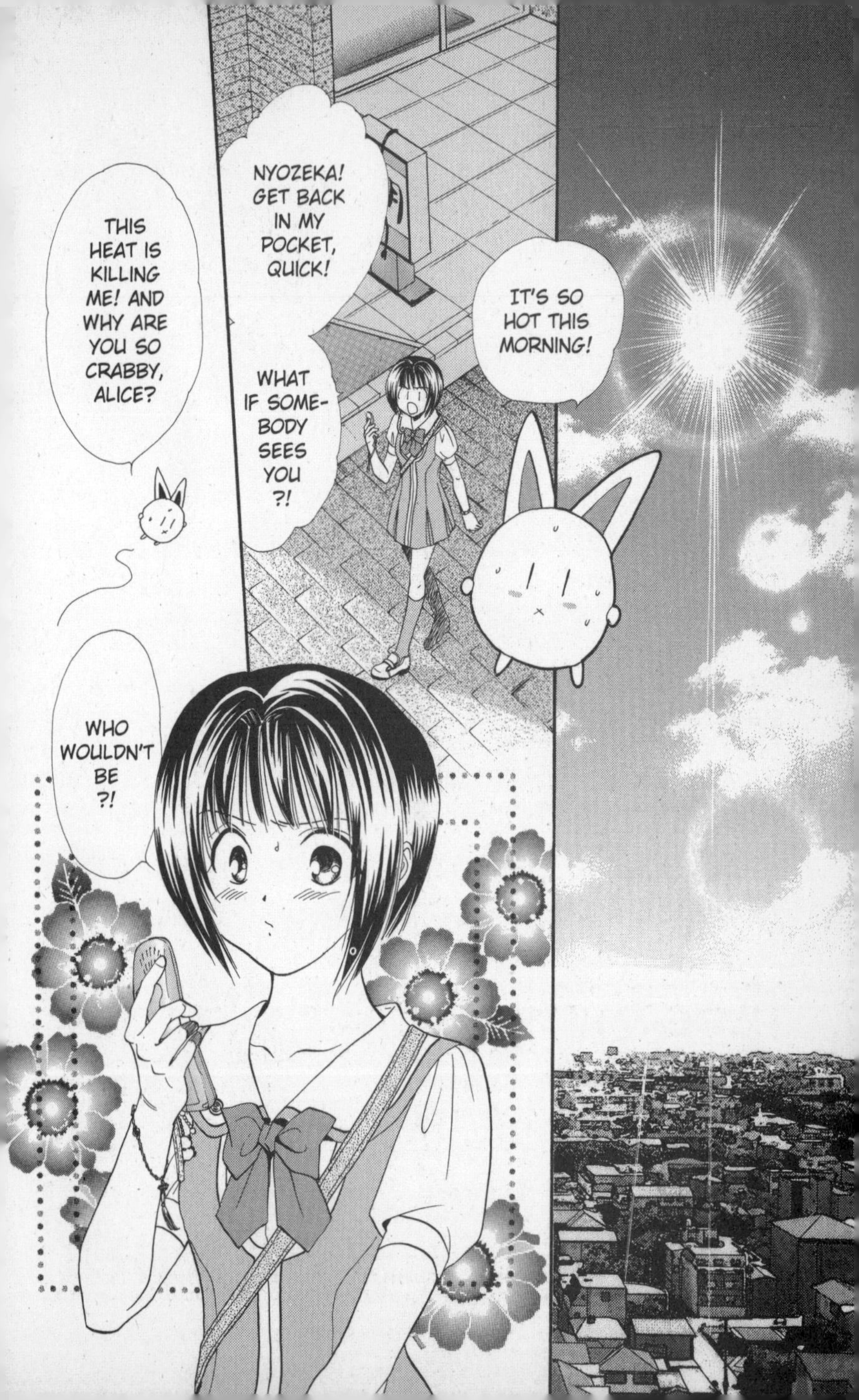
IT'S SO HOT THIS MORNING!
NYOZEKA! GET BACK IN MY POCKET, QUICK!
WHAT IF SOME-BODY SEES YOU ?!
THIS HEAT IS KILLING ME! AND WHY ARE YOU SO CRABBY, ALICE?
WHO WOULDN'T BE ?!

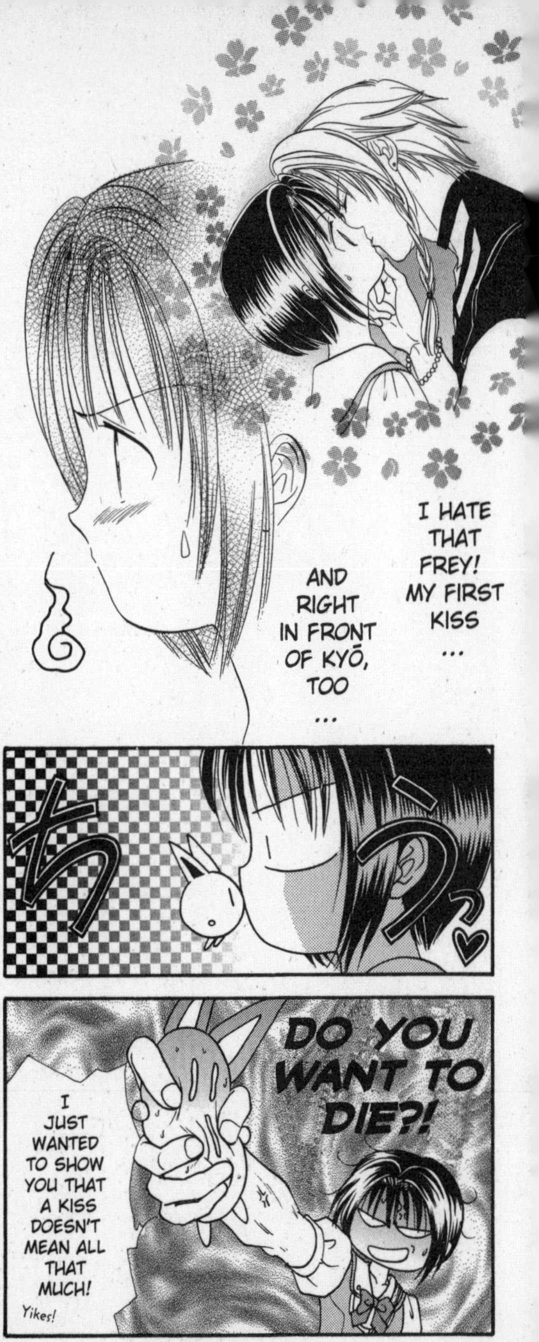
I HATE THAT FREY! MY FIRST KISS ...
AND RIGHT IN FRONT OF KYŌ, TOO ...
DO YOU WANT TO DIE?!
I JUST WANTED TO SHOW YOU THAT A KISS DOESN'T MEAN ALL THAT MUCH!
Yikes!

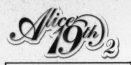

I'm kind of happy that there are so many fantasy movies coming out this winter!
I've already seen Harry Potter. Next, there's Lord of the Rings, and Atlantis... (Today is December 12.) There are so many movies to see! At New Year's, there's going to be a bunch of movies on Sky Perfect TV! All those movies! So give me a break from work!!! I've got videos piling up that need watching! And video games, too! Ah, and books!!
Now, to change the subject, I've been seeing the dentist all summer. It's because I got a cavity in my lower wisdom tooth!
My teeth have been quite good, so until the age of 17, I never had a cavity or saw a dentist. And when I went to the dentist for the first time, I supposedly had that lower wisdom tooth removed.
But then how did I get a cavity there? When I told the dentist this last time that my wisdom tooth must have grown back, they all laughed at me. Darn it, I was tricked!!
Anyway, I'll never forget this 3 hour major surgery that I just had. When it was all over, I couldn't help telling everybody, "They did it without giving me any anesthesia!!"
Actually, they did give me a shot, but it had no effect on me. I'm sure those who've experienced it will understand. Just a touch on a nerve is major pain! And this lasted 3 hours!! I struggled like crazy and yelled!! The dental assistant had to hold my hand. In my pain, I screamed out, "Am I going into labor?!!" The assistant burst out laughing. But even under these extreme circumstances, the mind thinks of all kinds of things.

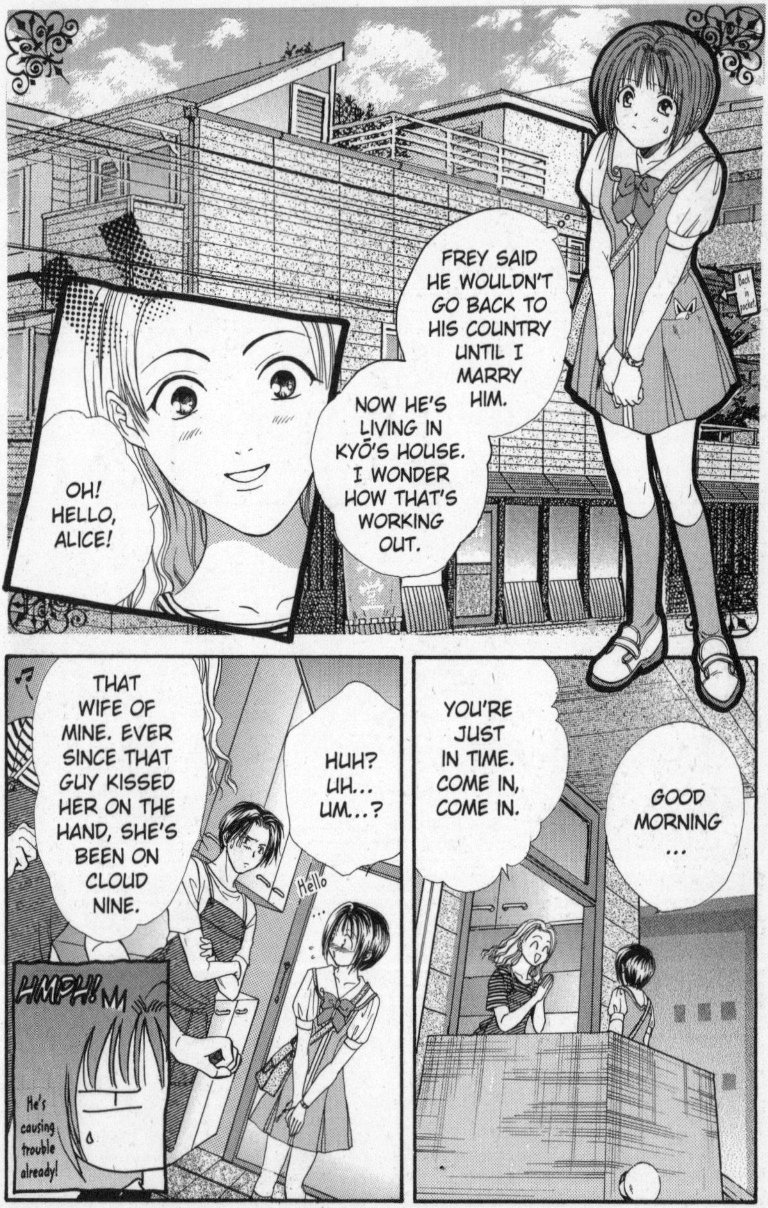
FREY SAID HE WOULDN'T GO BACK TO HIS COUNTRY UNTIL I MARRY HIM.
NOW HE'S LIVING IN KYŌ'S HOUSE. I WONDER HOW THAT'S WORKING OUT.
Back in pocket
OH! HELLO, ALICE!
GOOD MORNING ...
YOU'RE JUST IN TIME. COME IN, COME IN.
HUH? UH... UM...?
Hello ...
THAT WIFE OF MINE. EVER SINCE THAT GUY KISSED HER ON THE HAND, SHE'S BEEN ON CLOUD NINE.
HMPH!
He's causing trouble already!

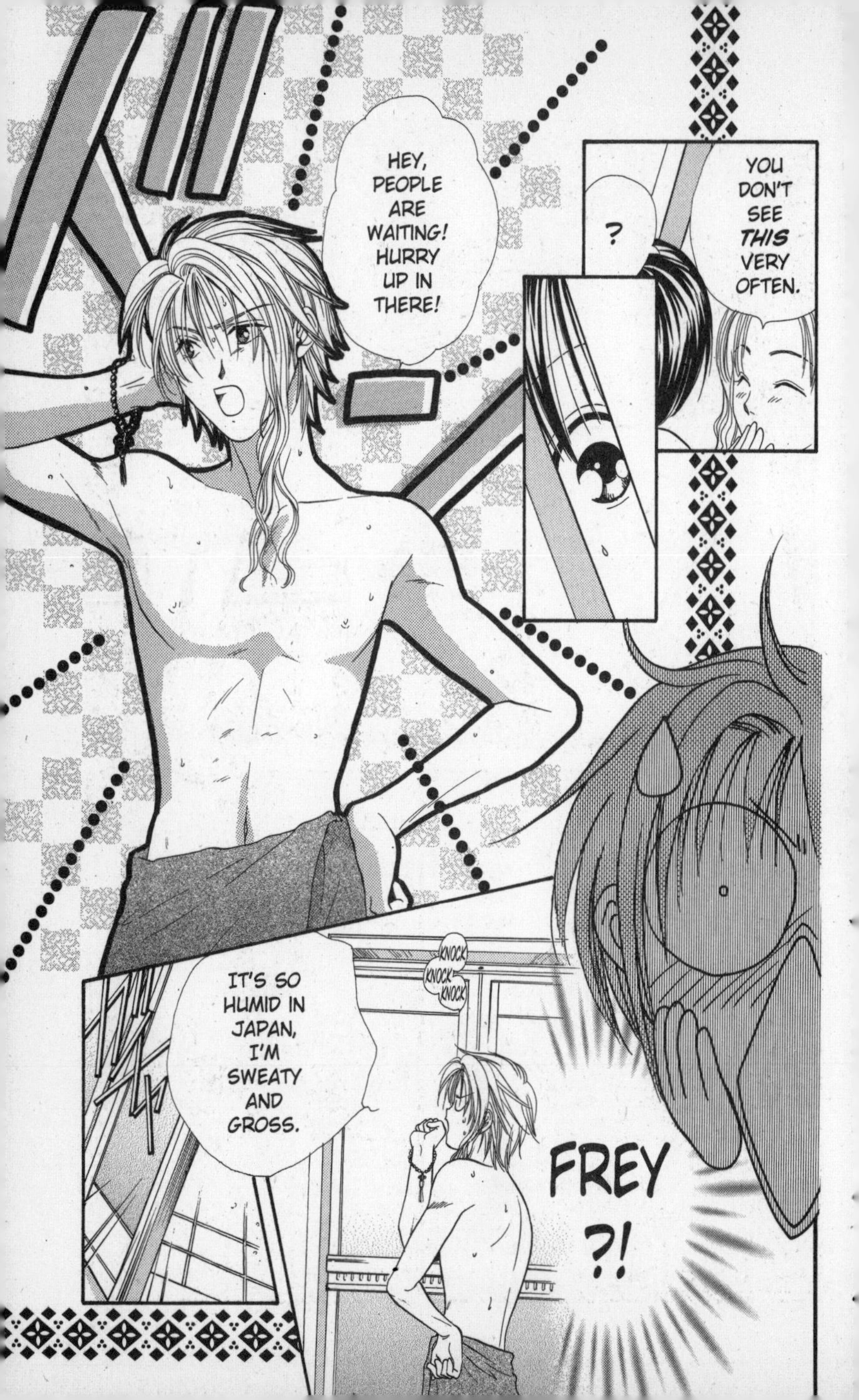
YOU DON'T SEE *THIS* VERY OFTEN.
?
HEY, PEOPLE ARE WAITING! HURRY UP IN THERE!
FREY ?!
KNOCK KNOCK KNOCK
IT'S SO HUMID IN JAPAN, I'M SWEATY AND GROSS.

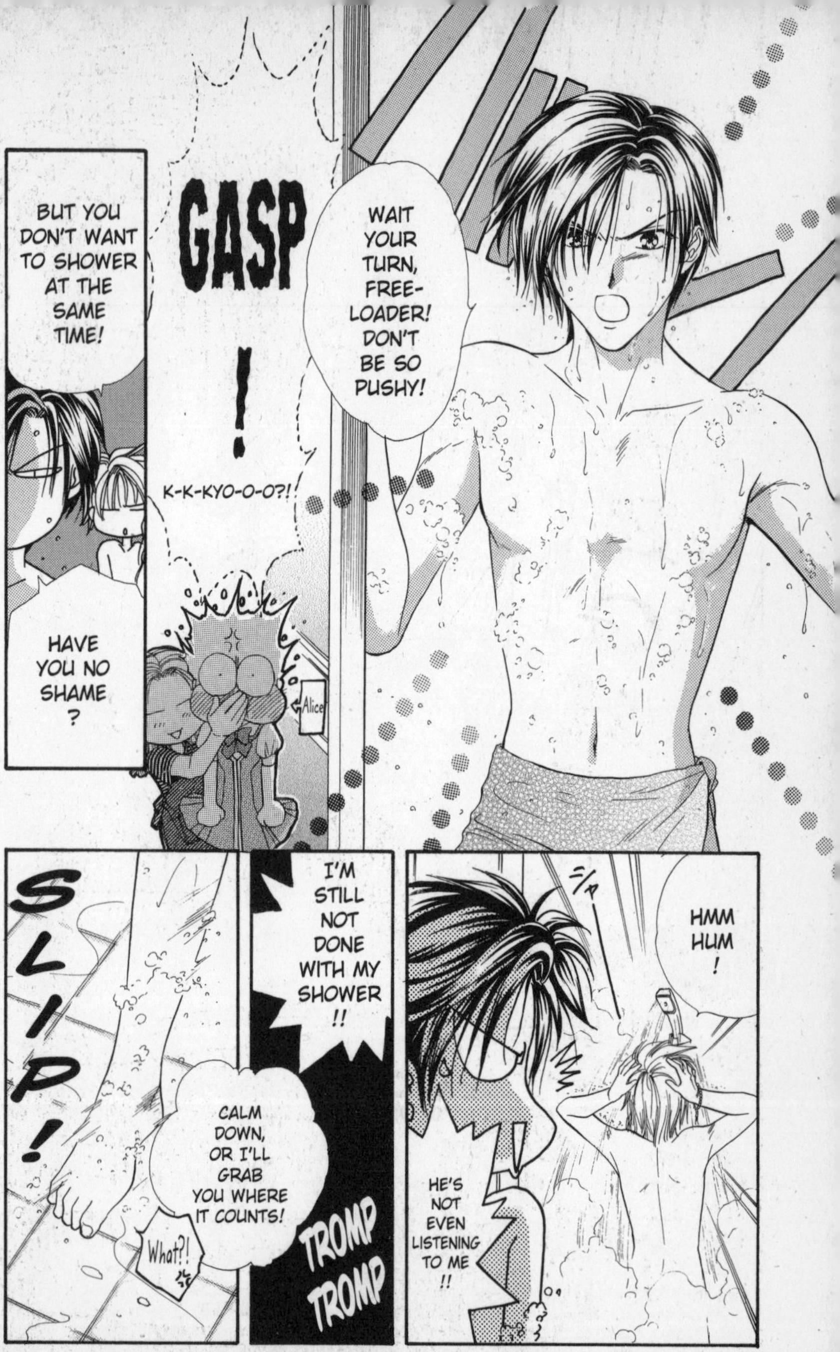
WAIT YOUR TURN, FREE-LOADER! DON'T BE SO PUSHY!
GASP!
K-K-KYO-O-O?!
BUT YOU DON'T WANT TO SHOWER AT THE SAME TIME!
HAVE YOU NO SHAME?
HMM HUM!
HE'S NOT EVEN LISTENING TO ME!!
I'M STILL NOT DONE WITH MY SHOWER!!
TROMP TROMP
SLIP!
CALM DOWN, OR I'LL GRAB YOU WHERE IT COUNTS!
What?!

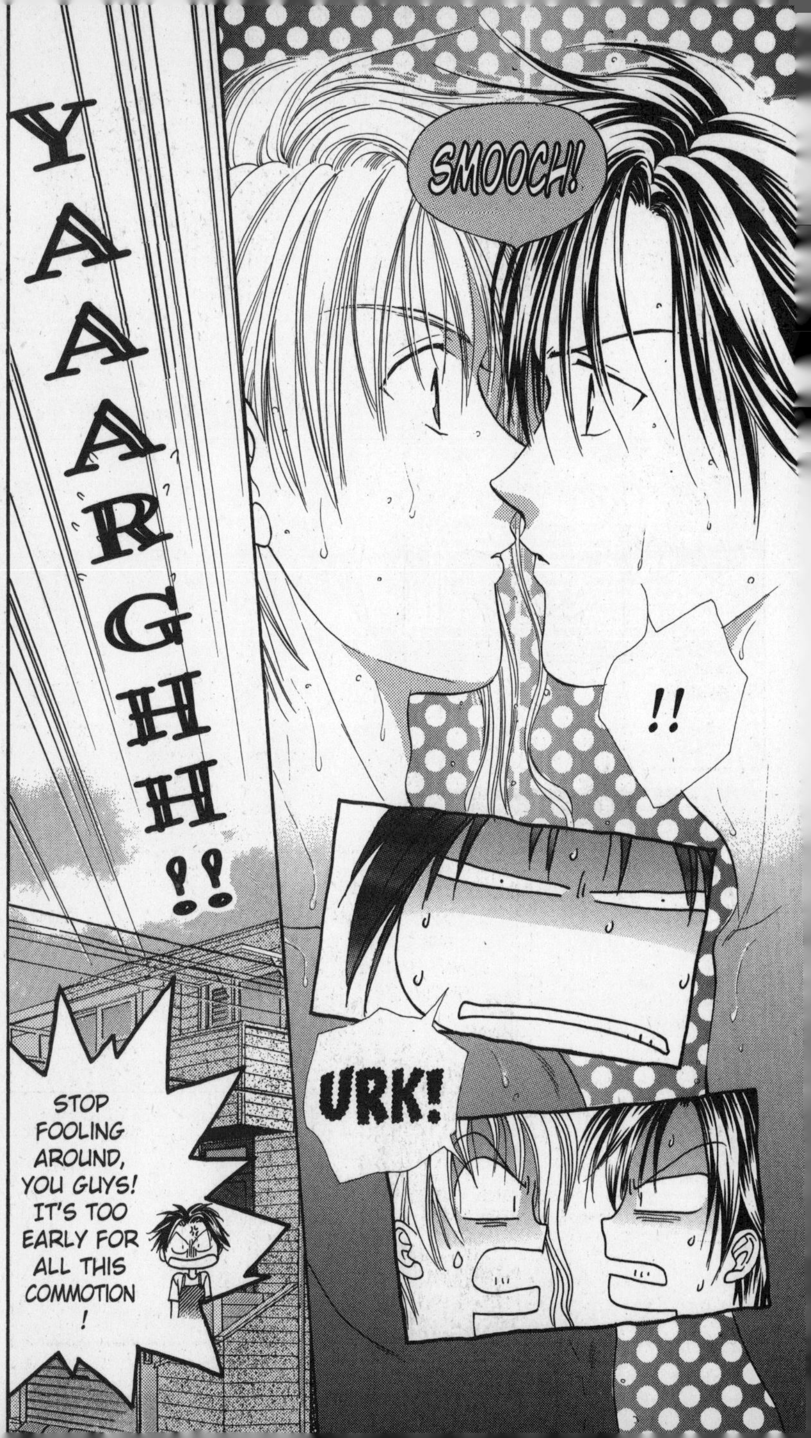
SMOOCH!
!!
URK!
YAAARGHH!!
STOP FOOLING AROUND, YOU GUYS! IT'S TOO EARLY FOR ALL THIS COMMOTION!

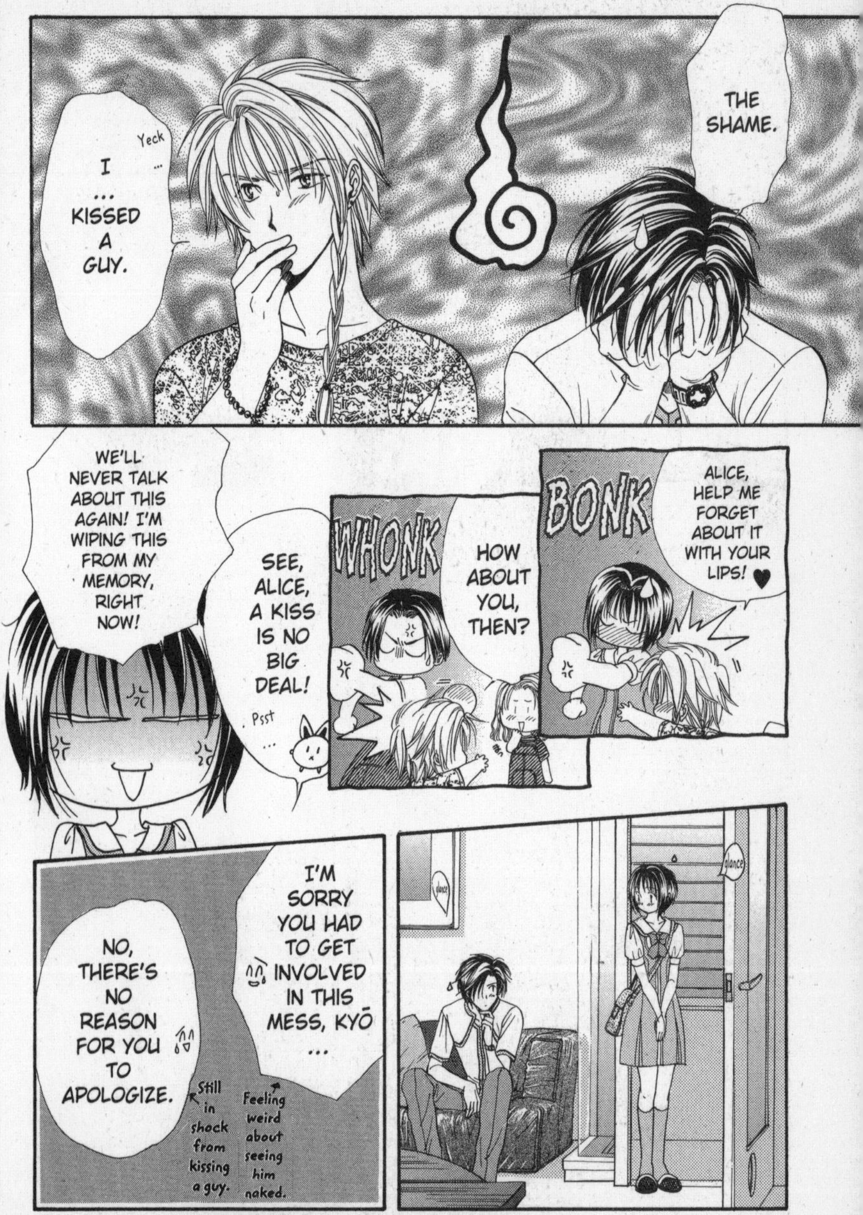
THE SHAME.
Yeck ...
I ... KISSED A GUY.
BONK
ALICE, HELP ME FORGET ABOUT IT WITH YOUR LIPS! ♥
WHONK
HOW ABOUT YOU, THEN?
SEE, ALICE, A KISS IS NO BIG DEAL!
Psst ...
WE'LL NEVER TALK ABOUT THIS AGAIN! I'M WIPING THIS FROM MY MEMORY, RIGHT NOW!
glance
glance
I'M SORRY YOU HAD TO GET INVOLVED IN THIS MESS, KYŌ ...
Feeling weird about seeing him naked.
NO, THERE'S NO REASON FOR YOU TO APOLOGIZE.
Still in shock from kissing a guy.

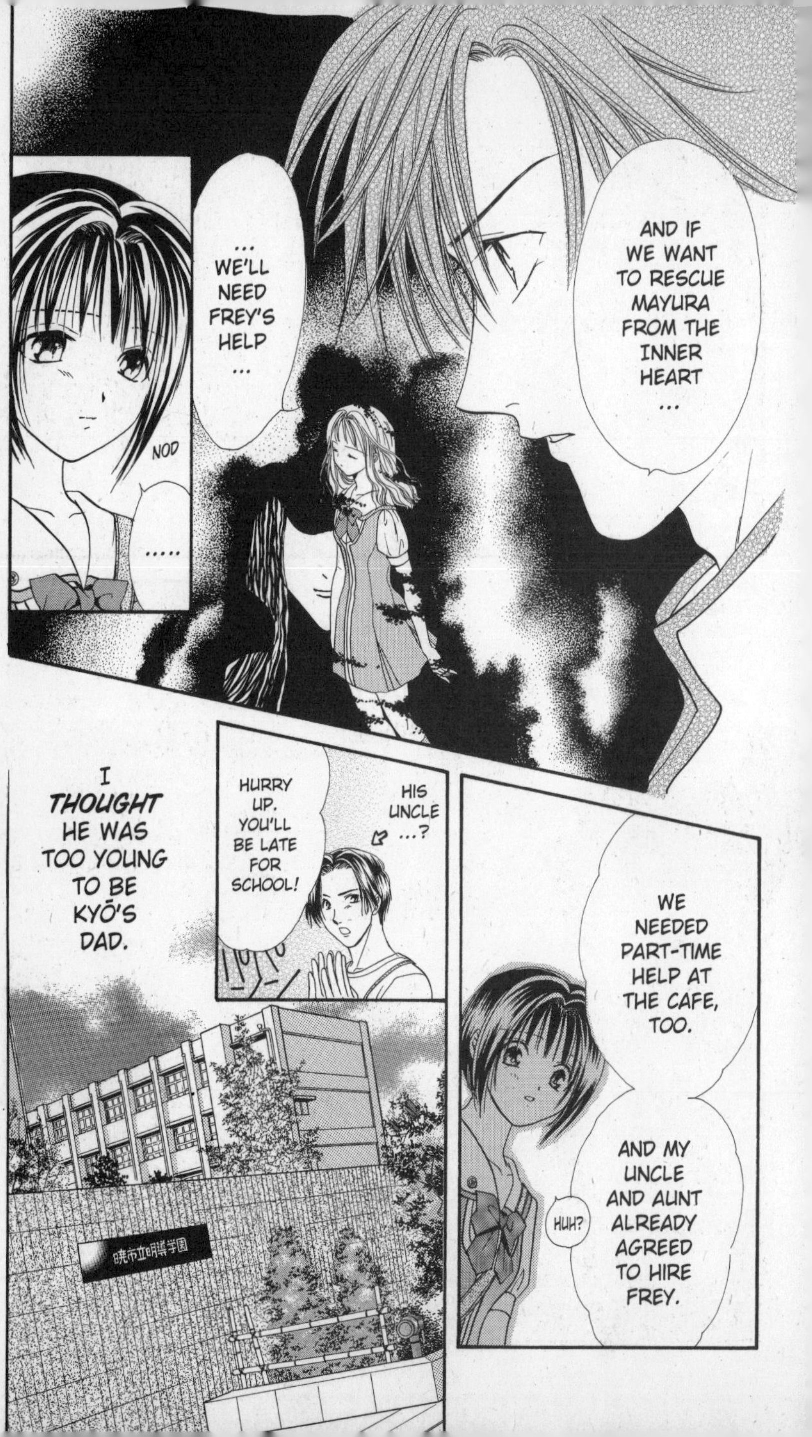
AND IF WE WANT TO RESCUE MAYURA FROM THE INNER HEART ...
... WE'LL NEED FREY'S HELP ...
NOD
.....
WE NEEDED PART-TIME HELP AT THE CAFE, TOO.
AND MY UNCLE AND AUNT ALREADY AGREED TO HIRE FREY.
HUH?
HURRY UP. YOU'LL BE LATE FOR SCHOOL!
HIS UNCLE ...?
I *THOUGHT* HE WAS TOO YOUNG TO BE KYŌ'S DAD.
暁市立明導学園

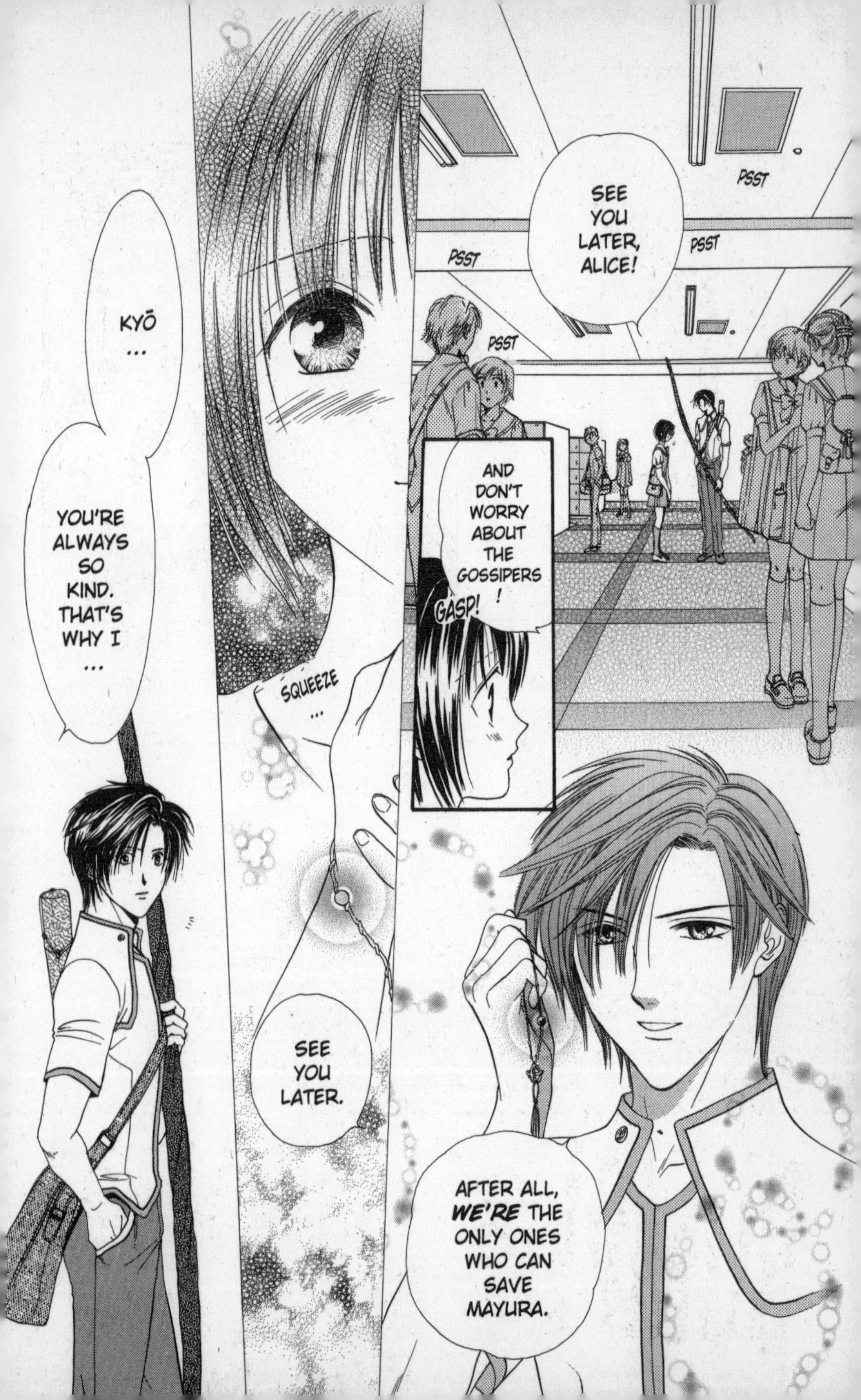
SEE YOU LATER, ALICE!
PSST
PSST
PSST
PSST
AND DON'T WORRY ABOUT THE GOSSIPERS!
GASP!
AFTER ALL, ***WE'RE*** THE ONLY ONES WHO CAN SAVE MAYURA.
SQUEEZE ...
SEE YOU LATER.
KYŌ ...
YOU'RE ALWAYS SO KIND. THAT'S WHY I ...

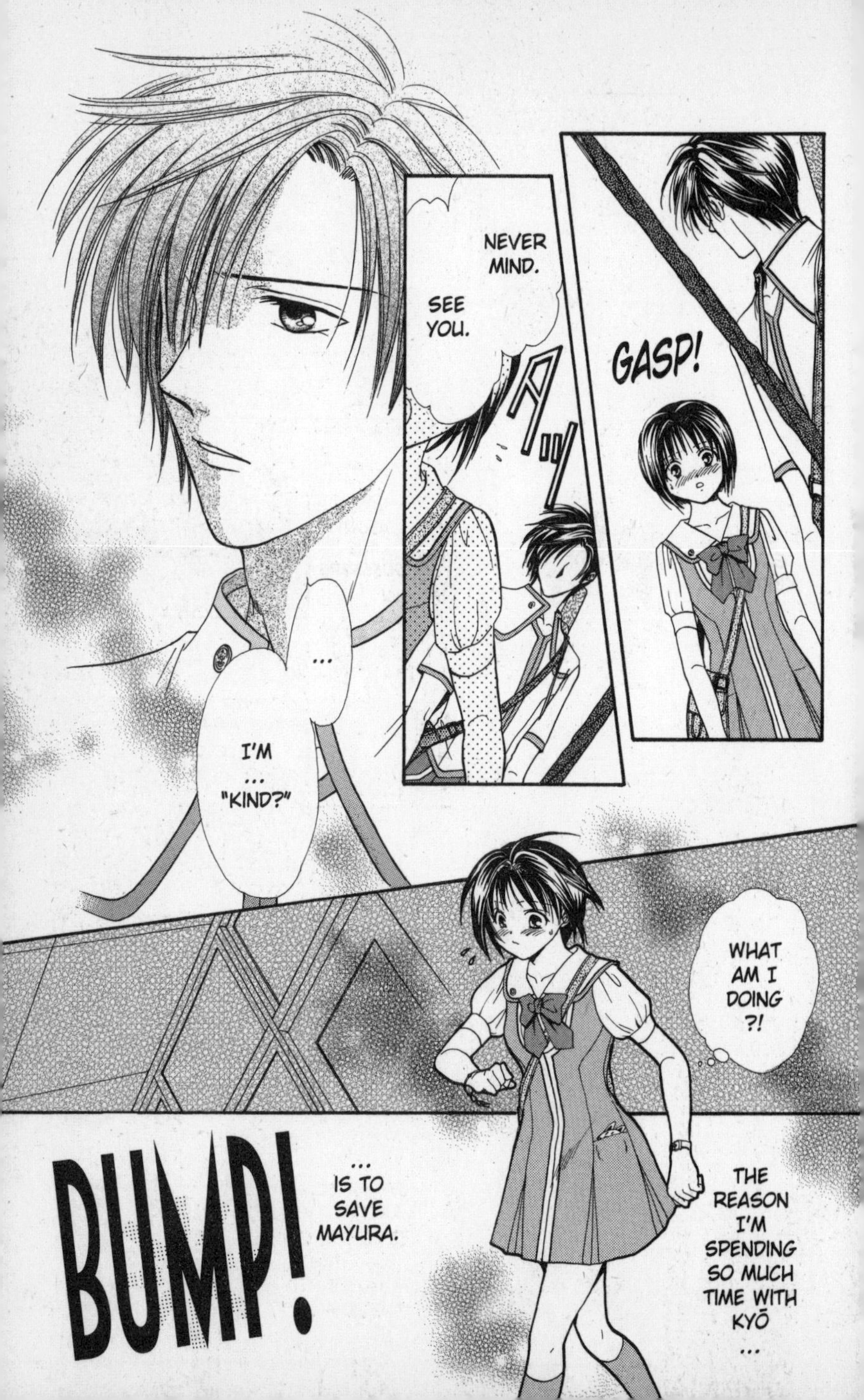
GASP!
NEVER MIND.
SEE YOU.
...
I'M ... "KIND?"
WHAT AM I DOING ?!
THE REASON I'M SPENDING SO MUCH TIME WITH KYŌ ...
... IS TO SAVE MAYURA.
BUMP!

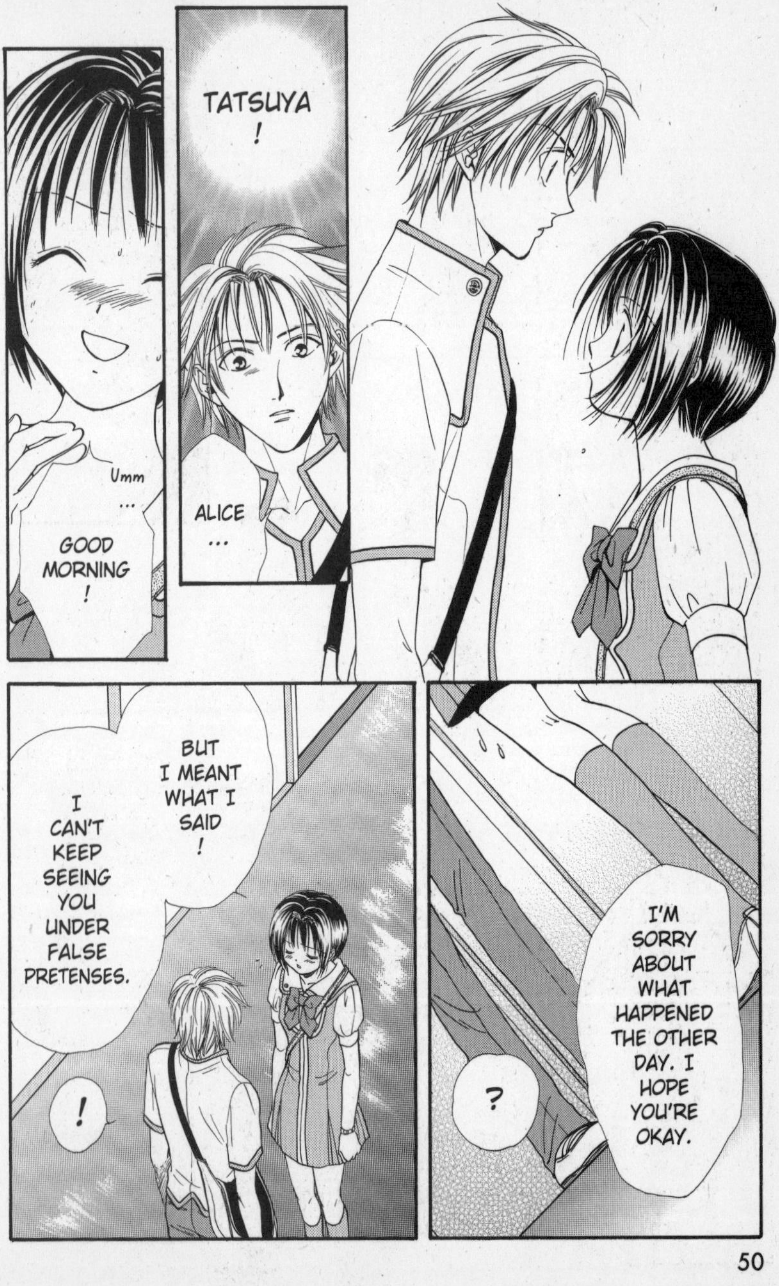
TATSUYA !
ALICE ...
Umm ...
GOOD MORNING !
I'M SORRY ABOUT WHAT HAPPENED THE OTHER DAY. I HOPE YOU'RE OKAY.
?
BUT I MEANT WHAT I SAID !
I CAN'T KEEP SEEING YOU UNDER FALSE PRETENSES.
!

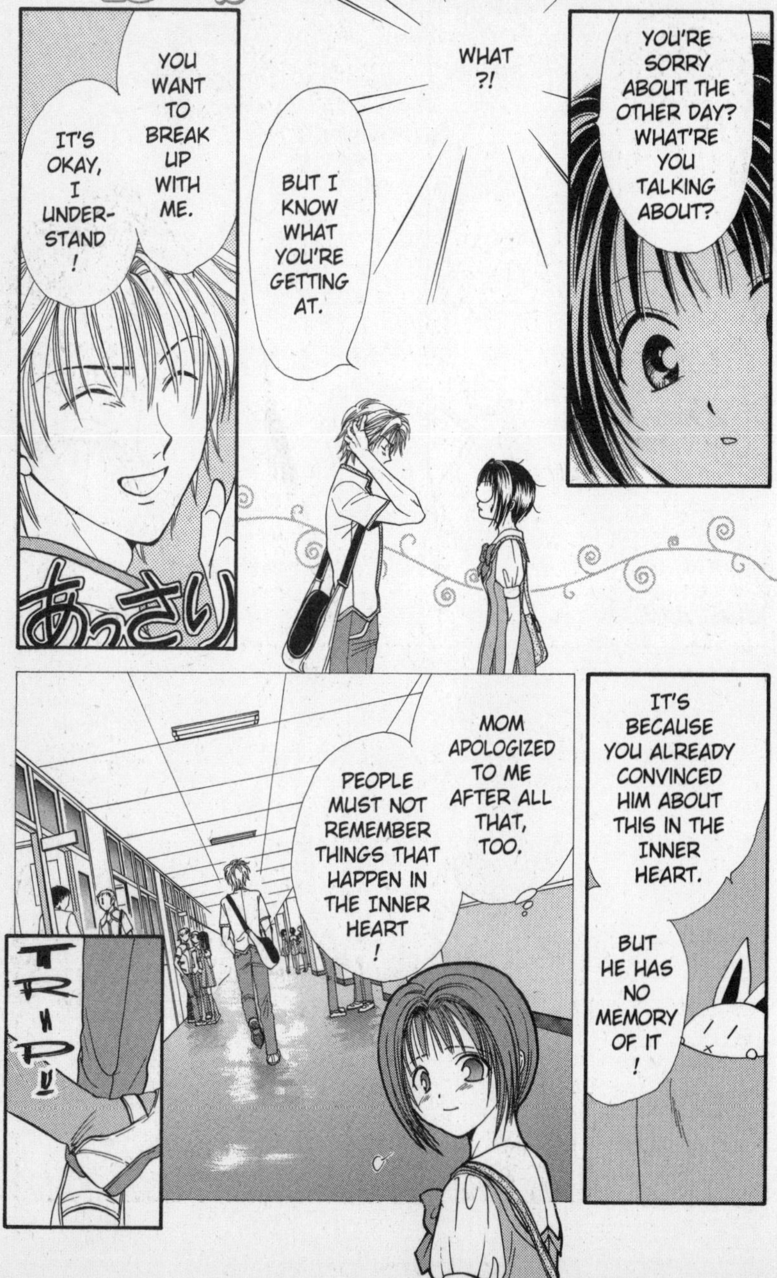
YOU'RE SORRY ABOUT THE OTHER DAY? WHAT'RE YOU TALKING ABOUT?
WHAT ?!
BUT I KNOW WHAT YOU'RE GETTING AT.
YOU WANT TO BREAK UP WITH ME.
IT'S OKAY, I UNDERSTAND!
あっさり
IT'S BECAUSE YOU ALREADY CONVINCED HIM ABOUT THIS IN THE INNER HEART.
BUT HE HAS NO MEMORY OF IT!
MOM APOLOGIZED TO ME AFTER ALL THAT, TOO.
PEOPLE MUST NOT REMEMBER THINGS THAT HAPPEN IN THE INNER HEART!
TRIP!!

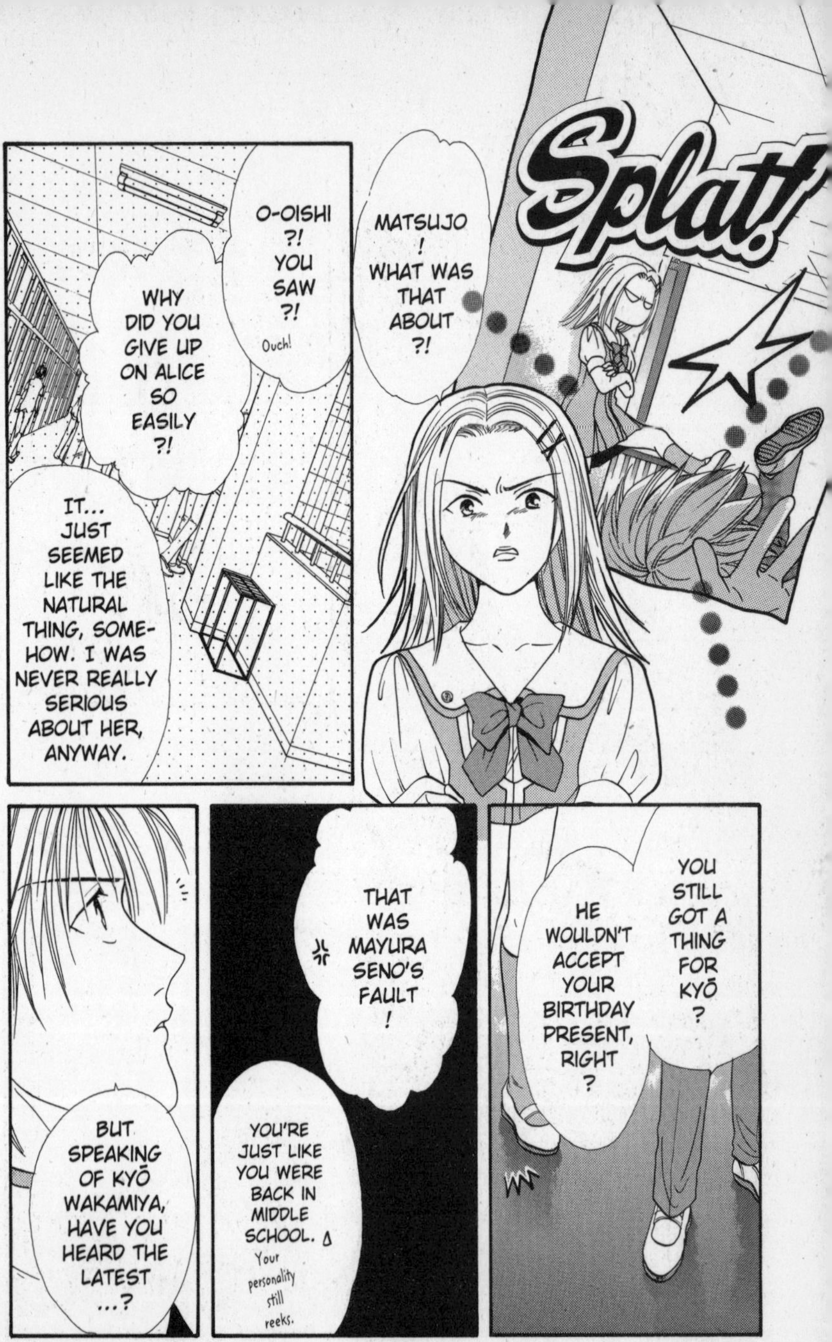
Splat!
MATSUJO! WHAT WAS THAT ABOUT?!
O-OISHI?! YOU SAW?!
Ouch!
WHY DID YOU GIVE UP ON ALICE SO EASILY?!
IT... JUST SEEMED LIKE THE NATURAL THING, SOMEHOW. I WAS NEVER REALLY SERIOUS ABOUT HER, ANYWAY.
YOU STILL GOT A THING FOR KYŌ?
HE WOULDN'T ACCEPT YOUR BIRTHDAY PRESENT, RIGHT?
THAT WAS MAYURA SENO'S FAULT!
YOU'RE JUST LIKE YOU WERE BACK IN MIDDLE SCHOOL.
Your personality still reeks.
BUT SPEAKING OF KYŌ WAKAMIYA, HAVE YOU HEARD THE LATEST ...?

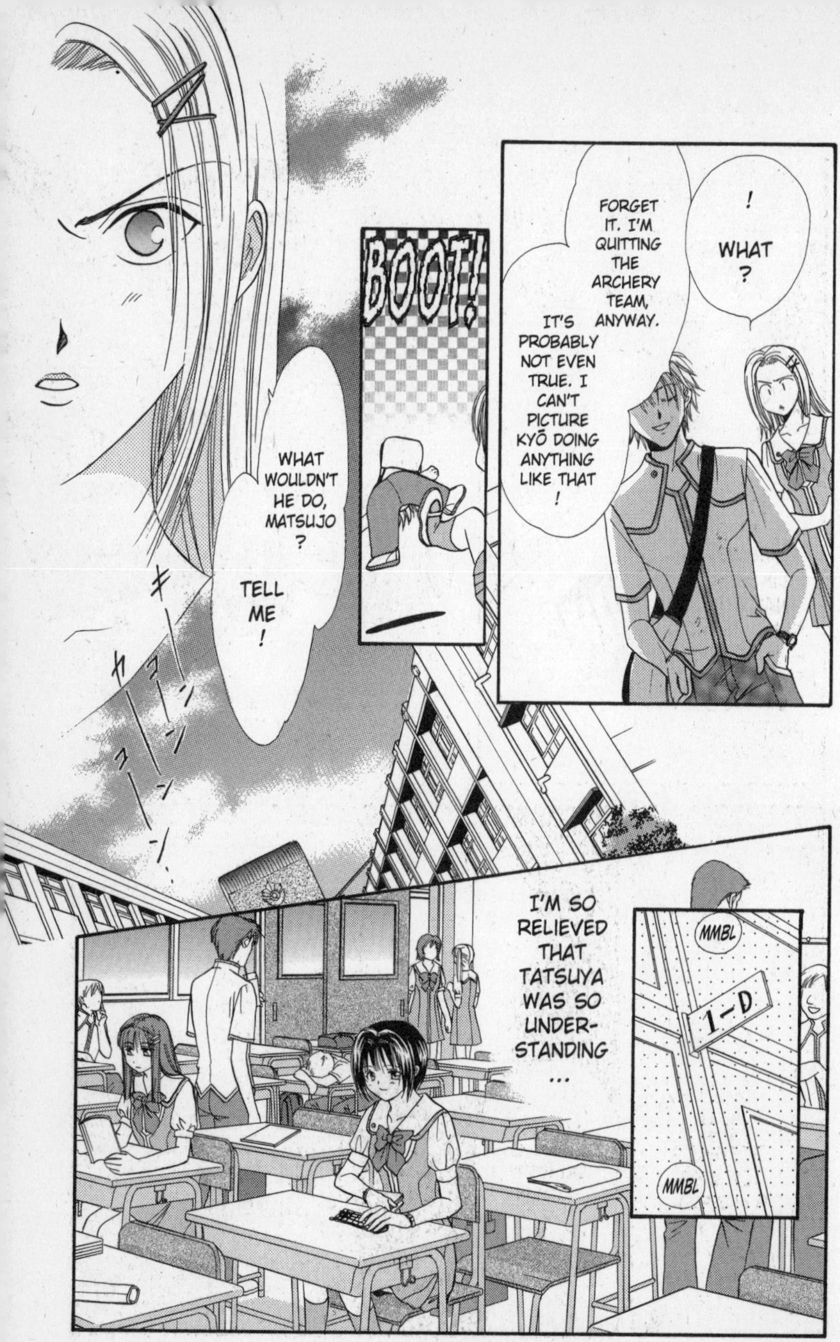
! WHAT?
FORGET IT. I'M QUITTING THE ARCHERY TEAM, ANYWAY.
IT'S PROBABLY NOT EVEN TRUE. I CAN'T PICTURE KYŌ DOING ANYTHING LIKE THAT!
BOOT!
WHAT WOULDN'T HE DO, MATSUJO?
TELL ME!
MMBL
1-D
MMBL
I'M SO RELIEVED THAT TATSUYA WAS SO UNDER-STANDING...

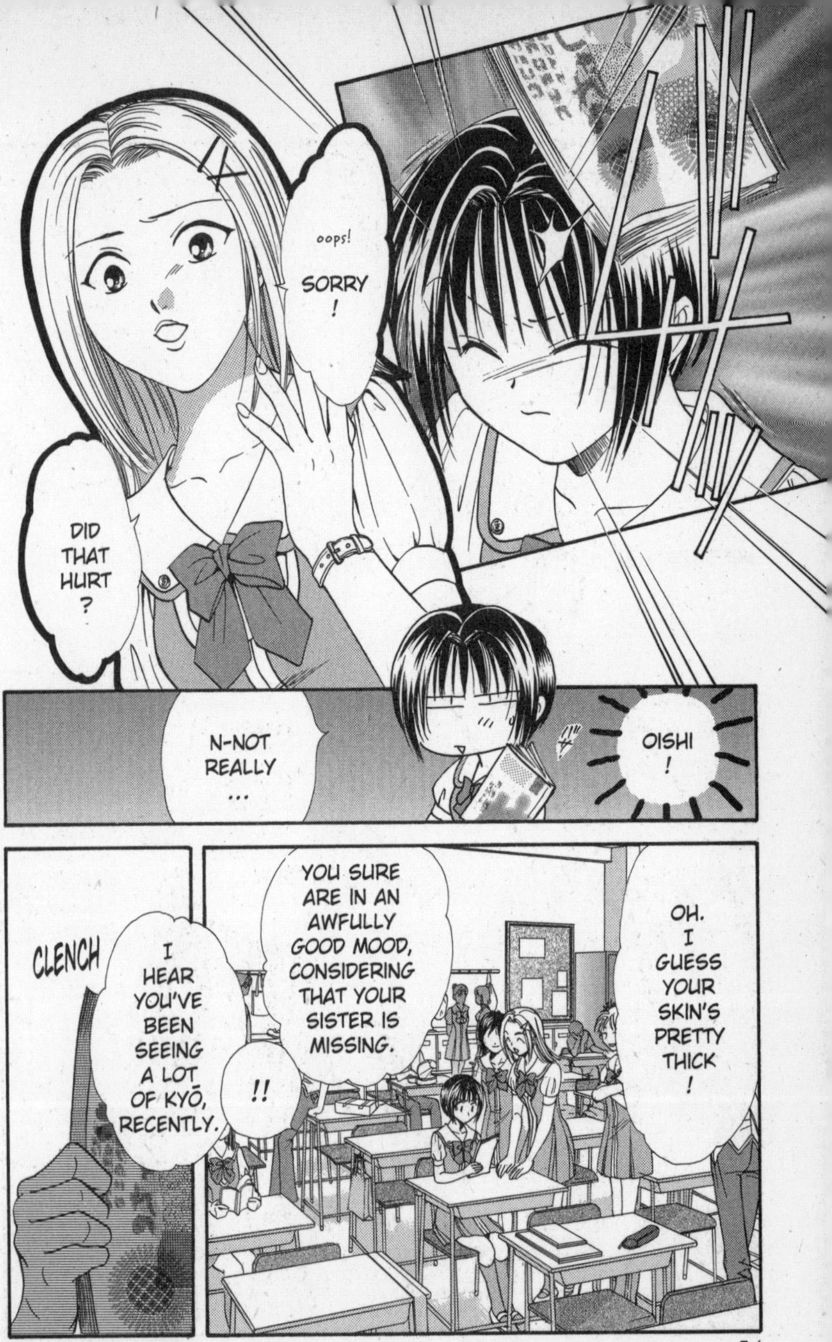
oops!
SORRY!
DID THAT HURT?
OISHI!
N-NOT REALLY...
OH. I GUESS YOUR SKIN'S PRETTY THICK!
YOU SURE ARE IN AN AWFULLY GOOD MOOD, CONSIDERING THAT YOUR SISTER IS MISSING.
!!
CLENCH
I HEAR YOU'VE BEEN SEEING A LOT OF KYŌ, RECENTLY.

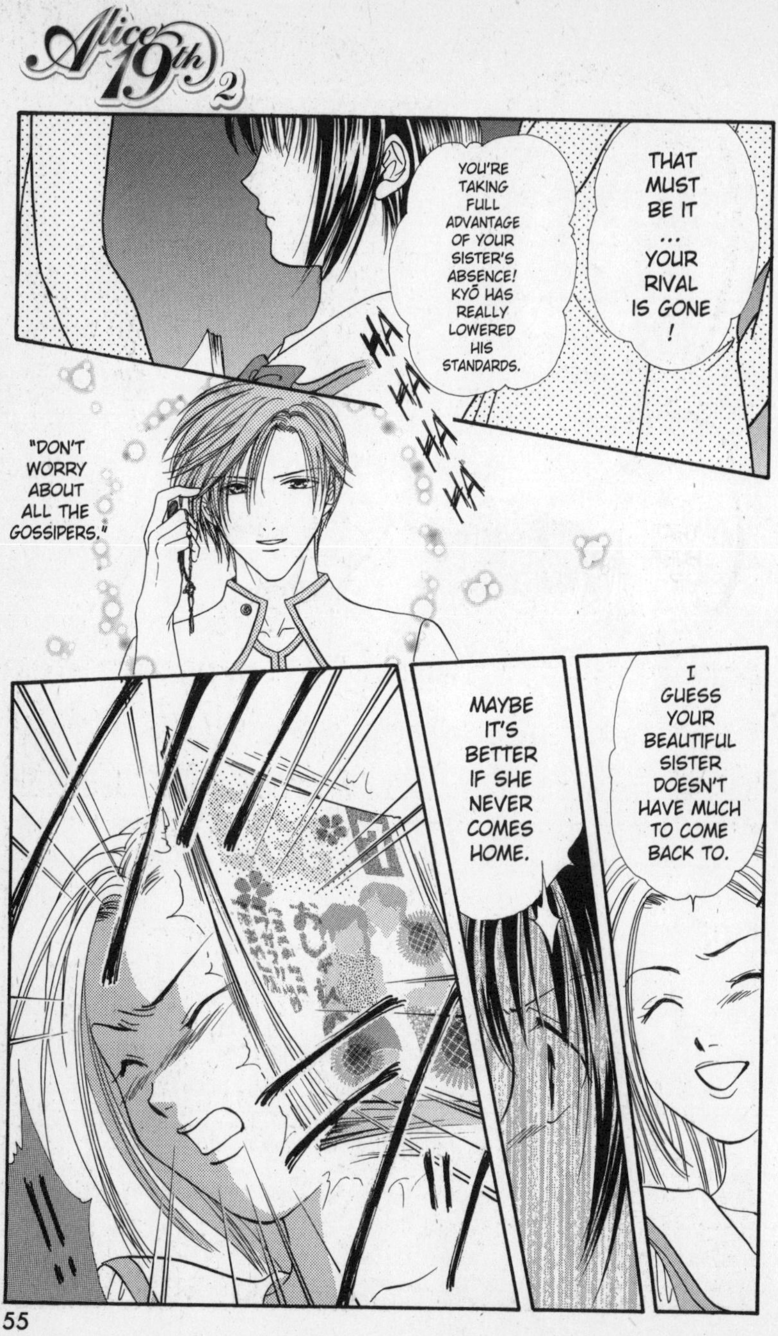
THAT MUST BE IT ... YOUR RIVAL IS GONE!
YOU'RE TAKING FULL ADVANTAGE OF YOUR SISTER'S ABSENCE! KYŌ HAS REALLY LOWERED HIS STANDARDS.
HA HA HA HA HA
"DON'T WORRY ABOUT ALL THE GOSSIPERS."
I GUESS YOUR BEAUTIFUL SISTER DOESN'T HAVE MUCH TO COME BACK TO.
MAYBE IT'S BETTER IF SHE NEVER COMES HOME.

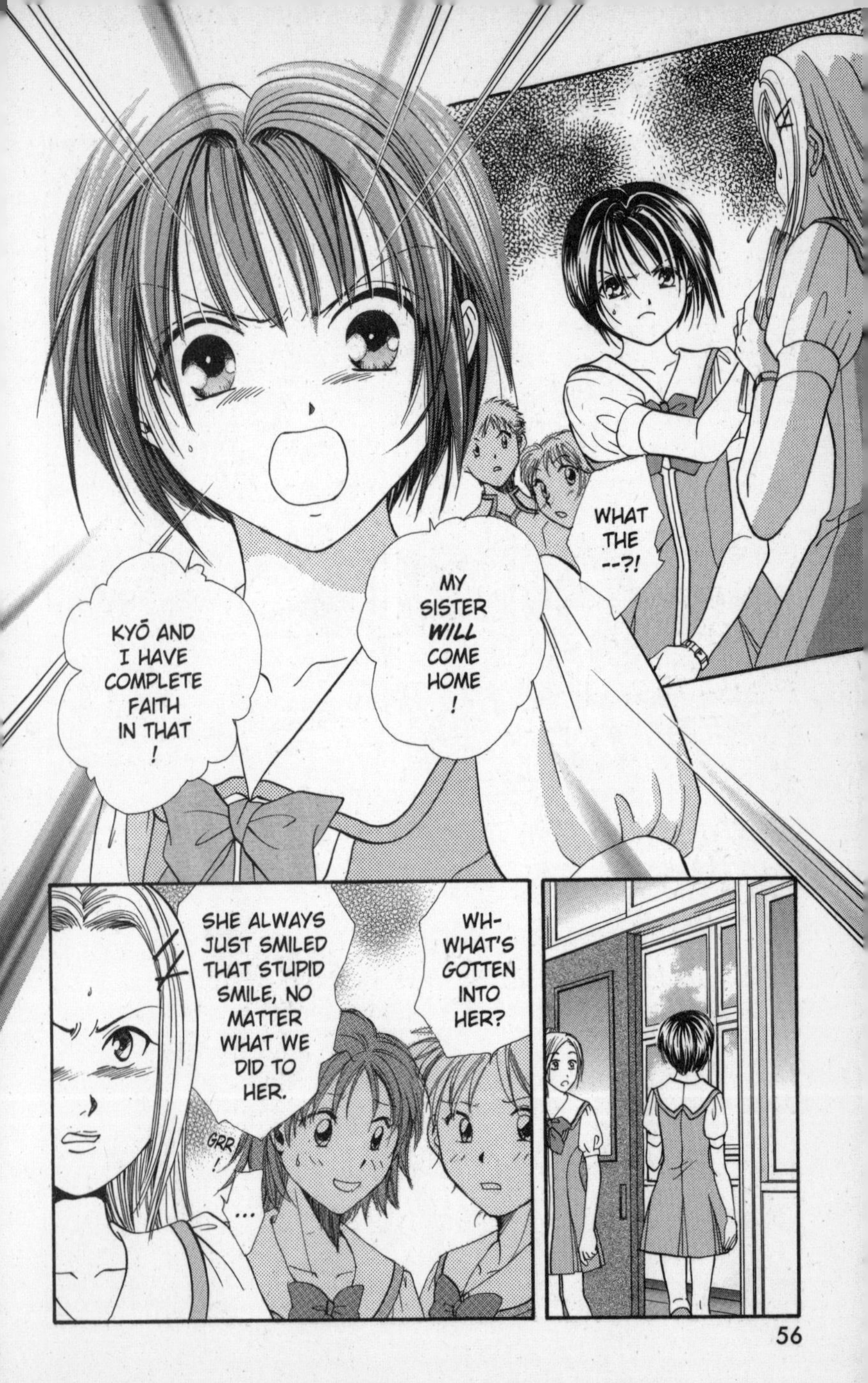
WHAT THE --?!
MY SISTER WILL COME HOME!
KYŌ AND I HAVE COMPLETE FAITH IN THAT!
WH- WHAT'S GOTTEN INTO HER?
SHE ALWAYS JUST SMILED THAT STUPID SMILE, NO MATTER WHAT WE DID TO HER.
GRR!
...

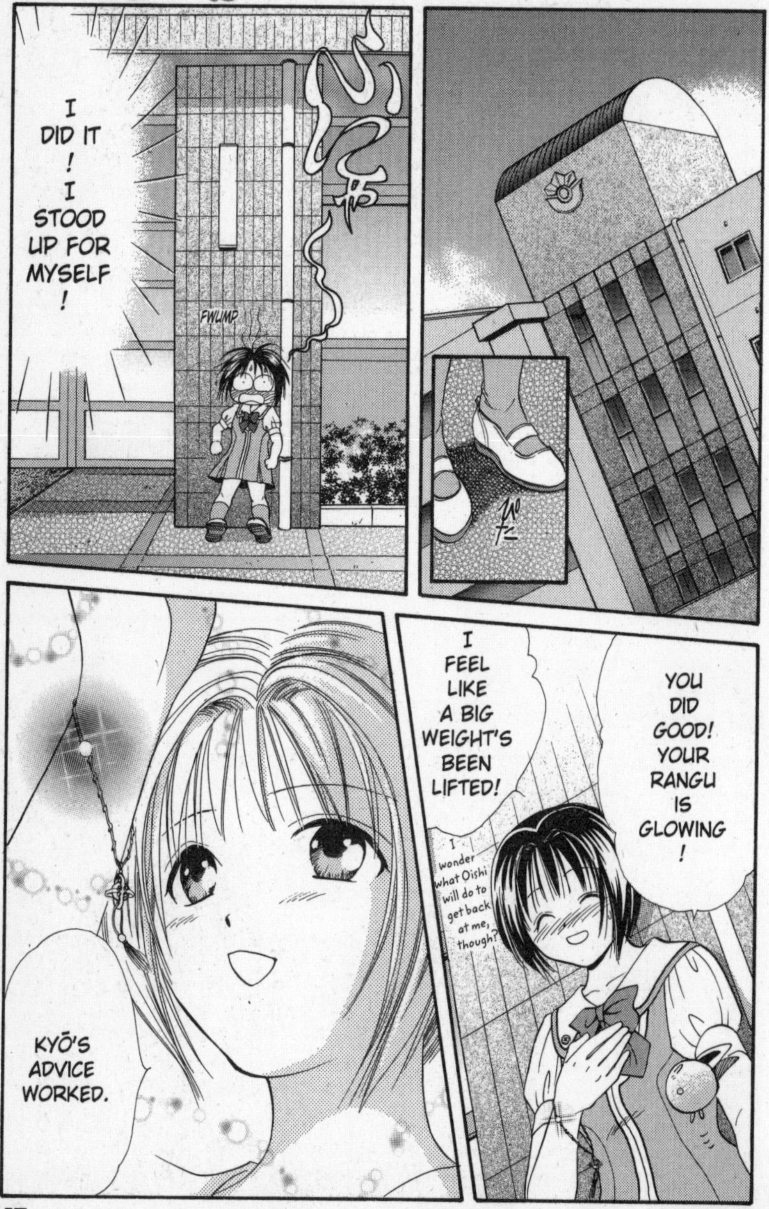
I DID IT! I STOOD UP FOR MYSELF!
FWUMP
I FEEL LIKE A BIG WEIGHT'S BEEN LIFTED!
YOU DID GOOD! YOUR RANGU IS GLOWING!
I wonder what Oishi will do to get back at me, though?
KYŌ'S ADVICE WORKED.

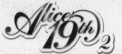

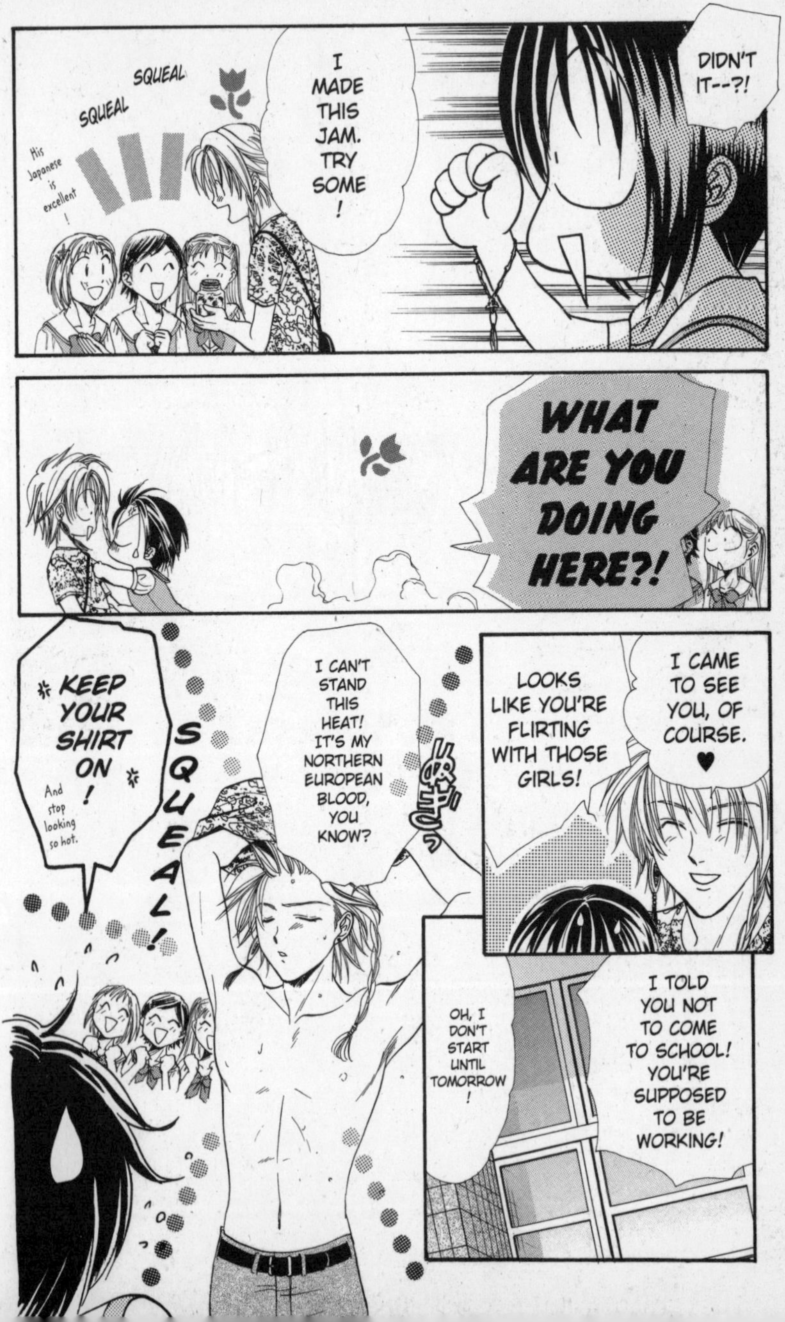
DIDN'T IT--?!
I MADE THIS JAM. TRY SOME!
SQUEAL
SQUEAL
His Japanese is excellent!
WHAT ARE YOU DOING HERE?!
I CAME TO SEE YOU, OF COURSE. ♥
LOOKS LIKE YOU'RE FLIRTING WITH THOSE GIRLS!
I TOLD YOU NOT TO COME TO SCHOOL! YOU'RE SUPPOSED TO BE WORKING!
OH, I DON'T START UNTIL TOMORROW!
I CAN'T STAND THIS HEAT! IT'S MY NORTHERN EUROPEAN BLOOD, YOU KNOW?
SQUEAL!
KEEP YOUR SHIRT ON!
And stop looking so hot.

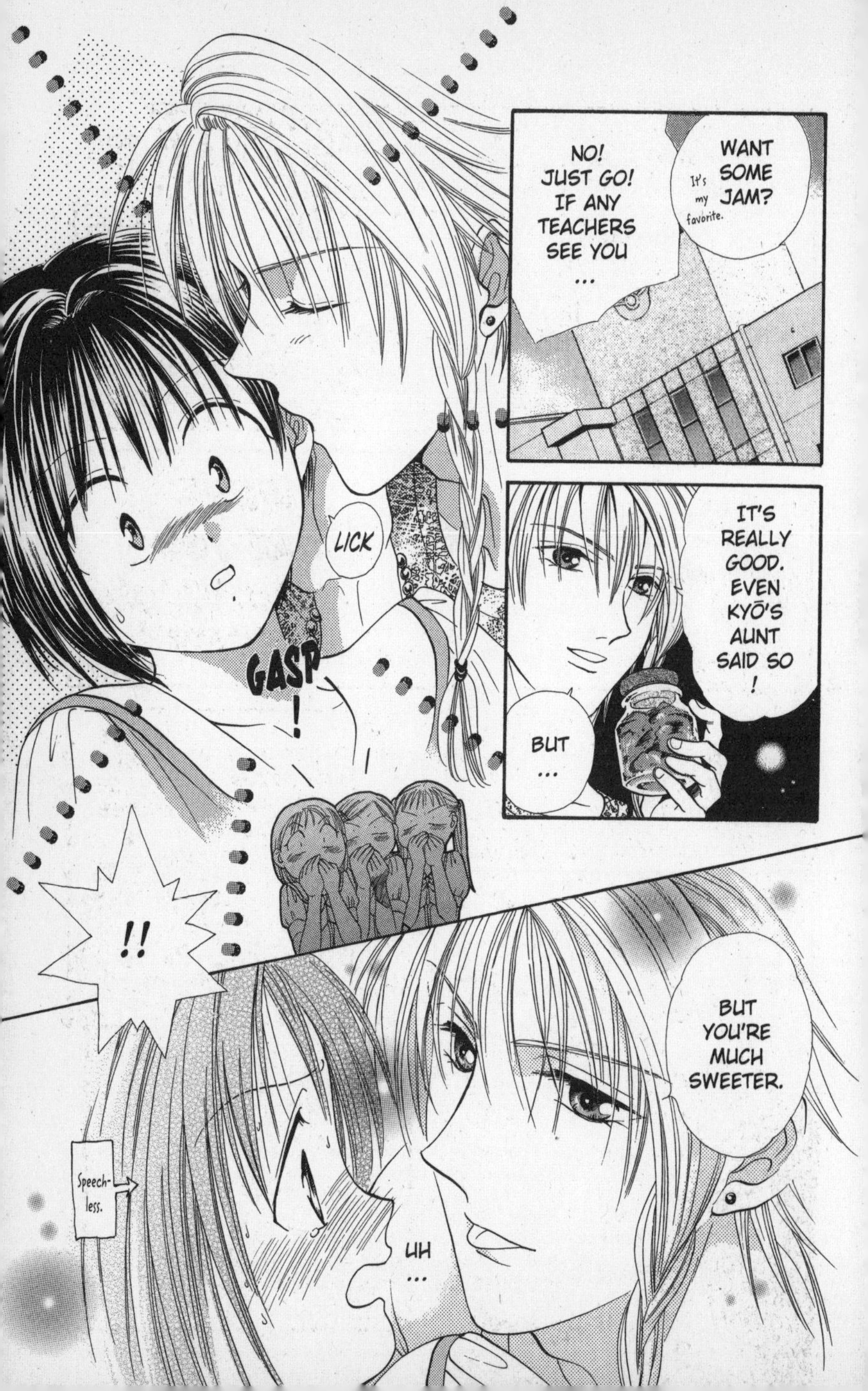
WANT SOME JAM?
It's my favorite.
NO! JUST GO! IF ANY TEACHERS SEE YOU ...
IT'S REALLY GOOD. EVEN KYŌ'S AUNT SAID SO!
BUT ...
LICK
GASP!
!!
BUT YOU'RE MUCH SWEETER.
Speech-less.
UH ...

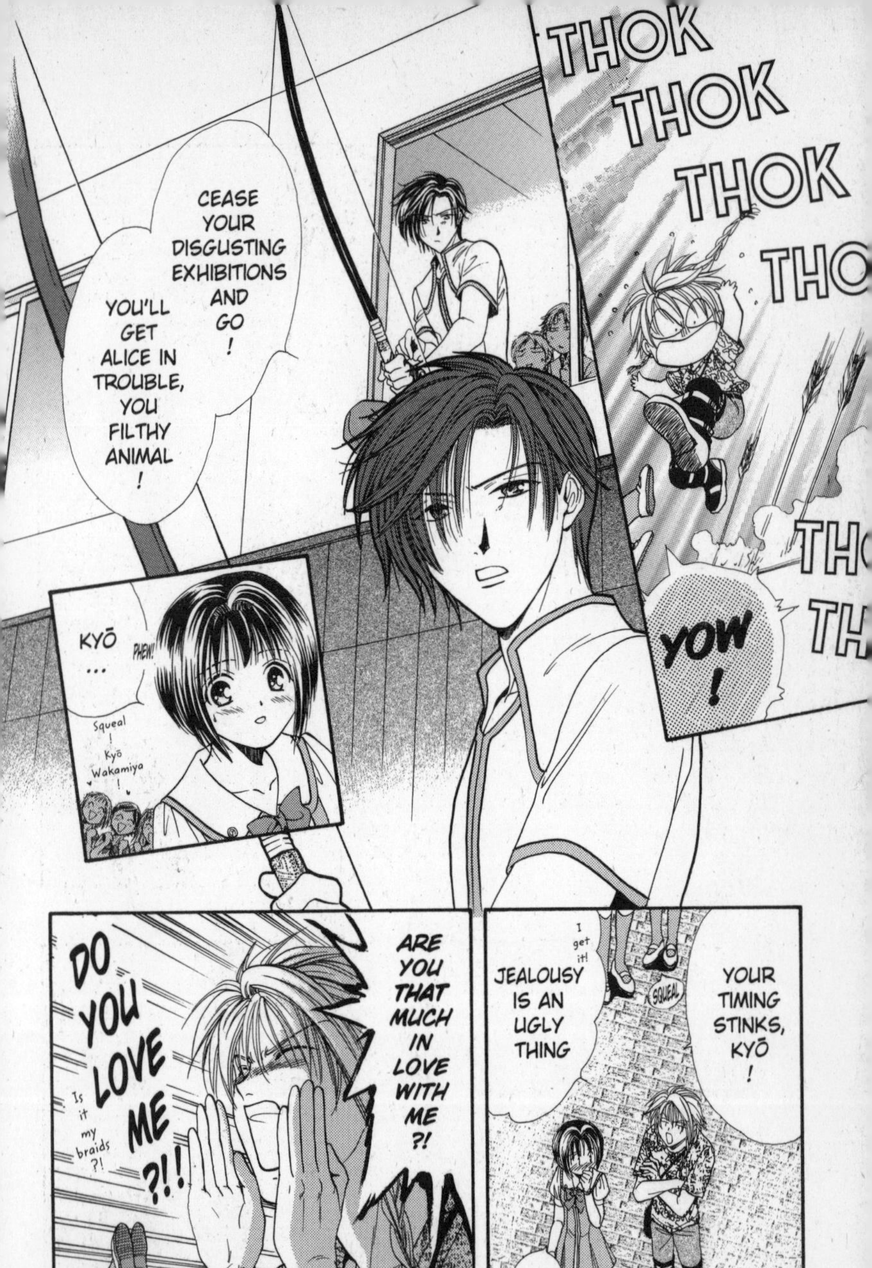
THOK THOK THOK THO
THO THO
YOW!
CEASE YOUR DISGUSTING EXHIBITIONS AND GO!
YOU'LL GET ALICE IN TROUBLE, YOU FILTHY ANIMAL!
KYŌ...
PHEW!
Squeal! Kyō Wakamiya!
YOUR TIMING STINKS, KYŌ!
JEALOUSY IS AN UGLY THING
I get it!
SQUEAL
!
ARE YOU THAT MUCH IN LOVE WITH ME?!
DO YOU LOVE ME?!!
Is it my braids?!

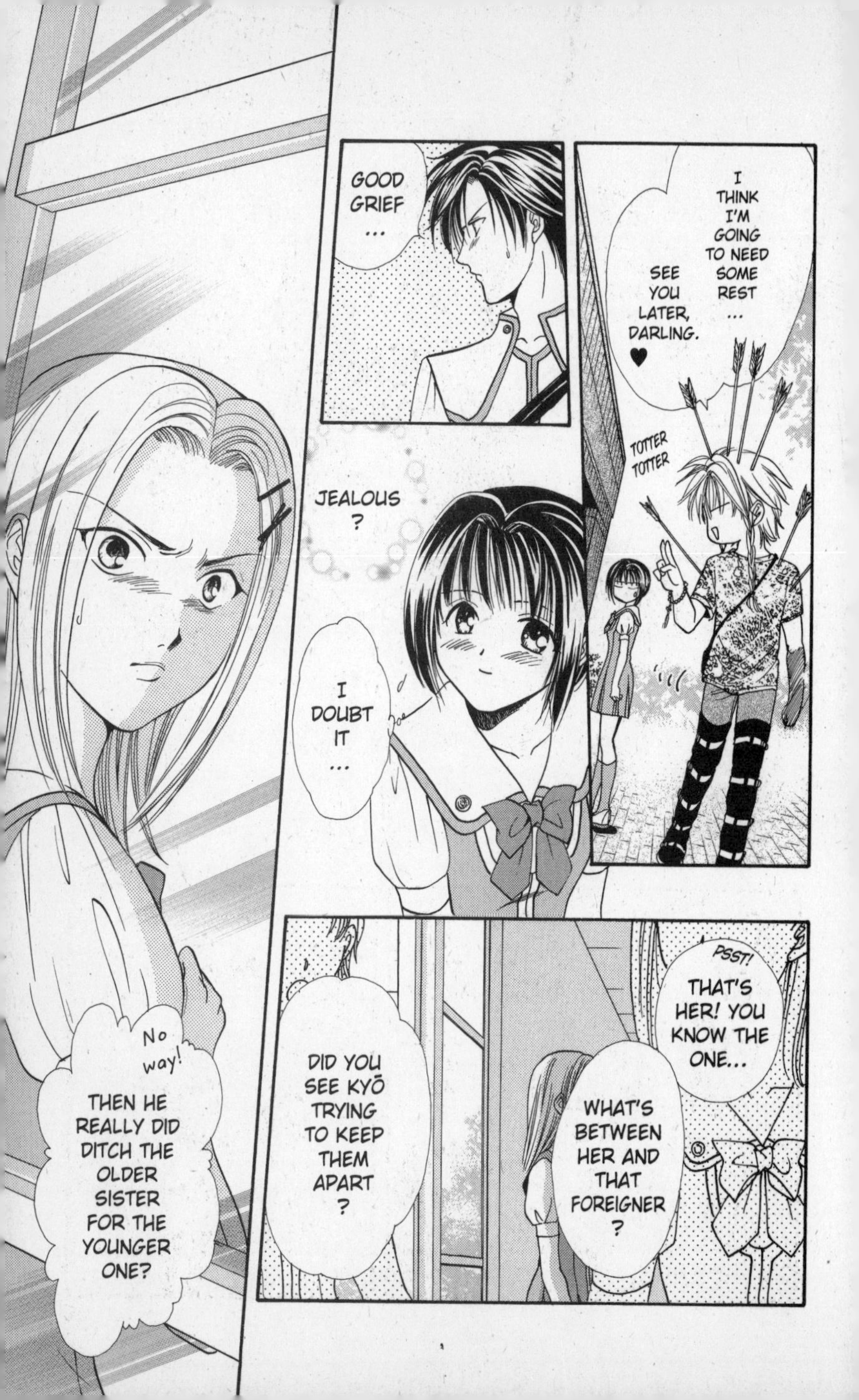
I THINK I'M GOING TO NEED SOME REST...
SEE YOU LATER, DARLING. ♥
TOTTER TOTTER
GOOD GRIEF...
JEALOUS?
I DOUBT IT...
PSST!
THAT'S HER! YOU KNOW THE ONE...
WHAT'S BETWEEN HER AND THAT FOREIGNER?
DID YOU SEE KYŌ TRYING TO KEEP THEM APART?
No way!
THEN HE REALLY DID DITCH THE OLDER SISTER FOR THE YOUNGER ONE?

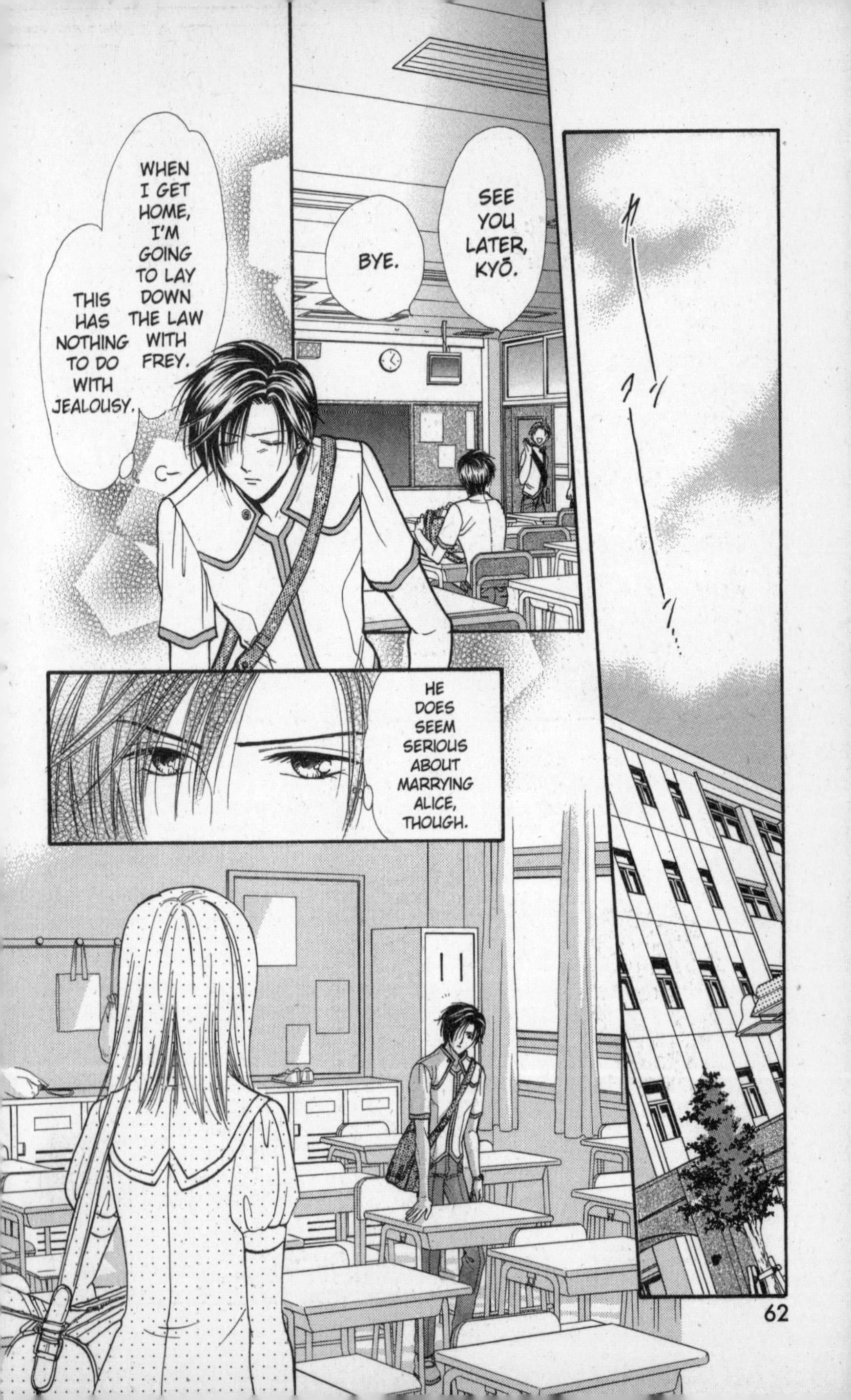
SEE YOU LATER, KYŌ.
BYE.
C—
WHEN I GET HOME, I'M GOING TO LAY DOWN THE LAW WITH FREY.
THIS HAS NOTHING TO DO WITH JEALOUSY.
HE DOES SEEM SERIOUS ABOUT MARRYING ALICE, THOUGH.

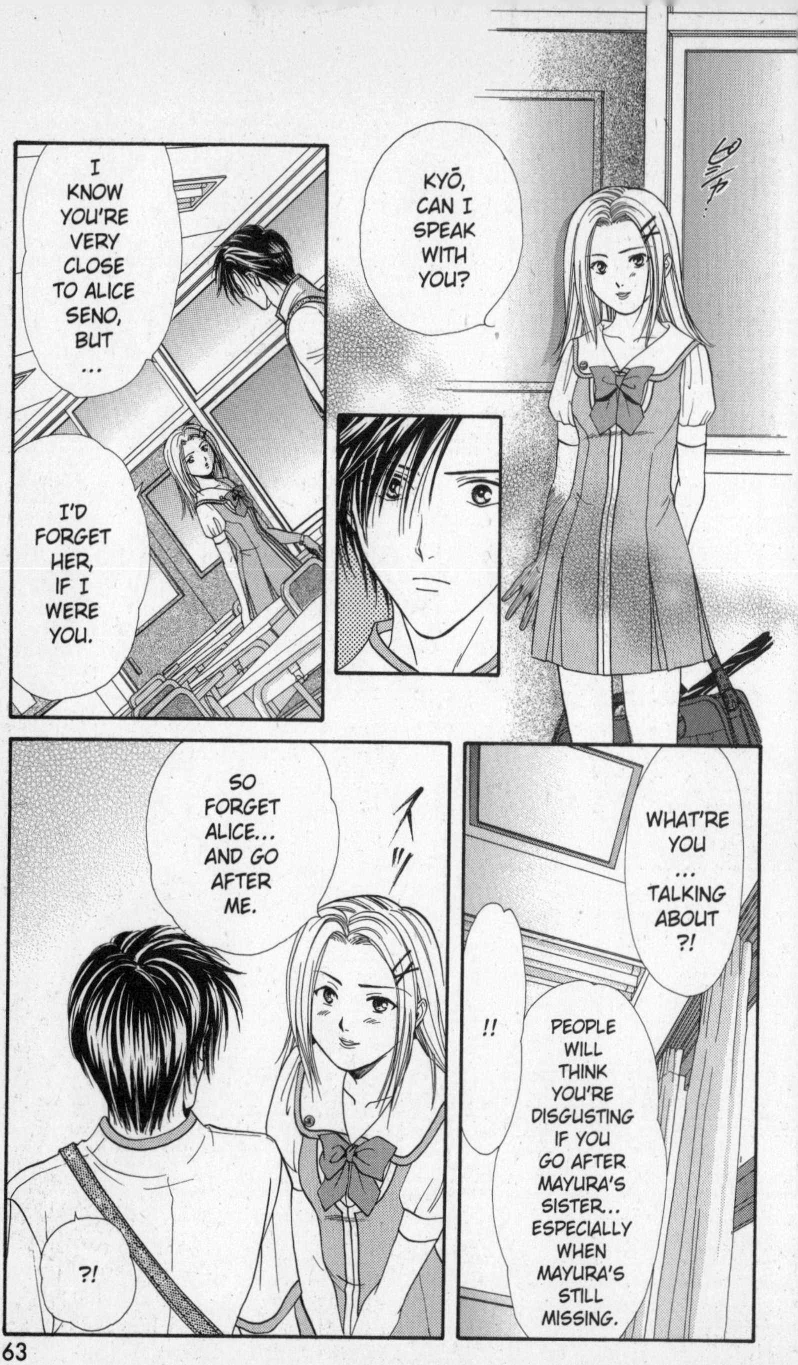
KYŌ, CAN I SPEAK WITH YOU?
I KNOW YOU'RE VERY CLOSE TO ALICE SENO, BUT ...
I'D FORGET HER, IF I WERE YOU.
WHAT'RE YOU ... TALKING ABOUT ?!
!!
PEOPLE WILL THINK YOU'RE DISGUSTING IF YOU GO AFTER MAYURA'S SISTER.. ESPECIALLY WHEN MAYURA'S STILL MISSING.
SO FORGET ALICE... AND GO AFTER ME.
?!

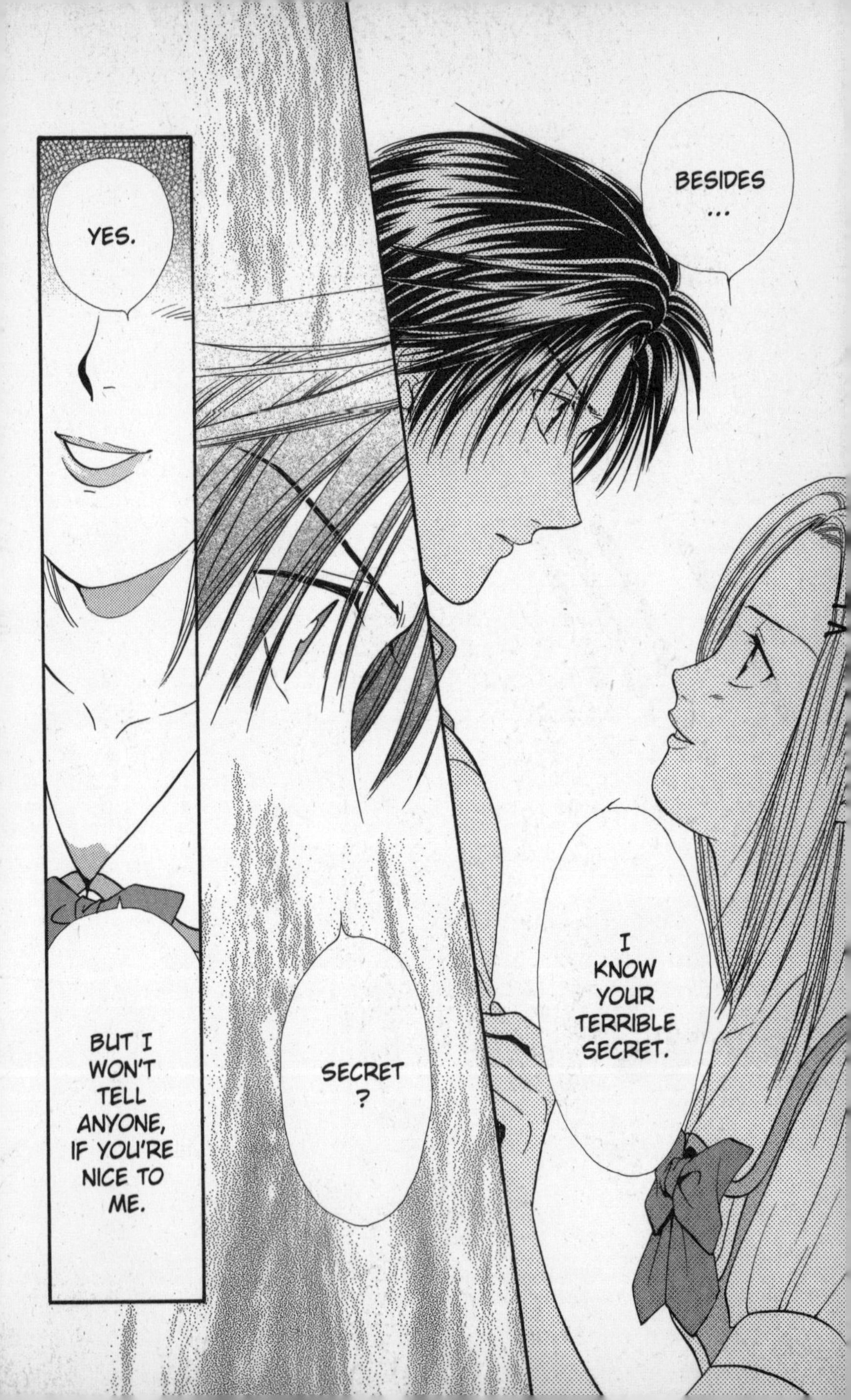
BESIDES ...
I KNOW YOUR TERRIBLE SECRET.
SECRET ?
YES.
BUT I WON'T TELL ANYONE, IF YOU'RE NICE TO ME.

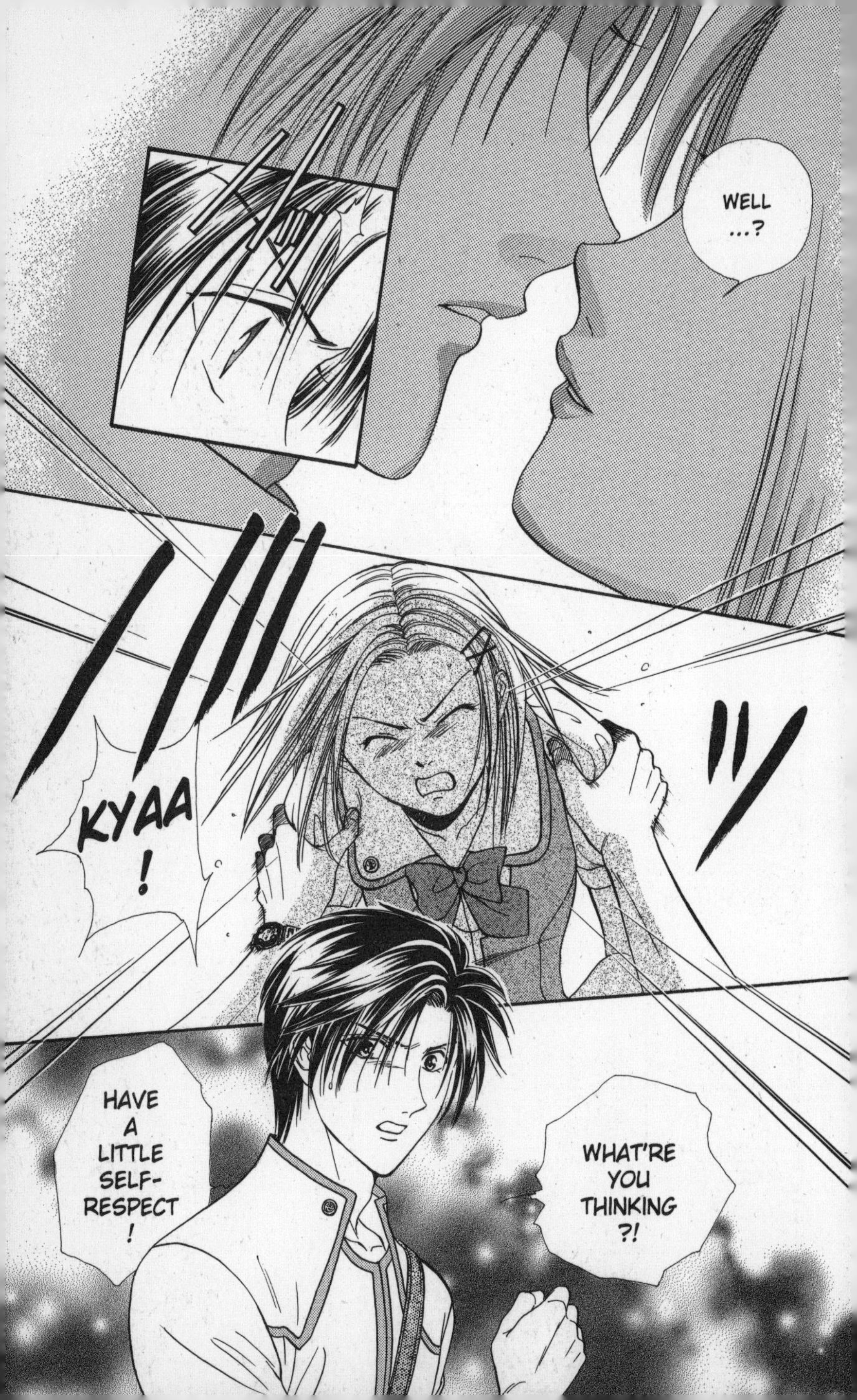
WELL ...?
KYAA!
WHAT'RE YOU THINKING ?!
HAVE A LITTLE SELF-RESPECT!

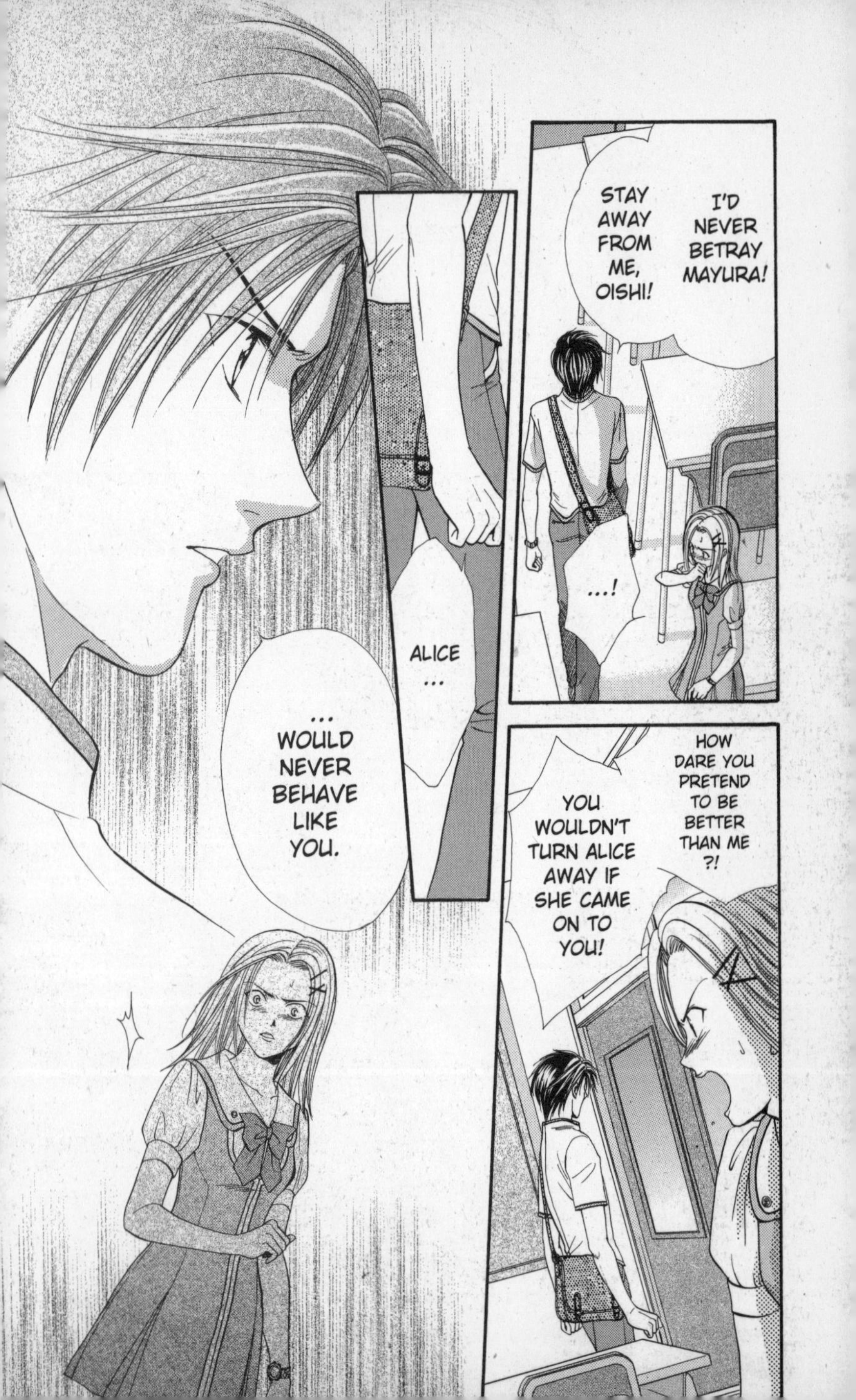
I'D NEVER BETRAY MAYURA!
STAY AWAY FROM ME, OISHI!
...!
HOW DARE YOU PRETEND TO BE BETTER THAN ME ?!
YOU WOULDN'T TURN ALICE AWAY IF SHE CAME ON TO YOU!
ALICE ...
... WOULD NEVER BEHAVE LIKE YOU.

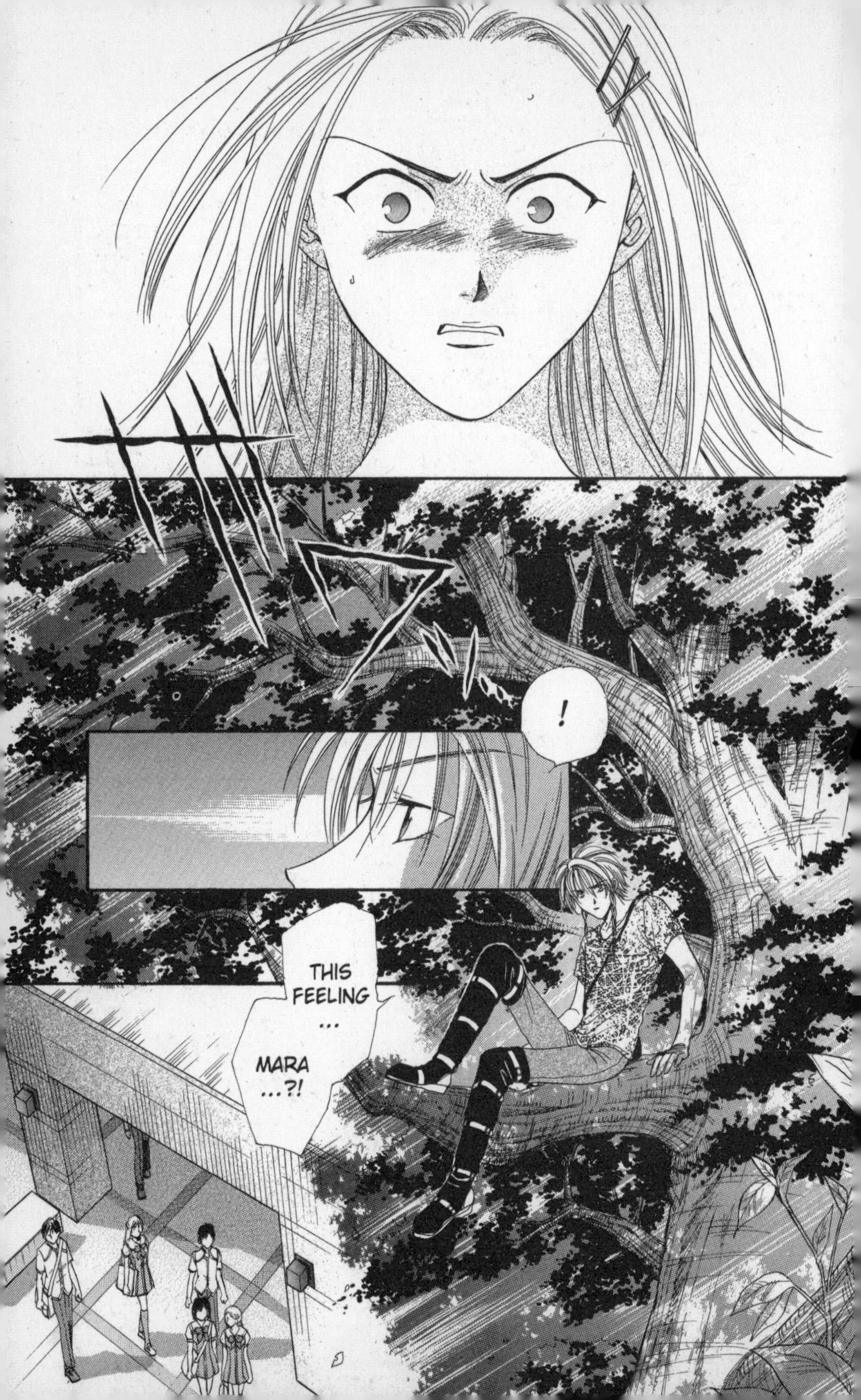
!
THIS FEELING ... MARA ...?!

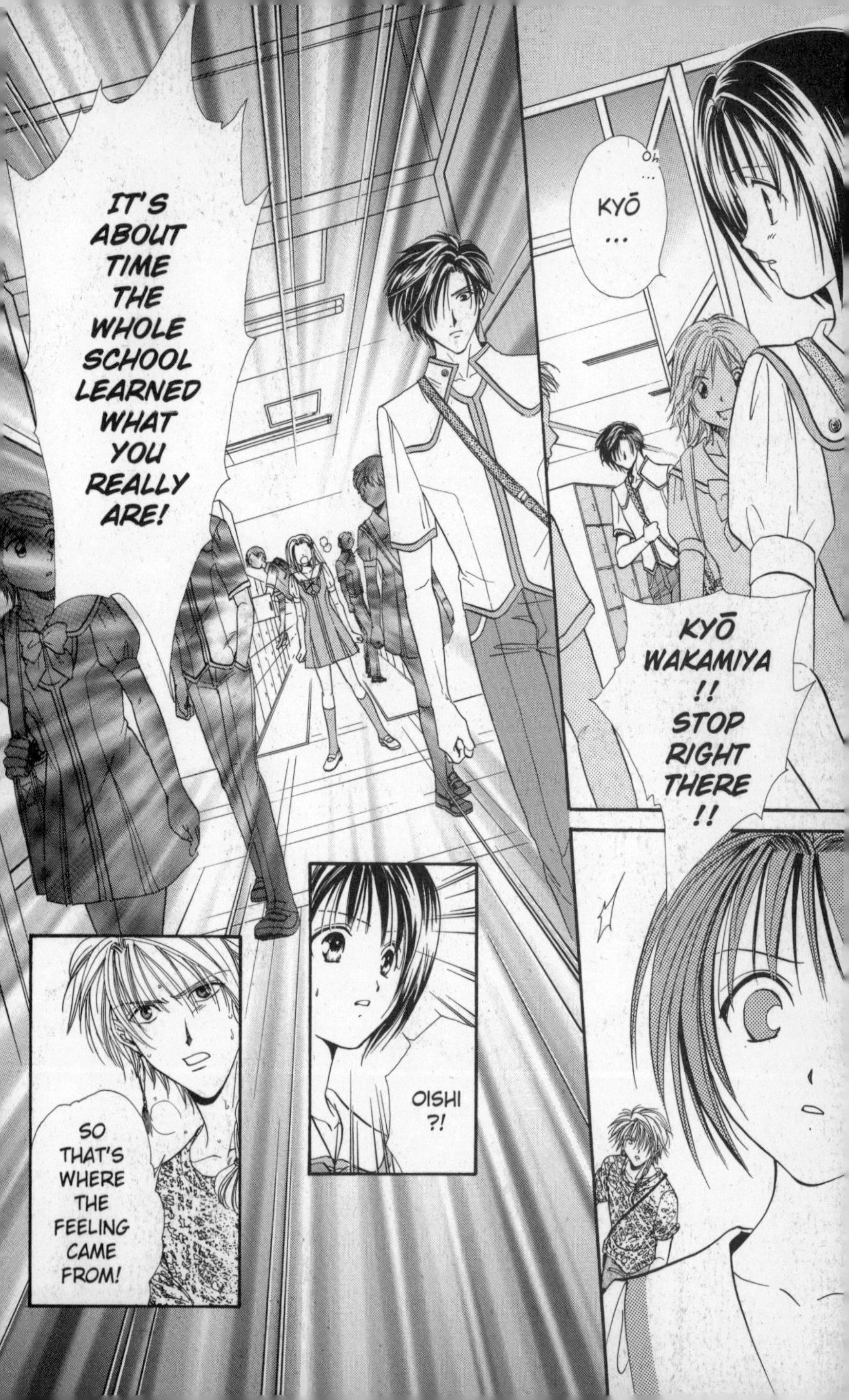

Oh... KYŌ ...
KYŌ WAKAMIYA !! STOP RIGHT THERE !!
IT'S ABOUT TIME THE WHOLE SCHOOL LEARNED WHAT YOU REALLY ARE!
OISHI ?!
SO THAT'S WHERE THE FEELING CAME FROM!

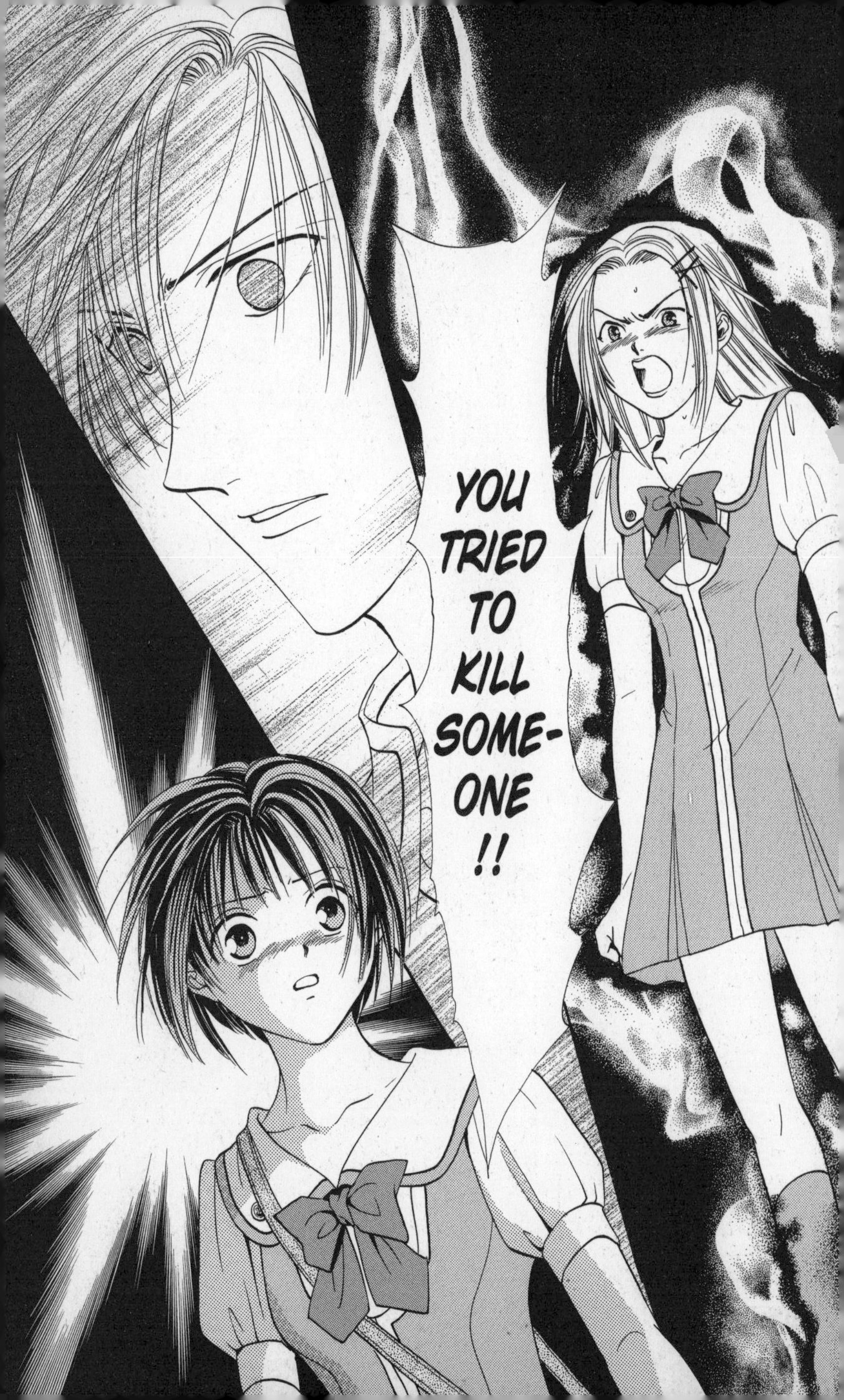
YOU TRIED TO KILL SOME-ONE !!

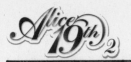

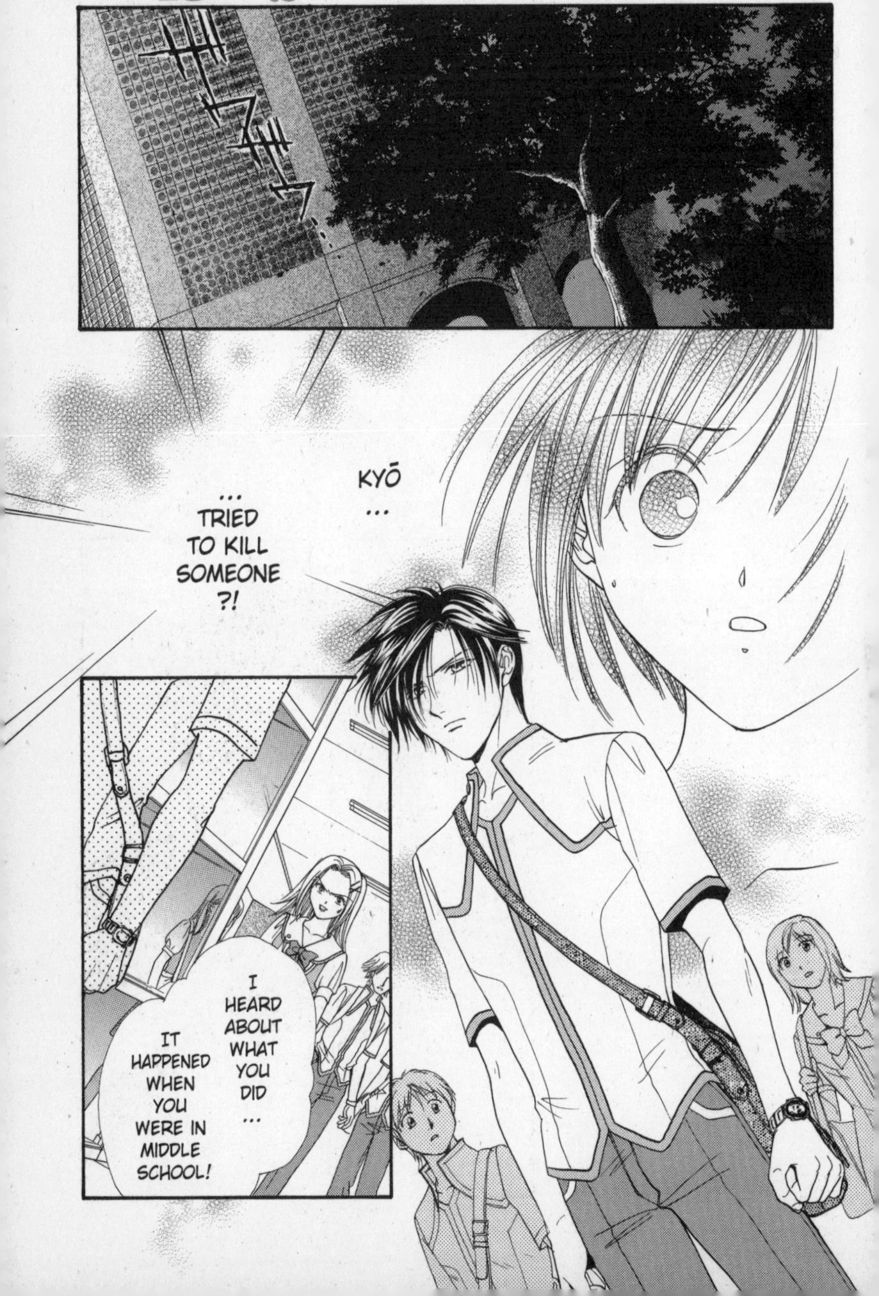
KYŌ ...
... TRIED TO KILL SOMEONE ?!
I HEARD ABOUT WHAT YOU DID ...
IT HAPPENED WHEN YOU WERE IN MIDDLE SCHOOL!

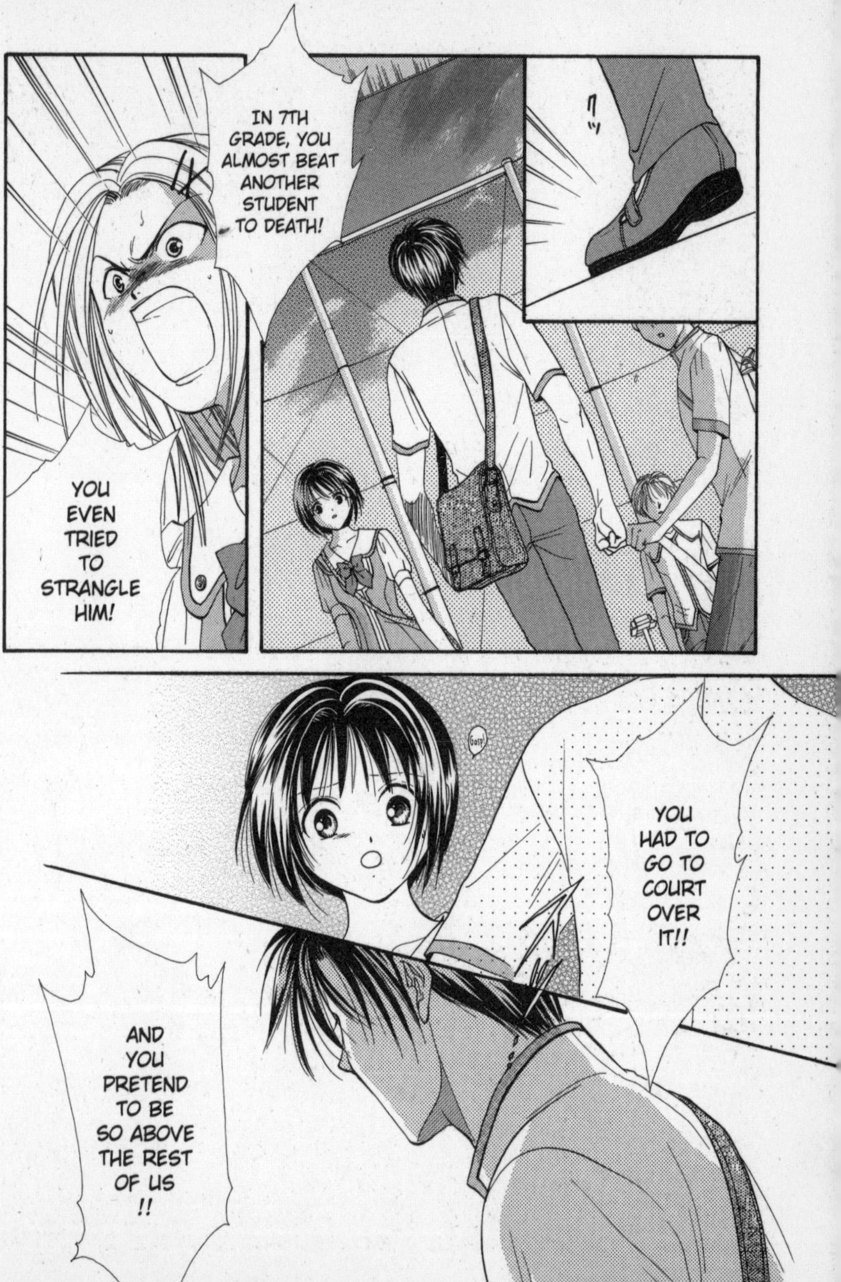
IN 7TH GRADE, YOU ALMOST BEAT ANOTHER STUDENT TO DEATH!
YOU EVEN TRIED TO STRANGLE HIM!
Gasp!
YOU HAD TO GO TO COURT OVER IT!!
AND YOU PRETEND TO BE SO ABOVE THE REST OF US !!

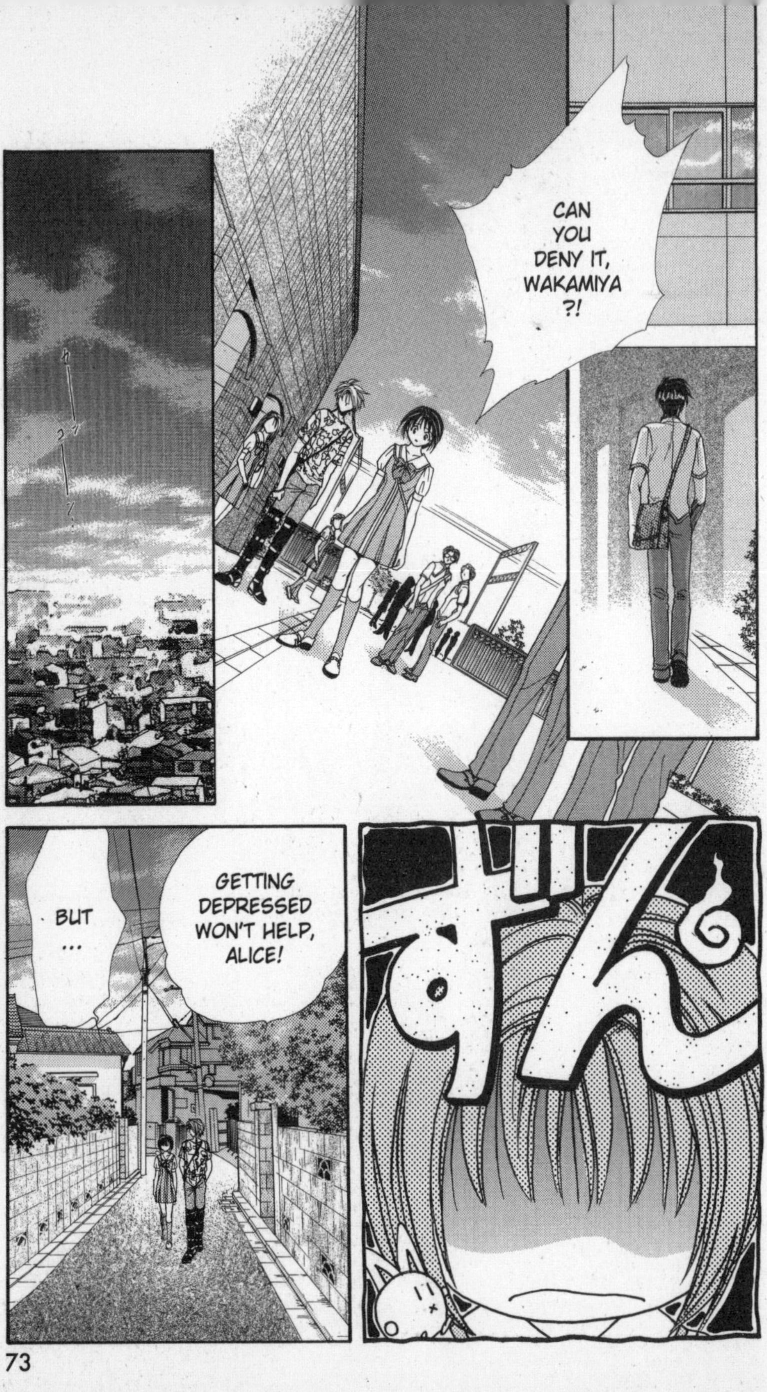
CAN YOU DENY IT, WAKAMIYA ?!
カーンコーン
GETTING DEPRESSED WON'T HELP, ALICE!
BUT ...

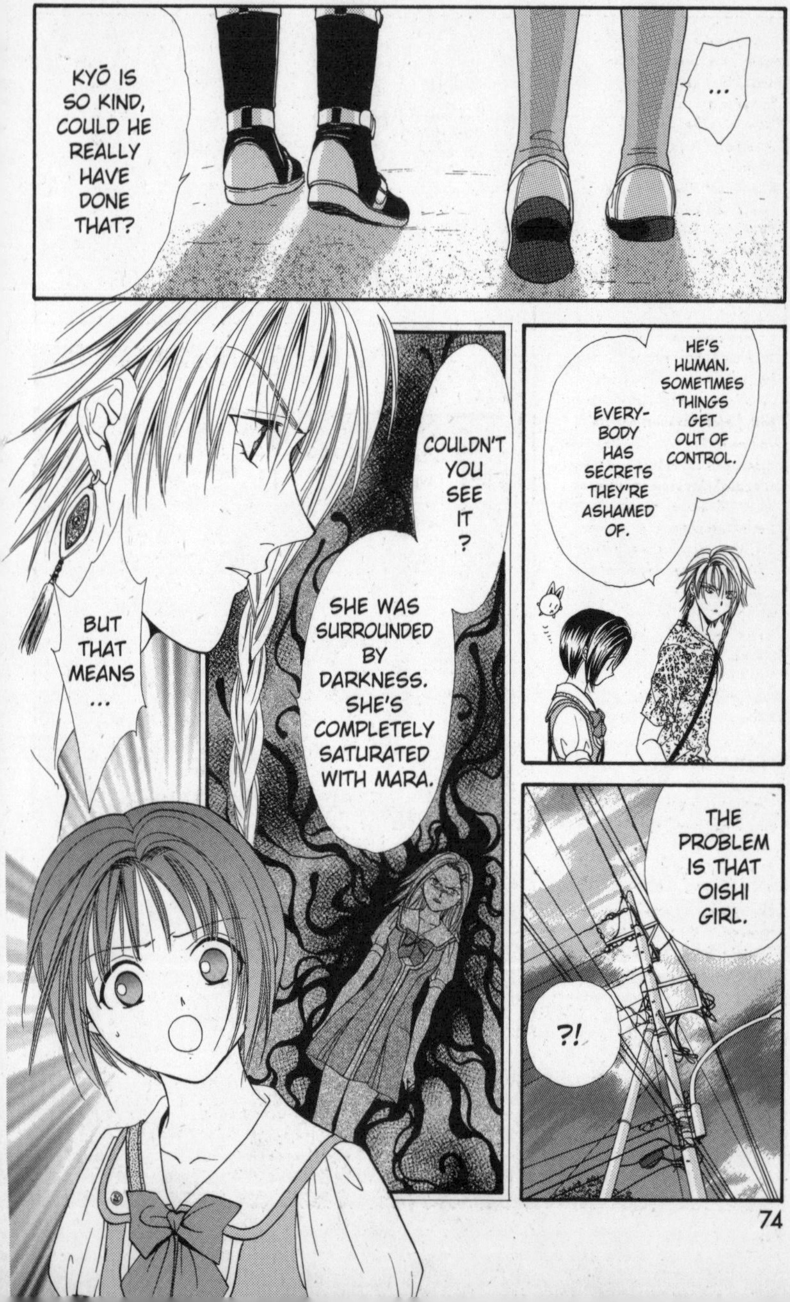
...
KYŌ IS SO KIND, COULD HE REALLY HAVE DONE THAT?
HE'S HUMAN. SOMETIMES THINGS GET OUT OF CONTROL.
EVERY-BODY HAS SECRETS THEY'RE ASHAMED OF.
THE PROBLEM IS THAT OISHI GIRL.
?!
COULDN'T YOU SEE IT?
SHE WAS SURROUNDED BY DARKNESS. SHE'S COMPLETELY SATURATED WITH MARA.
BUT THAT MEANS ...

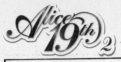

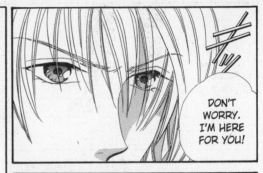

DON'T WORRY. I'M HERE FOR YOU!
FOR NOW, WE WAIT AND OBSERVE THE SITUATION.
PAT PAT
WE'LL DO SOMETHING WHEN WE HAVE A BETTER IDEA OF WHAT'S GOING ON!
SQUEEZE HUG
THANKS FOR WALKING ME HOME!
My pleasure
HE NEVER LEARNS, DOES HE?

I wondered if even childbirth could be more painful than dental torture. (Later, a friend told me the pain of labor might be preferable. No way!) Whoa!! I can't stand pain! I haven't got a masochistic bone in my body! I'm no masochist!! (What was I thinking?) In between, there was a bathroom break. Then they stopped midway to take x-rays. My consciousness was starting to slip. By the time we were going into the third hour, I could still feel the pain, but my brain was going numb. "I don't care, anymore. Just get it over with." Was it exhaustion? Isn't this what they say? It's like when a deer gets eaten by a lion. When it's caught, its brain produces a pleasure hormone in order to suppress the fear, and the deer dies in a euphoric state. Wrong! My brain produced no such substance! "Please! Hit me in the solar plexus and let me lose consciousness!" If I were a child, I would've screamed and cried. When it was finally over, my seat was dripping with perspiration, even though I was wearing jeans... There were various reasons that the anesthetic didn't work. Apparently the tooth in front of the wisdom tooth (Yes, the one where the cavity was filled when I was 17.) was rotten inside. The abscess had spread to the cavity in my wisdom tooth, so the gums hardened. This prevented the hypodermic needle from getting through all the way. It actually broke. What the heck...? That's why the painkiller they administered to the gums didn't work....Or so they said. It's unheard of! Undergoing surgery without anesthesia! Heh, heh, heh. Scary, isn't it? Would you be able to bear it?! I think of this as a weird tale of heroism.

Or maybe just rotten luck?

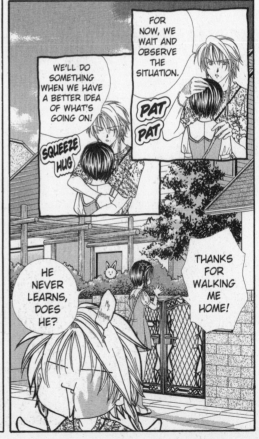

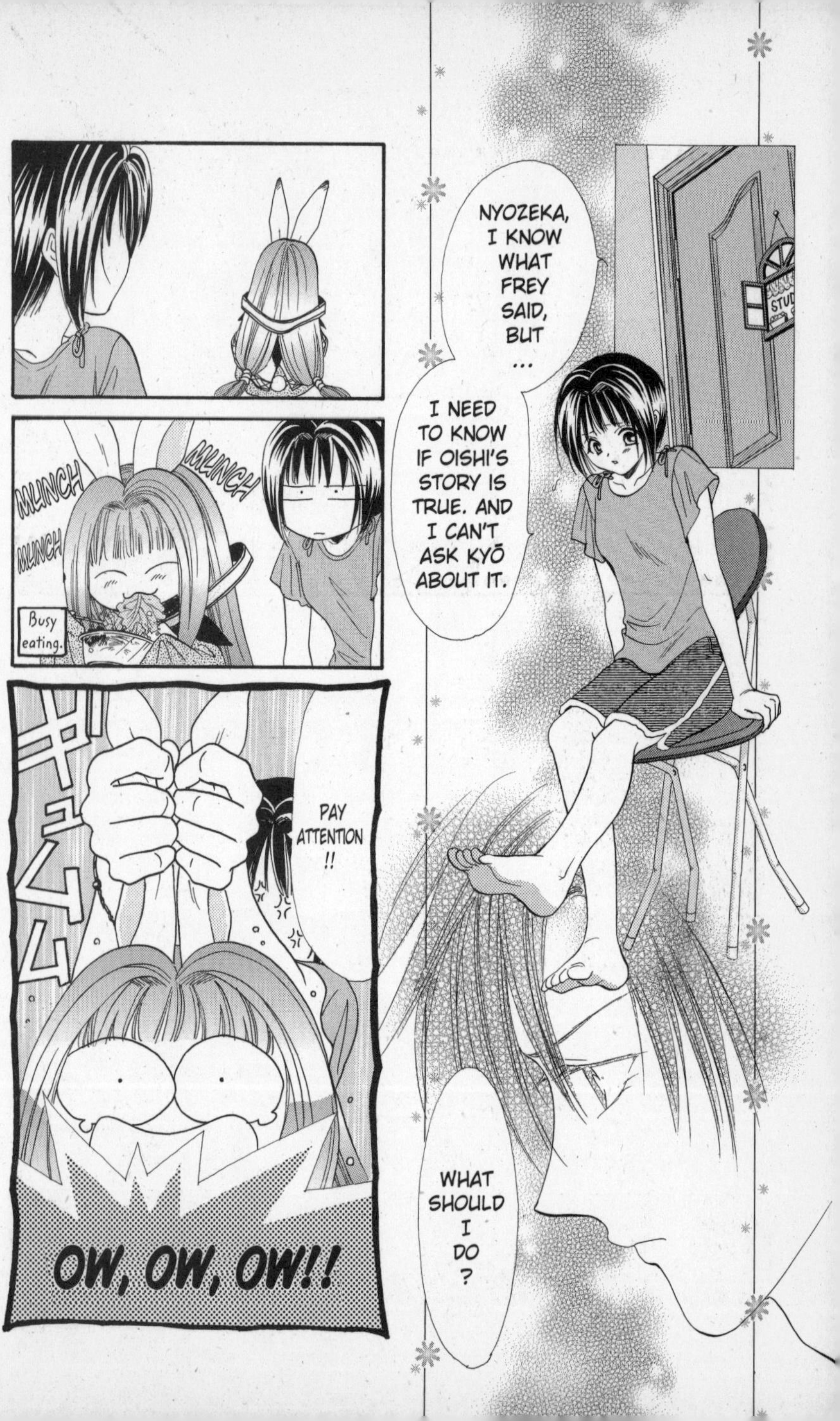
NYOZEKA, I KNOW WHAT FREY SAID, BUT ...
I NEED TO KNOW IF OISHI'S STORY IS TRUE. AND I CAN'T ASK KYŌ ABOUT IT.
WHAT SHOULD I DO?
MUNCH
MUNCH
MUNCH
Busy eating.
ギュムム
PAY ATTENTION !!
OW, OW, OW!!

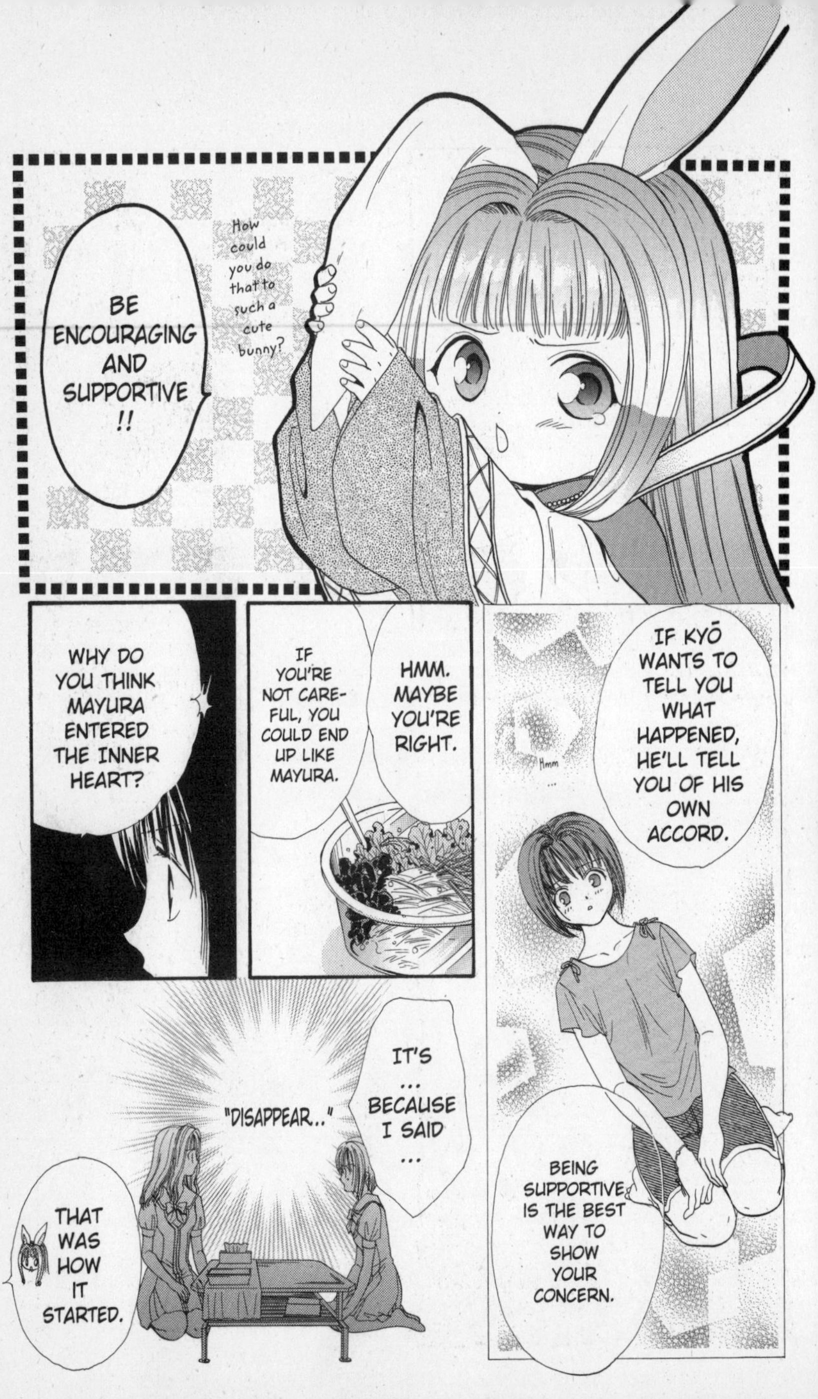
How could you do that to such a cute bunny?
BE ENCOURAGING AND SUPPORTIVE !!
IF KYŌ WANTS TO TELL YOU WHAT HAPPENED, HE'LL TELL YOU OF HIS OWN ACCORD.
Hmm ...
BEING SUPPORTIVE IS THE BEST WAY TO SHOW YOUR CONCERN.
HMM. MAYBE YOU'RE RIGHT.
IF YOU'RE NOT CARE-FUL, YOU COULD END UP LIKE MAYURA.
WHY DO YOU THINK MAYURA ENTERED THE INNER HEART?
IT'S ... BECAUSE I SAID ...
"DISAPPEAR.."
THAT WAS HOW IT STARTED.

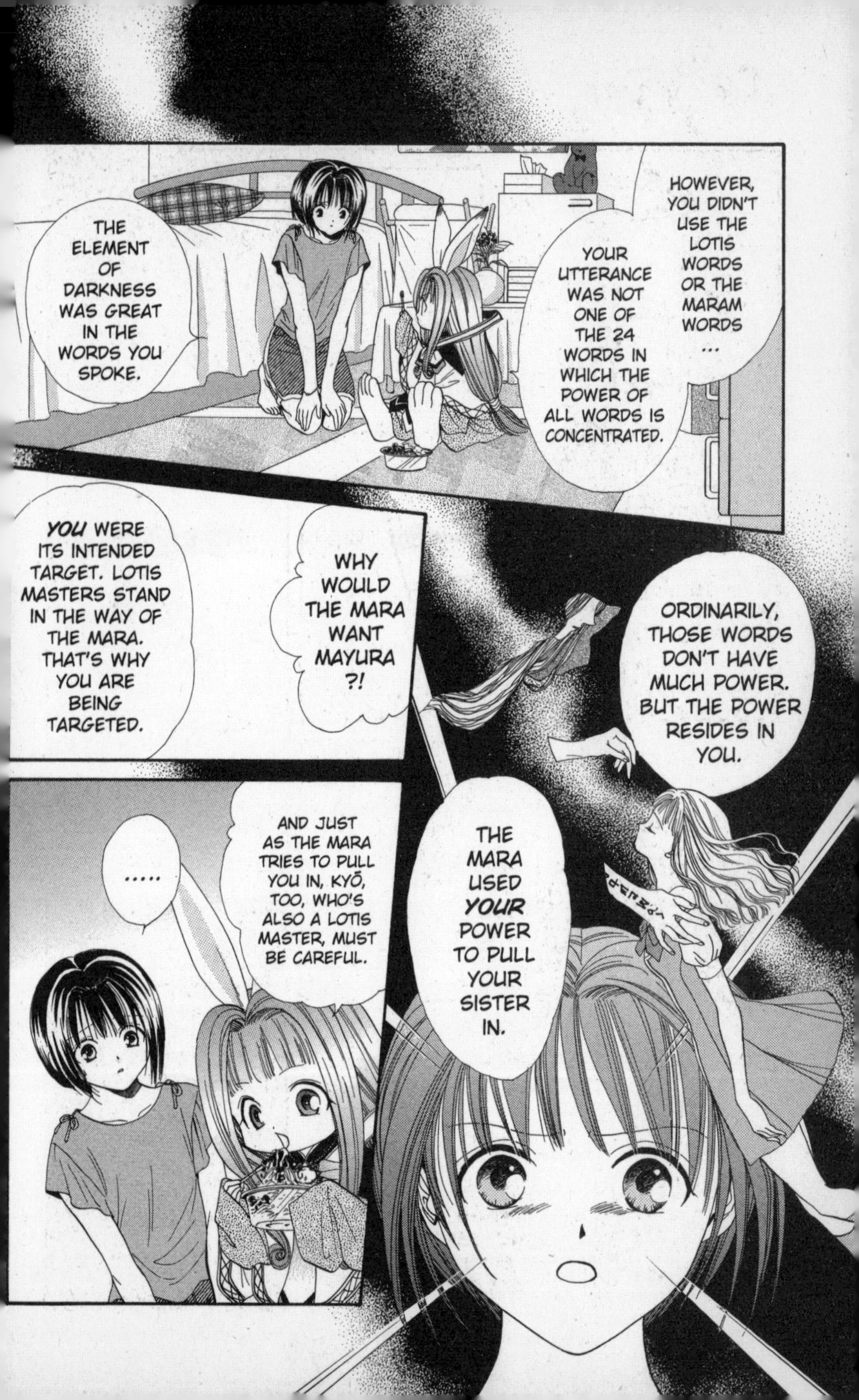
HOWEVER, YOU DIDN'T USE THE LOTIS WORDS OR THE MARAM WORDS ...
YOUR UTTERANCE WAS NOT ONE OF THE 24 WORDS IN WHICH THE POWER OF ALL WORDS IS CONCENTRATED.
THE ELEMENT OF DARKNESS WAS GREAT IN THE WORDS YOU SPOKE.
ORDINARILY, THOSE WORDS DON'T HAVE MUCH POWER. BUT THE POWER RESIDES IN YOU.
THE MARA USED *YOUR* POWER TO PULL YOUR SISTER IN.
WHY WOULD THE MARA WANT MAYURA ?!
YOU WERE ITS INTENDED TARGET. LOTIS MASTERS STAND IN THE WAY OF THE MARA. THAT'S WHY YOU ARE BEING TARGETED.
AND JUST AS THE MARA TRIES TO PULL YOU IN, KYŌ, TOO, WHO'S ALSO A LOTIS MASTER, MUST BE CAREFUL.
.....

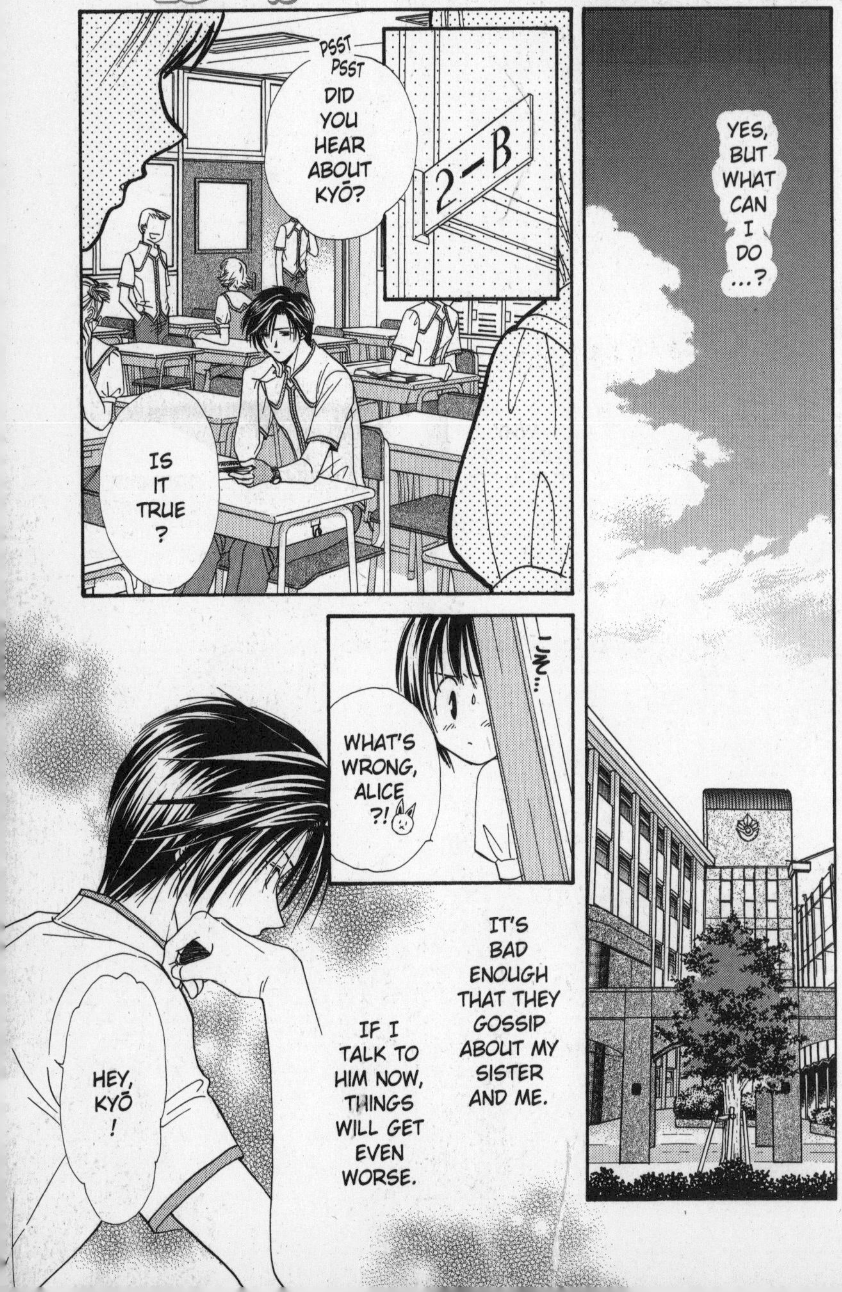
YES, BUT WHAT CAN I DO ...?
PSST PSST
DID YOU HEAR ABOUT KYŌ?
2-B
IS IT TRUE?
JUN...
WHAT'S WRONG, ALICE ?!
IT'S BAD ENOUGH THAT THEY GOSSIP ABOUT MY SISTER AND ME.
IF I TALK TO HIM NOW, THINGS WILL GET EVEN WORSE.
HEY, KYŌ!

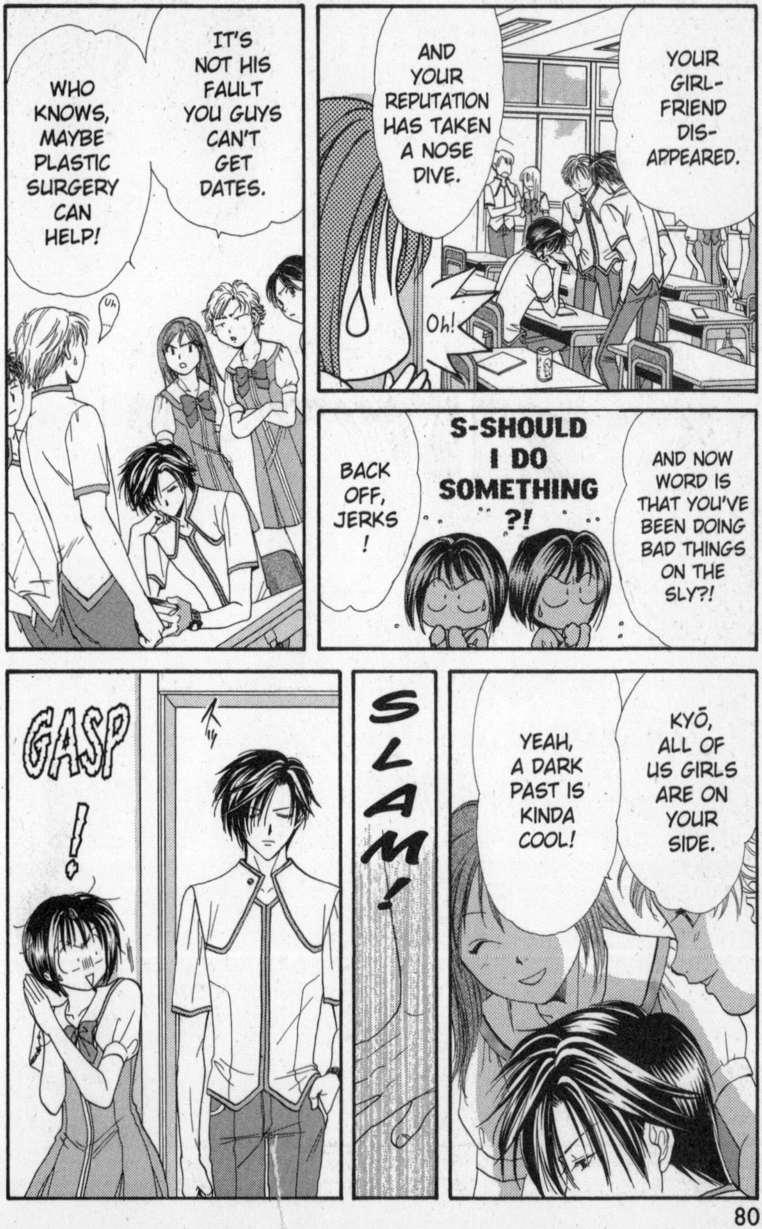
YOUR GIRLFRIEND DISAPPEARED.
AND YOUR REPUTATION HAS TAKEN A NOSE DIVE.
Oh!
AND NOW WORD IS THAT YOU'VE BEEN DOING BAD THINGS ON THE SLY?!
S-SHOULD I DO SOMETHING ?!
BACK OFF, JERKS!
IT'S NOT HIS FAULT YOU GUYS CAN'T GET DATES.
WHO KNOWS, MAYBE PLASTIC SURGERY CAN HELP!
Uh
KYŌ, ALL OF US GIRLS ARE ON YOUR SIDE.
YEAH, A DARK PAST IS KINDA COOL!
SLAM!
GASP!

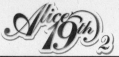

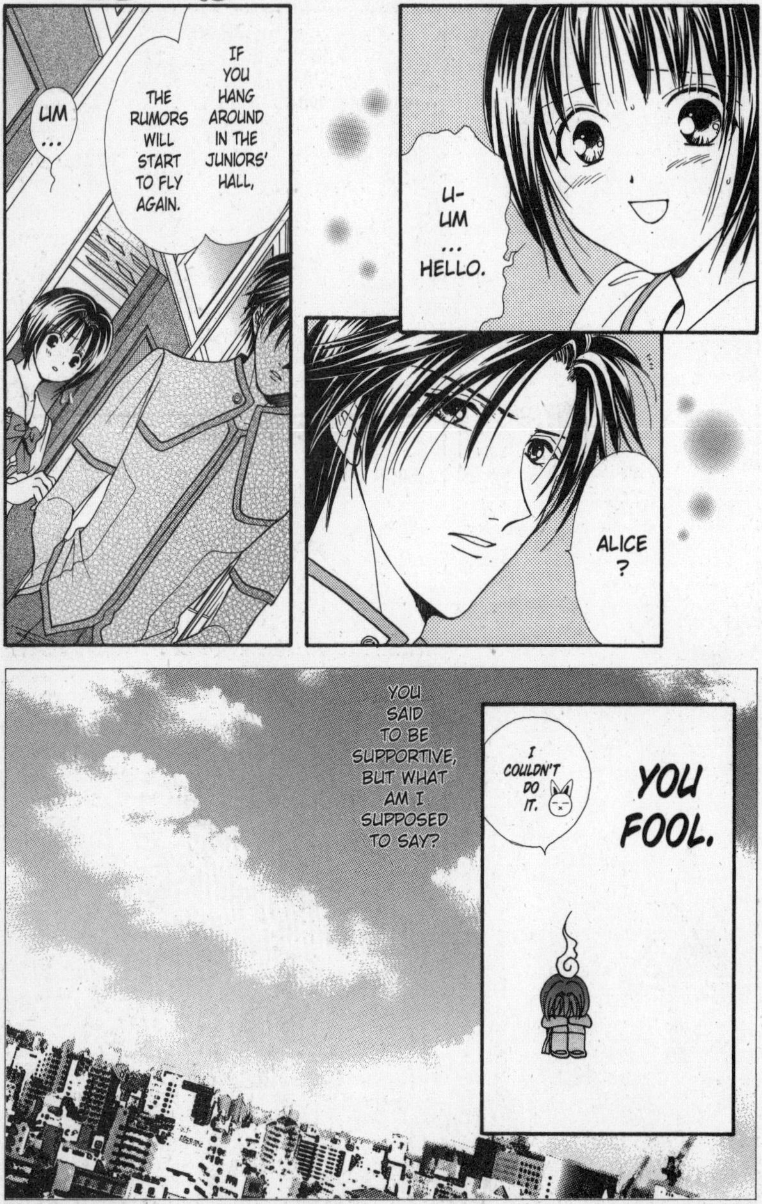
U-UM ... HELLO.
ALICE ?
IF YOU HANG AROUND IN THE JUNIORS' HALL,
THE RUMORS WILL START TO FLY AGAIN.
UM ...
YOU FOOL.
I COULDN'T DO IT.
YOU SAID TO BE SUPPORTIVE, BUT WHAT AM I SUPPOSED TO SAY?

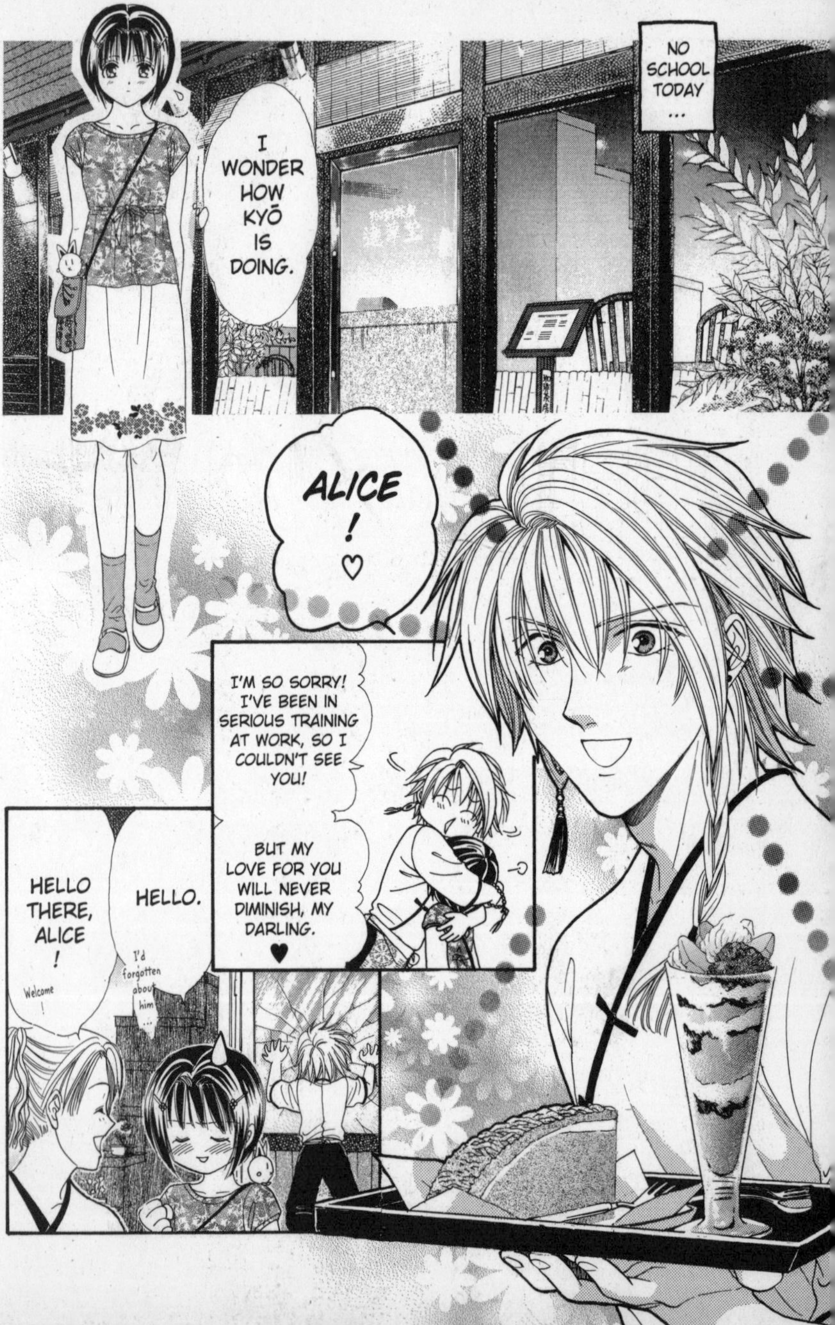
NO SCHOOL TODAY ...
I WONDER HOW KYŌ IS DOING.
ALICE! ♡
I'M SO SORRY! I'VE BEEN IN SERIOUS TRAINING AT WORK, SO I COULDN'T SEE YOU!
BUT MY LOVE FOR YOU WILL NEVER DIMINISH, MY DARLING. ♥
HELLO.
HELLO THERE, ALICE!
I'd forgotten about him ...
Welcome!

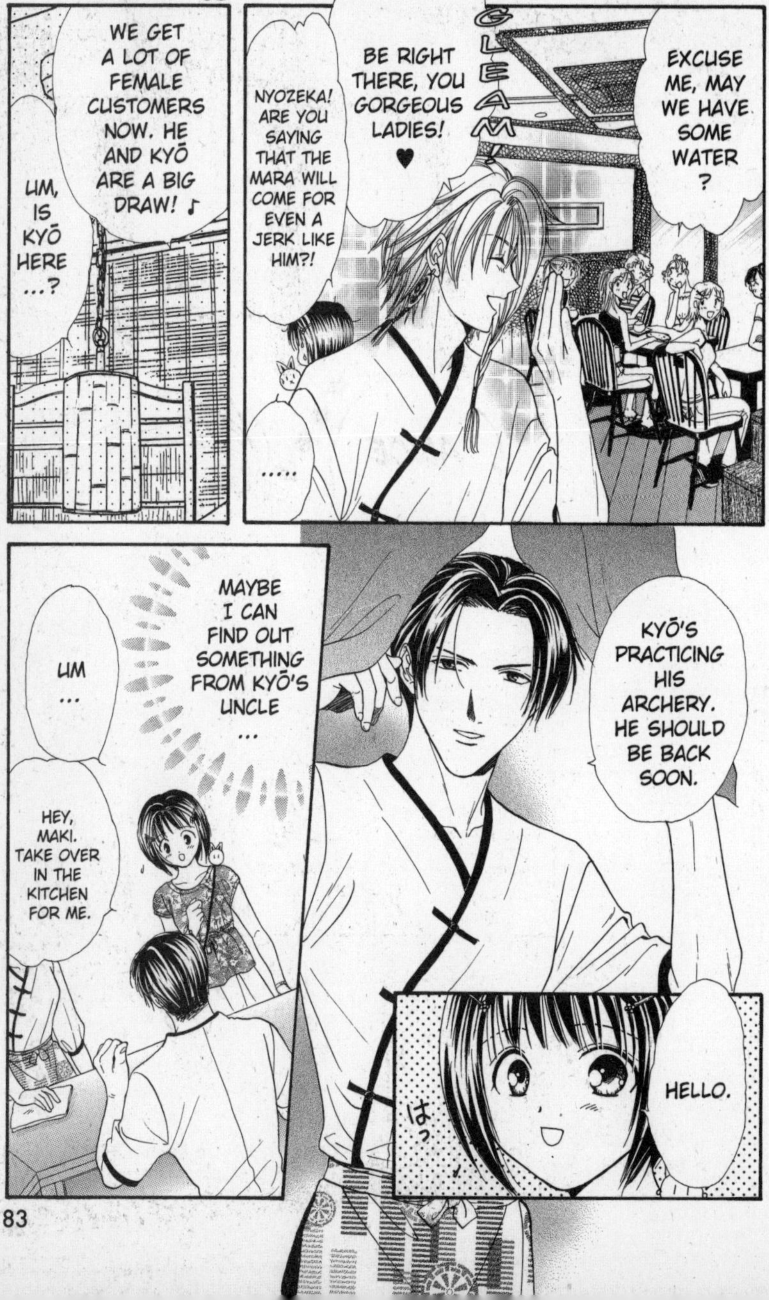
EXCUSE ME, MAY WE HAVE SOME WATER?
GLEAM!
BE RIGHT THERE, YOU GORGEOUS LADIES! ♥
NYOZEKA! ARE YOU SAYING THAT THE MARA WILL COME FOR EVEN A JERK LIKE HIM?!
.....
WE GET A LOT OF FEMALE CUSTOMERS NOW. HE AND KYŌ ARE A BIG DRAW! ♪
UM, IS KYŌ HERE ...?
KYŌ'S PRACTICING HIS ARCHERY. HE SHOULD BE BACK SOON.
HELLO.
はっ
MAYBE I CAN FIND OUT SOMETHING FROM KYŌ'S UNCLE ...
UM ...
HEY, MAKI. TAKE OVER IN THE KITCHEN FOR ME.

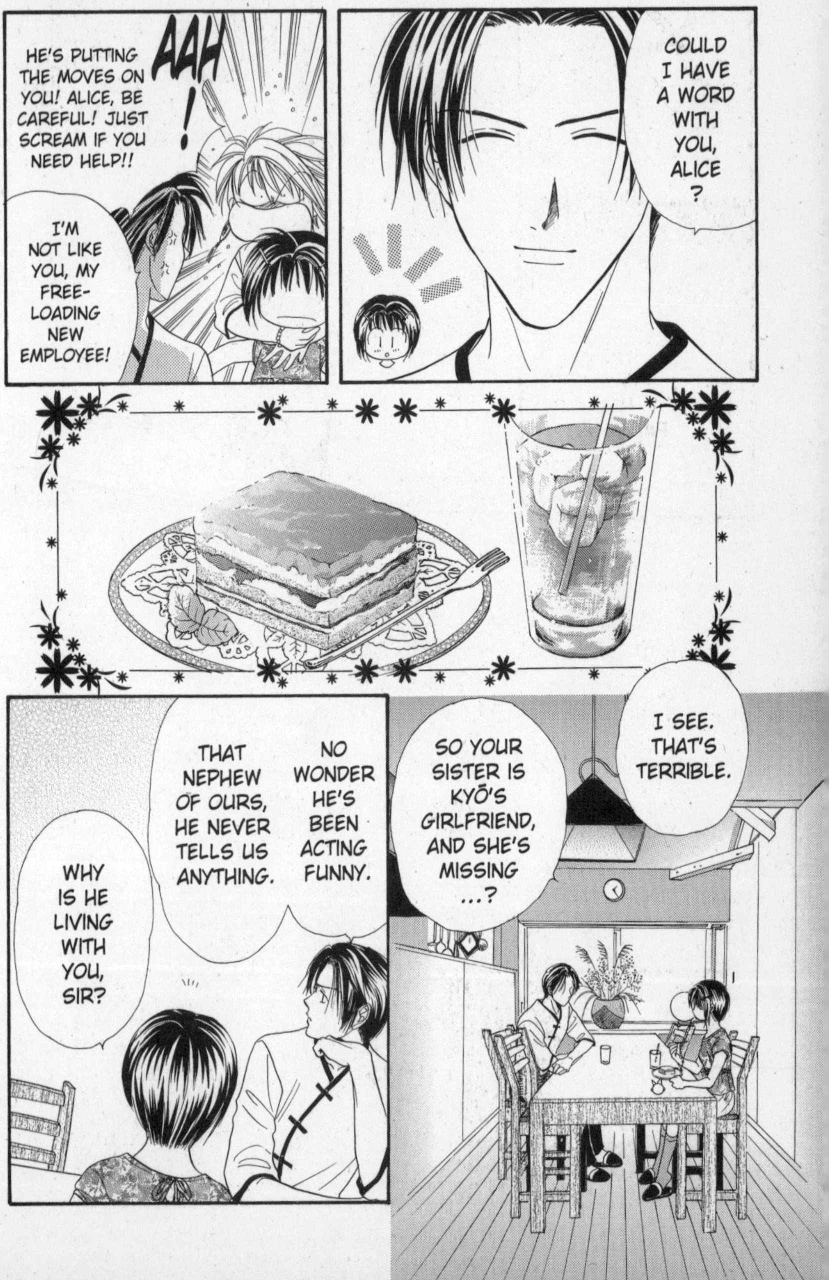
COULD I HAVE A WORD WITH YOU, ALICE?
AAH!
HE'S PUTTING THE MOVES ON YOU! ALICE, BE CAREFUL! JUST SCREAM IF YOU NEED HELP!!
I'M NOT LIKE YOU, MY FREE-LOADING NEW EMPLOYEE!
I SEE. THAT'S TERRIBLE.
SO YOUR SISTER IS KYŌ'S GIRLFRIEND, AND SHE'S MISSING...?
NO WONDER HE'S BEEN ACTING FUNNY.
THAT NEPHEW OF OURS, HE NEVER TELLS US ANYTHING.
WHY IS HE LIVING WITH YOU, SIR?

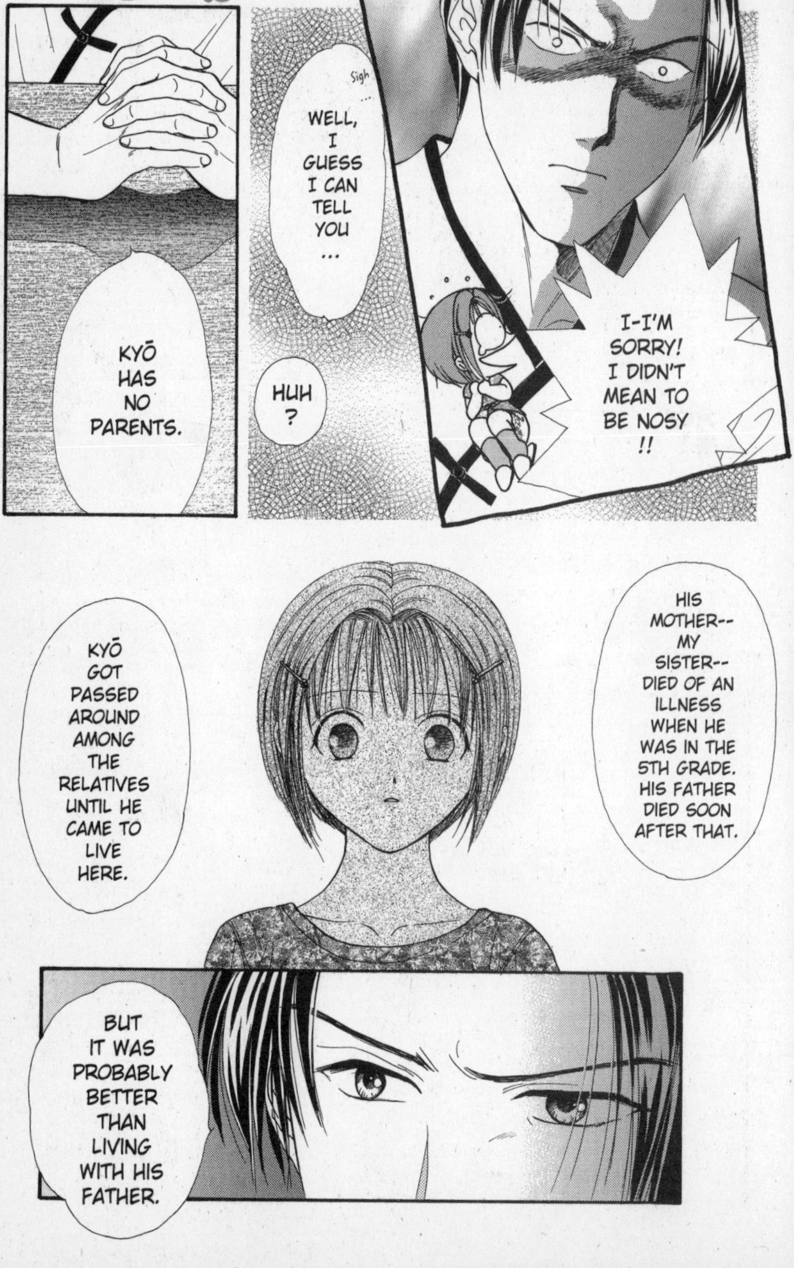
I-I'M SORRY! I DIDN'T MEAN TO BE NOSY!!
Sigh ...
WELL, I GUESS I CAN TELL YOU ...
HUH?
KYŌ HAS NO PARENTS.
HIS MOTHER--MY SISTER--DIED OF AN ILLNESS WHEN HE WAS IN THE 5TH GRADE. HIS FATHER DIED SOON AFTER THAT.
KYŌ GOT PASSED AROUND AMONG THE RELATIVES UNTIL HE CAME TO LIVE HERE.
BUT IT WAS PROBABLY BETTER THAN LIVING WITH HIS FATHER.

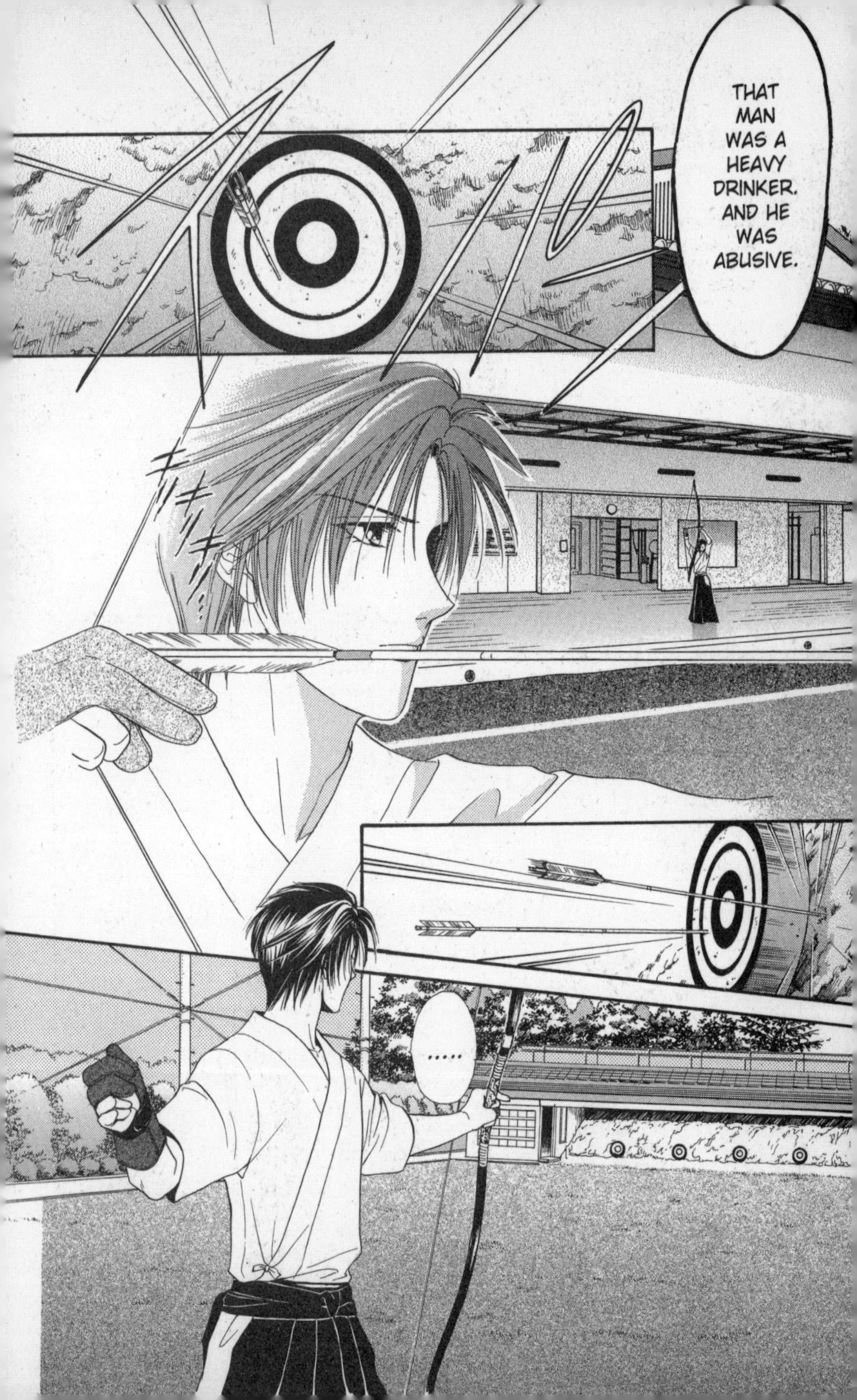
THAT MAN WAS A HEAVY DRINKER. AND HE WAS ABUSIVE.
......

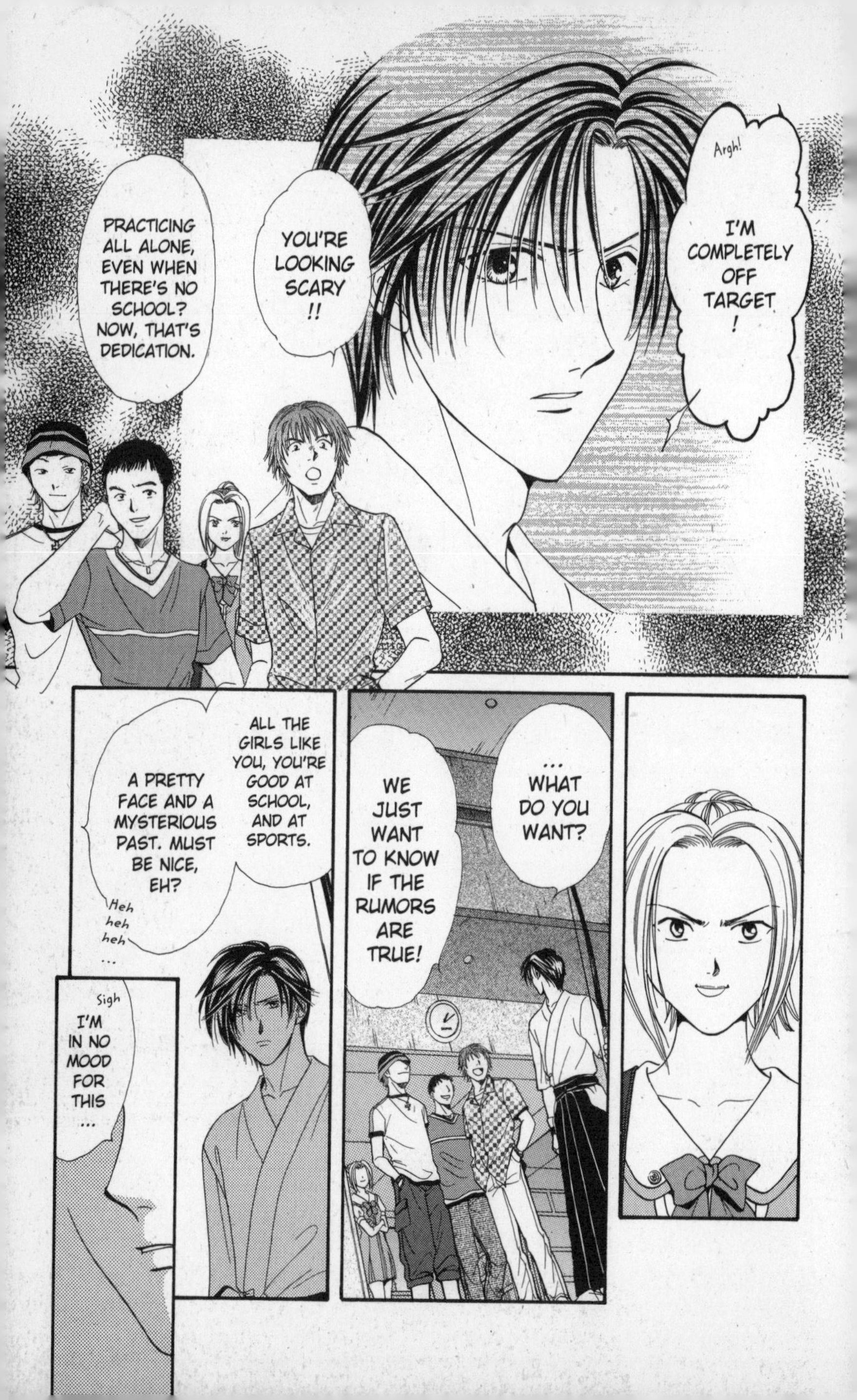
Argh!
I'M COMPLETELY OFF TARGET!
YOU'RE LOOKING SCARY!!
PRACTICING ALL ALONE, EVEN WHEN THERE'S NO SCHOOL? NOW, THAT'S DEDICATION.
... WHAT DO YOU WANT?
WE JUST WANT TO KNOW IF THE RUMORS ARE TRUE!
ALL THE GIRLS LIKE YOU, YOU'RE GOOD AT SCHOOL, AND AT SPORTS.
A PRETTY FACE AND A MYSTERIOUS PAST. MUST BE NICE, EH?
Heh heh heh...
Sigh
I'M IN NO MOOD FOR THIS...

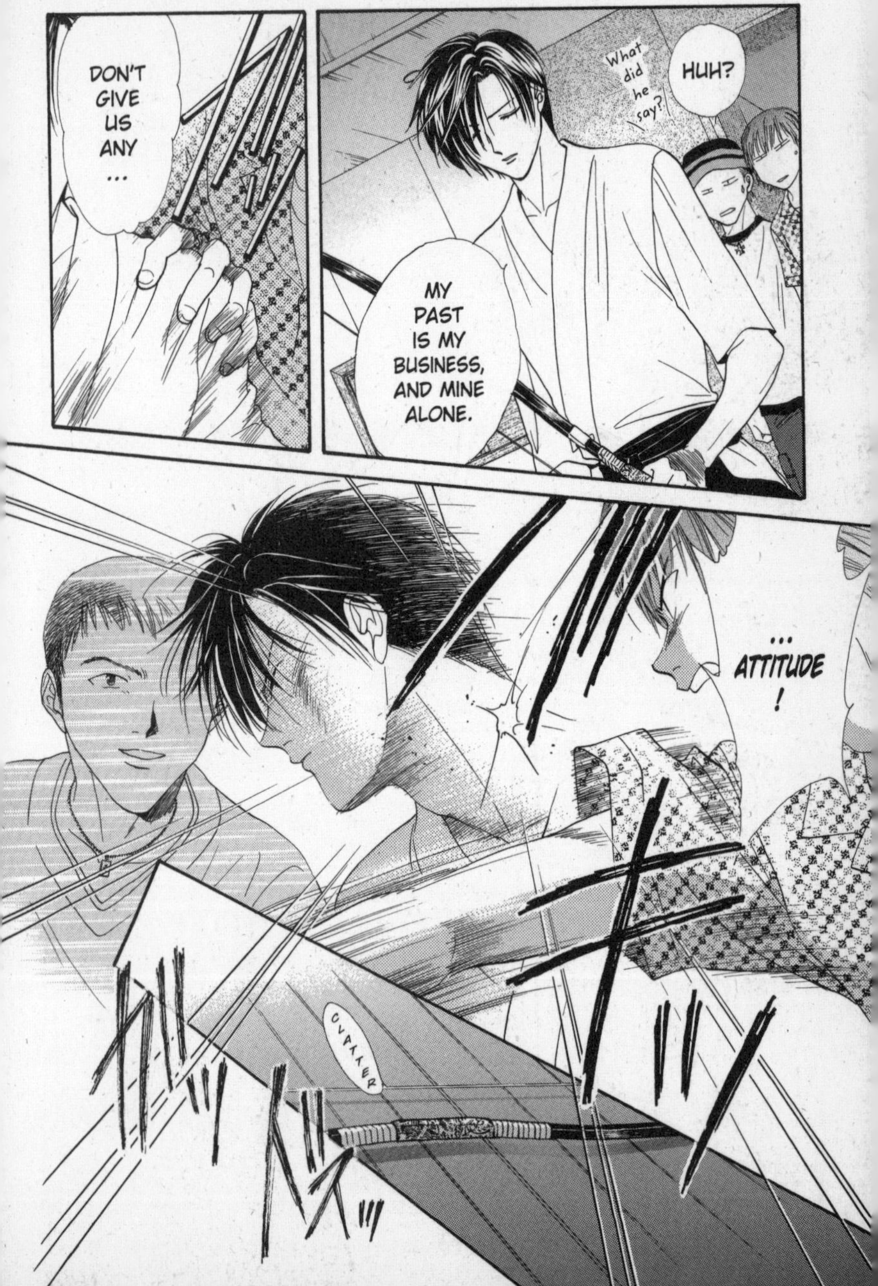
HUH?
What did he say?
MY PAST IS MY BUSINESS, AND MINE ALONE.
DON'T GIVE US ANY ...
... ATTITUDE!
CLATTER

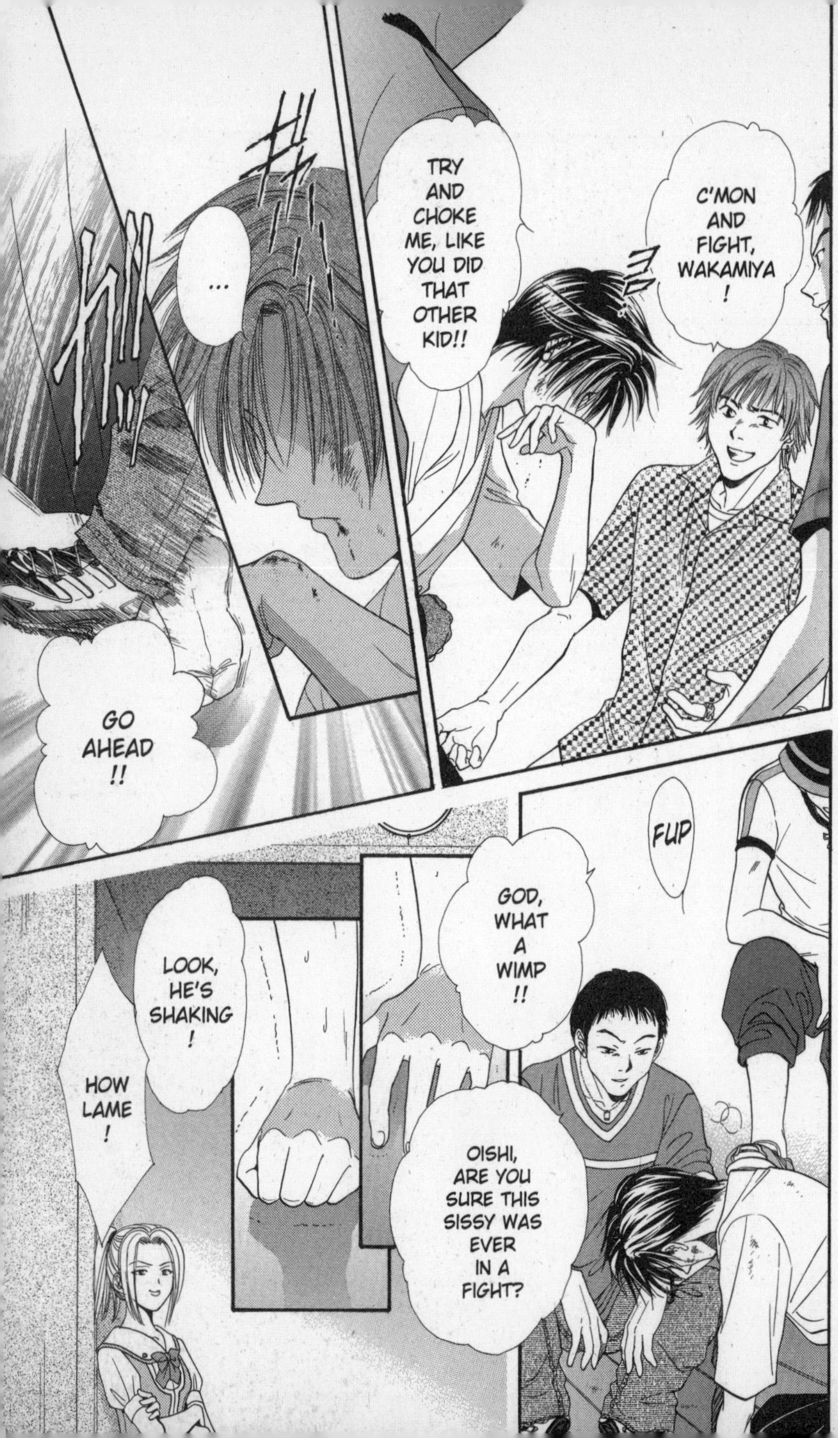
C'MON AND FIGHT, WAKAMIYA!
TRY AND CHOKE ME, LIKE YOU DID THAT OTHER KID!!
...
GO AHEAD!!
FUP
GOD, WHAT A WIMP!!
OISHI, ARE YOU SURE THIS SISSY WAS EVER IN A FIGHT?
LOOK, HE'S SHAKING!
HOW LAME!

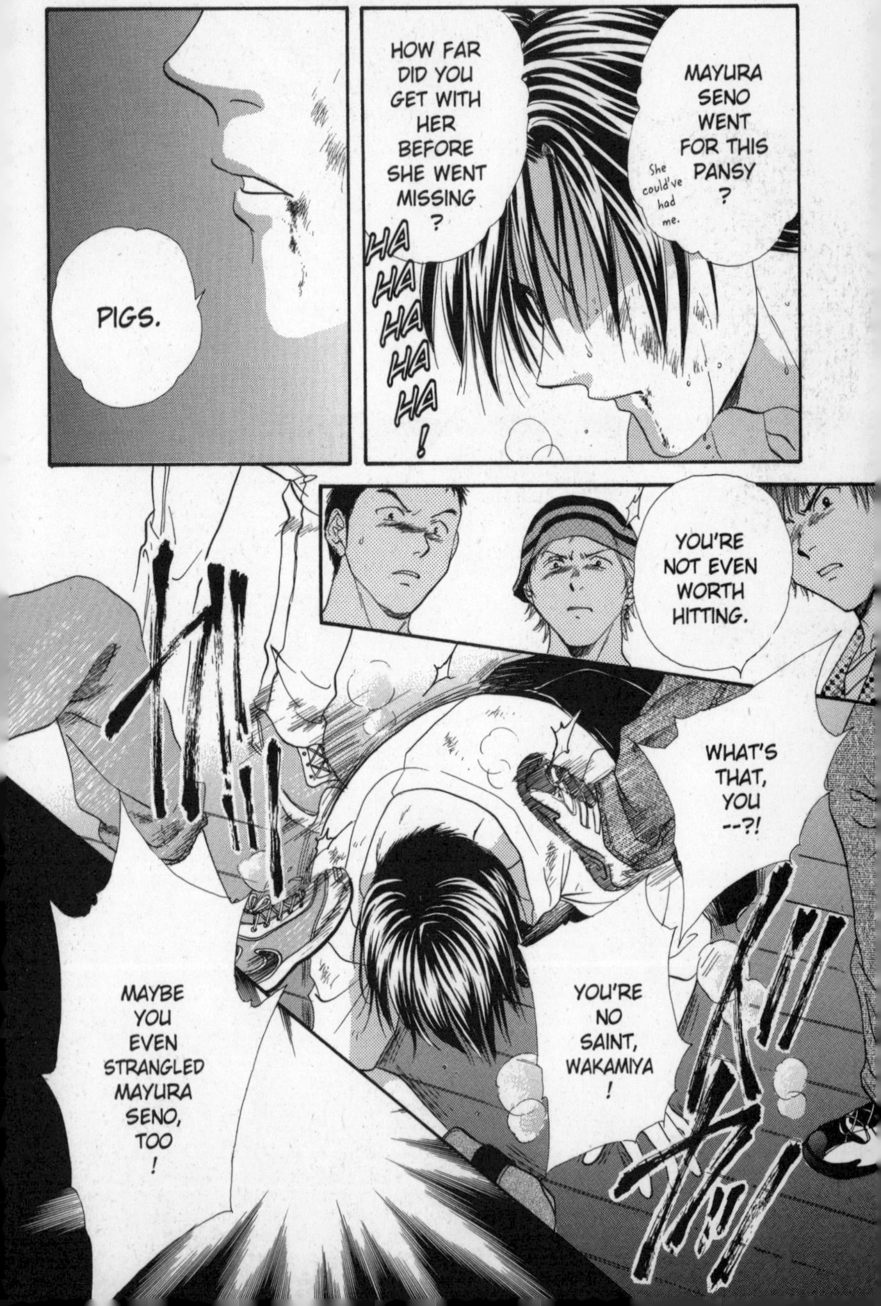
MAYURA SENO WENT FOR THIS PANSY?
She could've had me.
HOW FAR DID YOU GET WITH HER BEFORE SHE WENT MISSING?
HA HA HA HA HA!
PIGS.
YOU'RE NOT EVEN WORTH HITTING.
WHAT'S THAT, YOU --?!
YOU'RE NO SAINT, WAKAMIYA!
MAYBE YOU EVEN STRANGLED MAYURA SENO, TOO!

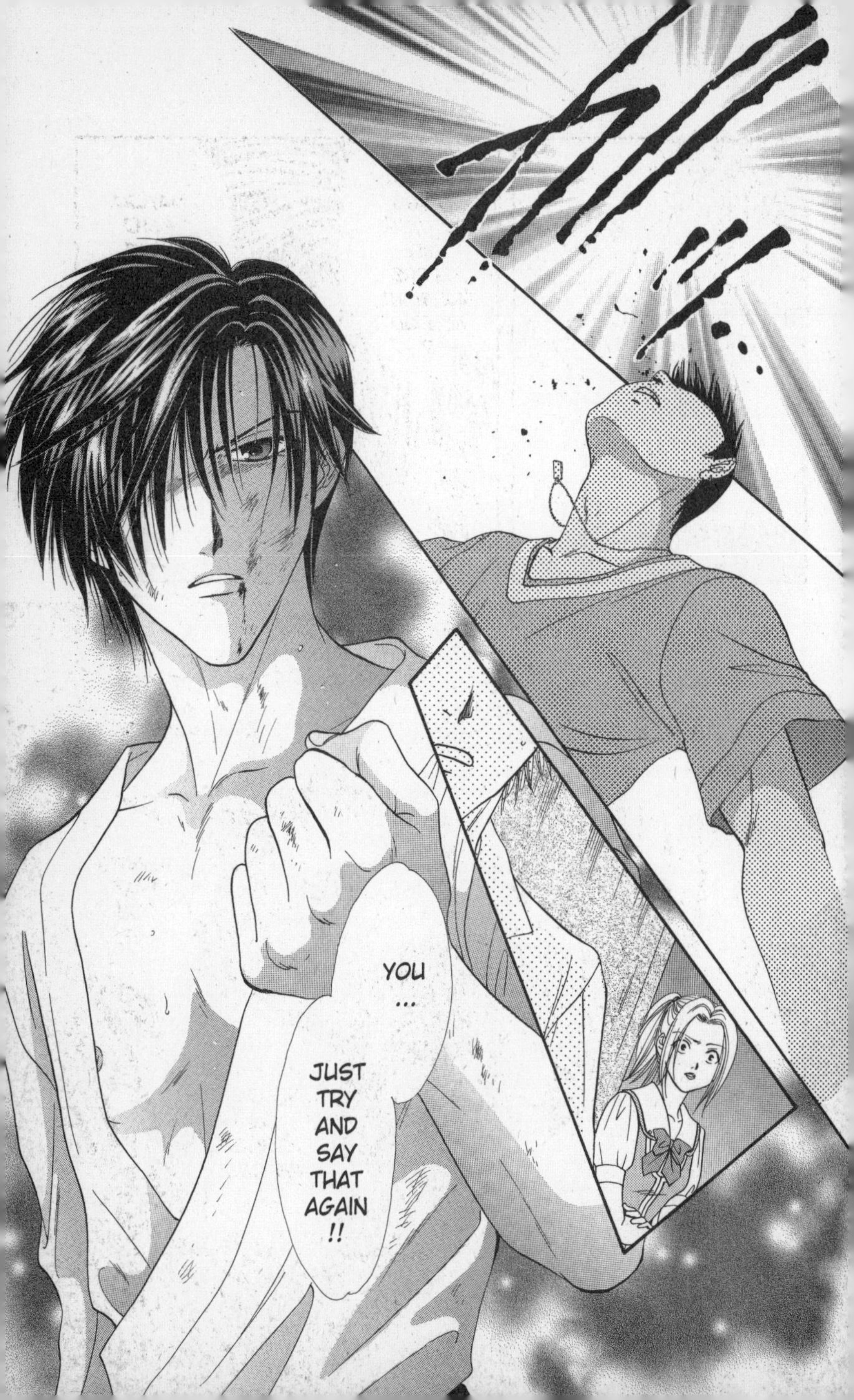
YOU ...
JUST TRY AND SAY THAT AGAIN !!

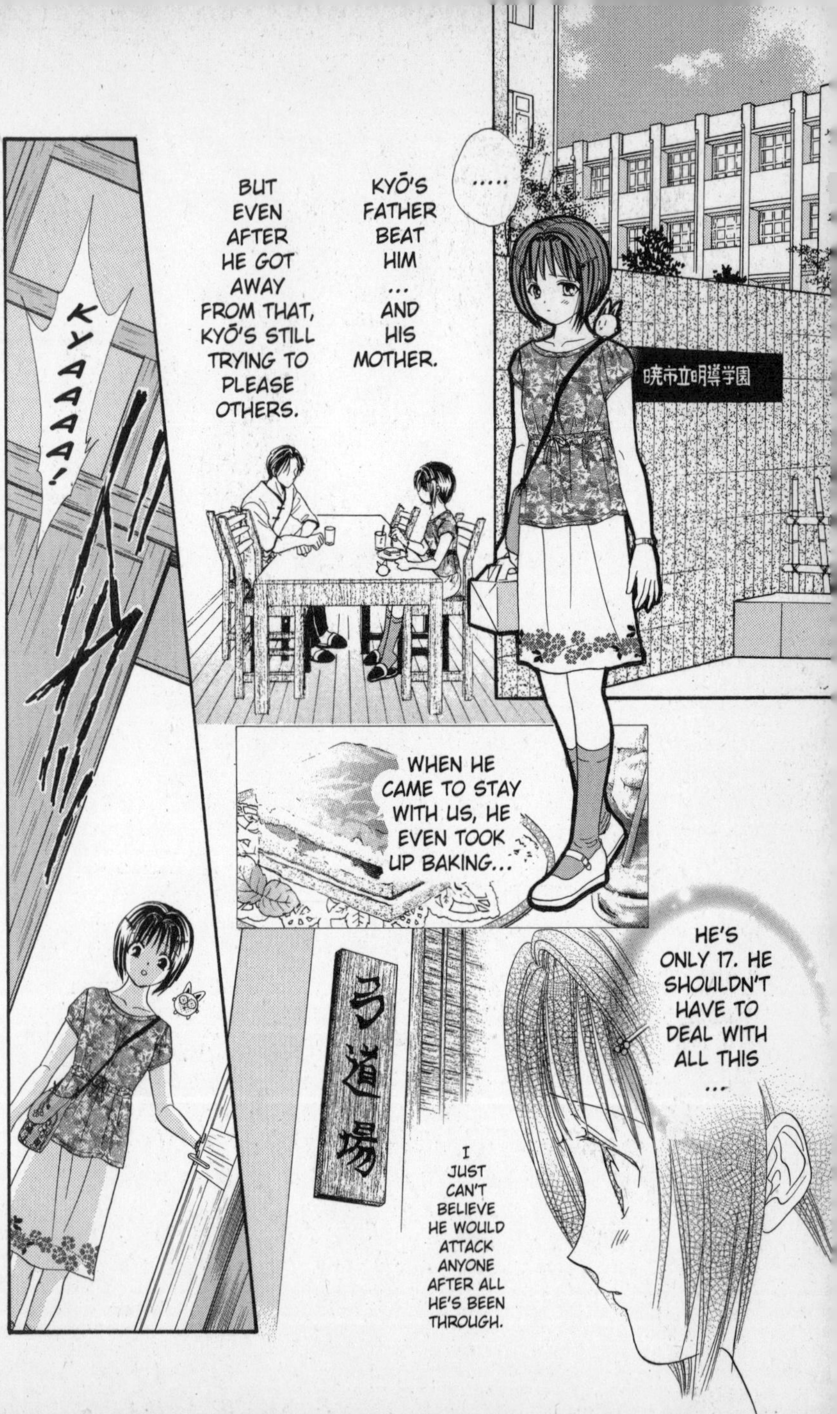
.....
暁市立明導学園
KYŌ'S FATHER BEAT HIM ... AND HIS MOTHER.
BUT EVEN AFTER HE GOT AWAY FROM THAT, KYŌ'S STILL TRYING TO PLEASE OTHERS.
WHEN HE CAME TO STAY WITH US, HE EVEN TOOK UP BAKING...
HE'S ONLY 17. HE SHOULDN'T HAVE TO DEAL WITH ALL THIS ...
I JUST CAN'T BELIEVE HE WOULD ATTACK ANYONE AFTER ALL HE'S BEEN THROUGH.
弓道場
KYAAAAA!

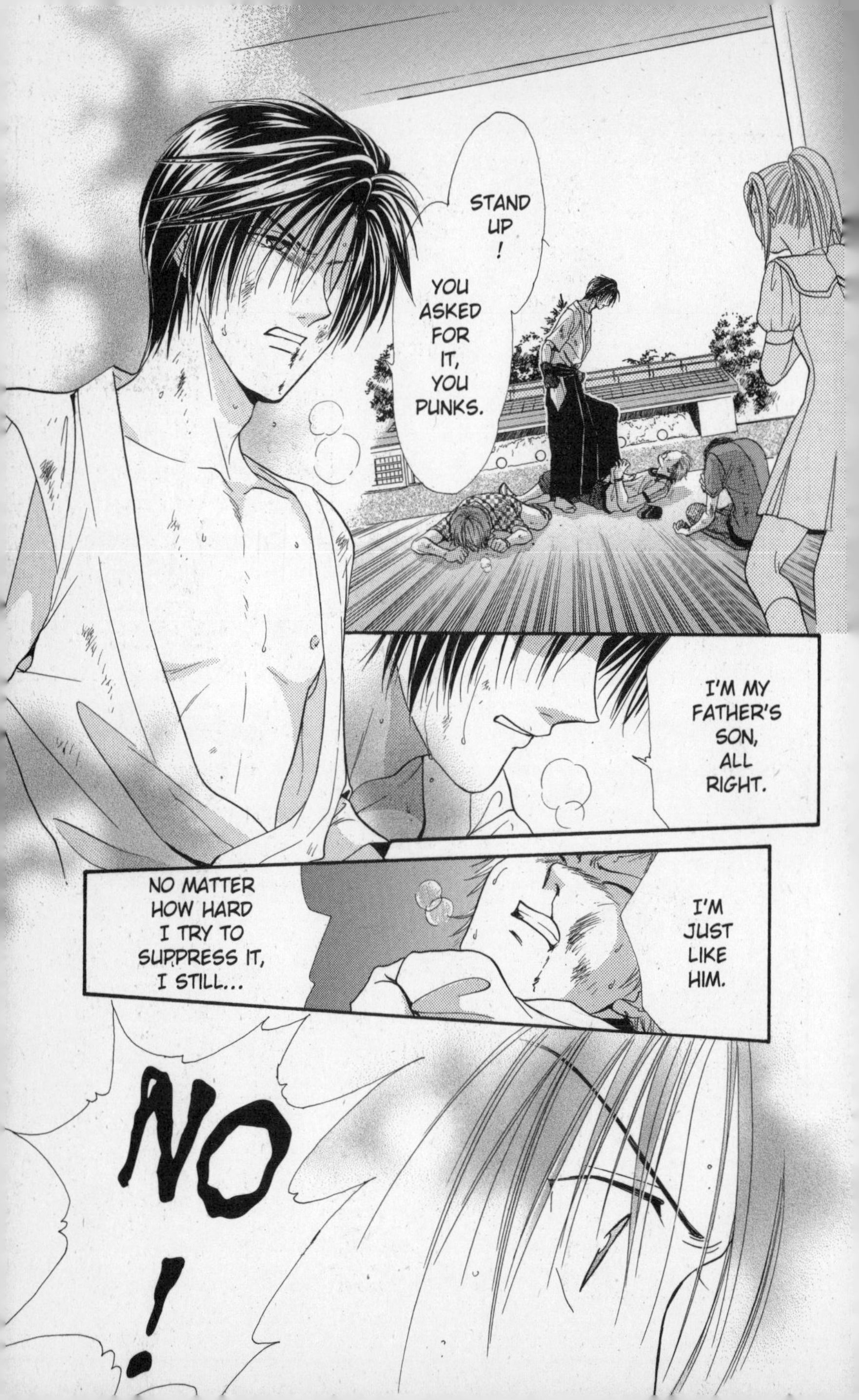
STAND UP!
YOU ASKED FOR IT, YOU PUNKS.
I'M MY FATHER'S SON, ALL RIGHT.
I'M JUST LIKE HIM.
NO MATTER HOW HARD I TRY TO SUPPRESS IT, I STILL...
NO!

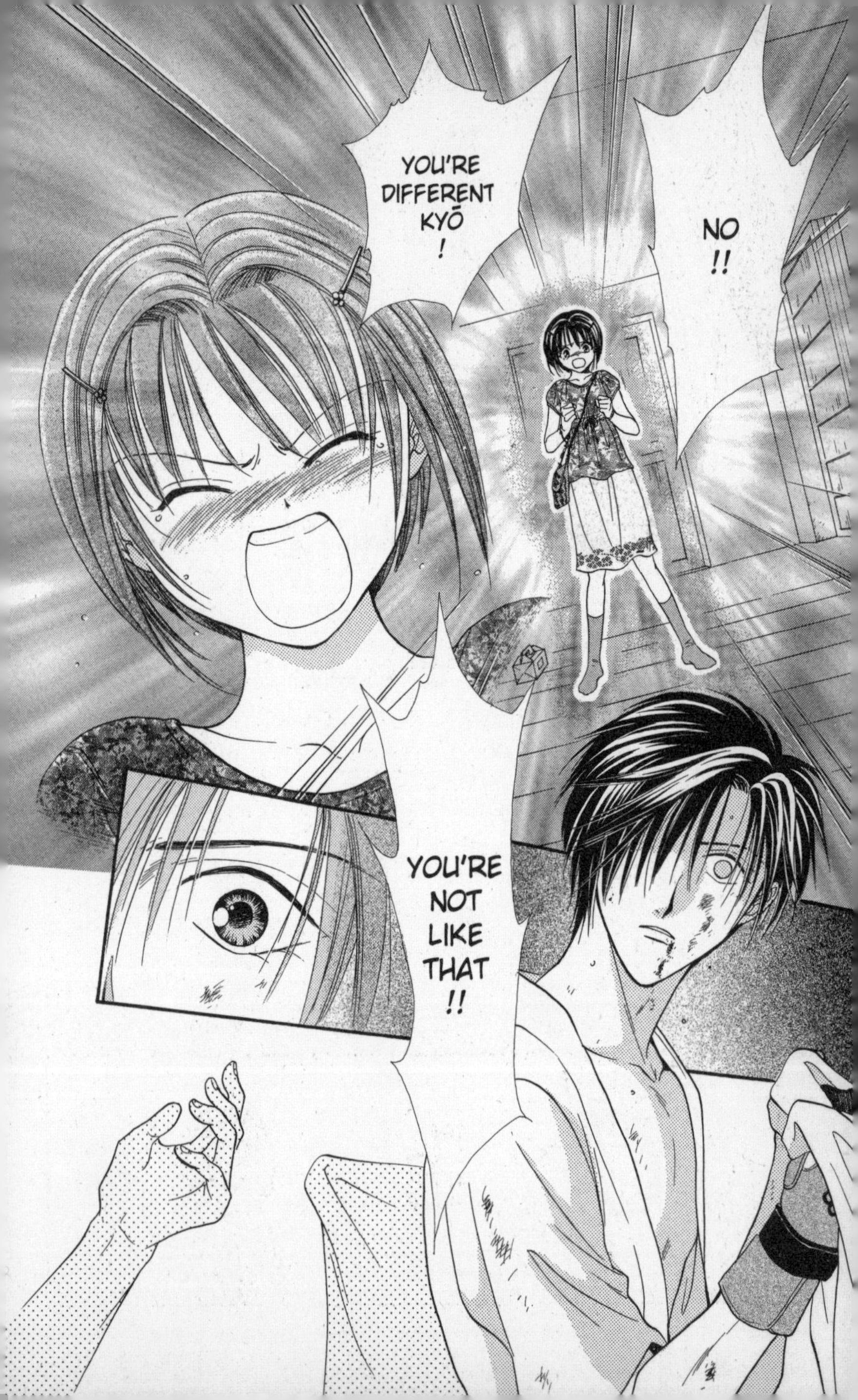
NO !!
YOU'RE DIFFERENT KYŌ !
YOU'RE NOT LIKE THAT !!

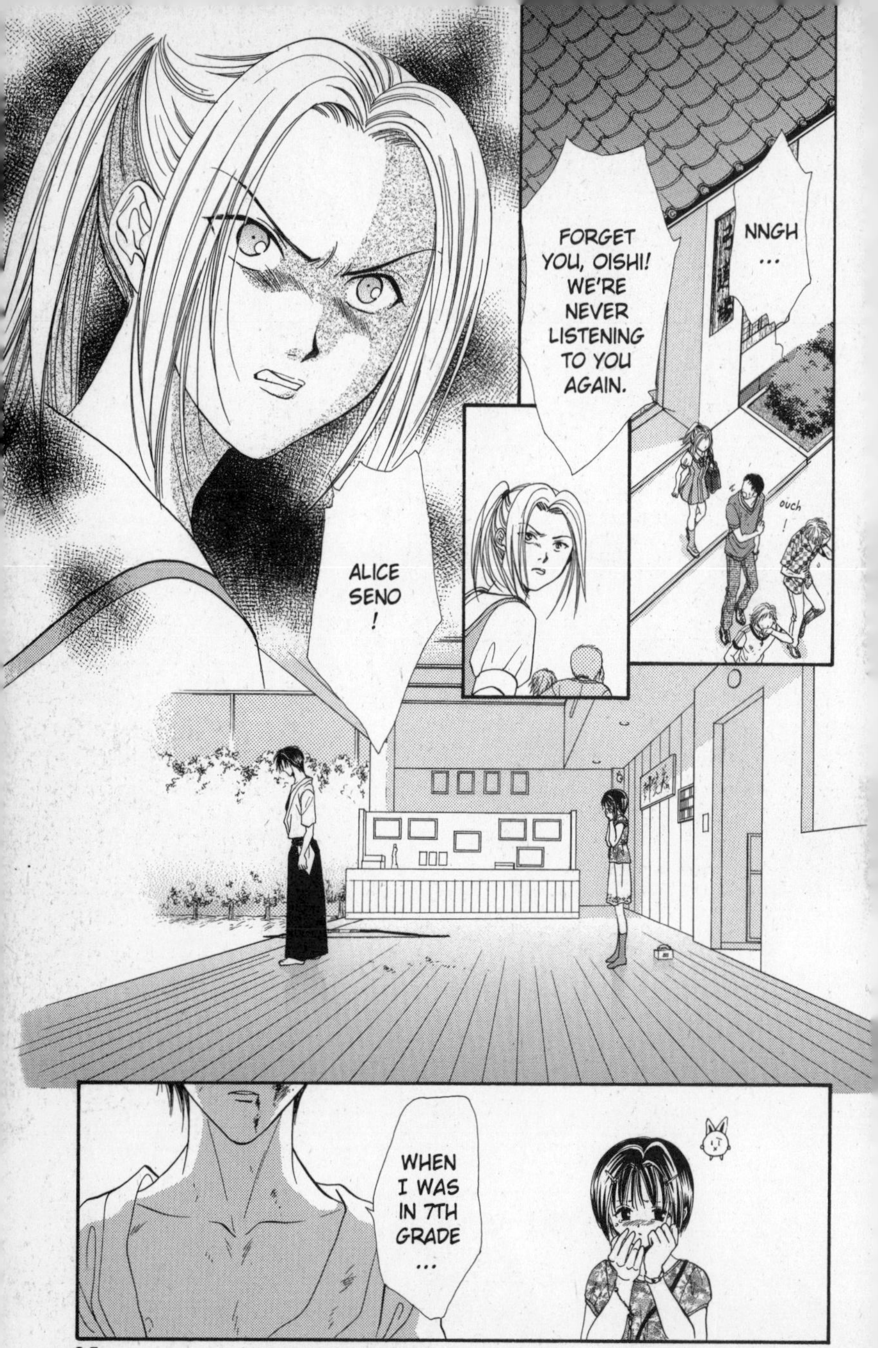
NNGH ...
ouch !
FORGET YOU, OISHI! WE'RE NEVER LISTENING TO YOU AGAIN.
ALICE SENO !
WHEN I WAS IN 7TH GRADE ...

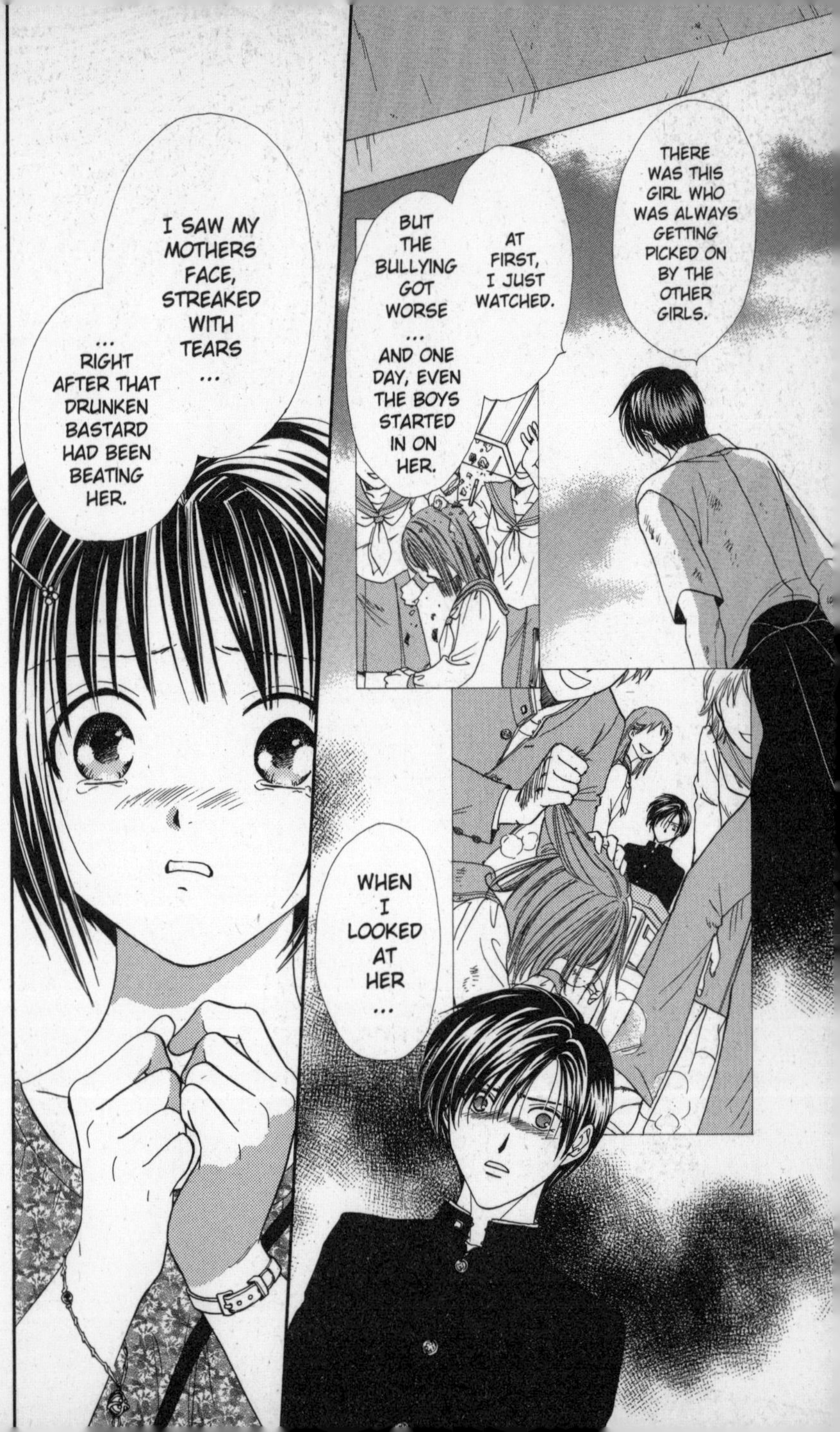
THERE WAS THIS GIRL WHO WAS ALWAYS GETTING PICKED ON BY THE OTHER GIRLS.
AT FIRST, I JUST WATCHED.
BUT THE BULLYING GOT WORSE ... AND ONE DAY, EVEN THE BOYS STARTED IN ON HER.
WHEN I LOOKED AT HER ...
I SAW MY MOTHERS FACE, STREAKED WITH TEARS ...
... RIGHT AFTER THAT DRUNKEN BASTARD HAD BEEN BEATING HER.

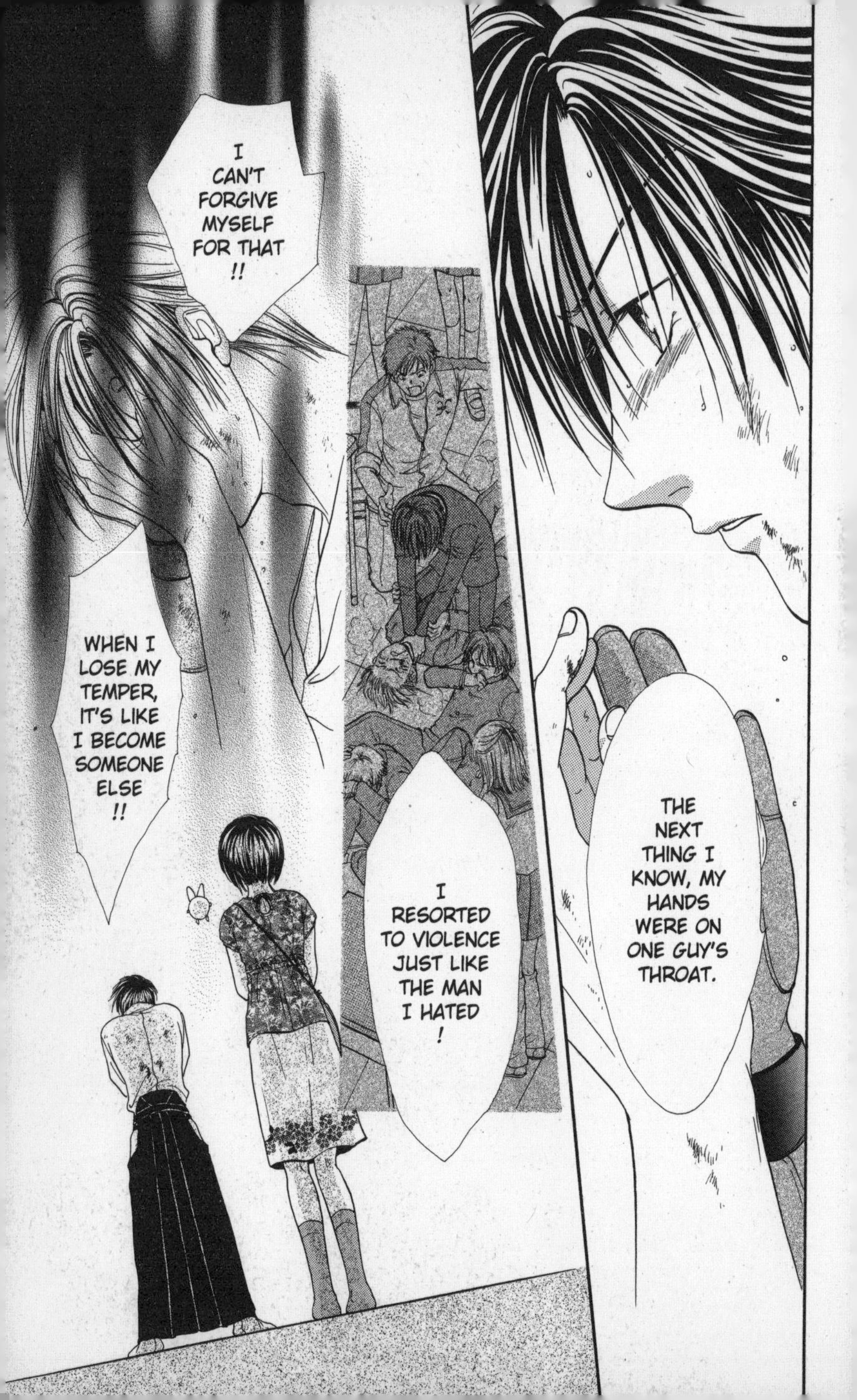
THE NEXT THING I KNOW, MY HANDS WERE ON ONE GUY'S THROAT.
I RESORTED TO VIOLENCE JUST LIKE THE MAN I HATED!
I CAN'T FORGIVE MYSELF FOR THAT!!
WHEN I LOSE MY TEMPER, IT'S LIKE I BECOME SOMEONE ELSE!!

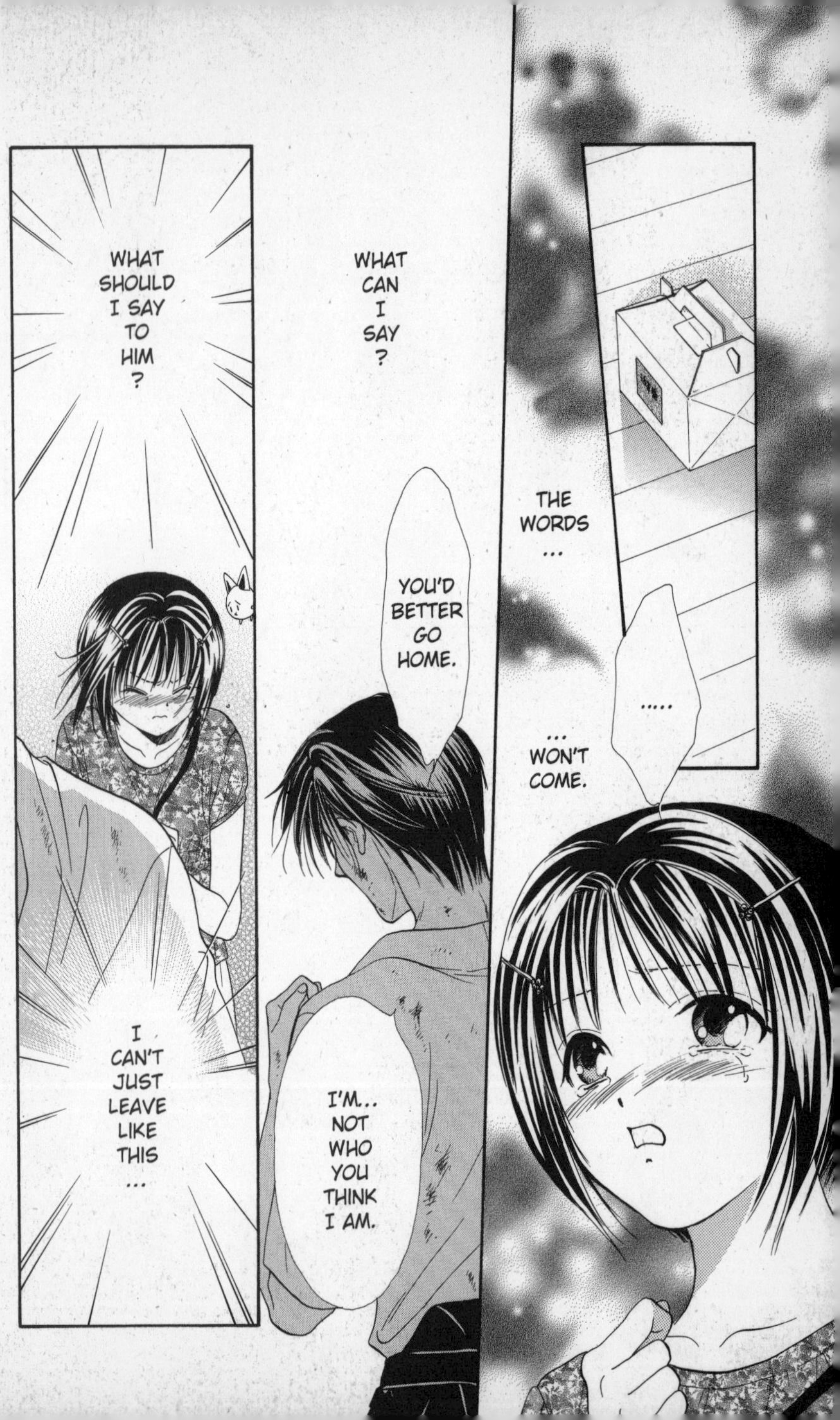
THE WORDS ...
.....
... WON'T COME.
WHAT CAN I SAY ?
YOU'D BETTER GO HOME.
I'M... NOT WHO YOU THINK I AM.
WHAT SHOULD I SAY TO HIM ?
I CAN'T JUST LEAVE LIKE THIS ...

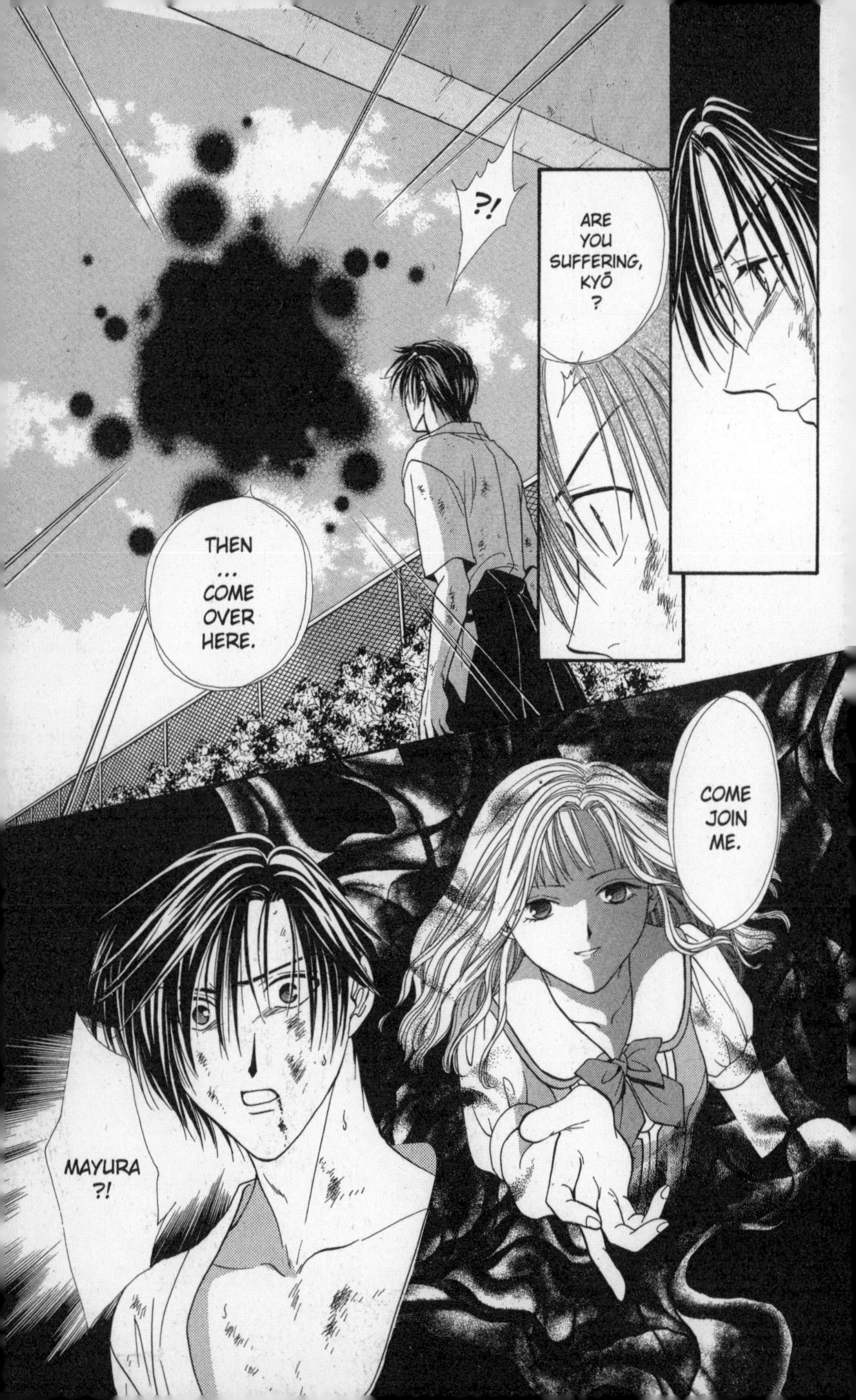
ARE YOU SUFFERING, KYŌ?
?!
THEN ... COME OVER HERE.
COME JOIN ME.
MAYURA ?!

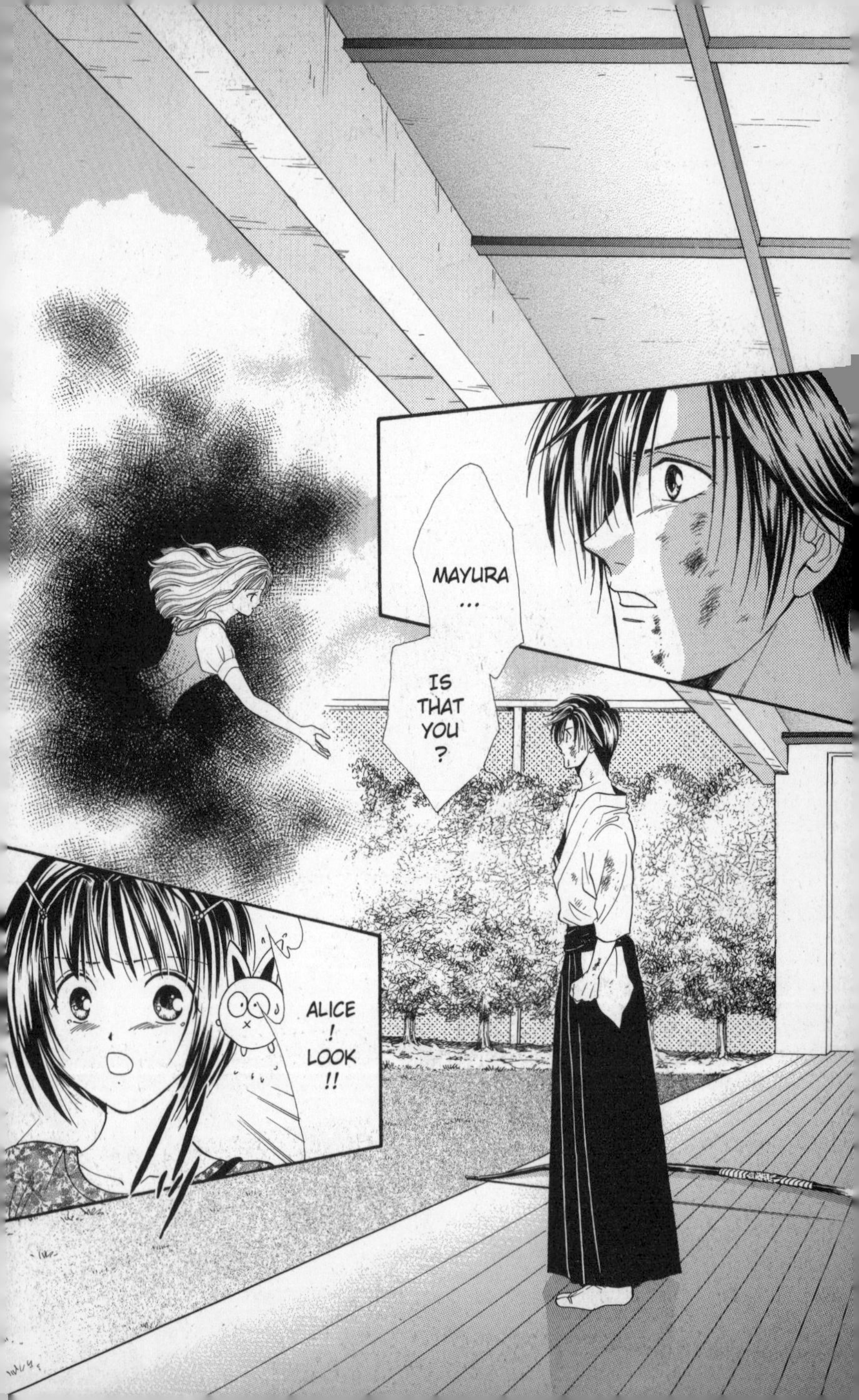
MAYURA ...
IS THAT YOU?
ALICE! LOOK!!

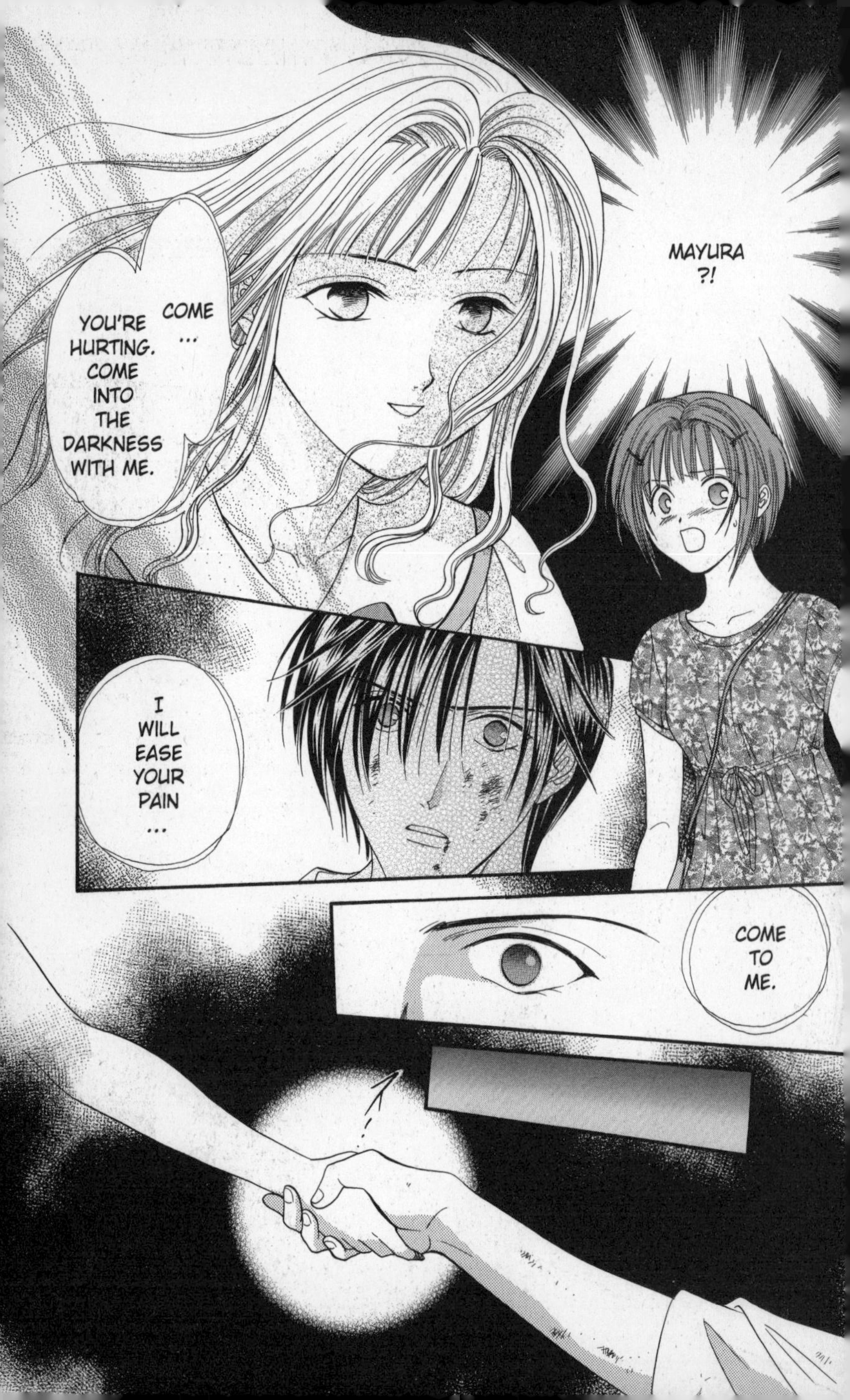
MAYURA ?!
COME ...
YOU'RE HURTING. COME INTO THE DARKNESS WITH ME.
I WILL EASE YOUR PAIN ...
COME TO ME.

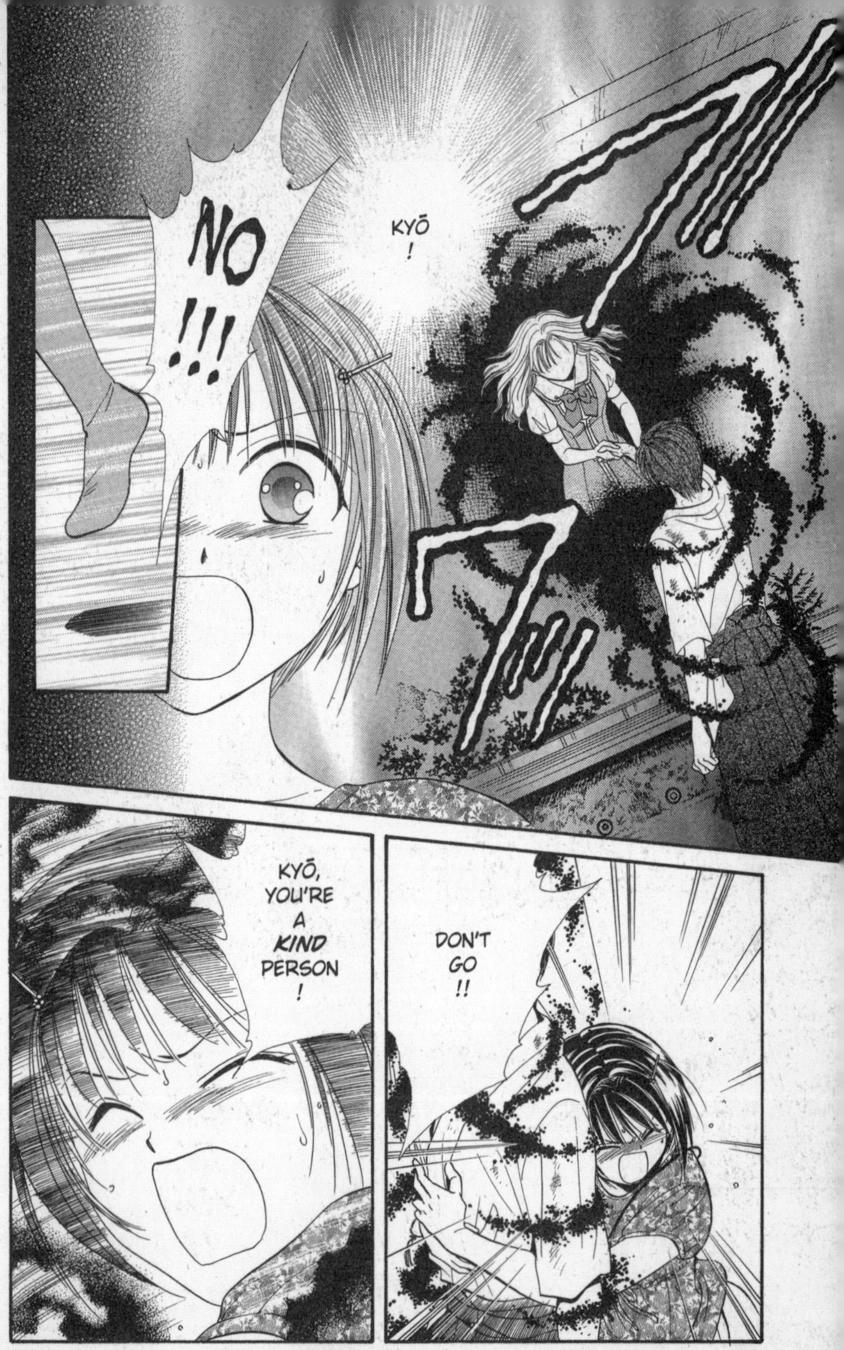
KYŌ !
NO !!!
DON'T GO !!
KYŌ, YOU'RE A *KIND* PERSON !

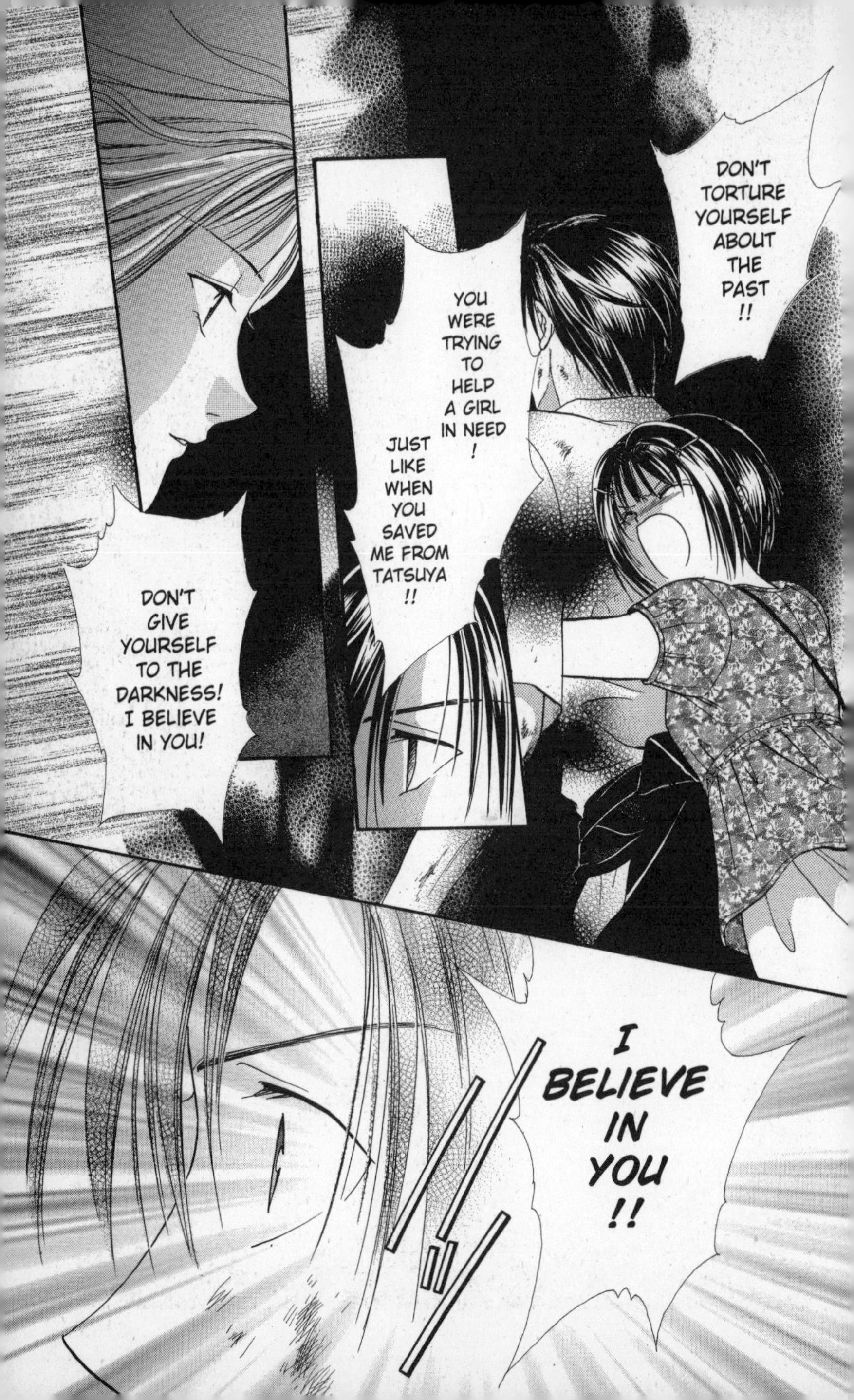
DON'T TORTURE YOURSELF ABOUT THE PAST!!
YOU WERE TRYING TO HELP A GIRL IN NEED!
JUST LIKE WHEN YOU SAVED ME FROM TATSUYA!!
DON'T GIVE YOURSELF TO THE DARKNESS! I BELIEVE IN YOU!
I BELIEVE IN YOU!!

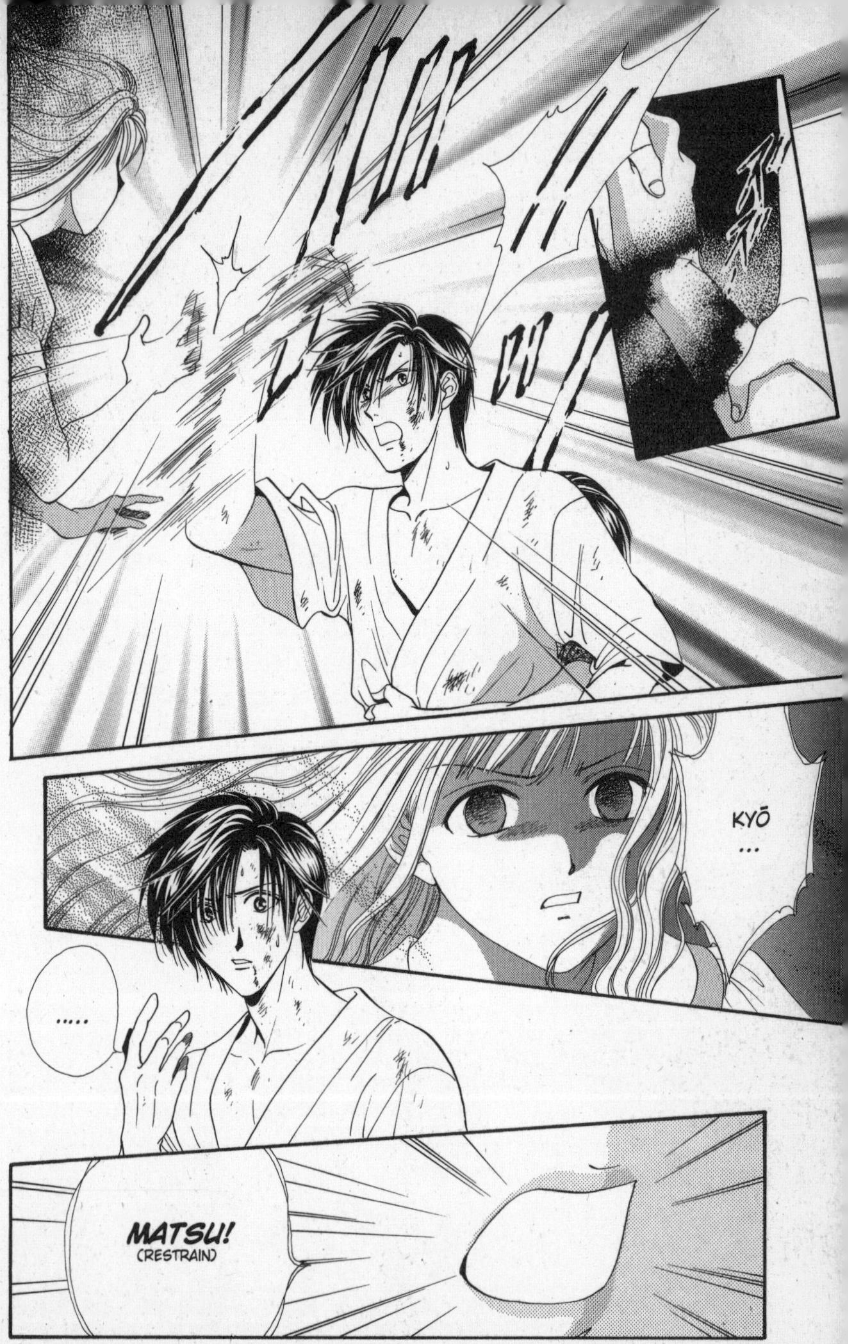
KYŌ
...
.....
MATSU!
(RESTRAIN)

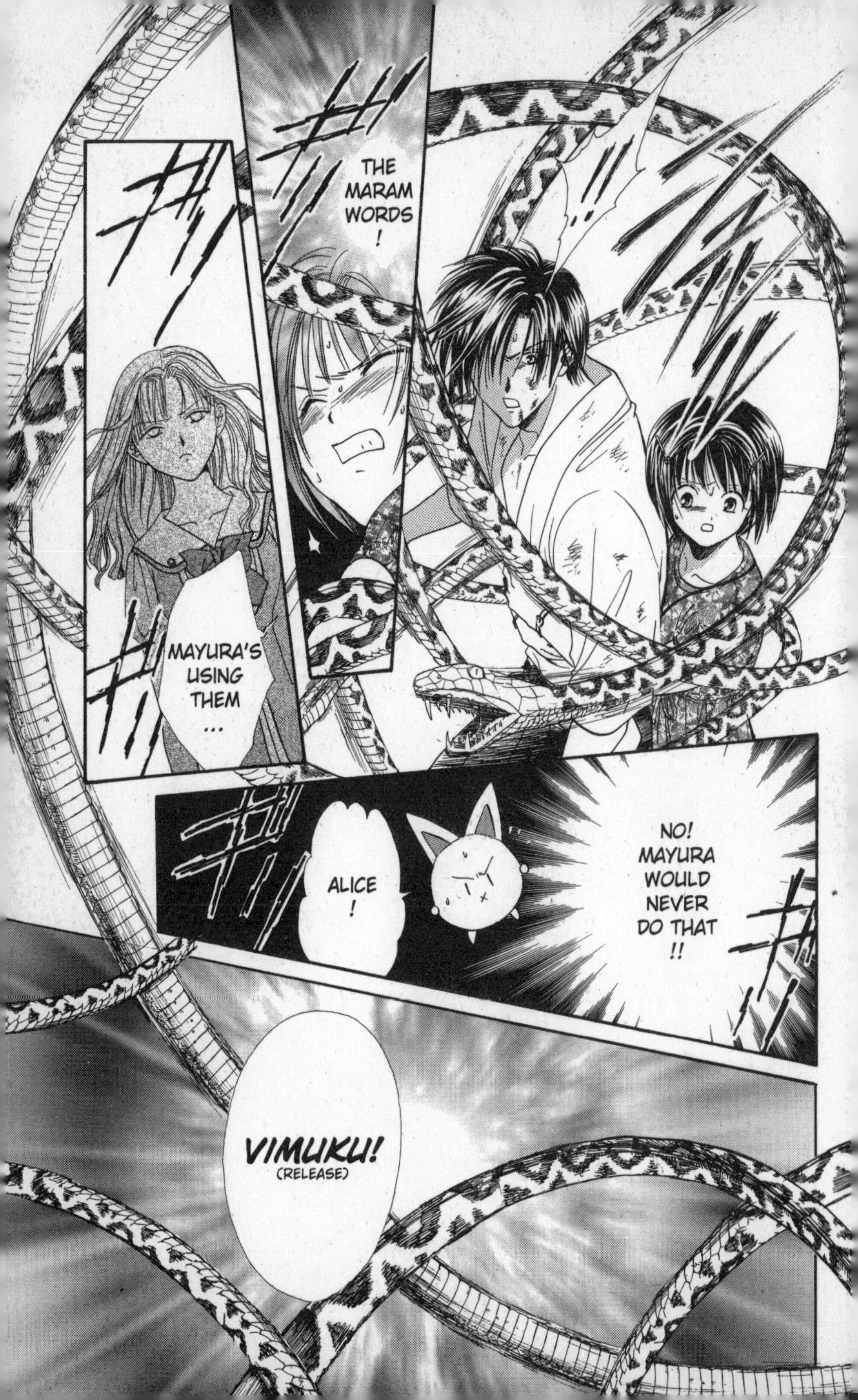
THE MARAM WORDS!
MAYURA'S USING THEM...
NO! MAYURA WOULD NEVER DO THAT!!
ALICE!
VIMUKU!
(RELEASE)

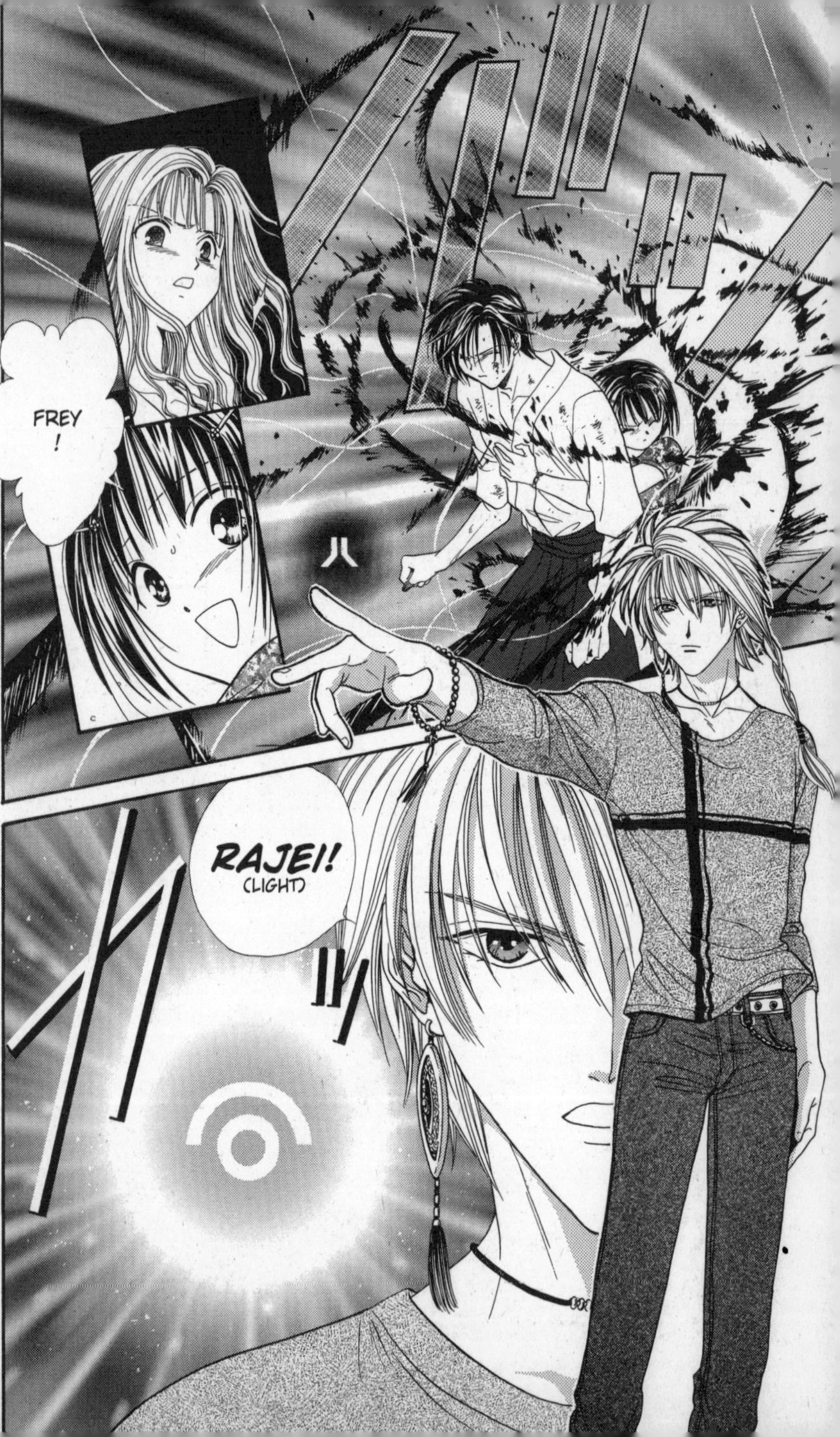
FREY!
RAJEI! (LIGHT)

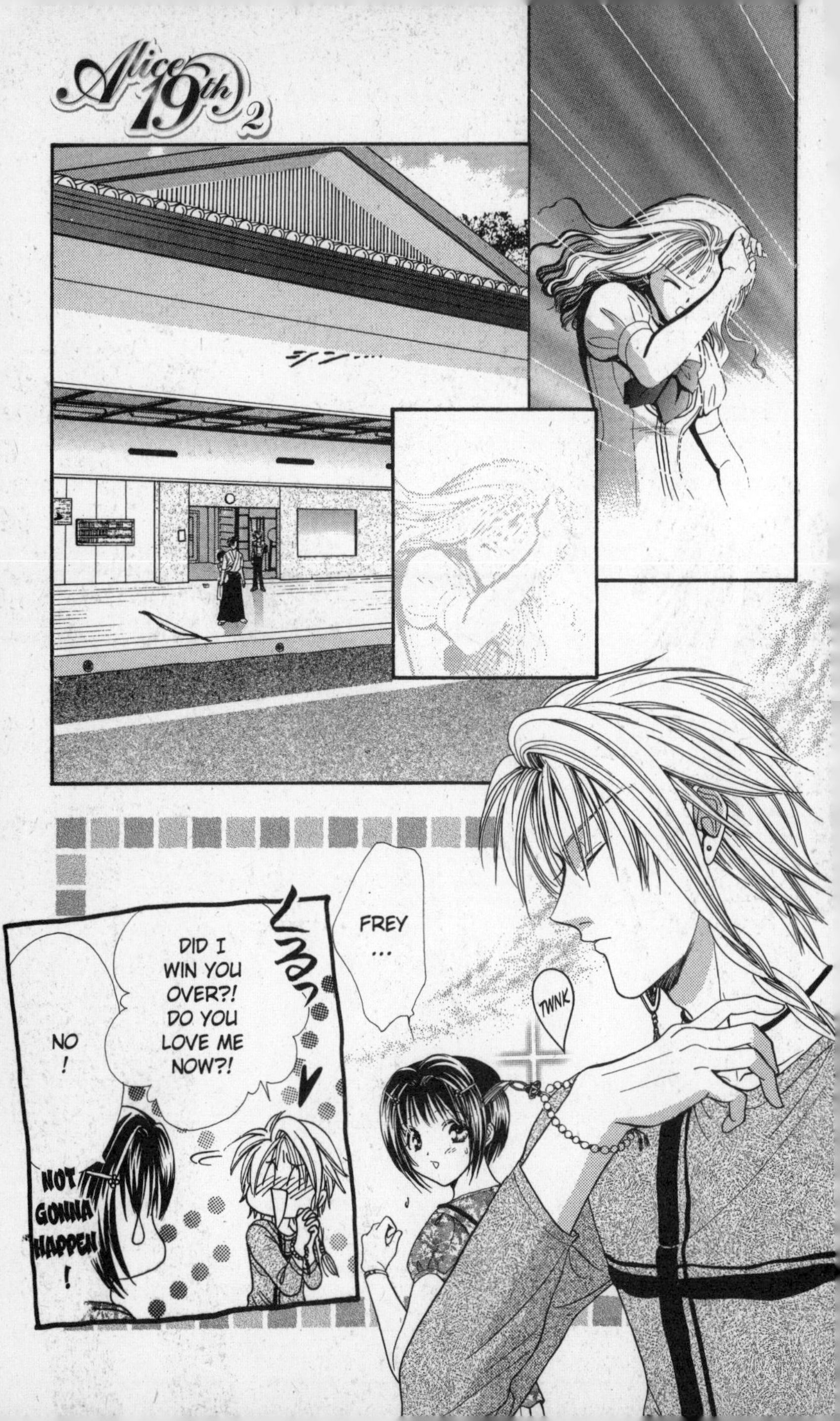
シン…
FREY ...
TWNK
くるっ
DID I WIN YOU OVER?! DO YOU LOVE ME NOW?!
NO!
NOT GONNA HAPPEN!

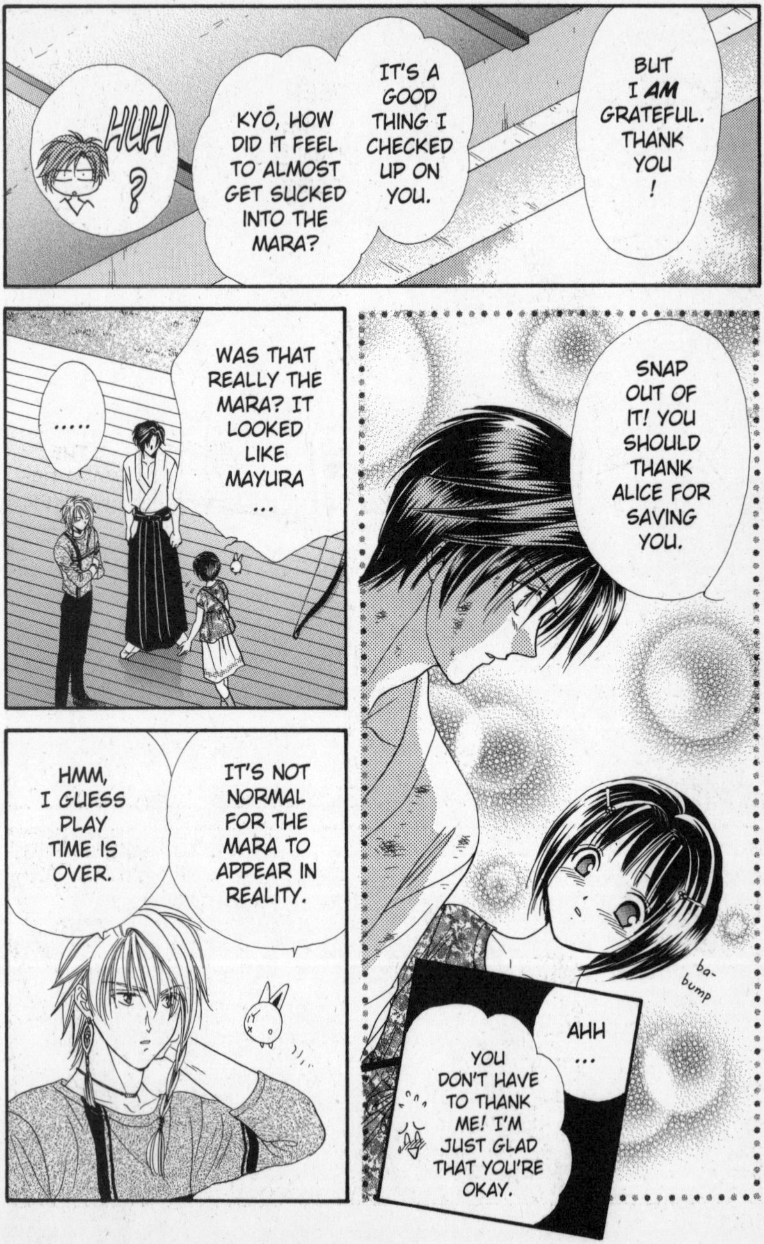
BUT I **AM** GRATEFUL. THANK YOU!
IT'S A GOOD THING I CHECKED UP ON YOU.
KYŌ, HOW DID IT FEEL TO ALMOST GET SUCKED INTO THE MARA?
HUH?
SNAP OUT OF IT! YOU SHOULD THANK ALICE FOR SAVING YOU.
ba-bump
AHH ...
YOU DON'T HAVE TO THANK ME! I'M JUST GLAD THAT YOU'RE OKAY.
WAS THAT REALLY THE MARA? IT LOOKED LIKE MAYURA ...
.....
IT'S NOT NORMAL FOR THE MARA TO APPEAR IN REALITY.
HMM, I GUESS PLAY TIME IS OVER.

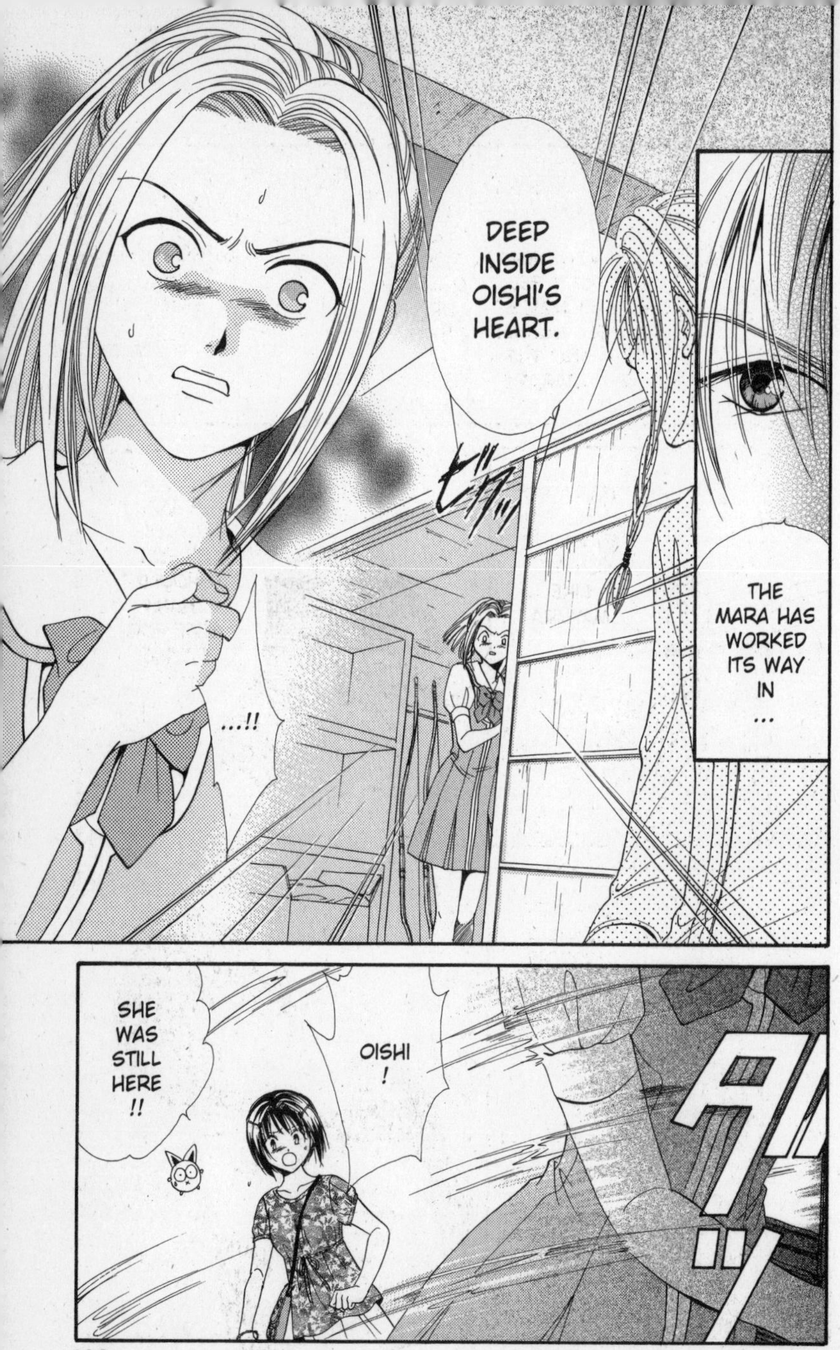
THE MARA HAS WORKED ITS WAY IN ...
DEEP INSIDE OISHI'S HEART.
ビクッ
...!!
タッ
OISHI !
SHE WAS STILL HERE !!

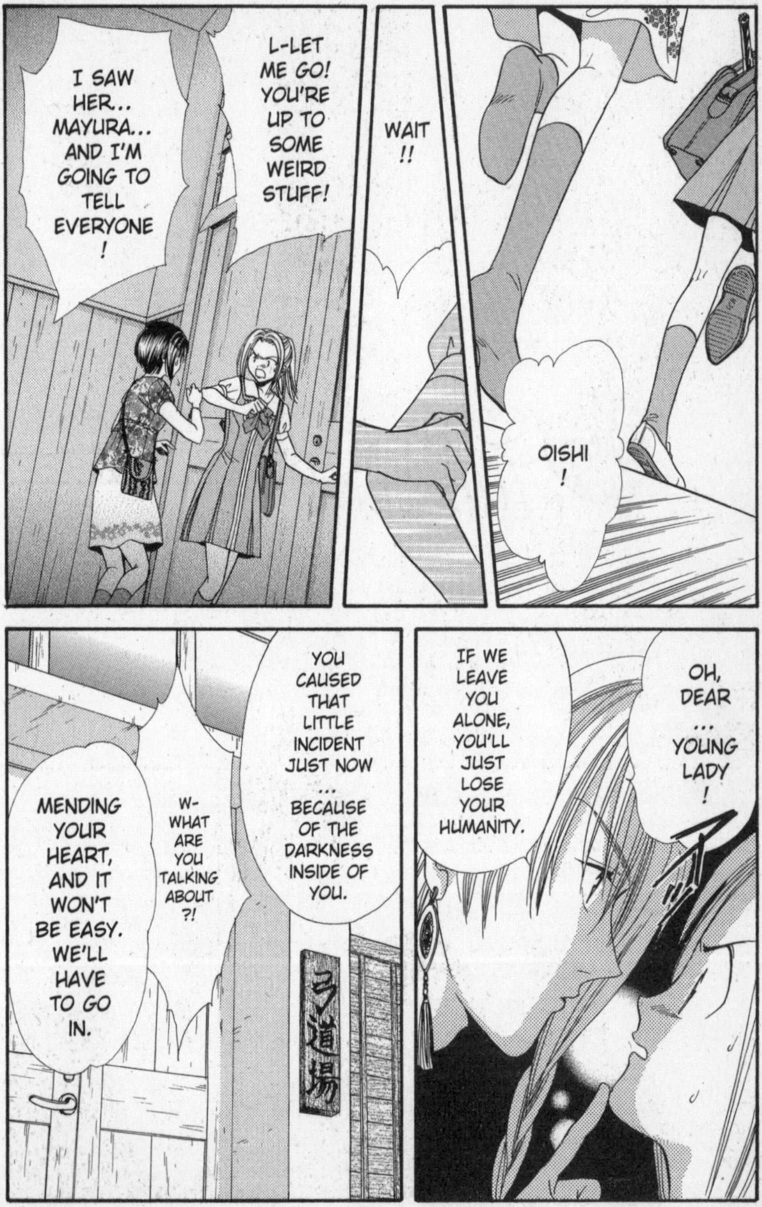
OISHI!
WAIT!!
L-LET ME GO! YOU'RE UP TO SOME WEIRD STUFF!
I SAW HER... MAYURA... AND I'M GOING TO TELL EVERYONE!
OH, DEAR... YOUNG LADY!
IF WE LEAVE YOU ALONE, YOU'LL JUST LOSE YOUR HUMANITY.
YOU CAUSED THAT LITTLE INCIDENT JUST NOW... BECAUSE OF THE DARKNESS INSIDE OF YOU.
W-WHAT ARE YOU TALKING ABOUT?!
MENDING YOUR HEART, AND IT WON'T BE EASY. WE'LL HAVE TO GO IN.
弓道場

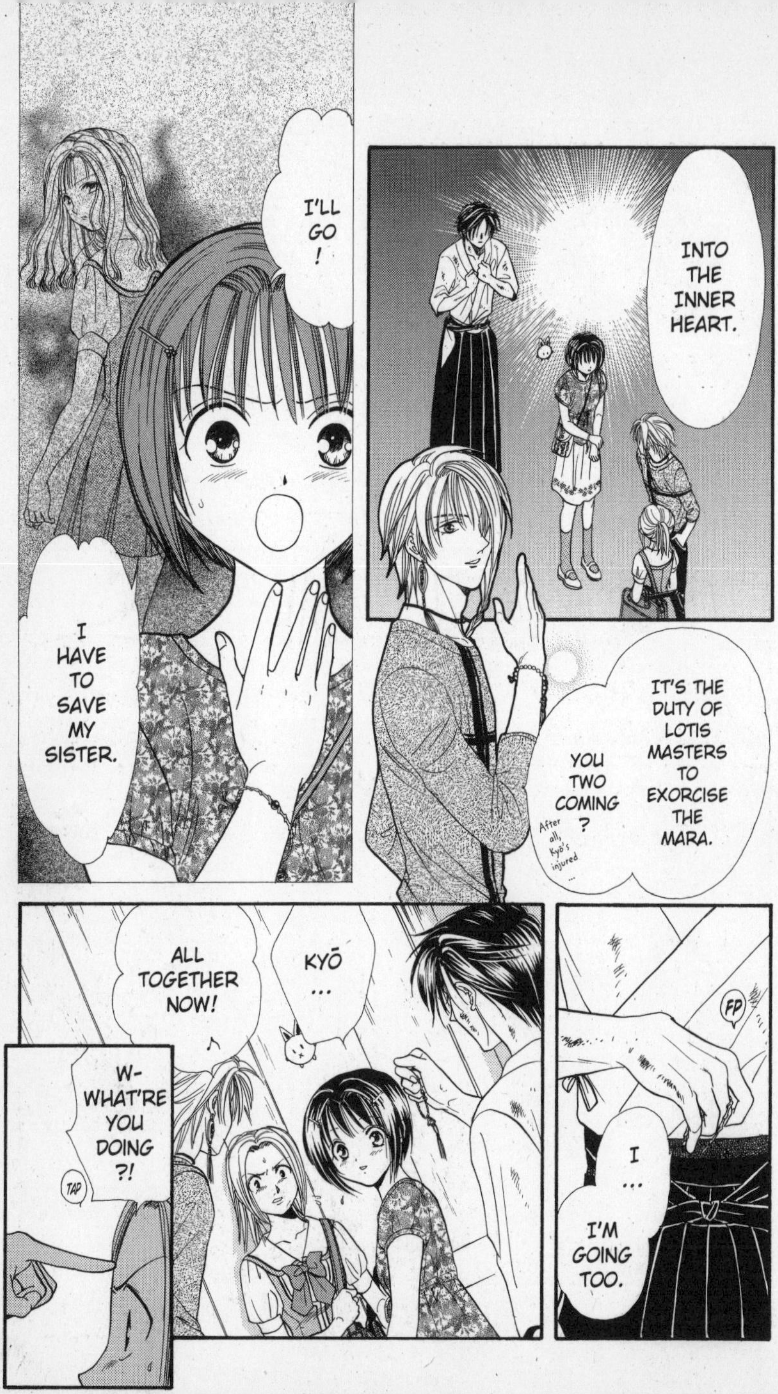
INTO THE INNER HEART.
IT'S THE DUTY OF LOTIS MASTERS TO EXORCISE THE MARA.
YOU TWO COMING?
After all, Kyō's injured...
I'LL GO!
I HAVE TO SAVE MY SISTER.
FP
I... I'M GOING TOO.
KYŌ...
ALL TOGETHER NOW!
W-WHAT'RE YOU DOING?!
TAP

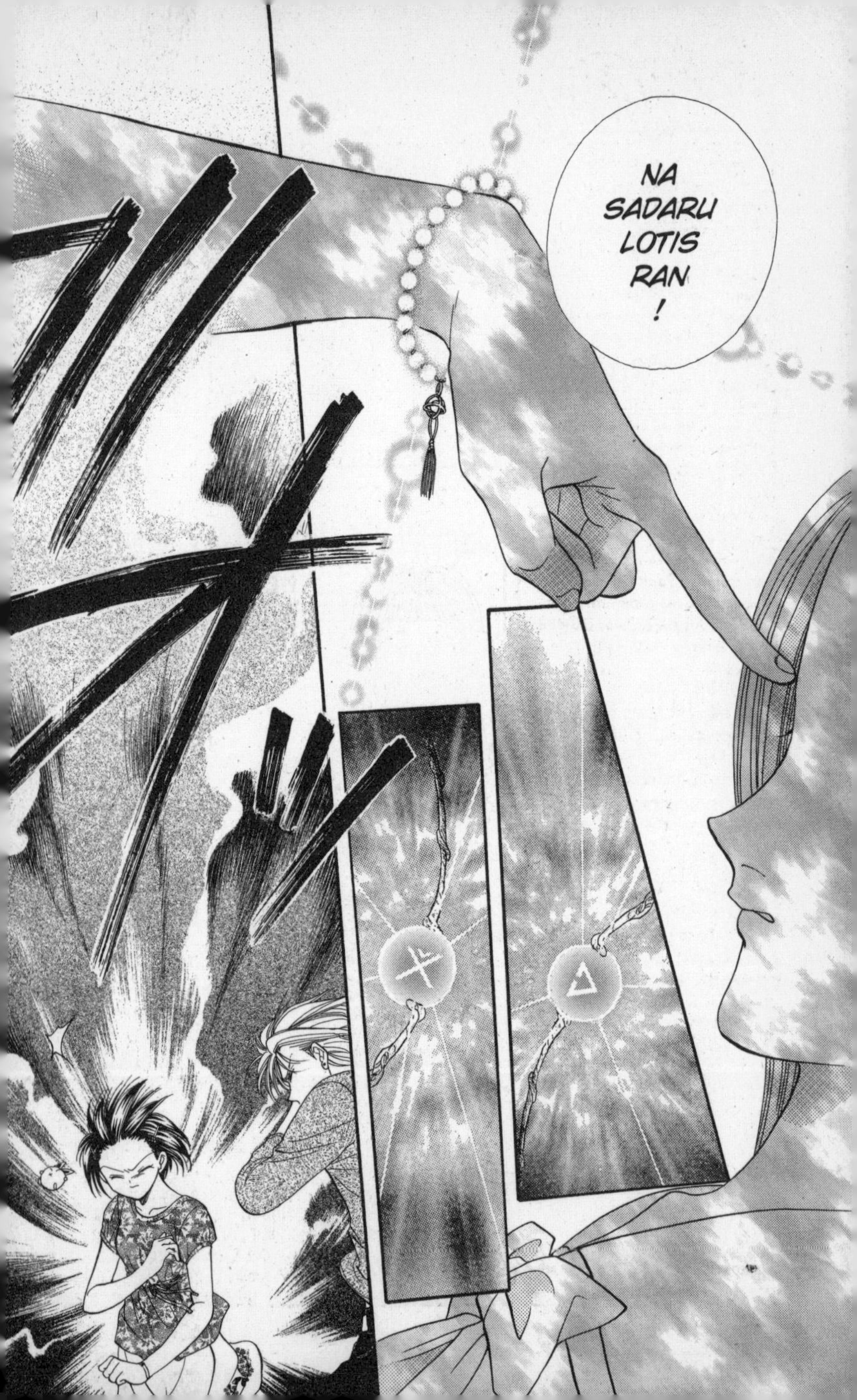
NA SADARU LOTIS RAN !

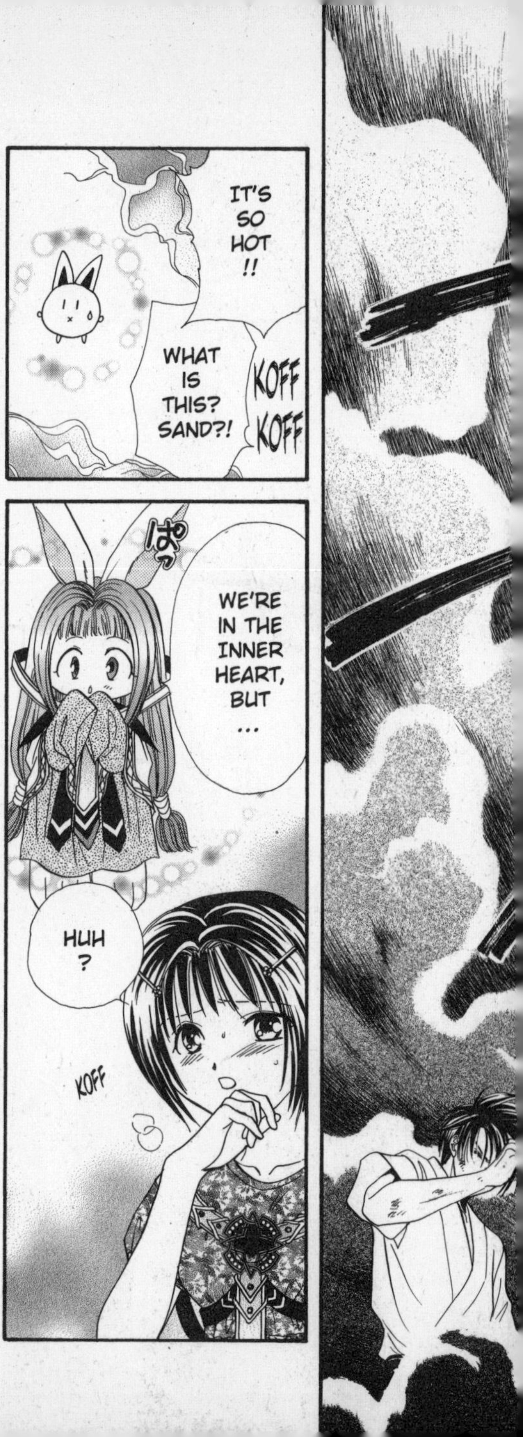
IT'S SO HOT !!
WHAT IS THIS? SAND?!
KOFF KOFF
ぱっ
WE'RE IN THE INNER HEART, BUT ...
HUH ?
KOFF

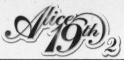

Now then! When this book (Japanese tankobon) is released the first volume of the Fushigi Yûgi OAV will be on sale. I recently attended an event for it.
Many thanks to those who came. The most interesting part was the forum with the voice actors. They were so funny.
Who would have thought that ten years later, there'd still be talk about this... ᵕ.ᵕ
A friend asked me to attend a "Fushigi Yûgi Only Event." Gathered there were members of dojinshi clubs. I also made a quick appearance several years ago... Back then, no one recognized me until halfway into it. This time, I was spotted the moment I walked in! ☺ Maybe I'm going out into the public too much?
I'm sorry that a big line for autographs disrupted the bingo game.
I was trying to be nonchalant. A lot of people gave me their own books... Many of you are very talented. You created all kinds of character merchandise, too. The best were the rice crackers with the laser illustrations of Tamahome, Nuriko, and Chichiri on them! And after the event, I was pleasantly surprised that the organizers of the event sent me even more of them! There was even kompeito candy. They were delicious. Thank you very much...But you're probably not reading this. But those types of events really do make me happy! ♪

♥ I wanted to go to the one in Osaka too!

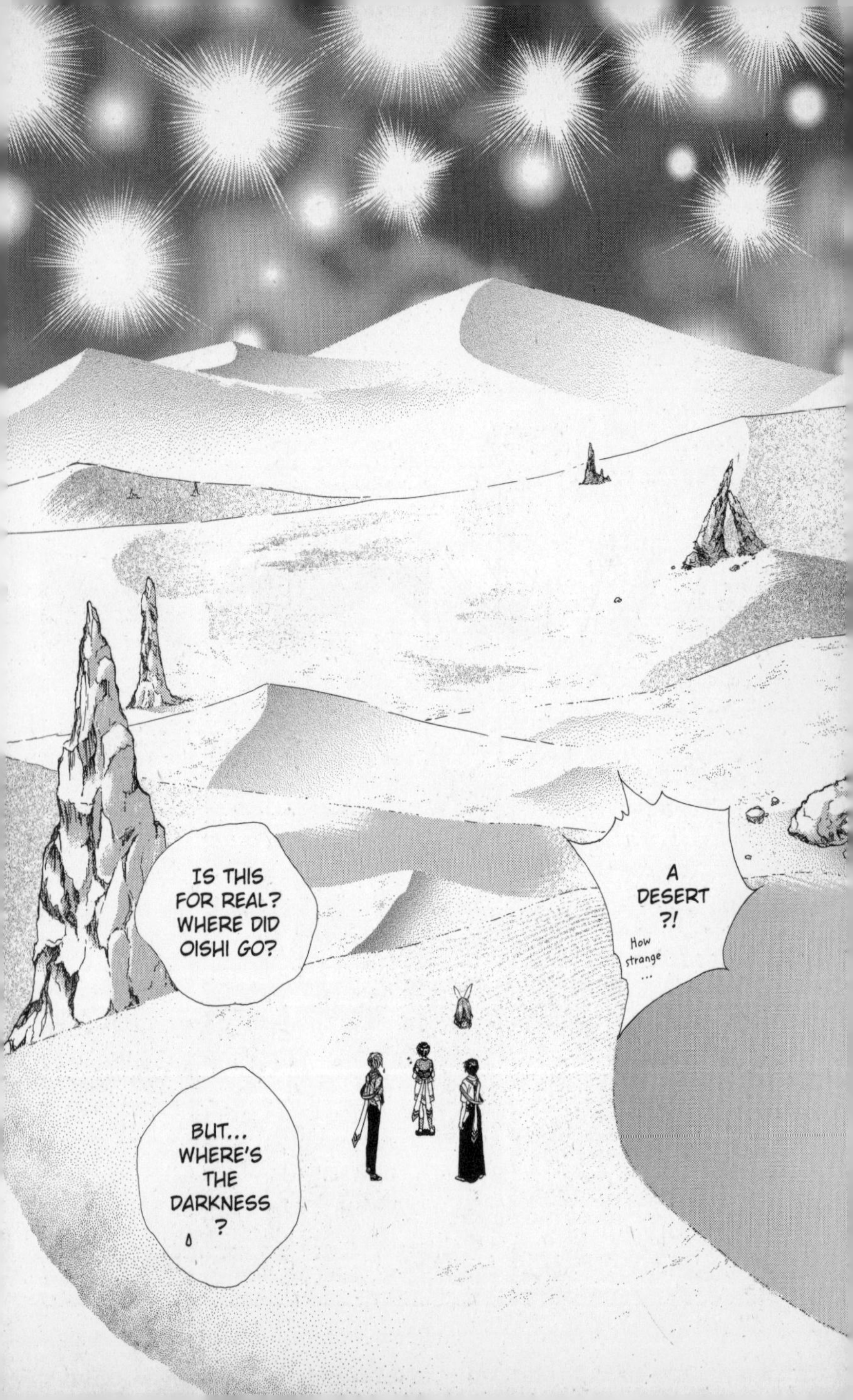
A DESERT ?!
How strange ...
IS THIS FOR REAL? WHERE DID OISHI GO?
BUT... WHERE'S THE DARKNESS ?

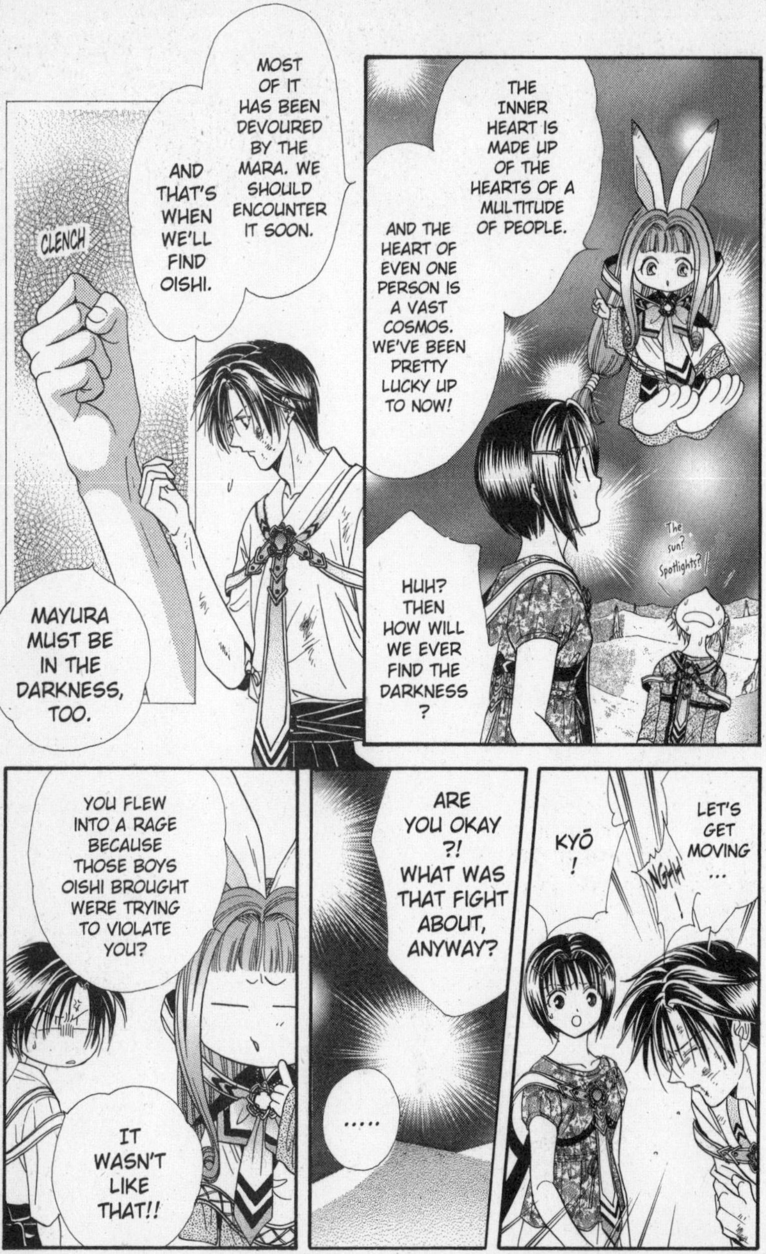
THE INNER HEART IS MADE UP OF THE HEARTS OF A MULTITUDE OF PEOPLE.
AND THE HEART OF EVEN ONE PERSON IS A VAST COSMOS. WE'VE BEEN PRETTY LUCKY UP TO NOW!
The sun? Spotlights?
HUH? THEN HOW WILL WE EVER FIND THE DARKNESS?
MOST OF IT HAS BEEN DEVOURED BY THE MARA. WE SHOULD ENCOUNTER IT SOON.
AND THAT'S WHEN WE'LL FIND OISHI.
CLENCH
MAYURA MUST BE IN THE DARKNESS, TOO.
LET'S GET MOVING...
KYŌ!
NGHH!
ARE YOU OKAY?! WHAT WAS THAT FIGHT ABOUT, ANYWAY?
.....
YOU FLEW INTO A RAGE BECAUSE THOSE BOYS OISHI BROUGHT WERE TRYING TO VIOLATE YOU?
IT WASN'T LIKE THAT!!

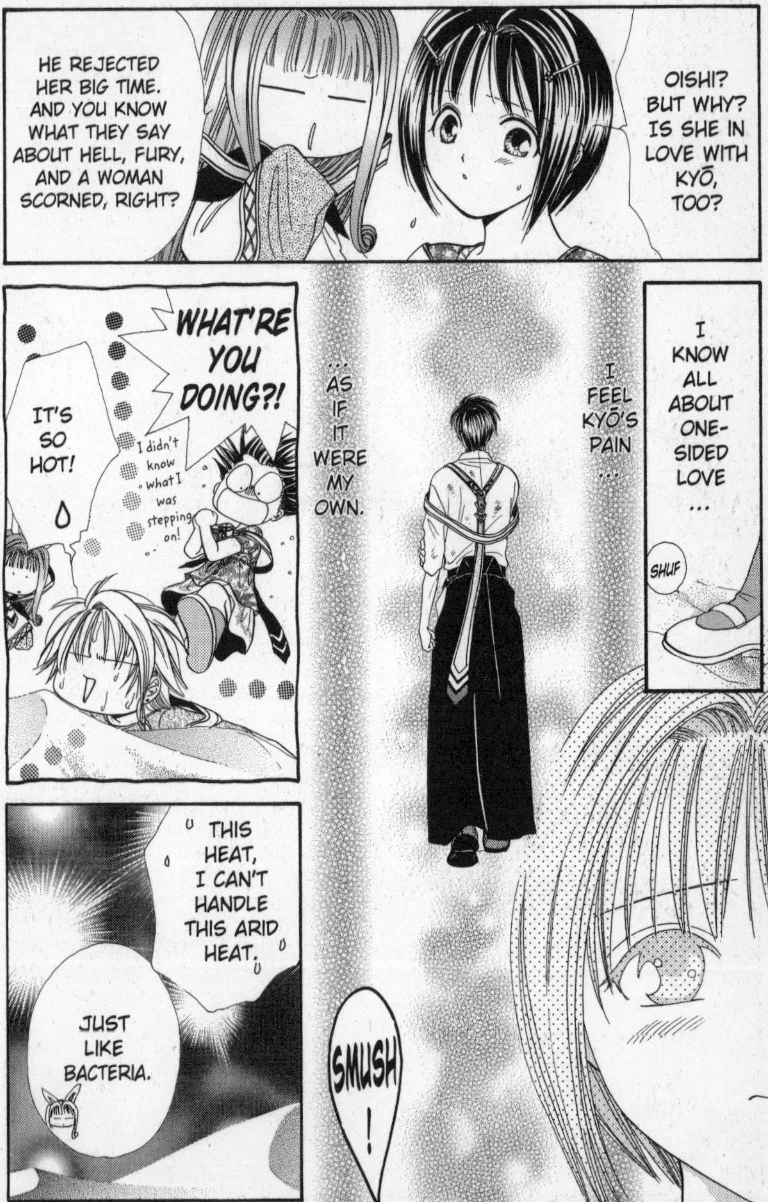
OISHI? BUT WHY? IS SHE IN LOVE WITH KYŌ, TOO?
HE REJECTED HER BIG TIME. AND YOU KNOW WHAT THEY SAY ABOUT HELL, FURY, AND A WOMAN SCORNED, RIGHT?
I KNOW ALL ABOUT ONE-SIDED LOVE...
SHUF
I FEEL KYŌ'S PAIN...
...AS IF IT WERE MY OWN.
SMUSH!
WHAT'RE YOU DOING?!
I didn't know what I was stepping on!
IT'S SO HOT!
THIS HEAT, I CAN'T HANDLE THIS ARID HEAT.
JUST LIKE BACTERIA.

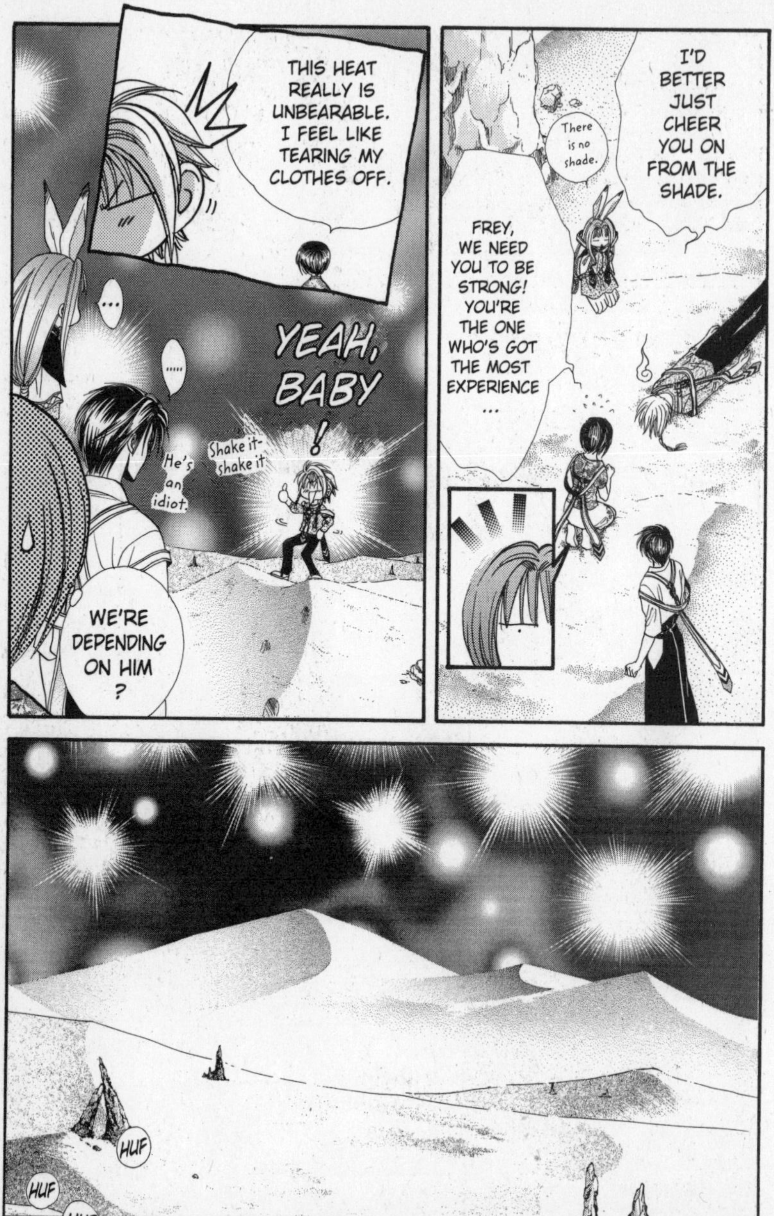
I'D BETTER JUST CHEER YOU ON FROM THE SHADE.
There is no shade.
FREY, WE NEED YOU TO BE STRONG! YOU'RE THE ONE WHO'S GOT THE MOST EXPERIENCE ...
THIS HEAT REALLY IS UNBEARABLE. I FEEL LIKE TEARING MY CLOTHES OFF.
YEAH, BABY!
Shake it-shake it
...
......
He's an idiot.
WE'RE DEPENDING ON HIM?
HUF
HUF
HUF

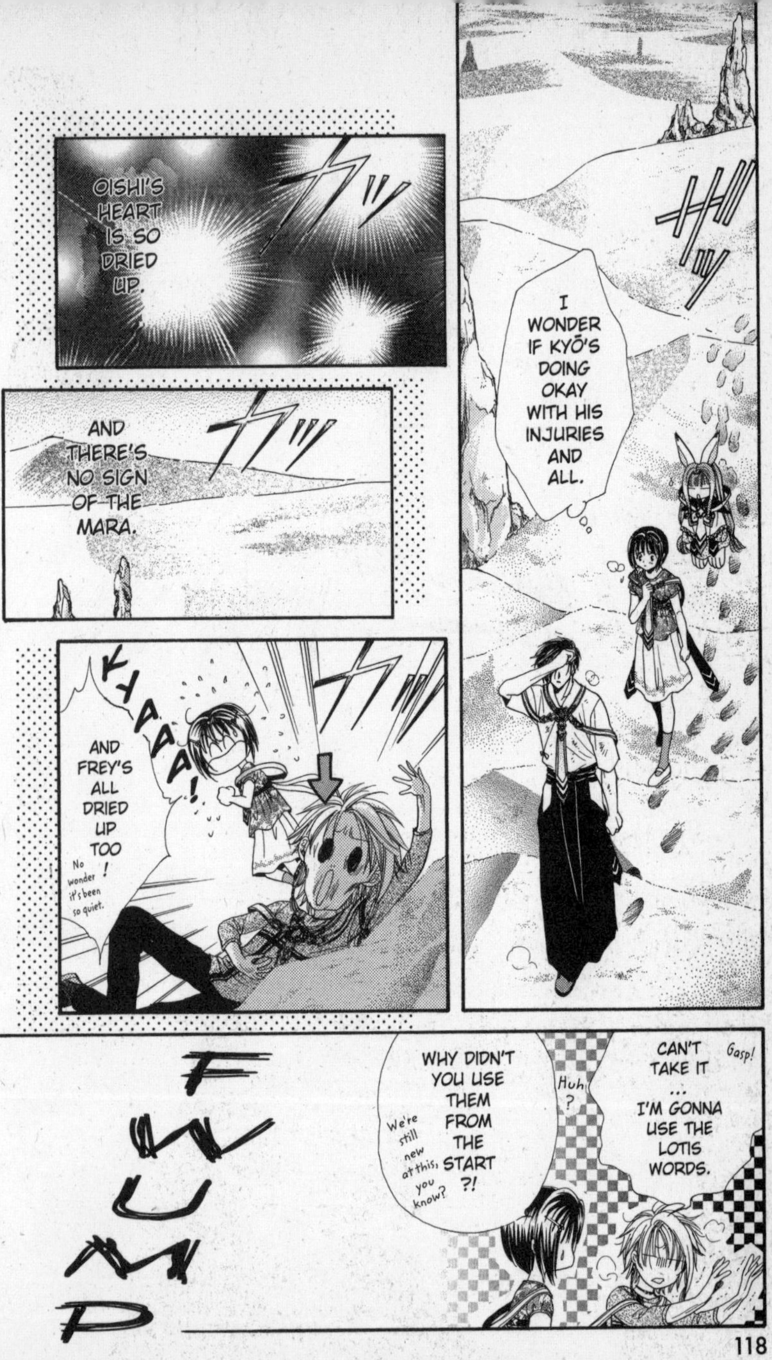
I WONDER IF KYŌ'S DOING OKAY WITH HIS INJURIES AND ALL.
OISHI'S HEART IS SO DRIED UP.
AND THERE'S NO SIGN OF THE MARA.
KYAAAA!
AND FREY'S ALL DRIED UP TOO!
No wonder it's been so quiet.
Gasp!
CAN'T TAKE IT ... I'M GONNA USE THE LOTIS WORDS.
Huh?
WHY DIDN'T YOU USE THEM FROM THE START?!
We're still new at this, you know?
FWUMP

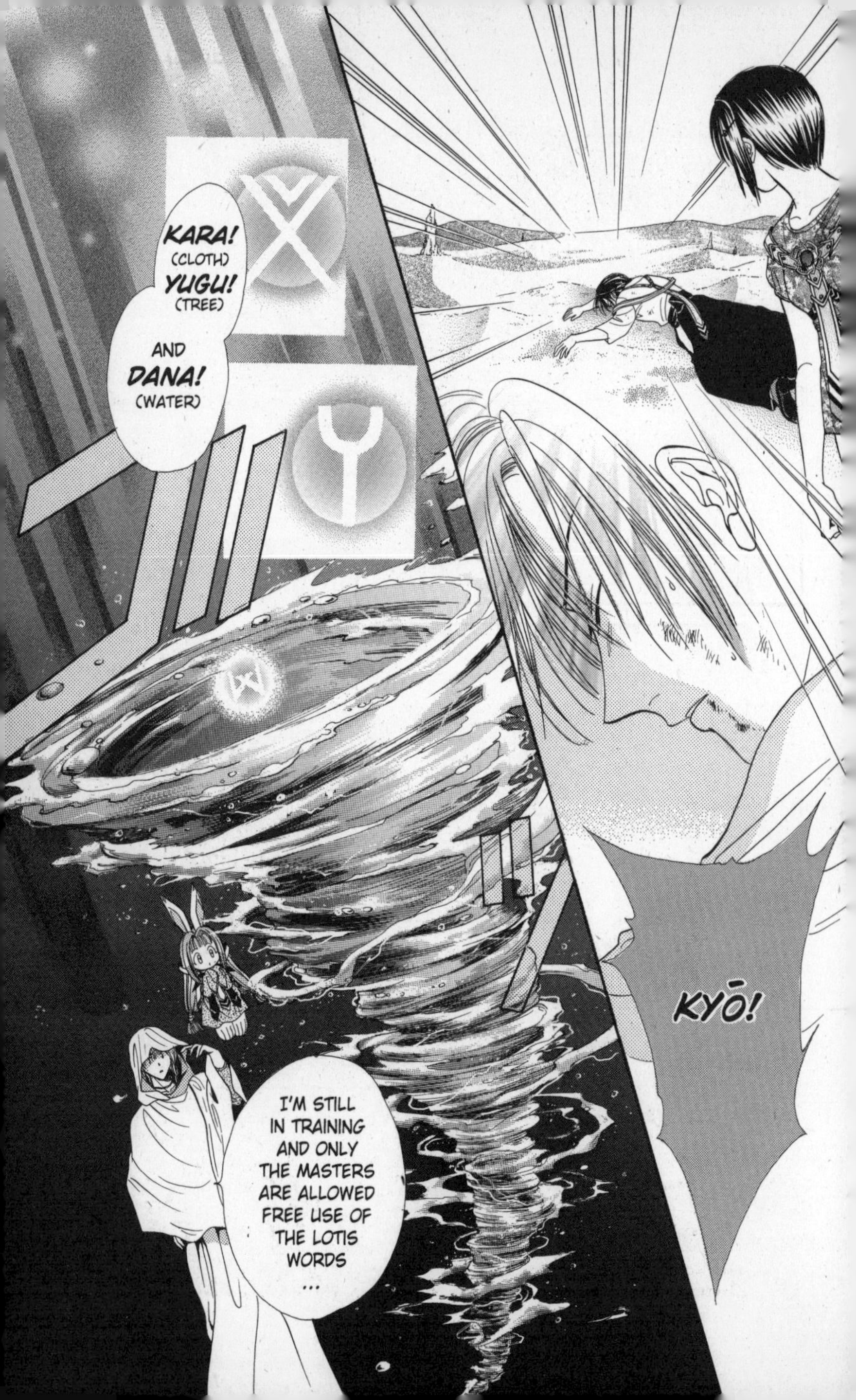
KYŌ!
KARA! (CLOTH)
YUGU! (TREE)
AND DANA! (WATER)
I'M STILL IN TRAINING AND ONLY THE MASTERS ARE ALLOWED FREE USE OF THE LOTIS WORDS ...

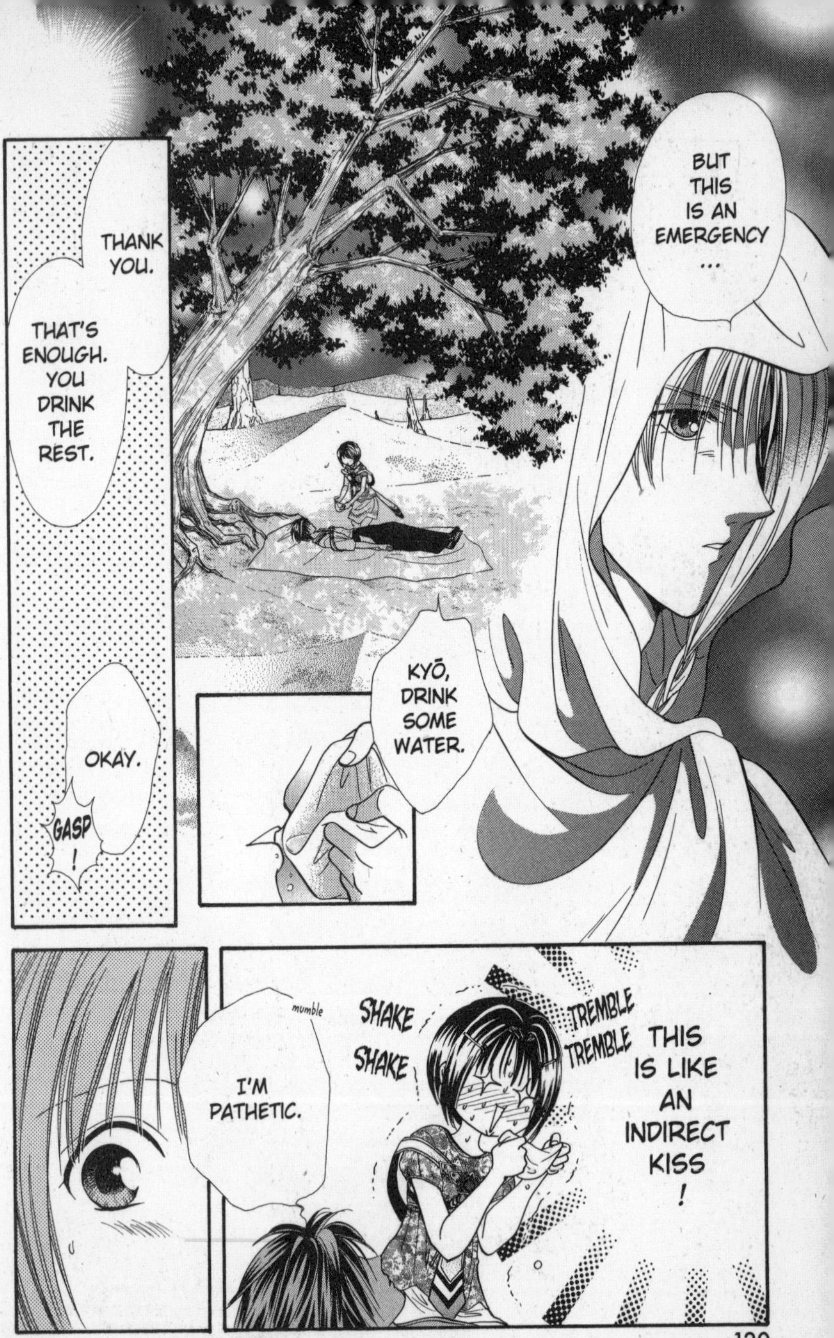
BUT THIS IS AN EMERGENCY ...
KYŌ, DRINK SOME WATER.
THANK YOU.
THAT'S ENOUGH. YOU DRINK THE REST.
OKAY.
GASP!
THIS IS LIKE AN INDIRECT KISS!
TREMBLE TREMBLE
SHAKE SHAKE
mumble
I'M PATHETIC.

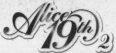

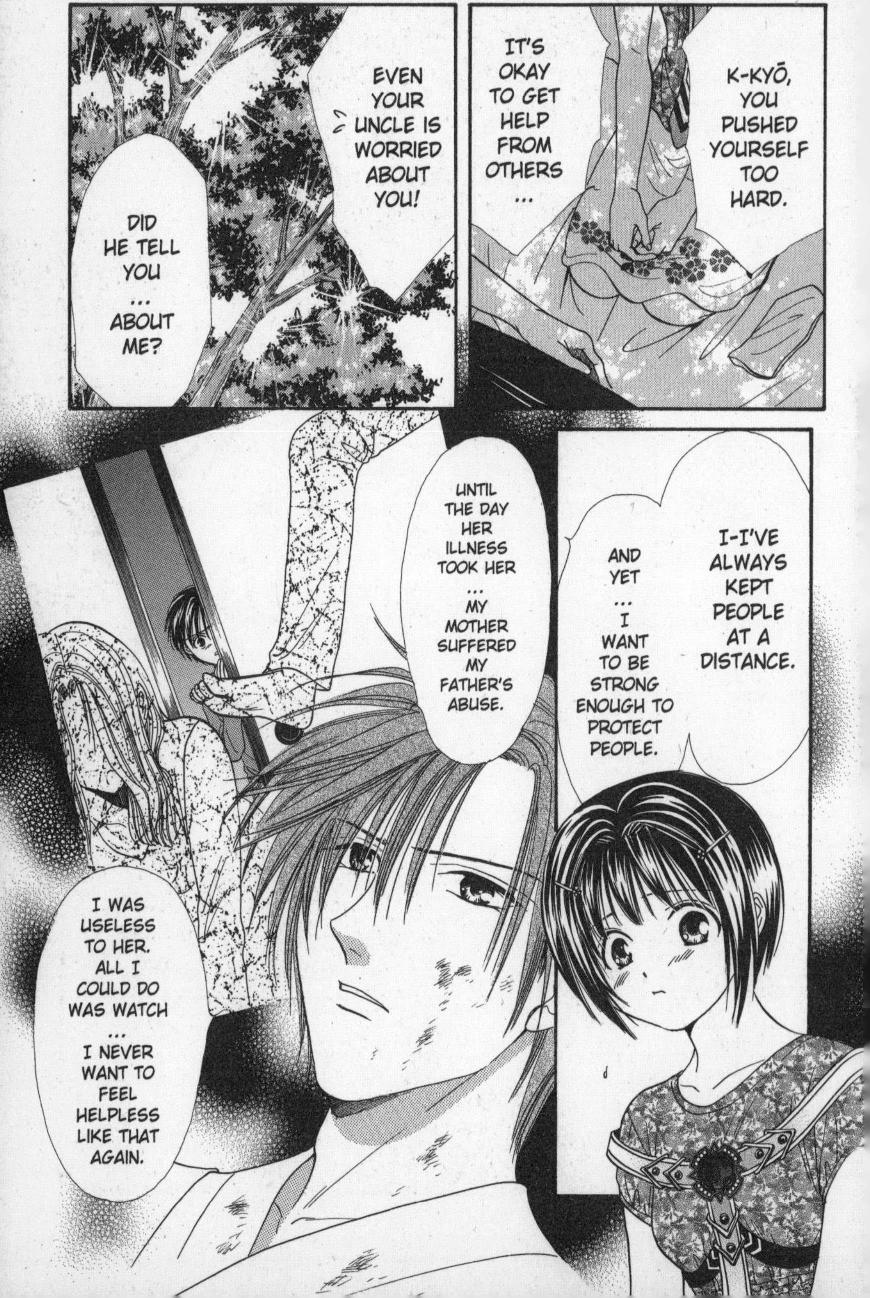
K-KYŌ, YOU PUSHED YOURSELF TOO HARD.
IT'S OKAY TO GET HELP FROM OTHERS ...
EVEN YOUR UNCLE IS WORRIED ABOUT YOU!
DID HE TELL YOU ... ABOUT ME?
I-I'VE ALWAYS KEPT PEOPLE AT A DISTANCE.
AND YET ... I WANT TO BE STRONG ENOUGH TO PROTECT PEOPLE.
UNTIL THE DAY HER ILLNESS TOOK HER ... MY MOTHER SUFFERED MY FATHER'S ABUSE.
I WAS USELESS TO HER. ALL I COULD DO WAS WATCH ... I NEVER WANT TO FEEL HELPLESS LIKE THAT AGAIN.

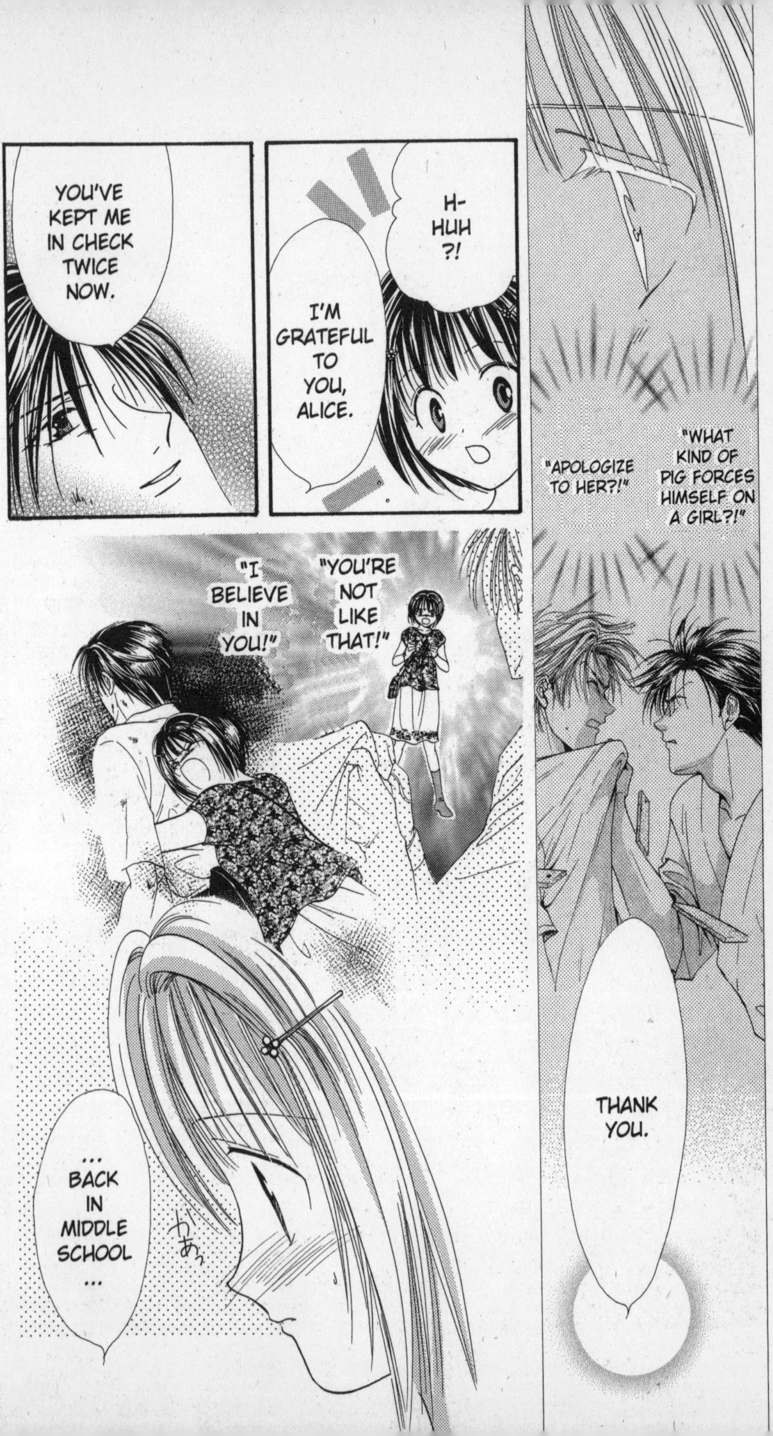
"WHAT KIND OF PIG FORCES HIMSELF ON A GIRL?!"
"APOLOGIZE TO HER?!"
THANK YOU.
H- HUH ?!
I'M GRATEFUL TO YOU, ALICE.
YOU'VE KEPT ME IN CHECK TWICE NOW.
"YOU'RE NOT LIKE THAT!"
"I BELIEVE IN YOU!"
... BACK IN MIDDLE SCHOOL ...
わあっ

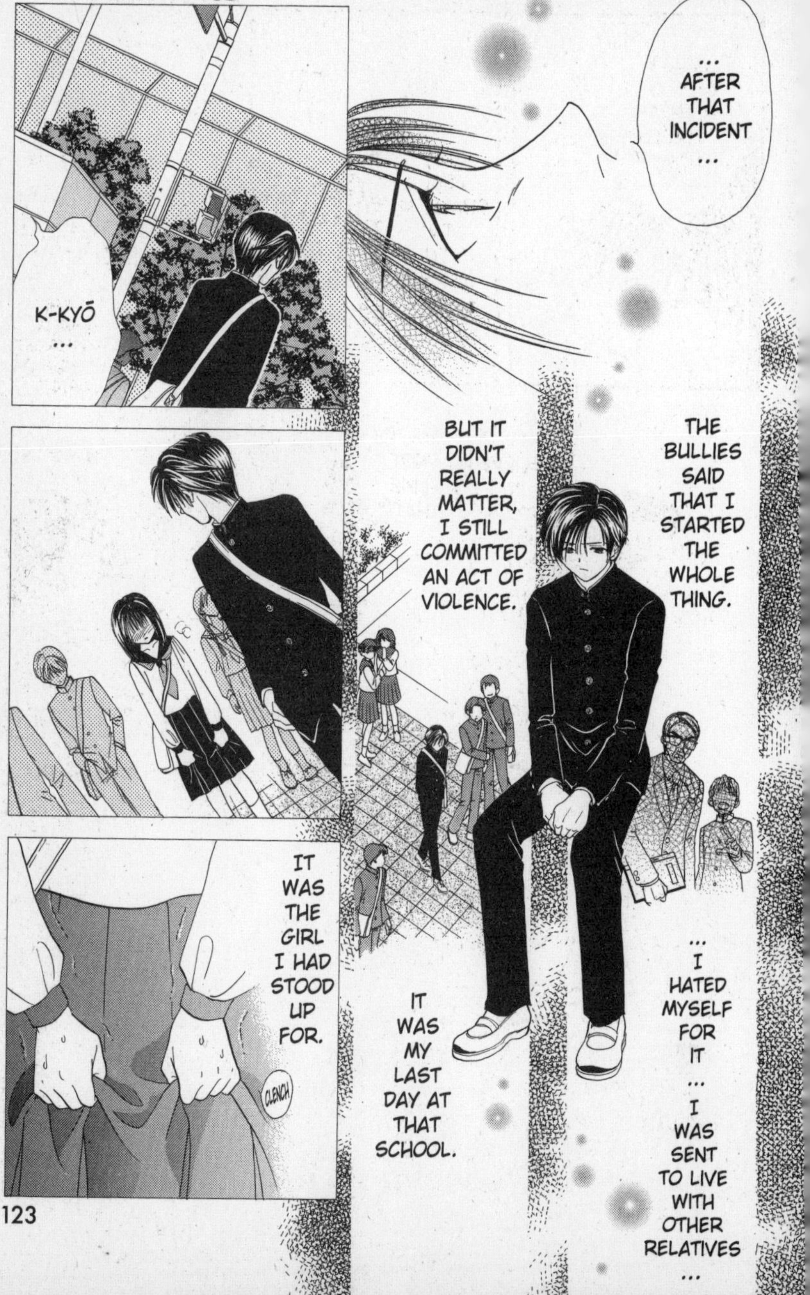
... AFTER THAT INCIDENT ...
THE BULLIES SAID THAT I STARTED THE WHOLE THING.
BUT IT DIDN'T REALLY MATTER, I STILL COMMITTED AN ACT OF VIOLENCE.
... I HATED MYSELF FOR IT ... I WAS SENT TO LIVE WITH OTHER RELATIVES ...
IT WAS MY LAST DAY AT THAT SCHOOL.
K-KYŌ ...
IT WAS THE GIRL I HAD STOOD UP FOR.
CLENCH

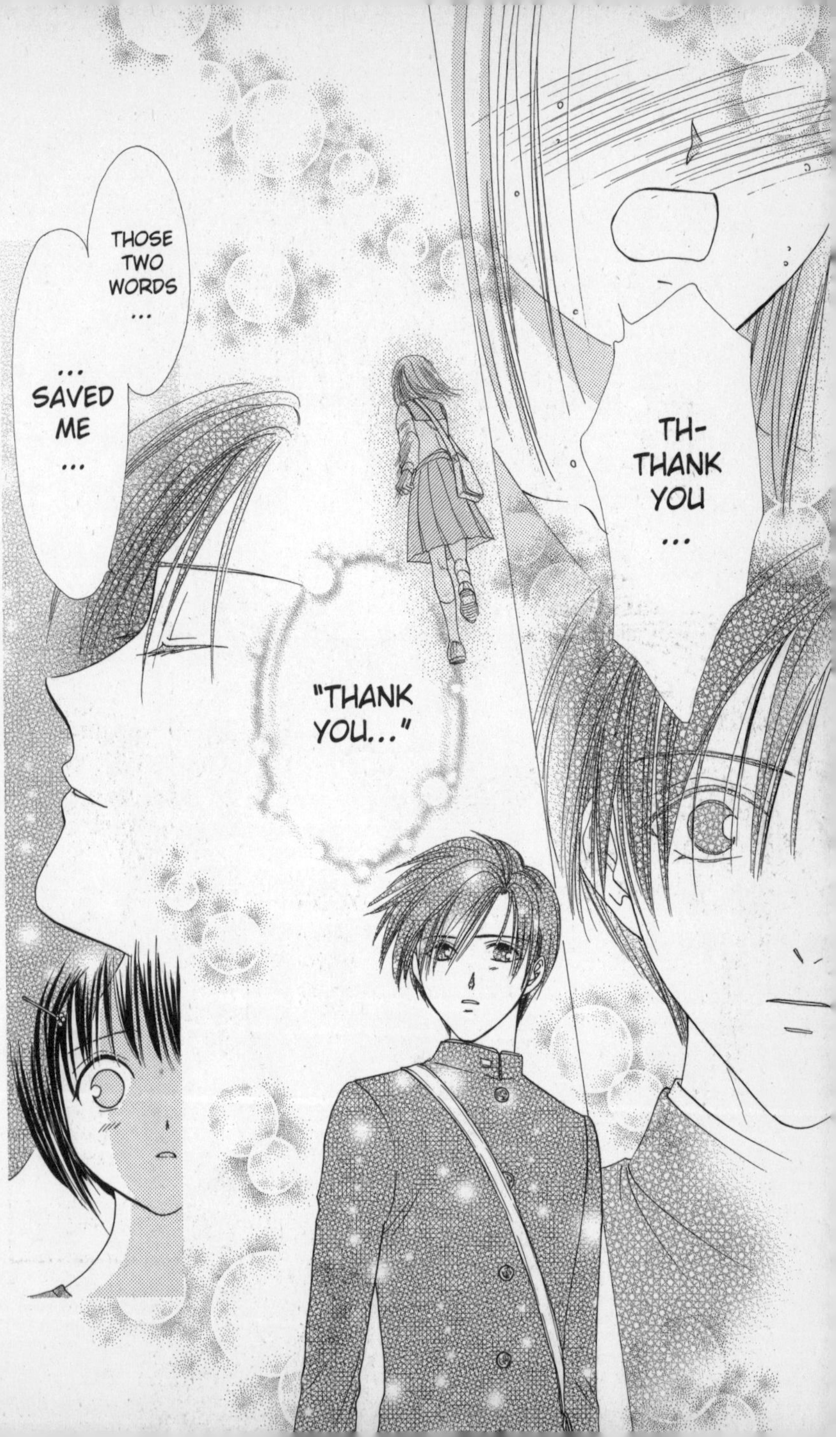
TH- THANK YOU ...
THOSE TWO WORDS ... ... SAVED ME ...
"THANK YOU..."

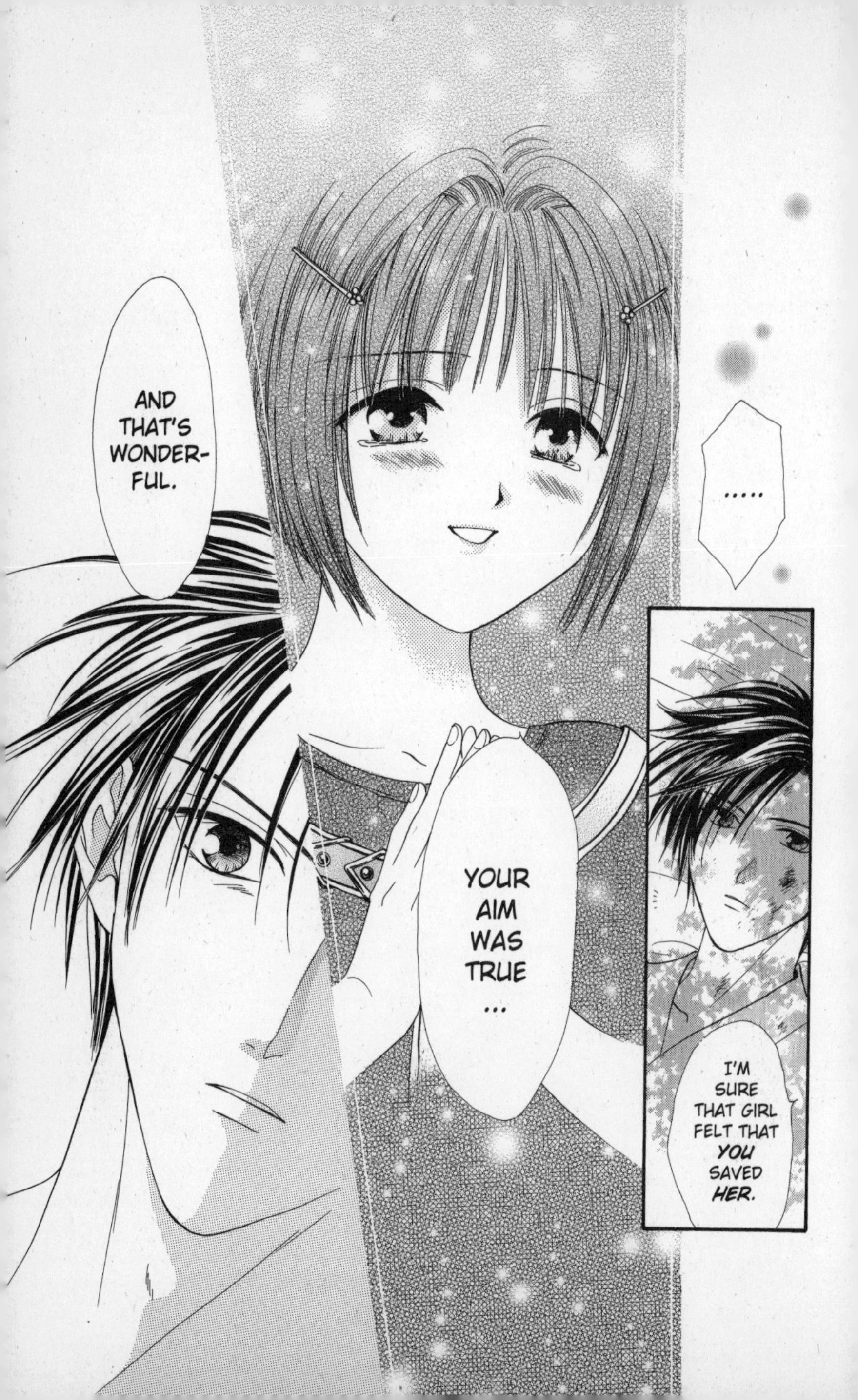
.....
I'M SURE THAT GIRL FELT THAT ***YOU*** SAVED ***HER.***
YOUR AIM WAS TRUE ...
AND THAT'S WONDER-FUL.

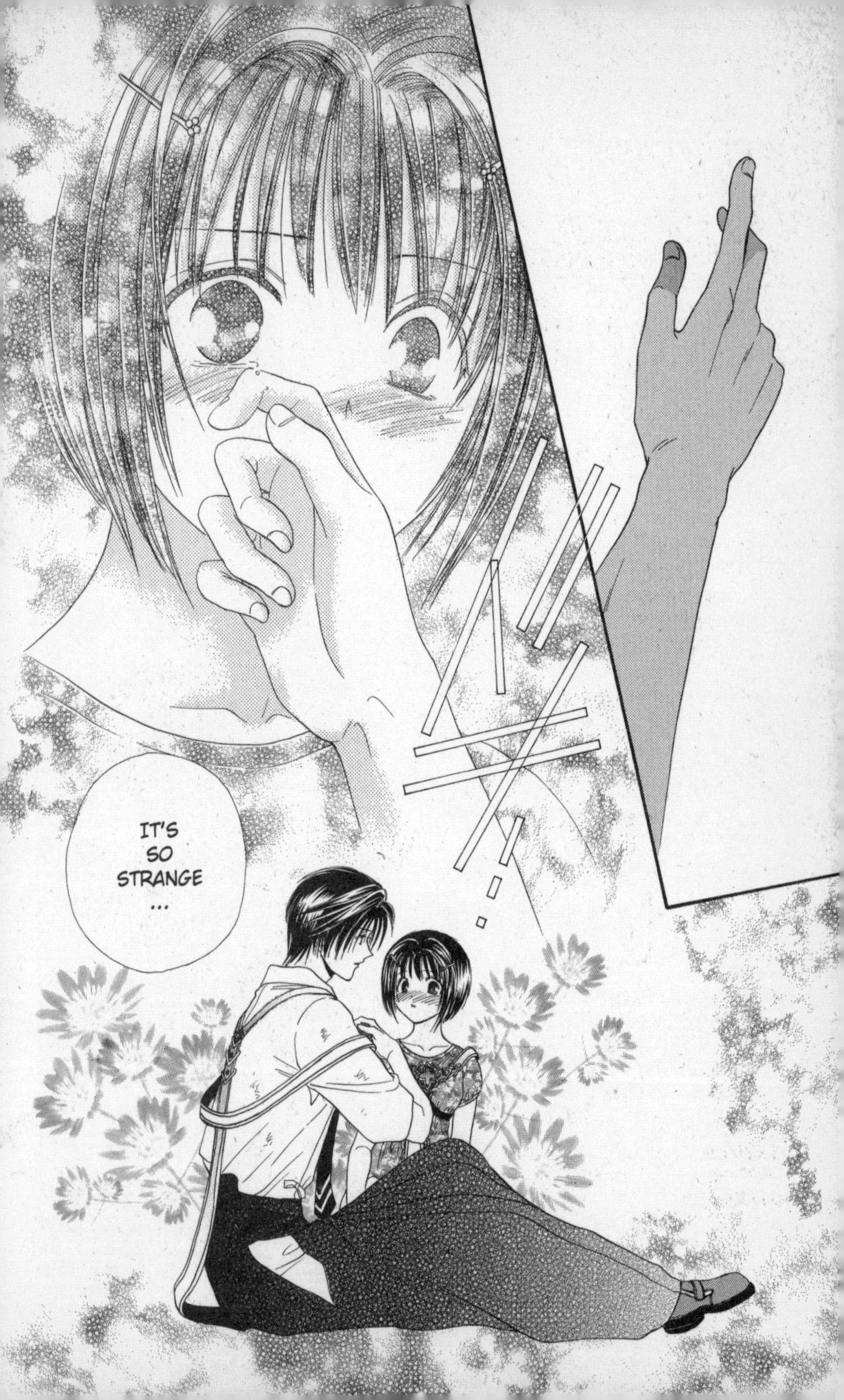
IT'S SO STRANGE ...

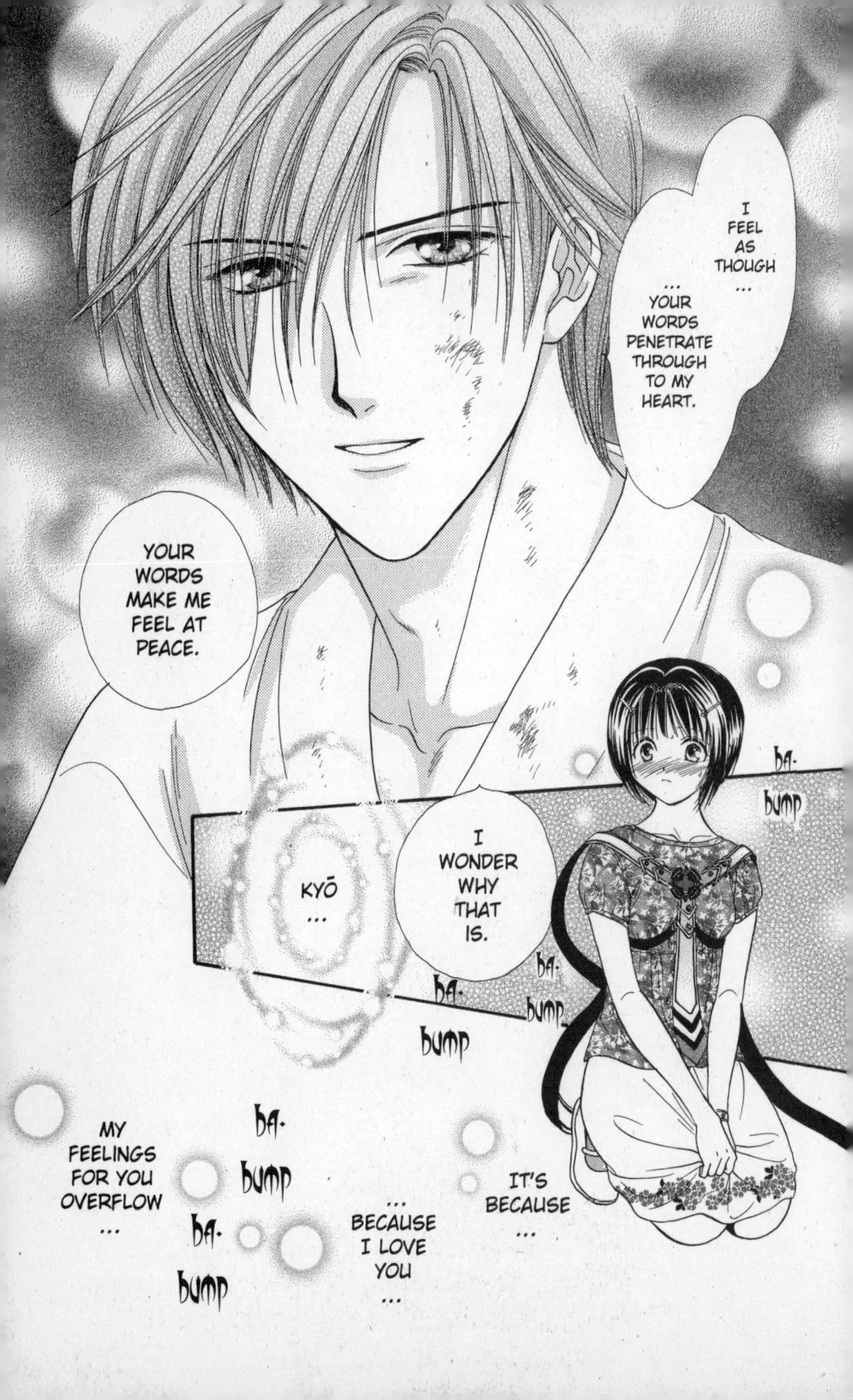
I FEEL AS THOUGH ... YOUR WORDS PENETRATE THROUGH TO MY HEART.
YOUR WORDS MAKE ME FEEL AT PEACE.
BA-BUMP
I WONDER WHY THAT IS.
KYŌ ...
BA-BUMP
BA-BUMP
IT'S BECAUSE ...
... BECAUSE I LOVE YOU ...
BA-BUMP
BA-BUMP
MY FEELINGS FOR YOU OVERFLOW ...

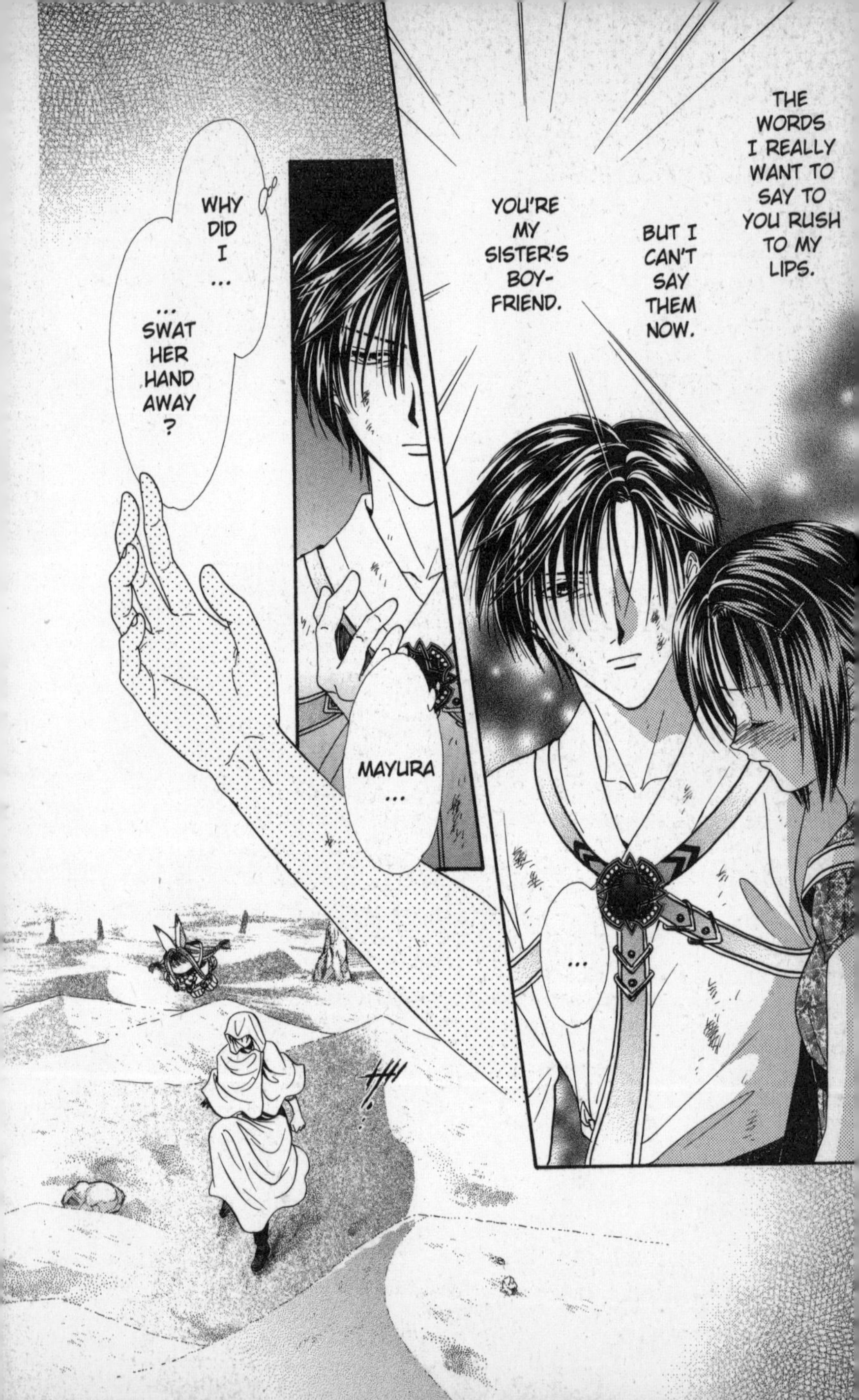
THE WORDS I REALLY WANT TO SAY TO YOU RUSH TO MY LIPS.
BUT I CAN'T SAY THEM NOW.
YOU'RE MY SISTER'S BOY-FRIEND.
...
MAYURA ...
WHY DID I ...
... SWAT HER HAND AWAY?

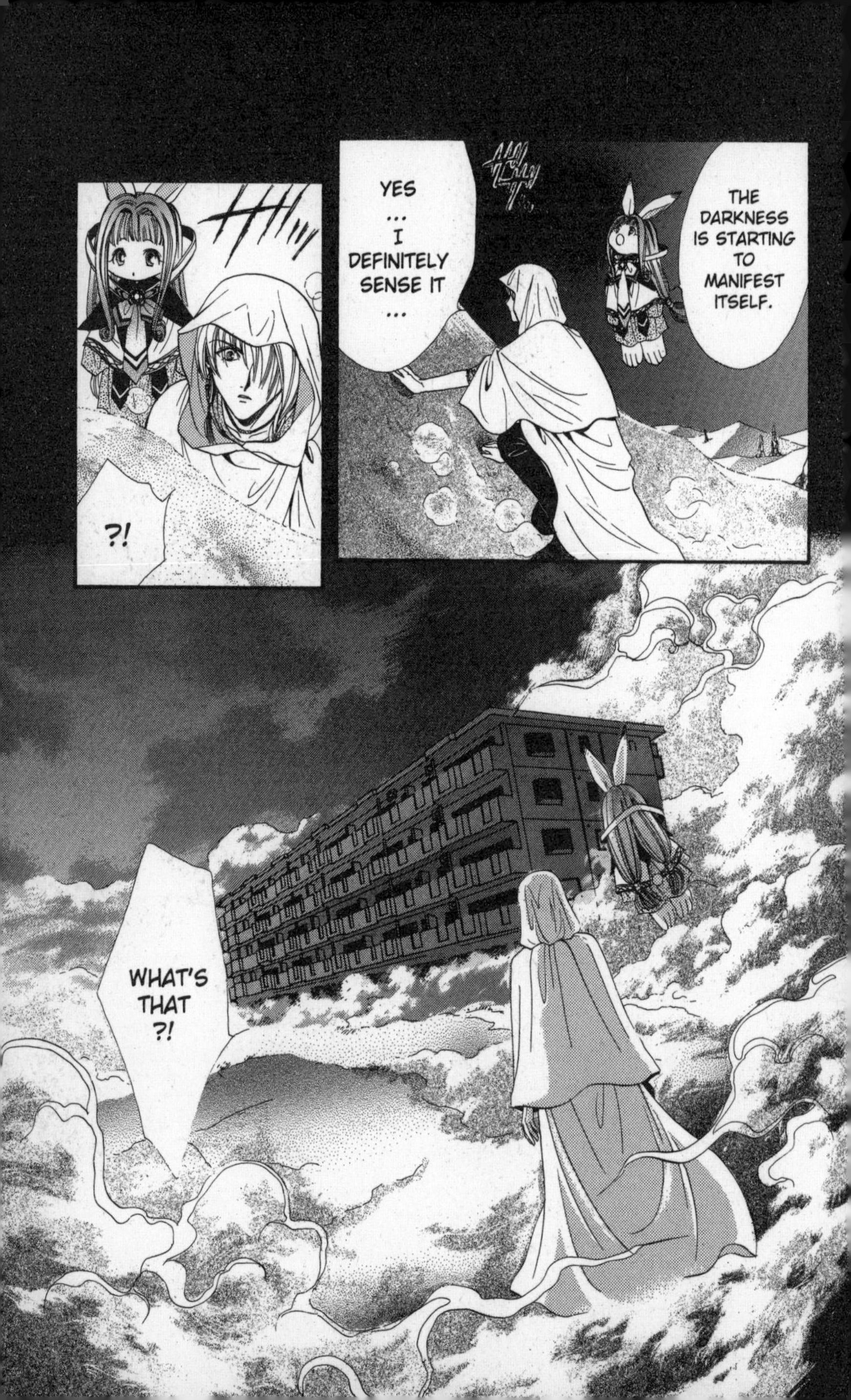
THE DARKNESS IS STARTING TO MANIFEST ITSELF.
YES ... I DEFINITELY SENSE IT ...
?!
WHAT'S THAT ?!

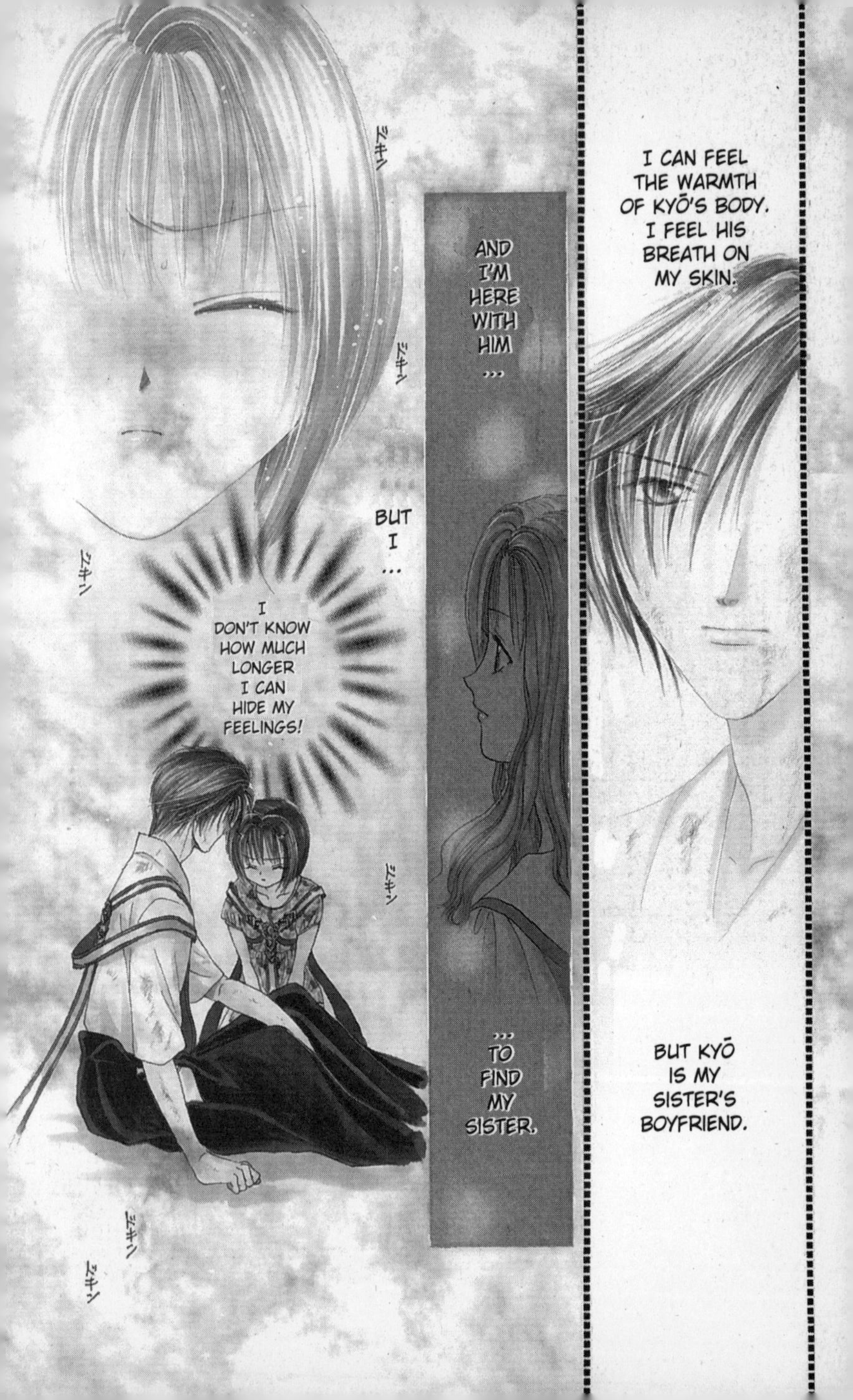
I CAN FEEL THE WARMTH OF KYŌ'S BODY. I FEEL HIS BREATH ON MY SKIN.
BUT KYŌ IS MY SISTER'S BOYFRIEND.
AND I'M HERE WITH HIM ...
... TO FIND MY SISTER.
BUT I ...
I DON'T KNOW HOW MUCH LONGER I CAN HIDE MY FEELINGS!

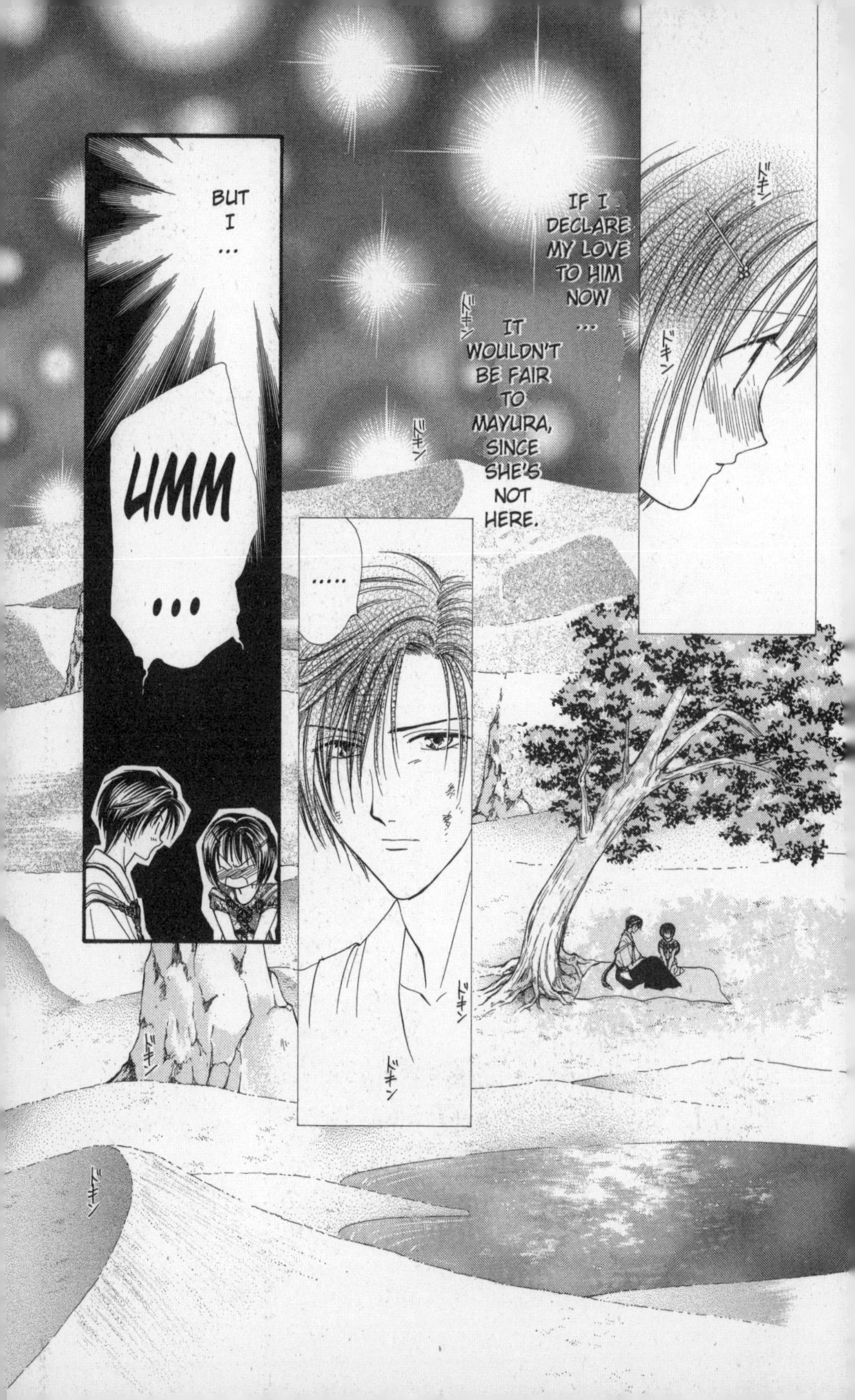

ドキン
ドキン
IF I DECLARE MY LOVE TO HIM NOW ...
IT WOULDN'T BE FAIR TO MAYURA, SINCE SHE'S NOT HERE.
ドキン
ドキン
.....
ドキン
ドキン
BUT I ...
UMM ...
ドキン
ドキン

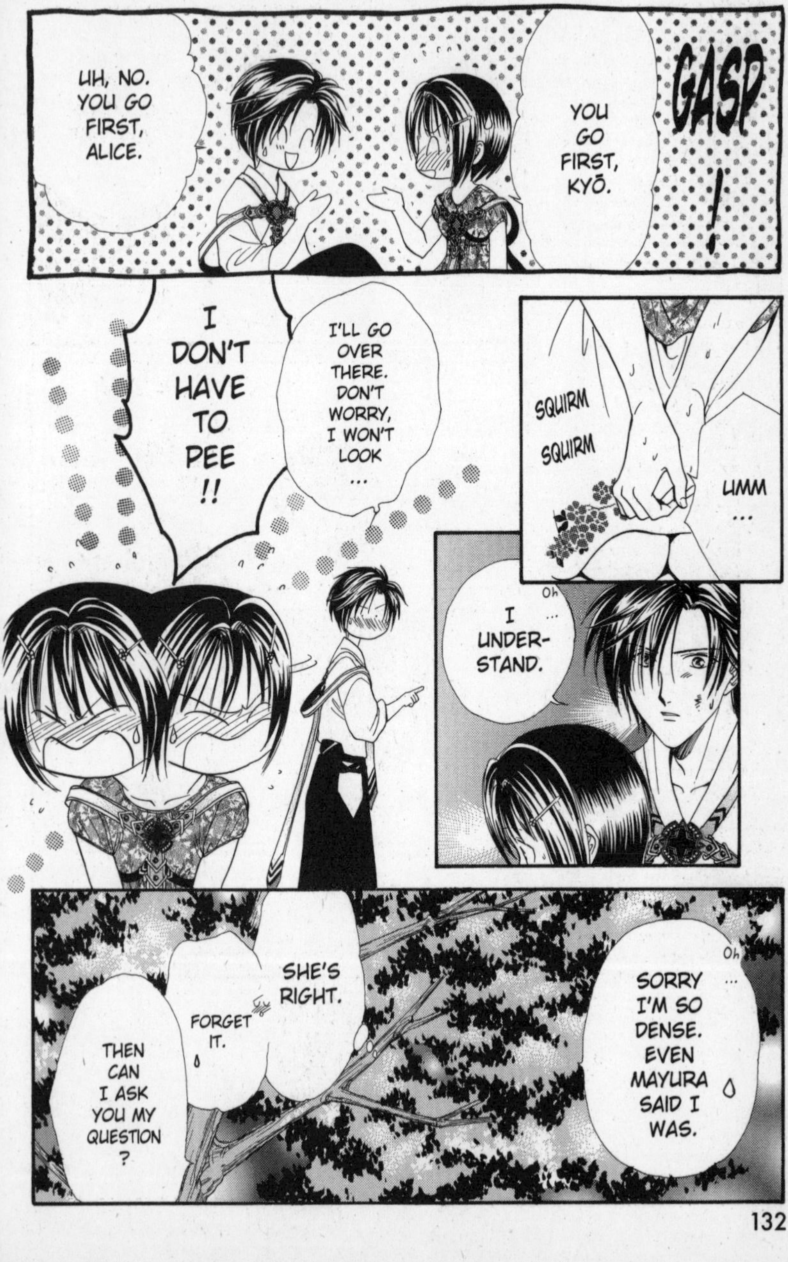
GASP!
YOU GO FIRST, KYŌ.
UH, NO. YOU GO FIRST, ALICE.
SQUIRM
SQUIRM
UMM ...
Oh ...
I UNDER-STAND.
I'LL GO OVER THERE. DON'T WORRY, I WON'T LOOK ...
I DON'T HAVE TO PEE !!
Oh ...
SORRY I'M SO DENSE. EVEN MAYURA SAID I WAS.
SHE'S RIGHT.
FORGET IT.
THEN CAN I ASK YOU MY QUESTION ?

ROLL ROLL ROLL
IS THERE SOMEONE YOU LIKE?
TATSUYA, MAYBE?
100% DENSE
NO, NOT HIM! THERE'S SOMEONE ELSE!
I SEE.
TELL ME, WHAT DOES THAT FEEL LIKE?

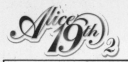

More talk about Fushigi Yûgi! The novels are continuing on. These will be stories included about Mitsukake and Chiriko. And that will make all seven characters. I wonder how far this will go.
But please don't ask me what happens next. Eikoden wasn't supposed to be a continuation of the series. It should end with volume 18. (At least Miaka's story.)
And that closes the discussion on Fushigi Yûgi.
I received a letter from a reader who wrote, "I was trying to tell someone I liked him. And inside I was saying, "Rangu" over and over again. It helped me to tell him how I felt!" That letter made me so happy!
Alice still can't make her declaration.
"If only I had told him back then..." is becoming a familiar phrase for Alice. Oh yes, on page 78 of Volume 1 (of the Japanese tankobon), the rune mark is missing on the jewel. It's been added in the subsequent printings, but to those of you who purchased the first printing, you have a collector's item (if you can consider it that). Sorry!
Alice 19th has so many little intricacies that even I forget. The hard part is when they enter the Inner Heart. You know the ribbon? My assistants thought it up. But it's such a pain!
And the mirror on their chests? Yes, it's a mirror.
I haven't had a chance to explain it, so I've left it alone. Eventually I'll have to include it somewhere. These details are truly problematic.

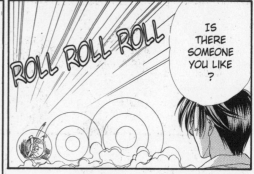

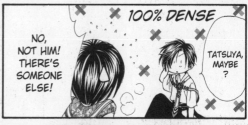

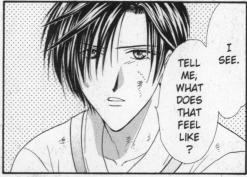

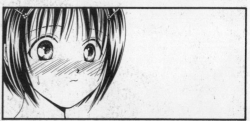

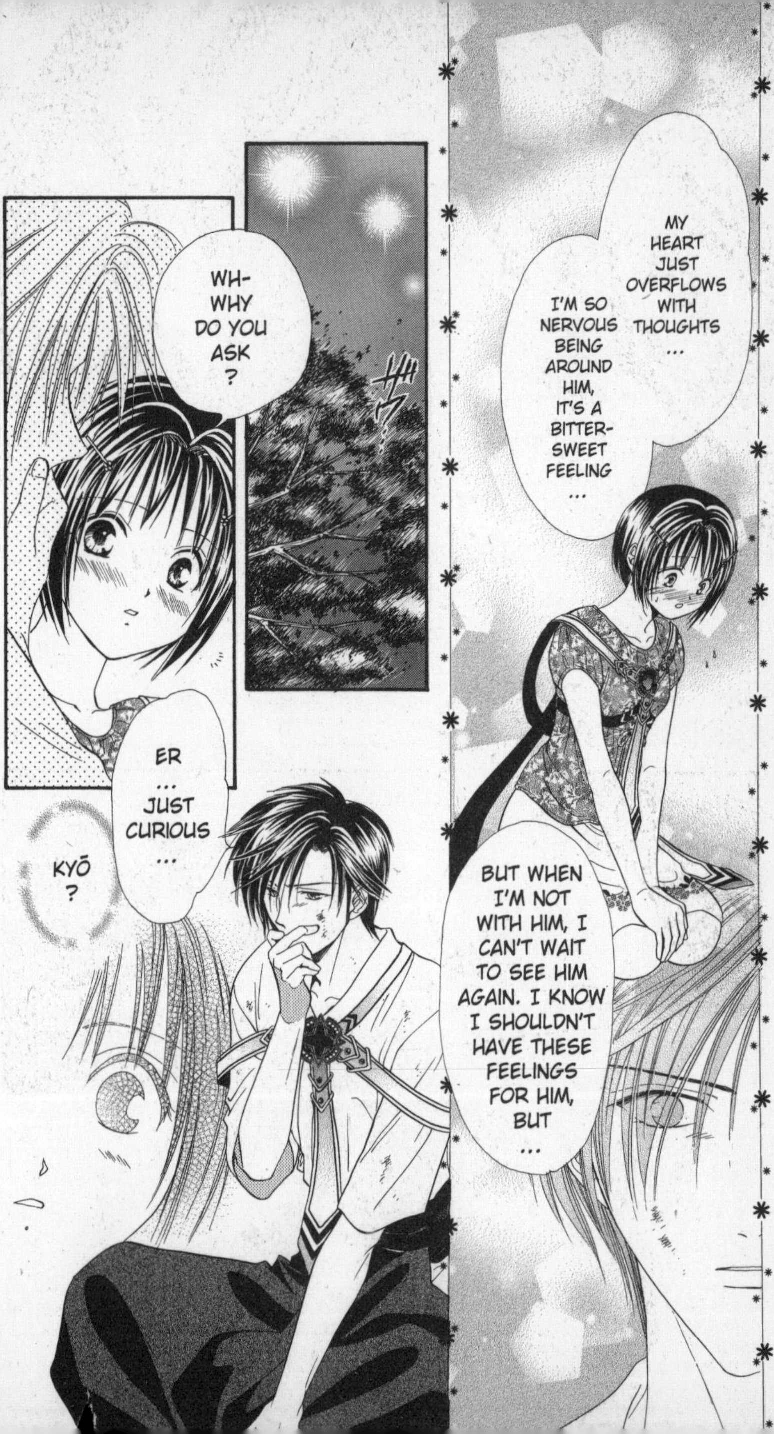
MY HEART JUST OVERFLOWS WITH THOUGHTS ...
I'M SO NERVOUS BEING AROUND HIM, IT'S A BITTER-SWEET FEELING ...
BUT WHEN I'M NOT WITH HIM, I CAN'T WAIT TO SEE HIM AGAIN. I KNOW I SHOULDN'T HAVE THESE FEELINGS FOR HIM, BUT ...
ザワ…
WH- WHY DO YOU ASK ?
ER ... JUST CURIOUS ...
KYŌ ?

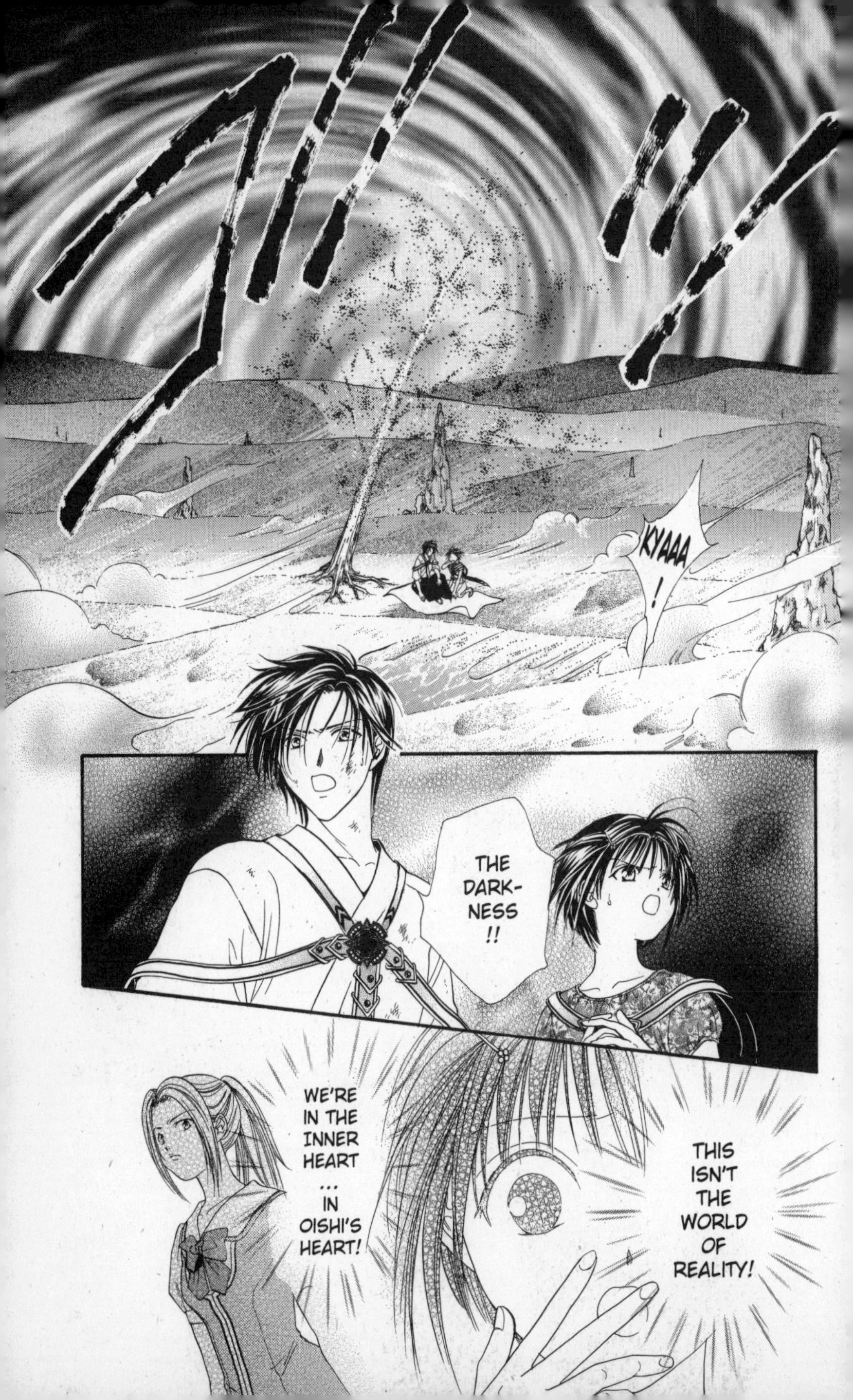
KYAAA!
THE DARKNESS!!
THIS ISN'T THE WORLD OF REALITY!
WE'RE IN THE INNER HEART... IN OISHI'S HEART!

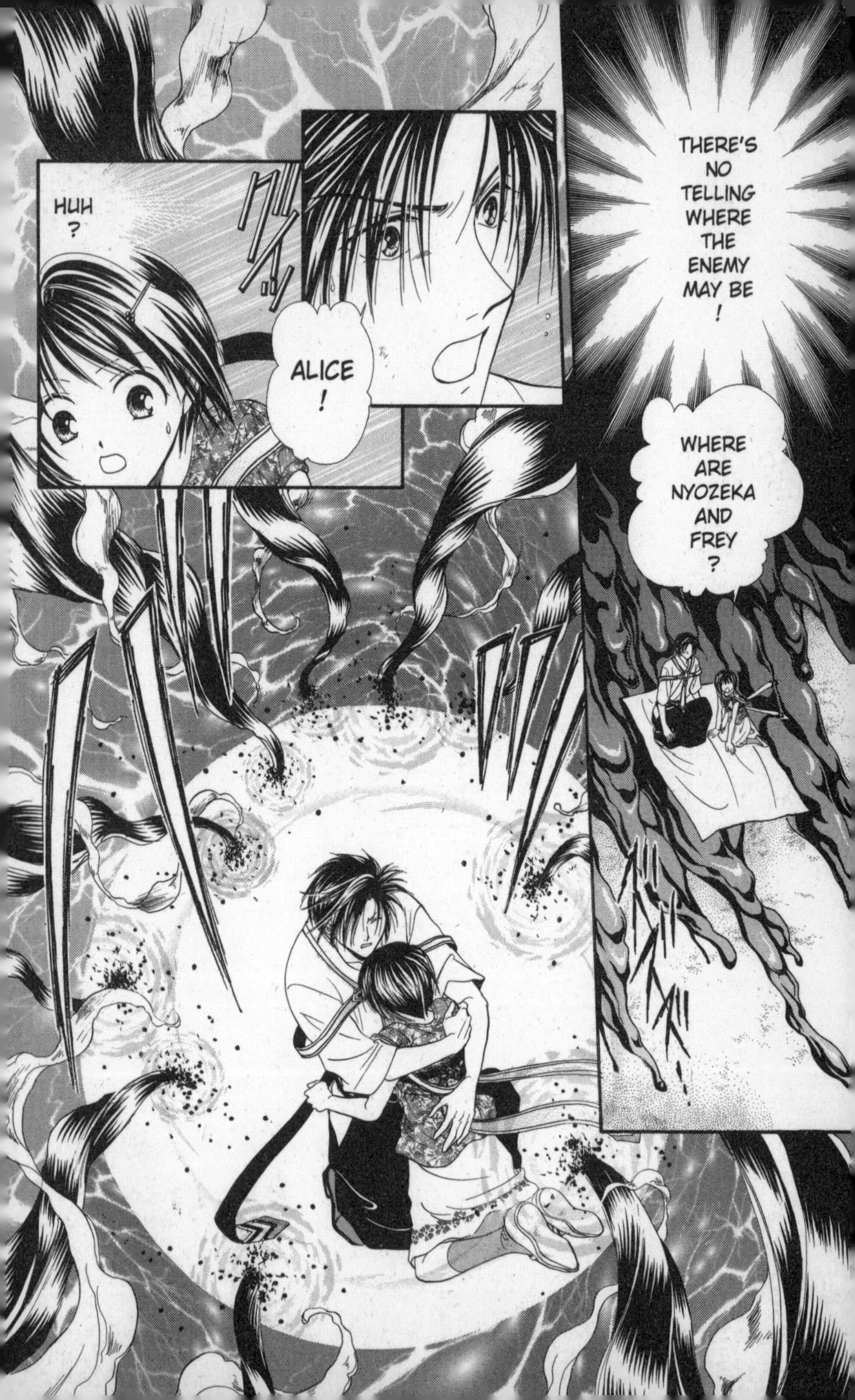
THERE'S NO TELLING WHERE THE ENEMY MAY BE!
WHERE ARE NYOZEKA AND FREY?
ALICE!
HUH?

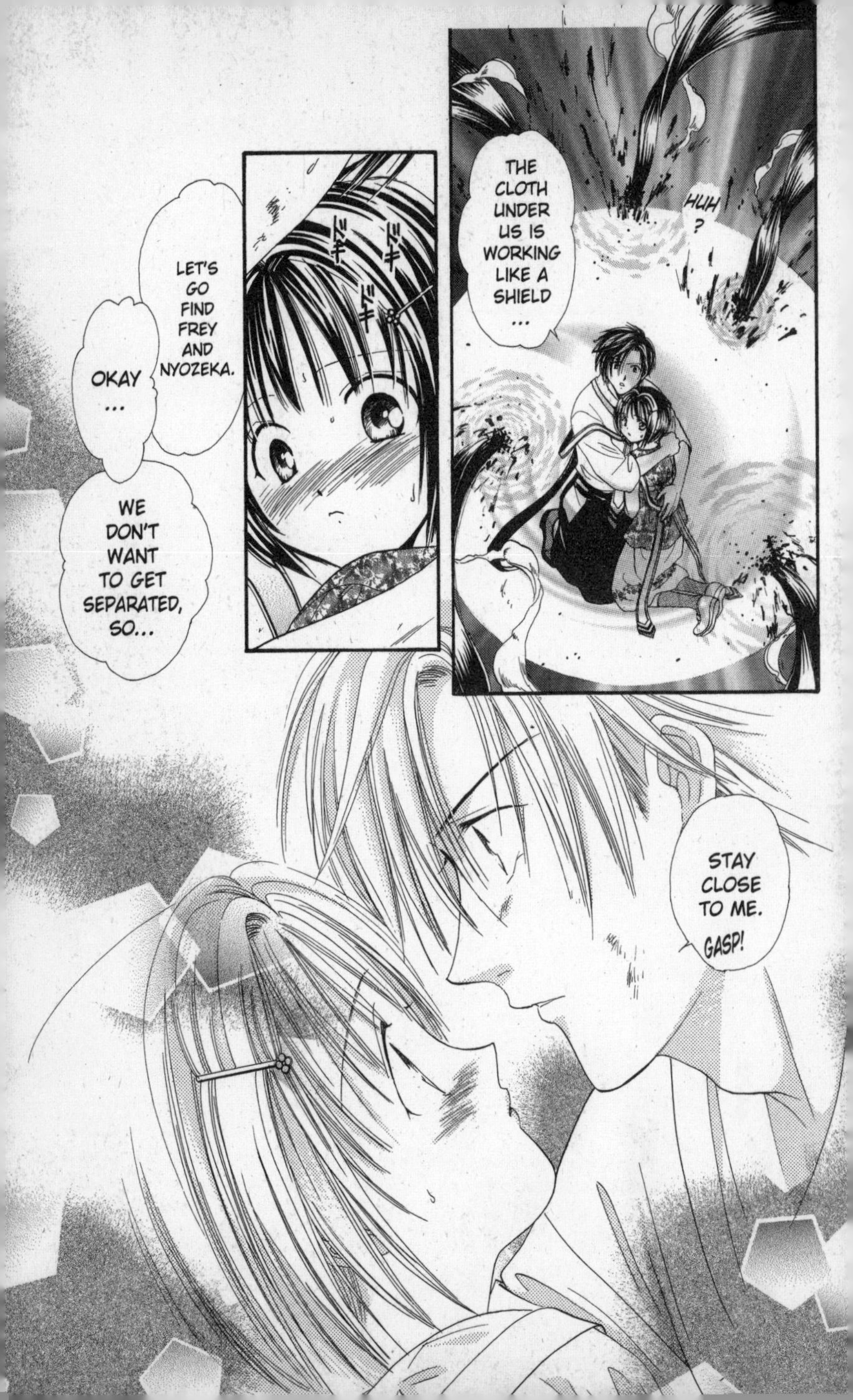
HUH?
THE CLOTH UNDER US IS WORKING LIKE A SHIELD...
ドキ ドキ
LET'S GO FIND FREY AND NYOZEKA.
OKAY...
WE DON'T WANT TO GET SEPARATED, SO...
STAY CLOSE TO ME.
GASP!

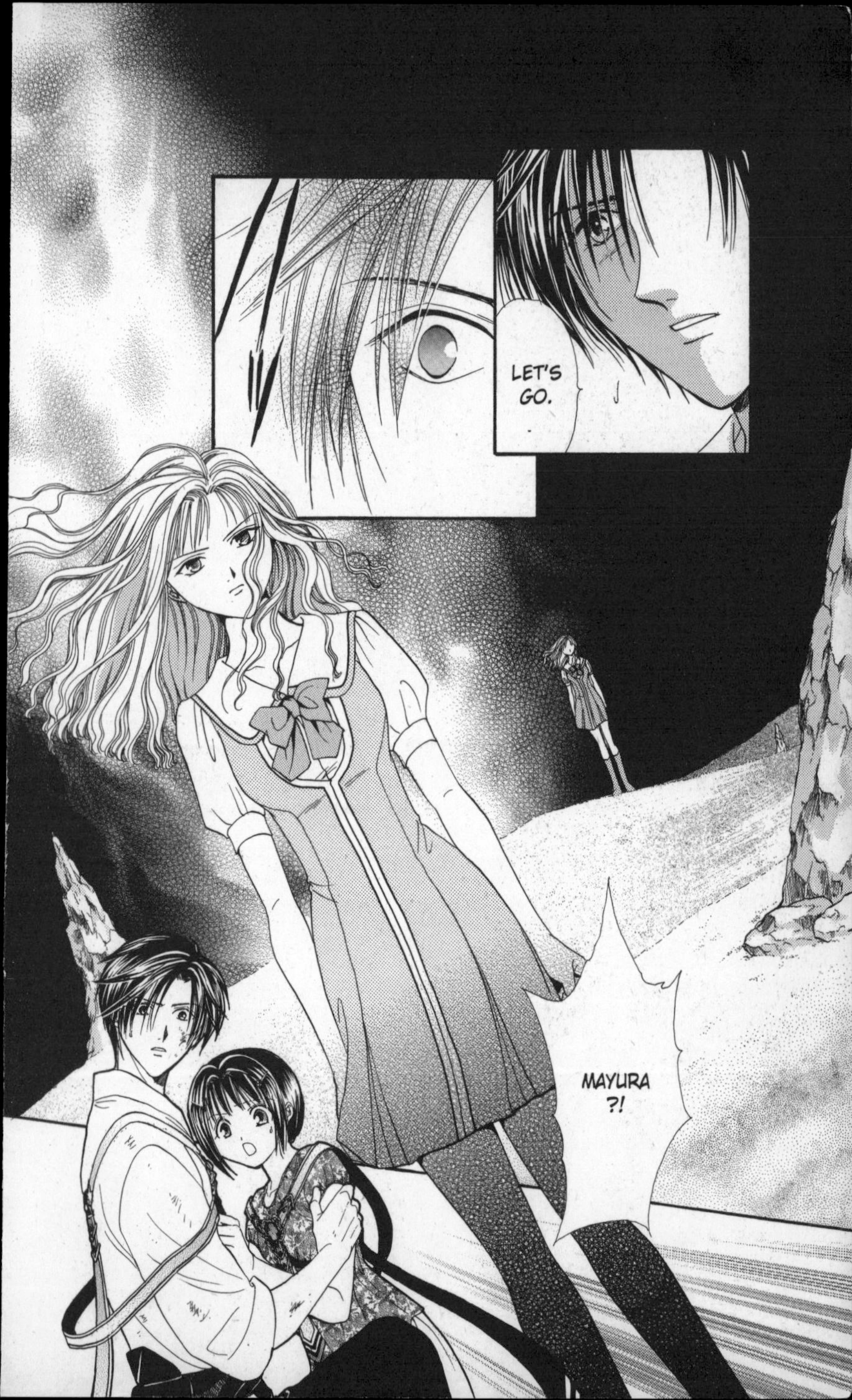
LET'S GO.
MAYURA ?!

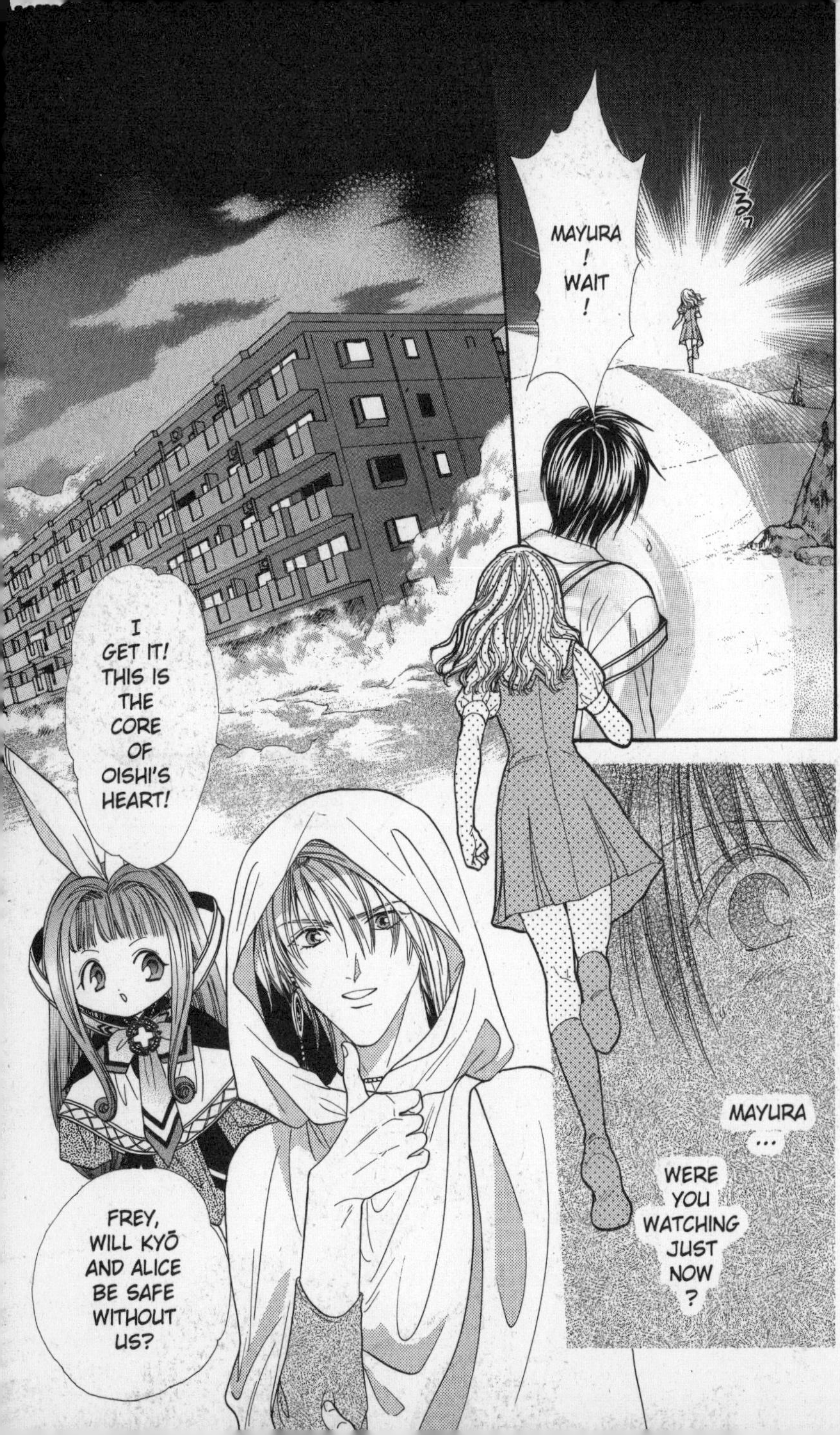

MAYURA! WAIT!
くるっ
MAYURA... WERE YOU WATCHING JUST NOW?
I GET IT! THIS IS THE CORE OF OISHI'S HEART!
FREY, WILL KYŌ AND ALICE BE SAFE WITHOUT US?

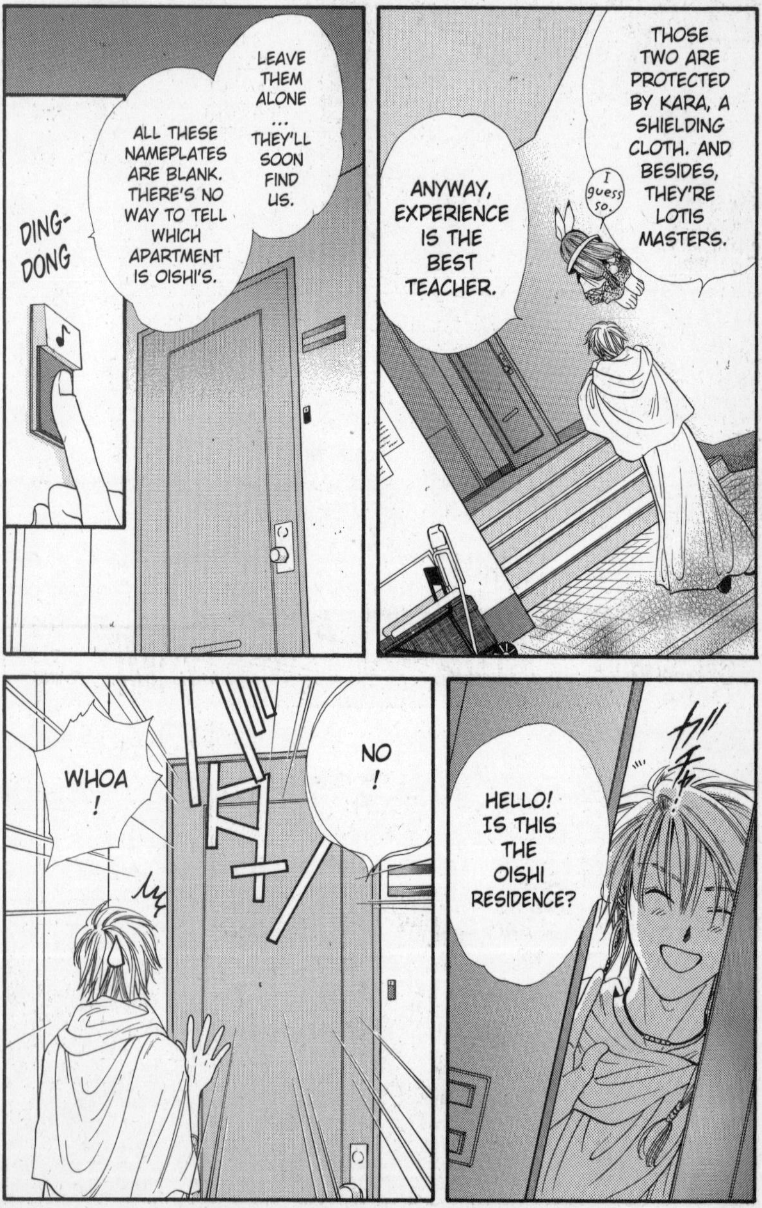
THOSE TWO ARE PROTECTED BY KARA, A SHIELDING CLOTH. AND BESIDES, THEY'RE LOTIS MASTERS.
I guess so.
ANYWAY, EXPERIENCE IS THE BEST TEACHER.
LEAVE THEM ALONE ... THEY'LL SOON FIND US.
ALL THESE NAMEPLATES ARE BLANK. THERE'S NO WAY TO TELL WHICH APARTMENT IS OISHI'S.
DING-DONG
HELLO! IS THIS THE OISHI RESIDENCE?
NO!
WHOA!

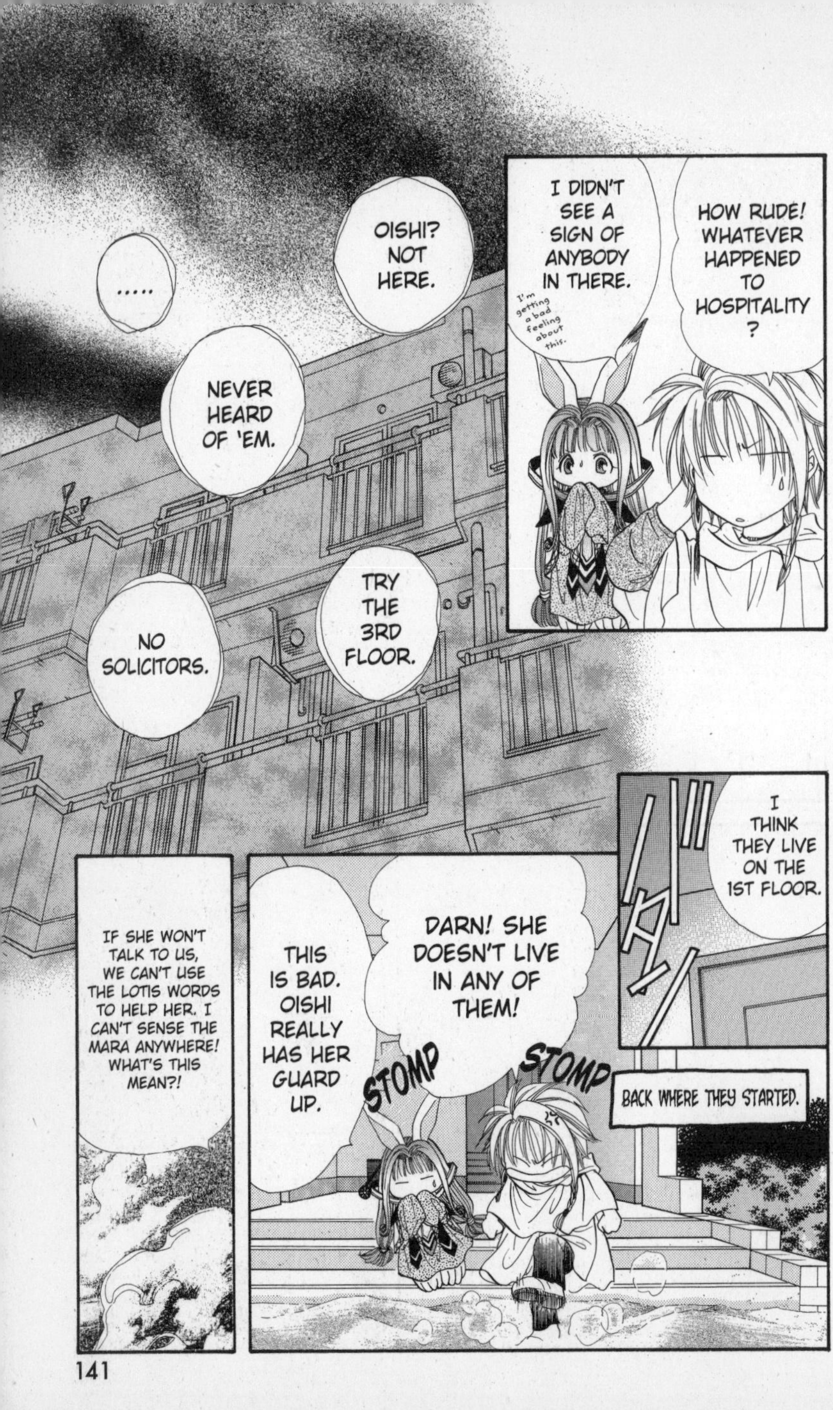
HOW RUDE! WHATEVER HAPPENED TO HOSPITALITY?
I DIDN'T SEE A SIGN OF ANYBODY IN THERE.
I'm getting a bad feeling about this.
OISHI? NOT HERE.
.....
NEVER HEARD OF 'EM.
TRY THE 3RD FLOOR.
NO SOLICITORS.
I THINK THEY LIVE ON THE 1ST FLOOR.
DARN! SHE DOESN'T LIVE IN ANY OF THEM!
STOMP
STOMP
BACK WHERE THEY STARTED.
THIS IS BAD. OISHI REALLY HAS HER GUARD UP.
IF SHE WON'T TALK TO US, WE CAN'T USE THE LOTIS WORDS TO HELP HER. I CAN'T SENSE THE MARA ANYWHERE! WHAT'S THIS MEAN?!

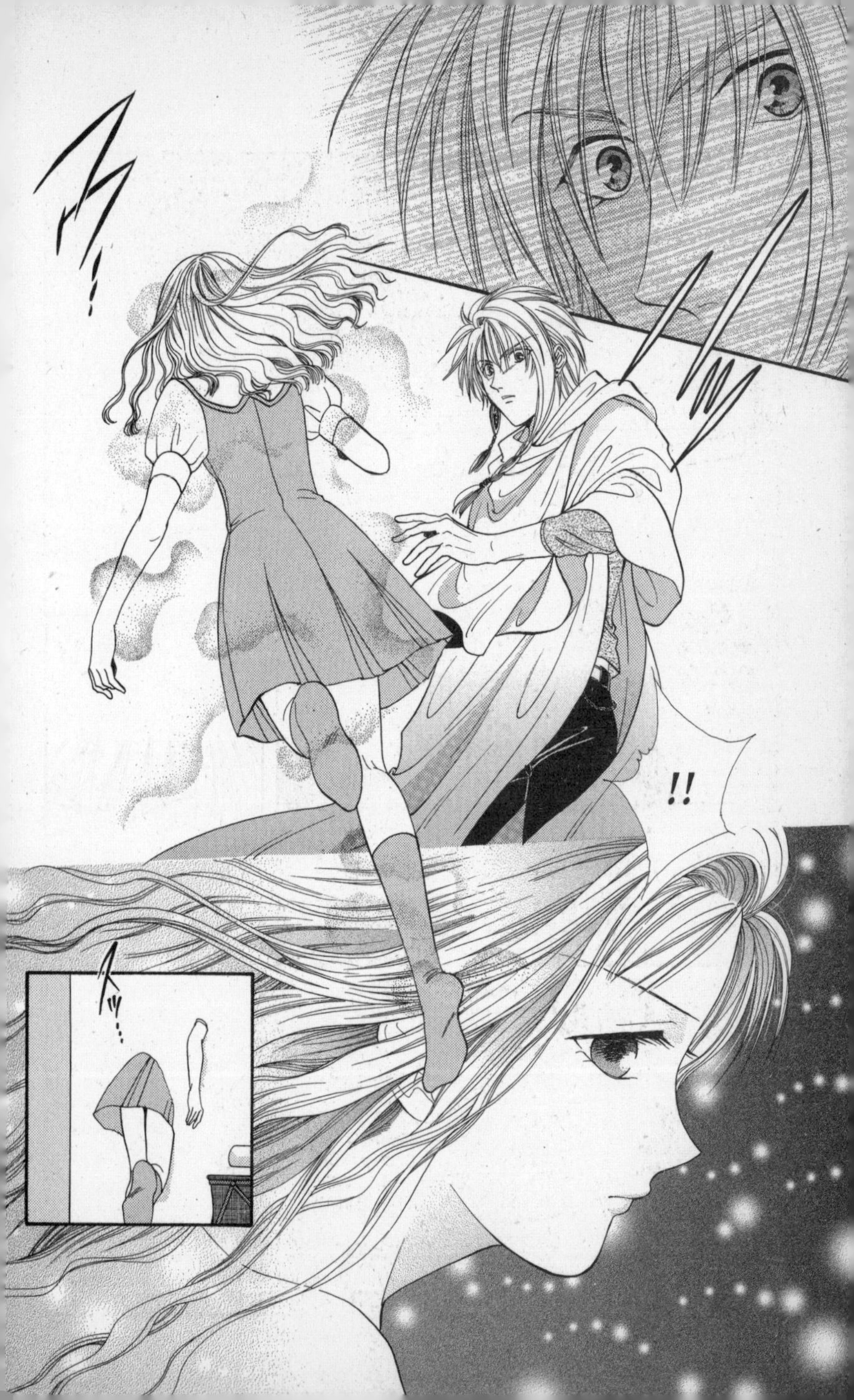
ハッ
スッ!!
!!
スッ…

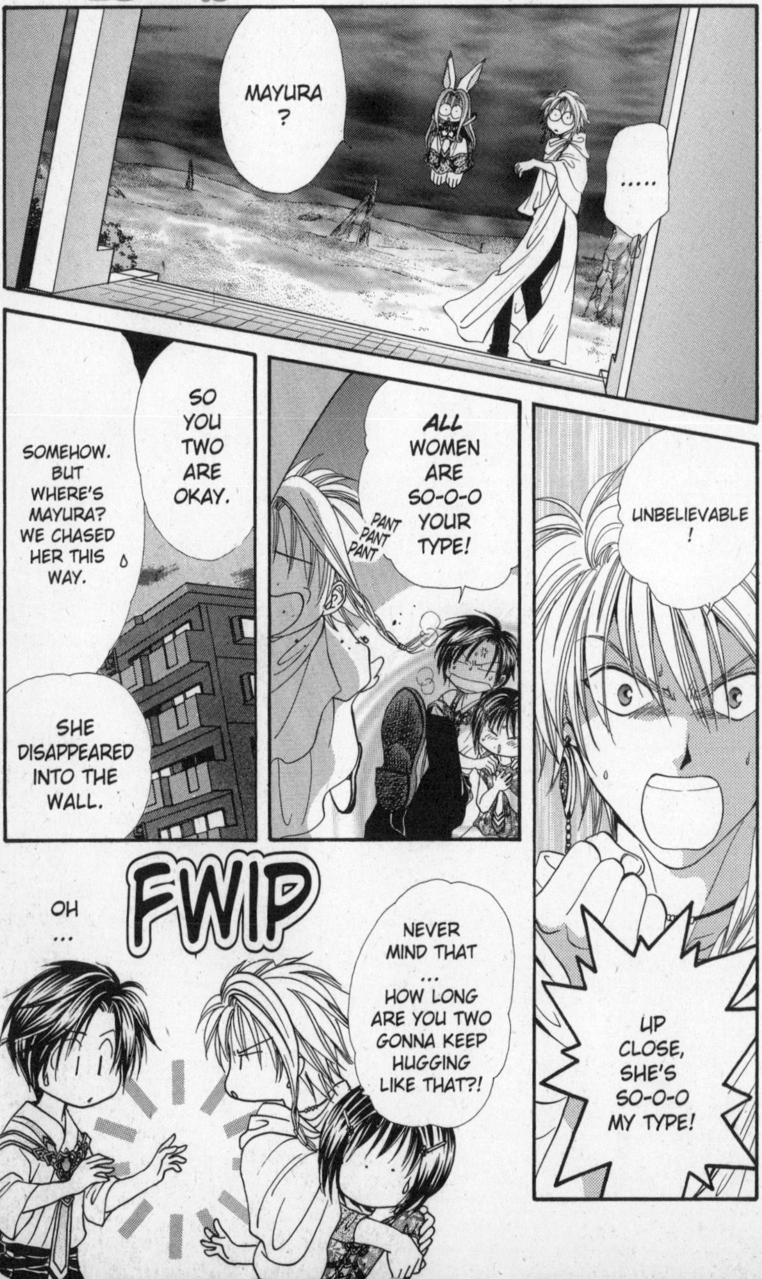
MAYURA ?
.....
UNBELIEVABLE !
UP CLOSE, SHE'S SO-O-O MY TYPE!
ALL WOMEN ARE SO-O-O YOUR TYPE!
PANT PANT PANT
SO YOU TWO ARE OKAY.
SOMEHOW. BUT WHERE'S MAYURA? WE CHASED HER THIS WAY.
SHE DISAPPEARED INTO THE WALL.
FWIP
NEVER MIND THAT ... HOW LONG ARE YOU TWO GONNA KEEP HUGGING LIKE THAT?!
OH ...

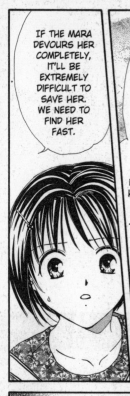

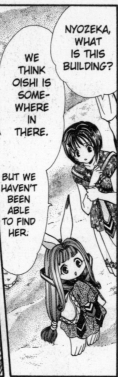

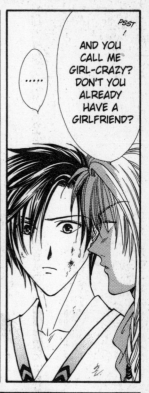

PSST!
AND YOU CALL ME GIRL-CRAZY? DON'T YOU ALREADY HAVE A GIRLFRIEND?
.....
NYOZEKA, WHAT IS THIS BUILDING?
WE THINK OISHI IS SOMEWHERE IN THERE.
BUT WE HAVEN'T BEEN ABLE TO FIND HER.
IF THE MARA DEVOURS HER COMPLETELY, IT'LL BE EXTREMELY DIFFICULT TO SAVE HER. WE NEED TO FIND HER FAST.
YOU TWO GO AFTER MAYURA ...
...!
NO! WE HAVE TO SAVE OISHI FIRST.
GASP!

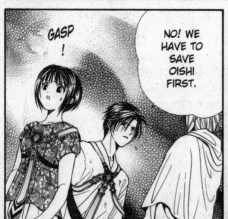

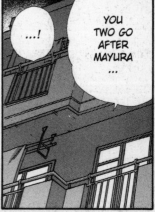

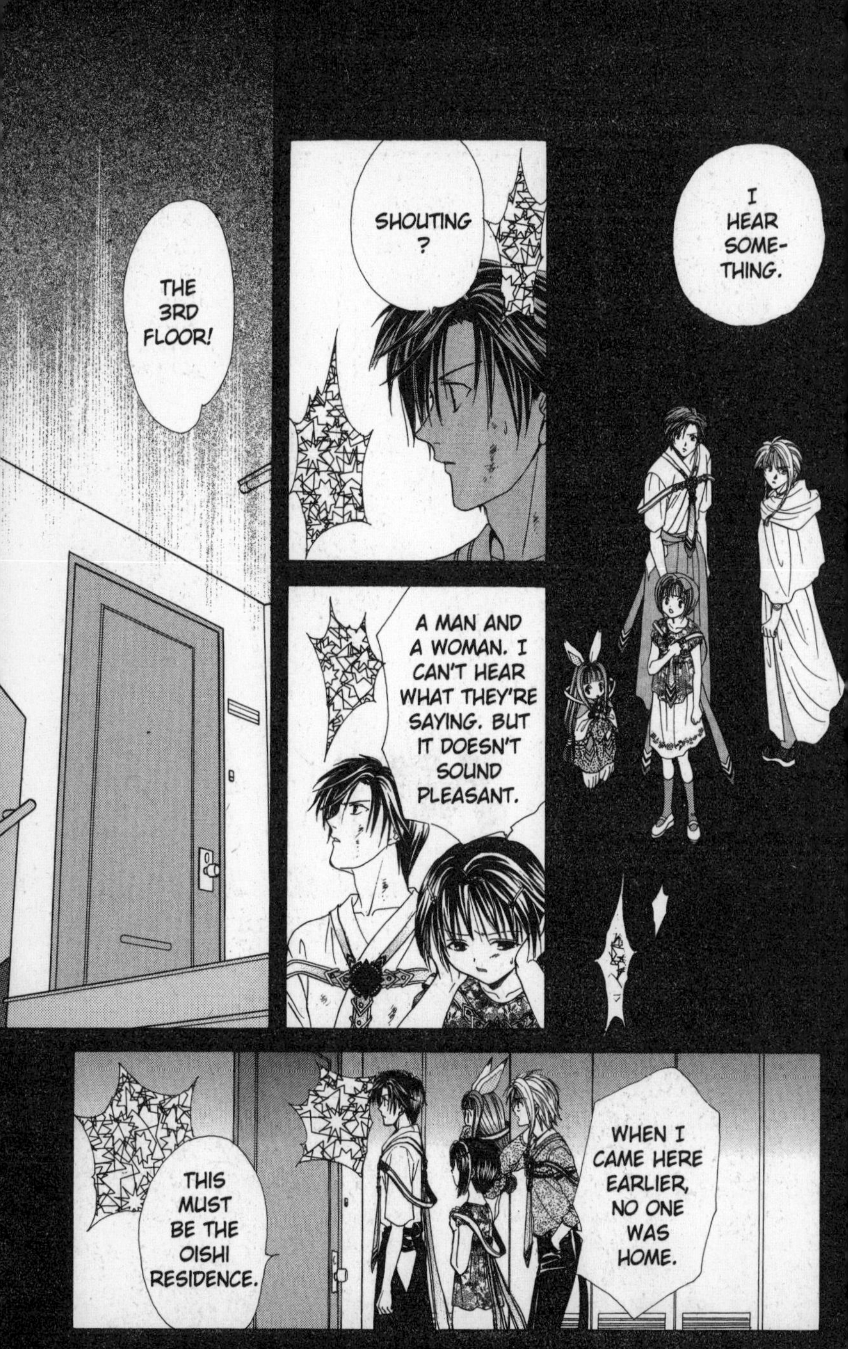
I HEAR SOMETHING.
SHOUTING?
A MAN AND A WOMAN. I CAN'T HEAR WHAT THEY'RE SAYING. BUT IT DOESN'T SOUND PLEASANT.
THE 3RD FLOOR!
WHEN I CAME HERE EARLIER, NO ONE WAS HOME.
THIS MUST BE THE OISHI RESIDENCE.

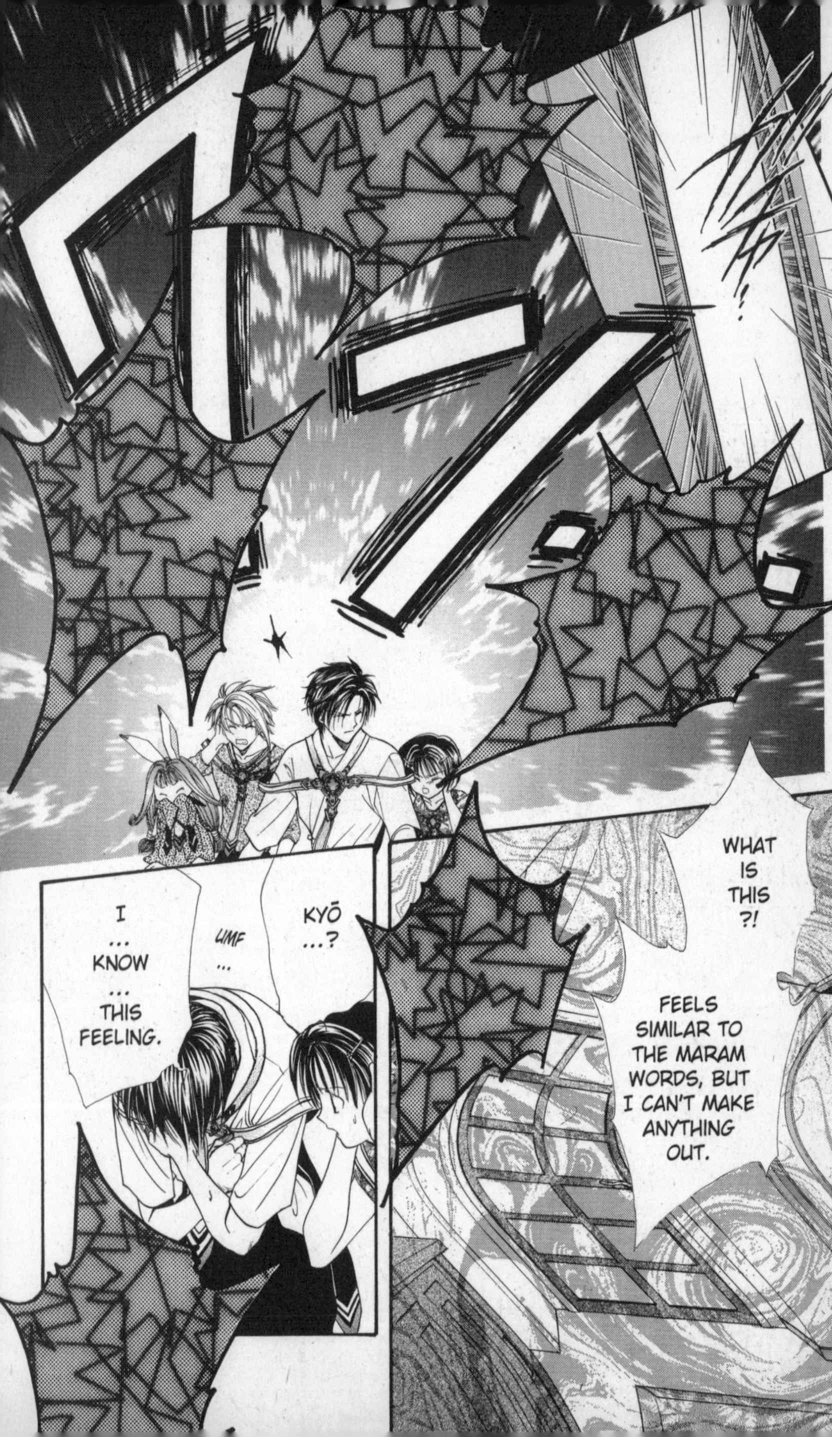
WHAT IS THIS?!
FEELS SIMILAR TO THE MARAM WORDS, BUT I CAN'T MAKE ANYTHING OUT.
KYŌ ...?
UMF ...
I ... KNOW ... THIS FEELING.

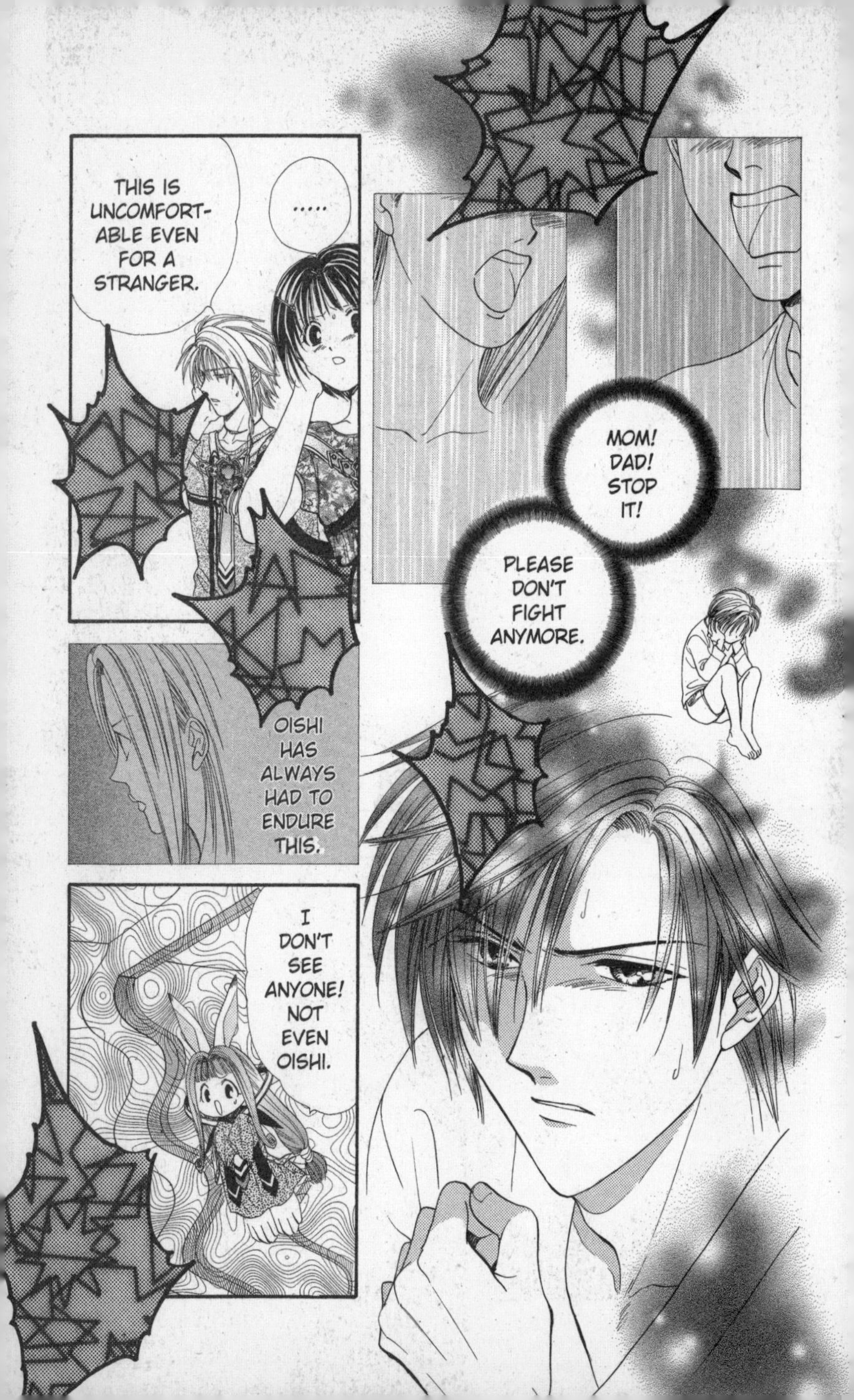
MOM! DAD! STOP IT!
PLEASE DON'T FIGHT ANYMORE.
.....
THIS IS UNCOMFORT-ABLE EVEN FOR A STRANGER.
OISHI HAS ALWAYS HAD TO ENDURE THIS.
I DON'T SEE ANYONE! NOT EVEN OISHI.

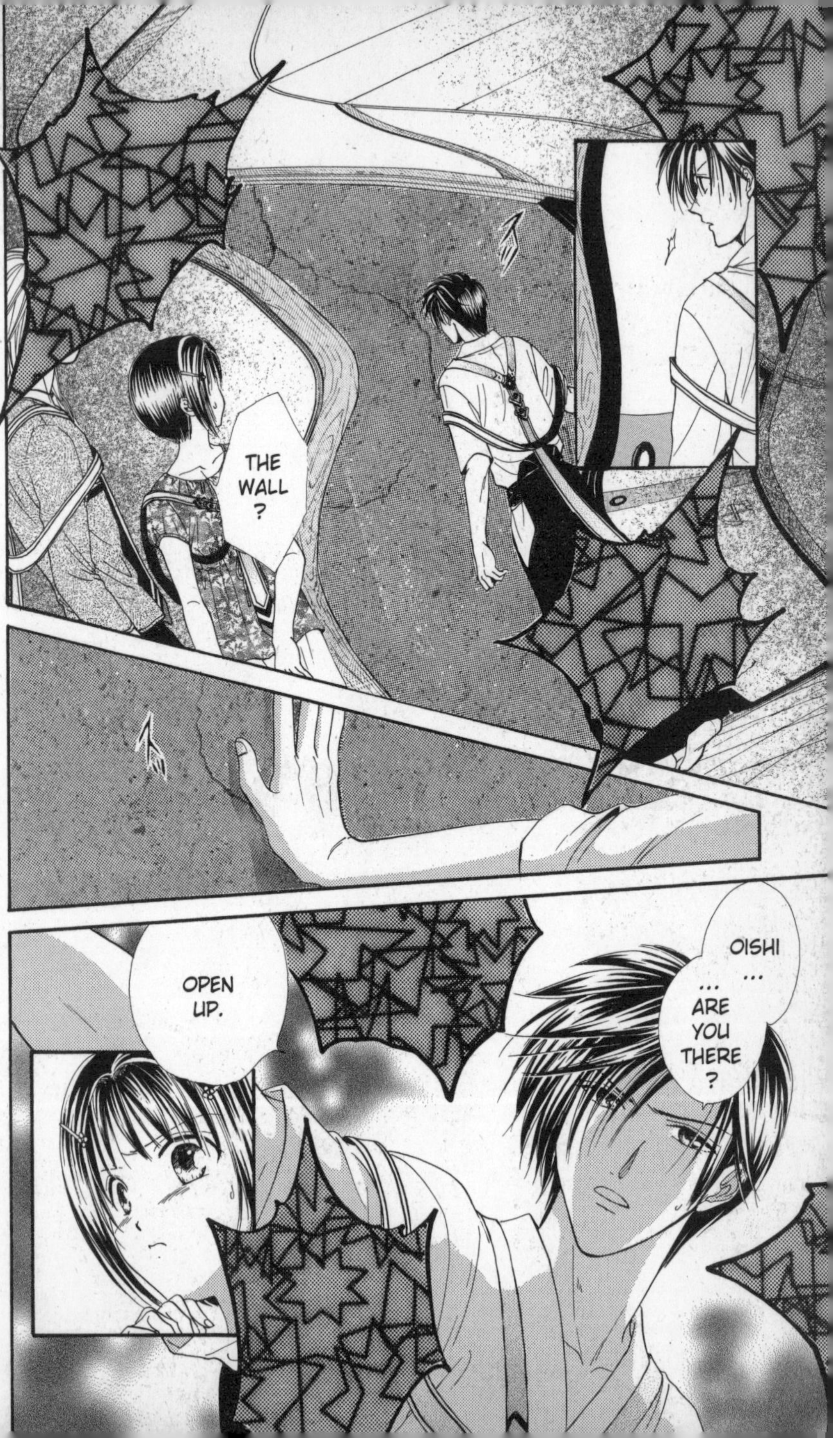
THE WALL ?
OISHI ... ... ARE YOU THERE ?
OPEN UP.

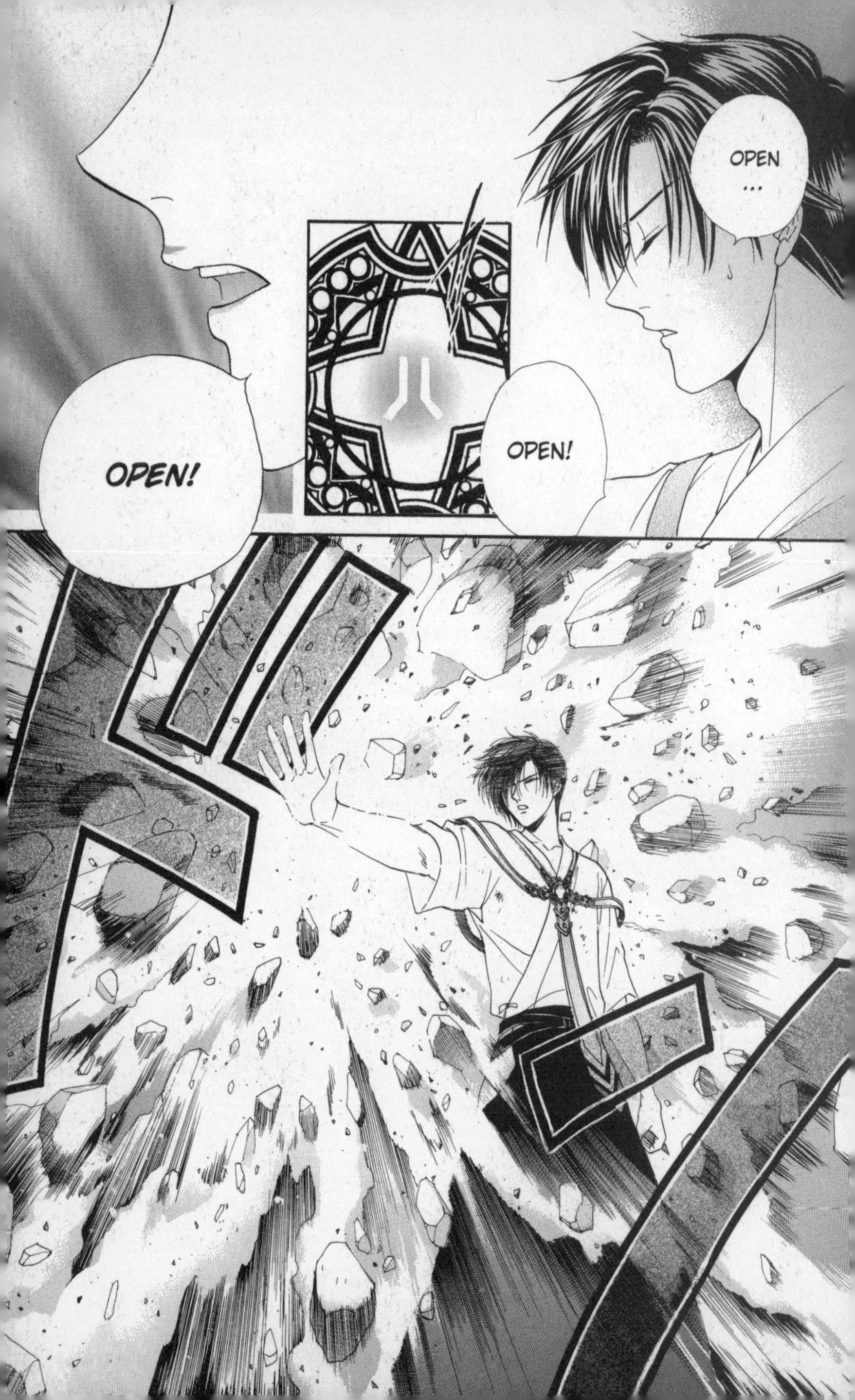
OPEN ...
OPEN!
OPEN!

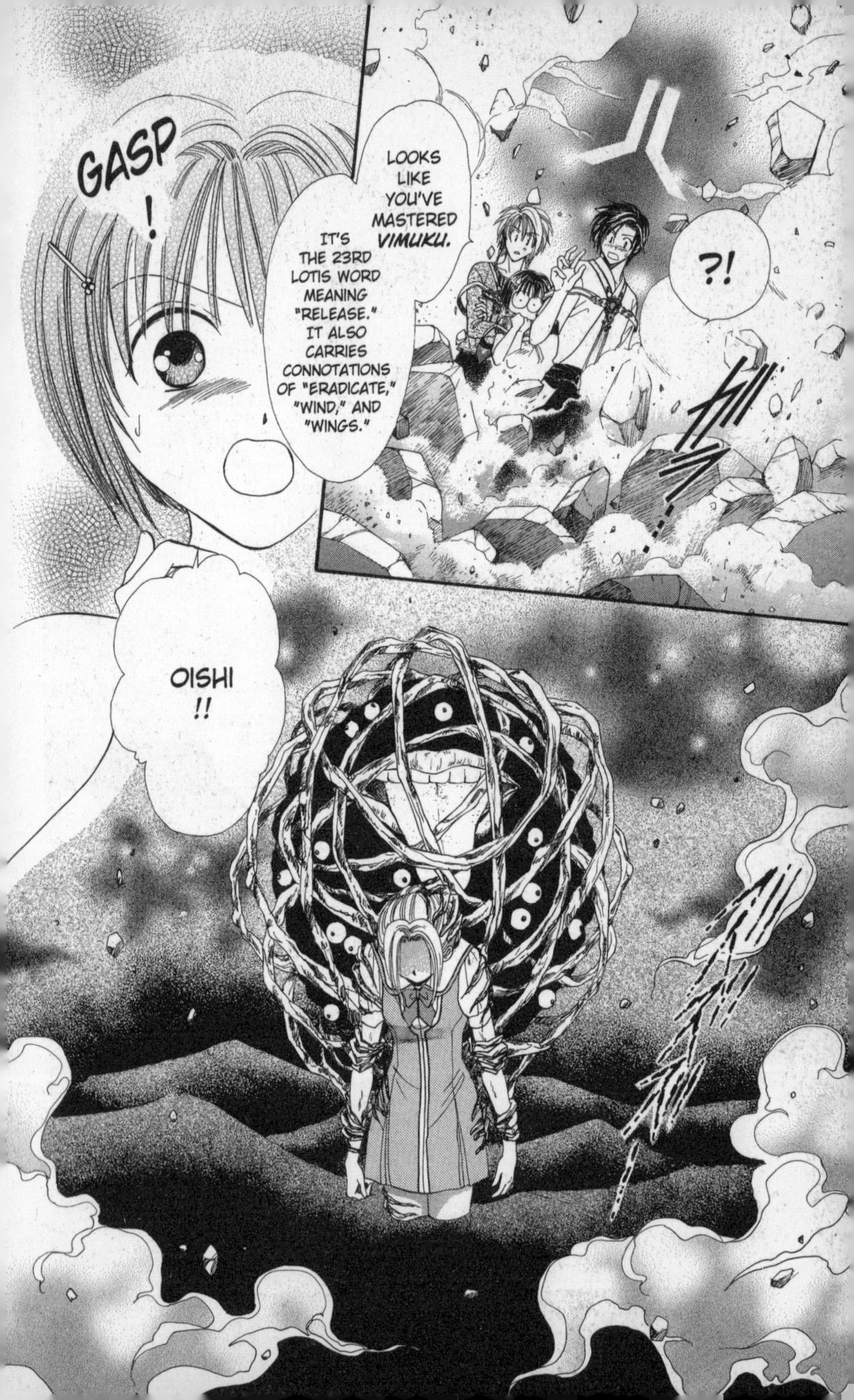
?!
LOOKS LIKE YOU'VE MASTERED VIMUKU.
IT'S THE 23RD LOTIS WORD MEANING "RELEASE." IT ALSO CARRIES CONNOTATIONS OF "ERADICATE," "WIND," AND "WINGS."
GASP
!
OISHI !!

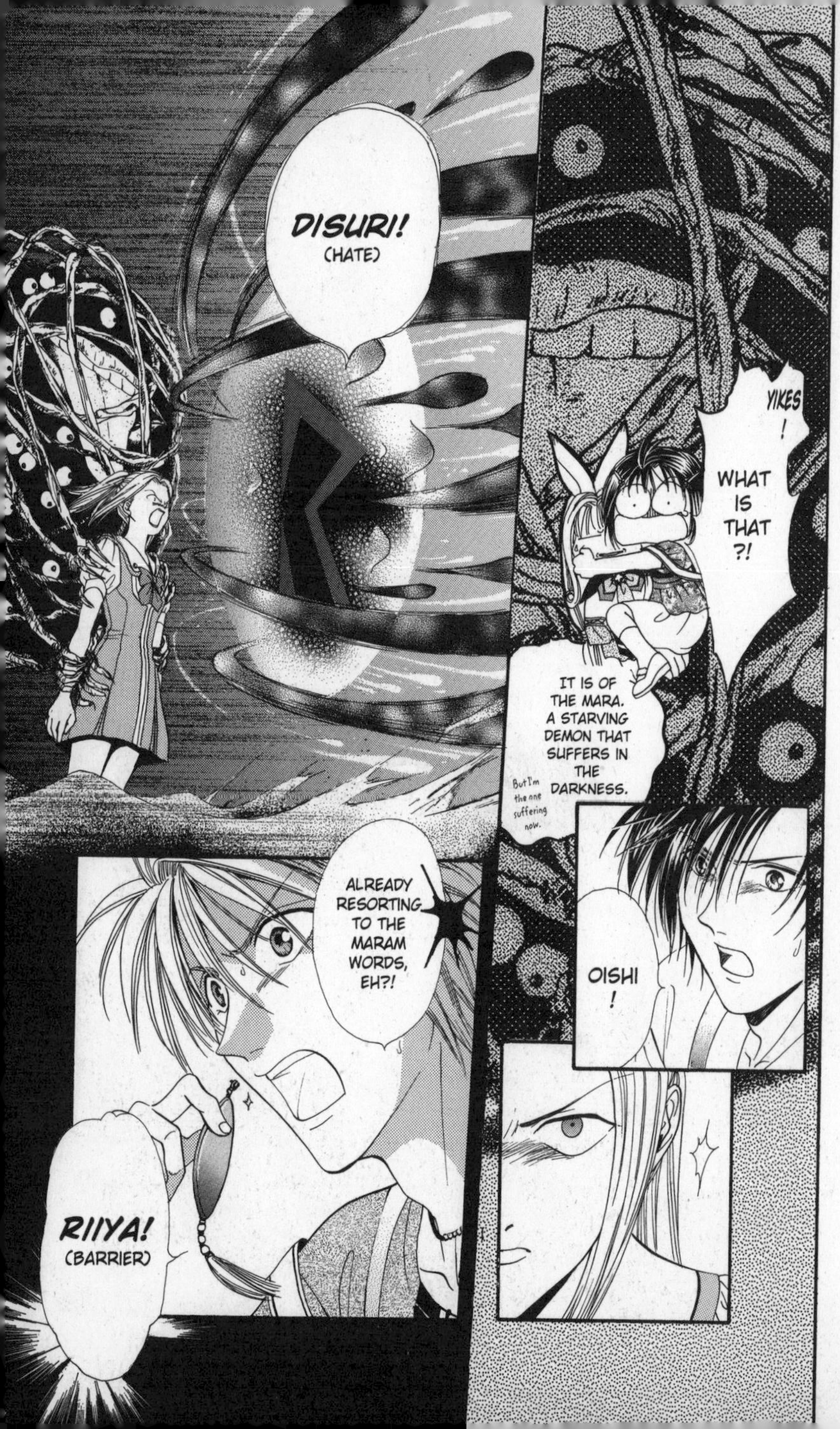
YIKES!
WHAT IS THAT?!
IT IS OF THE MARA. A STARVING DEMON THAT SUFFERS IN THE DARKNESS.
But I'm the one suffering now.
DISURI!
(HATE)
OISHI!
ALREADY RESORTING TO THE MARAM WORDS, EH?!
RIIYA!
(BARRIER)

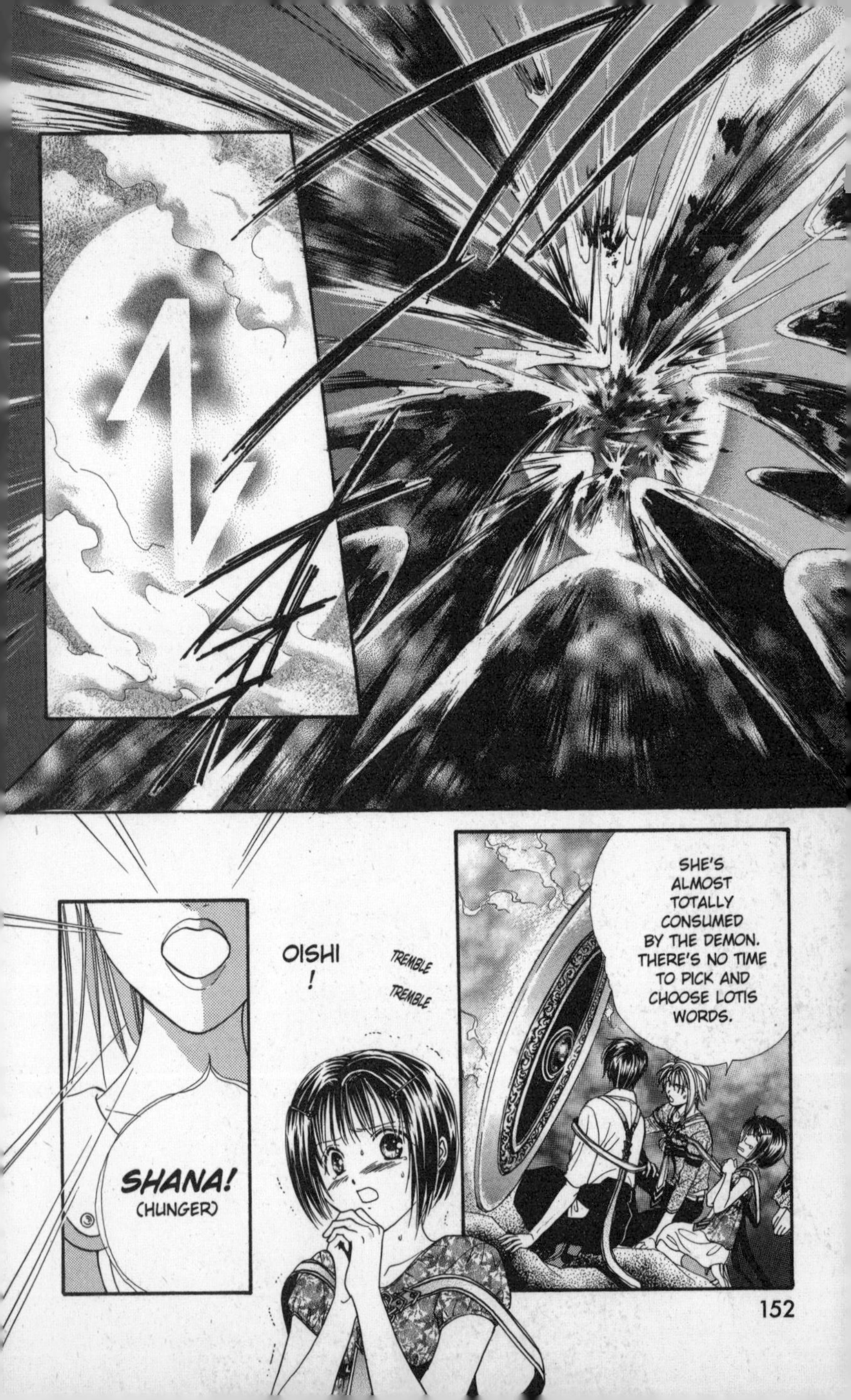
SHE'S ALMOST TOTALLY CONSUMED BY THE DEMON. THERE'S NO TIME TO PICK AND CHOOSE LOTIS WORDS.
OISHI!
TREMBLE
TREMBLE
SHANA!
(HUNGER)

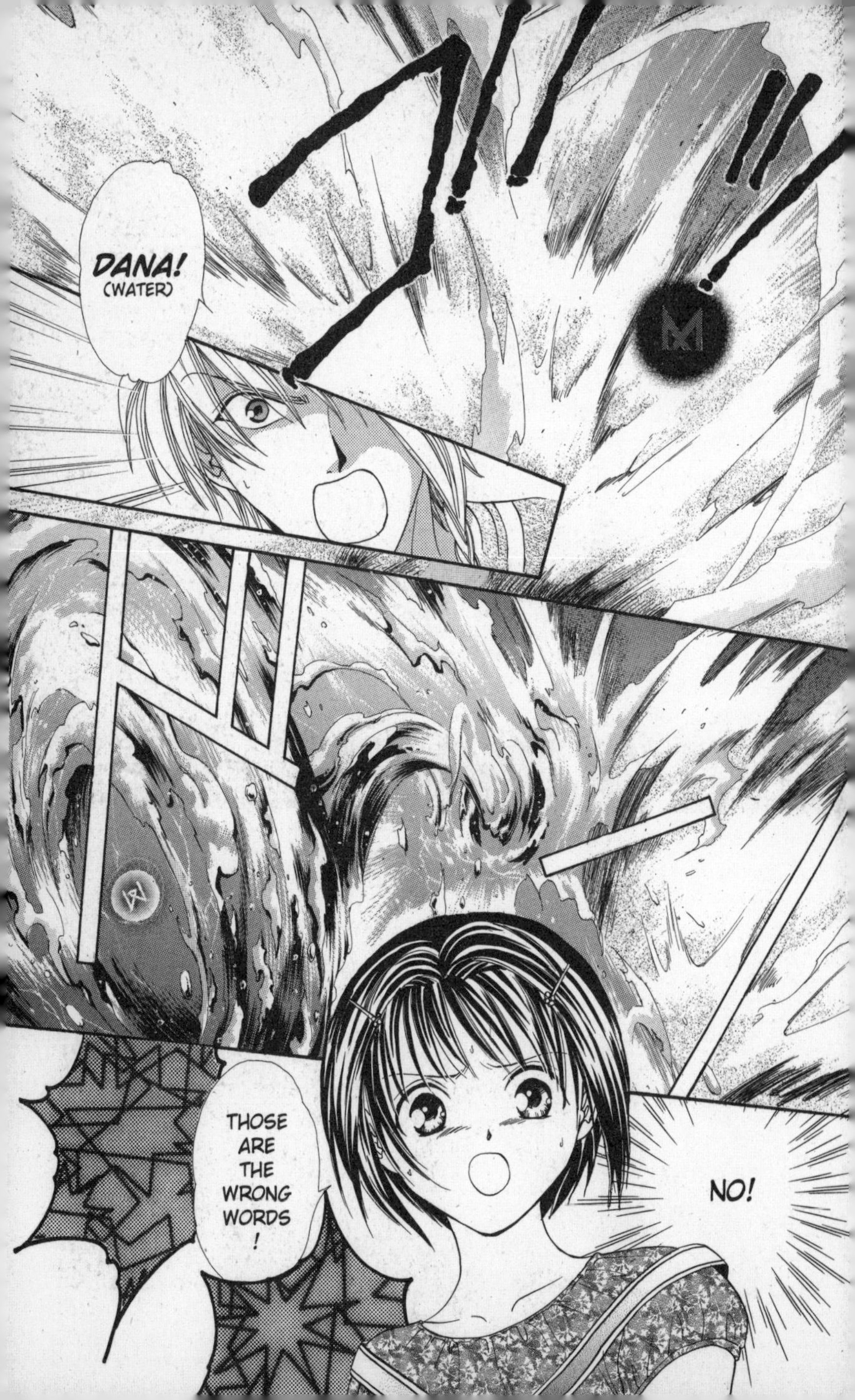
DANA!
(WATER)
NO!
THOSE ARE THE WRONG WORDS!

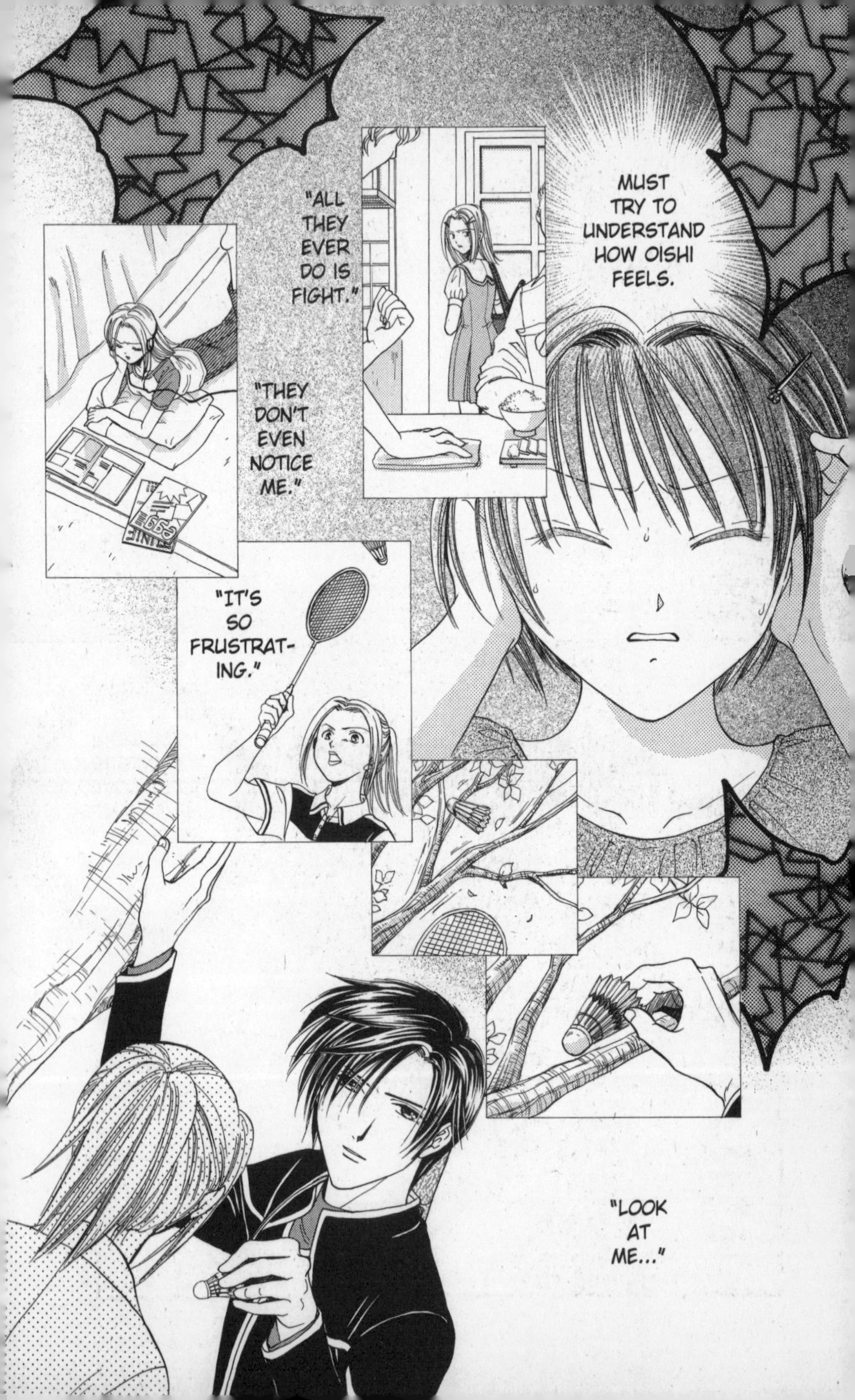
MUST TRY TO UNDERSTAND HOW OISHI FEELS.
"ALL THEY EVER DO IS FIGHT."
"THEY DON'T EVEN NOTICE ME."
"IT'S SO FRUSTRAT-ING."
"LOOK AT ME..."

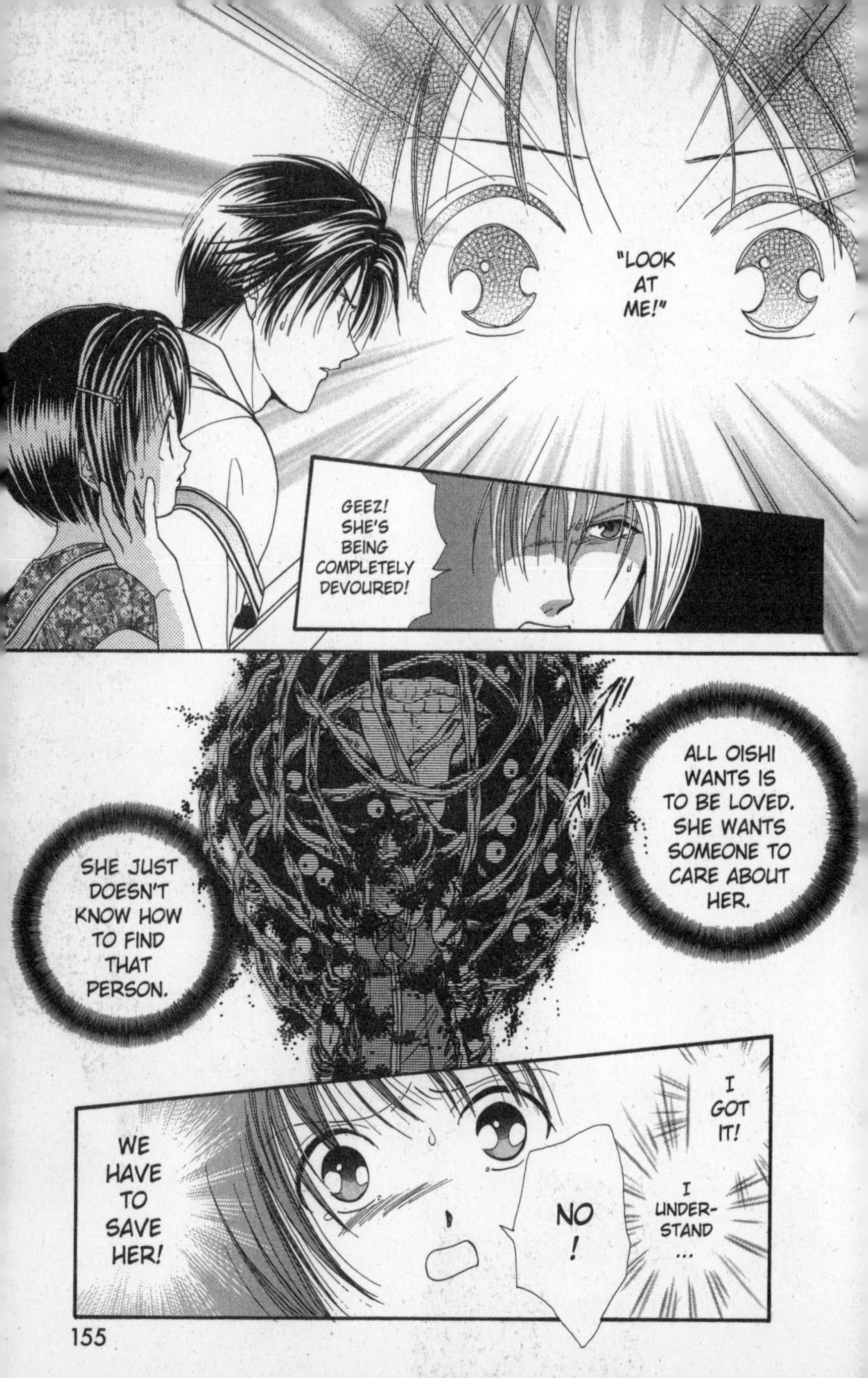
"LOOK AT ME!"
GEEZ! SHE'S BEING COMPLETELY DEVOURED!
ALL OISHI WANTS IS TO BE LOVED. SHE WANTS SOMEONE TO CARE ABOUT HER.
SHE JUST DOESN'T KNOW HOW TO FIND THAT PERSON.
I GOT IT!
I UNDER-STAND ...
NO!
WE HAVE TO SAVE HER!

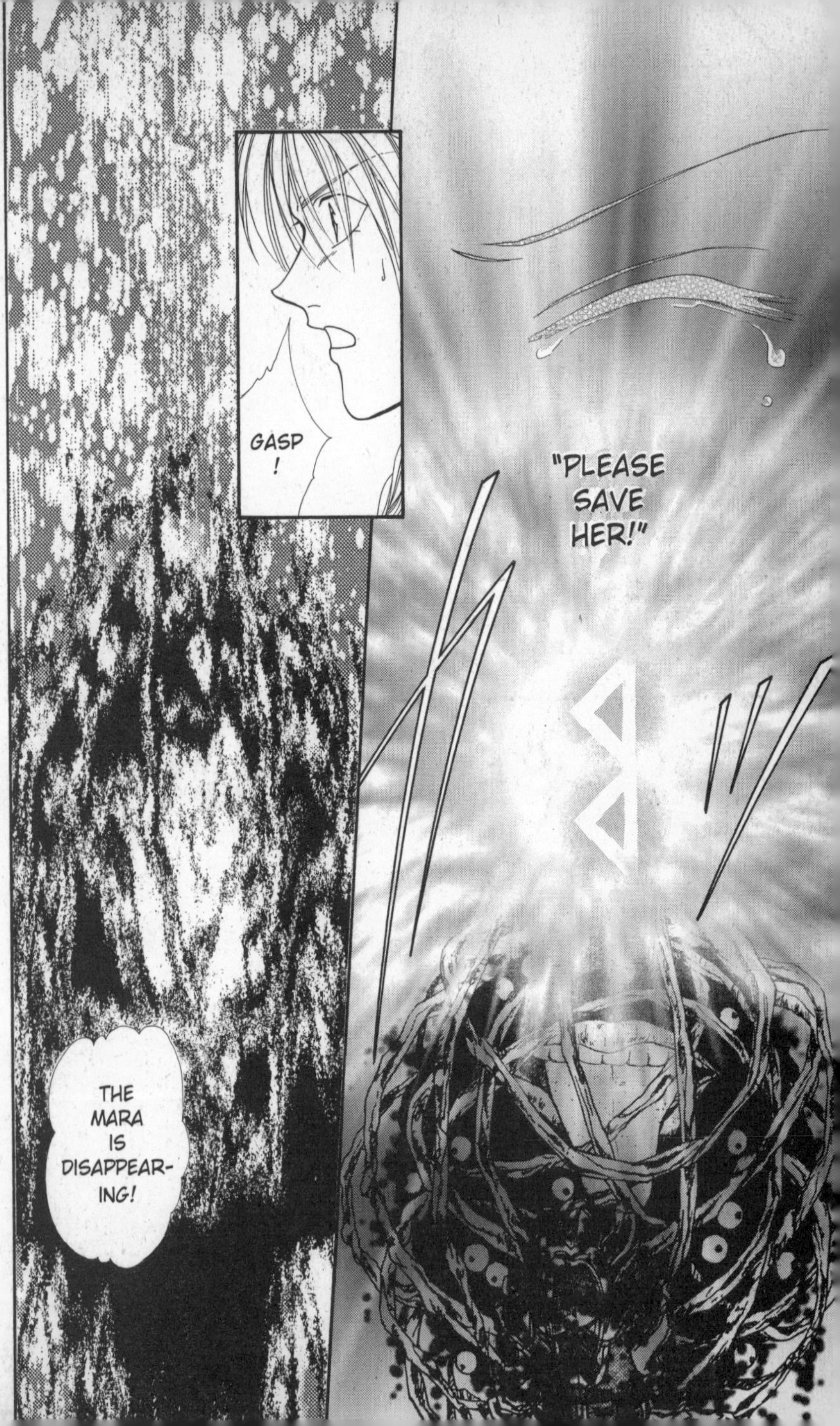
"PLEASE SAVE HER!"
GASP!
THE MARA IS DISAPPEARING!

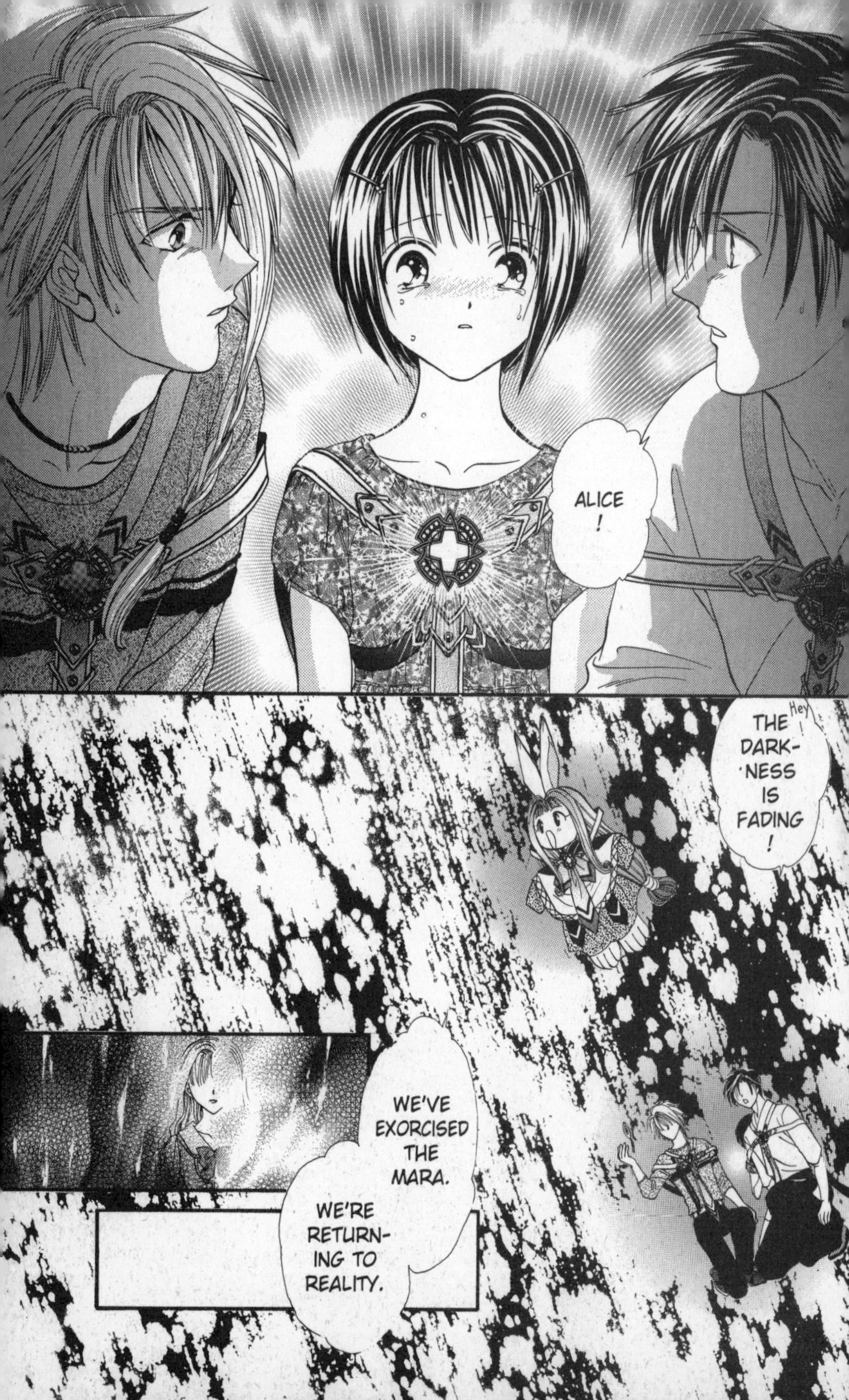
ALICE!
Hey!
THE DARK-NESS IS FADING!
WE'VE EXORCISED THE MARA.
WE'RE RETURN-ING TO REALITY.

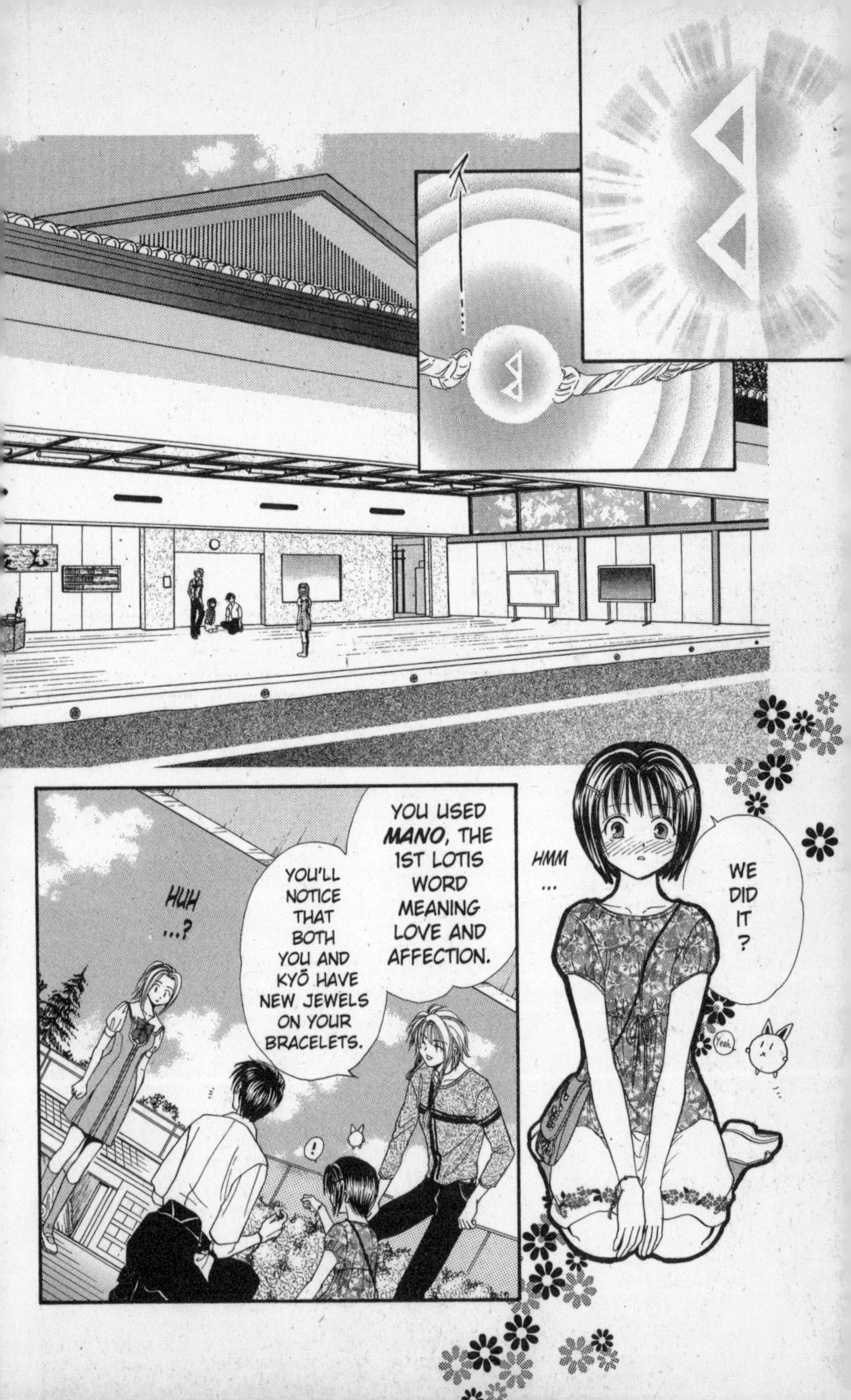

WE DID IT ?
HMM ...
Yeah.
YOU USED MANO, THE 1ST LOTIS WORD MEANING LOVE AND AFFECTION.
YOU'LL NOTICE THAT BOTH YOU AND KYŌ HAVE NEW JEWELS ON YOUR BRACELETS.
HUH ...?
!

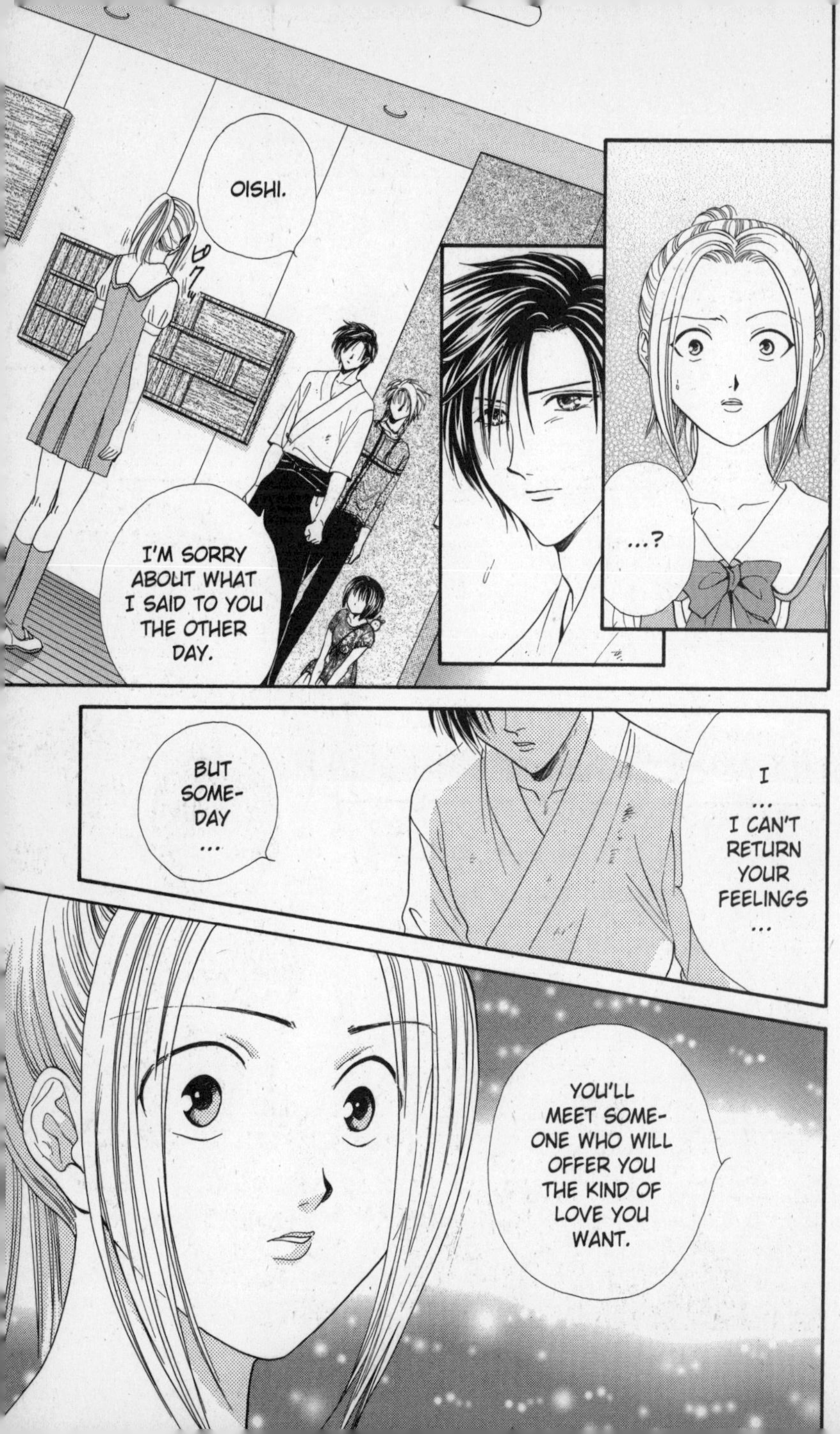
OISHI.
...?
I'M SORRY ABOUT WHAT I SAID TO YOU THE OTHER DAY.
I ... I CAN'T RETURN YOUR FEELINGS ...
BUT SOME-DAY ...
YOU'LL MEET SOME-ONE WHO WILL OFFER YOU THE KIND OF LOVE YOU WANT.

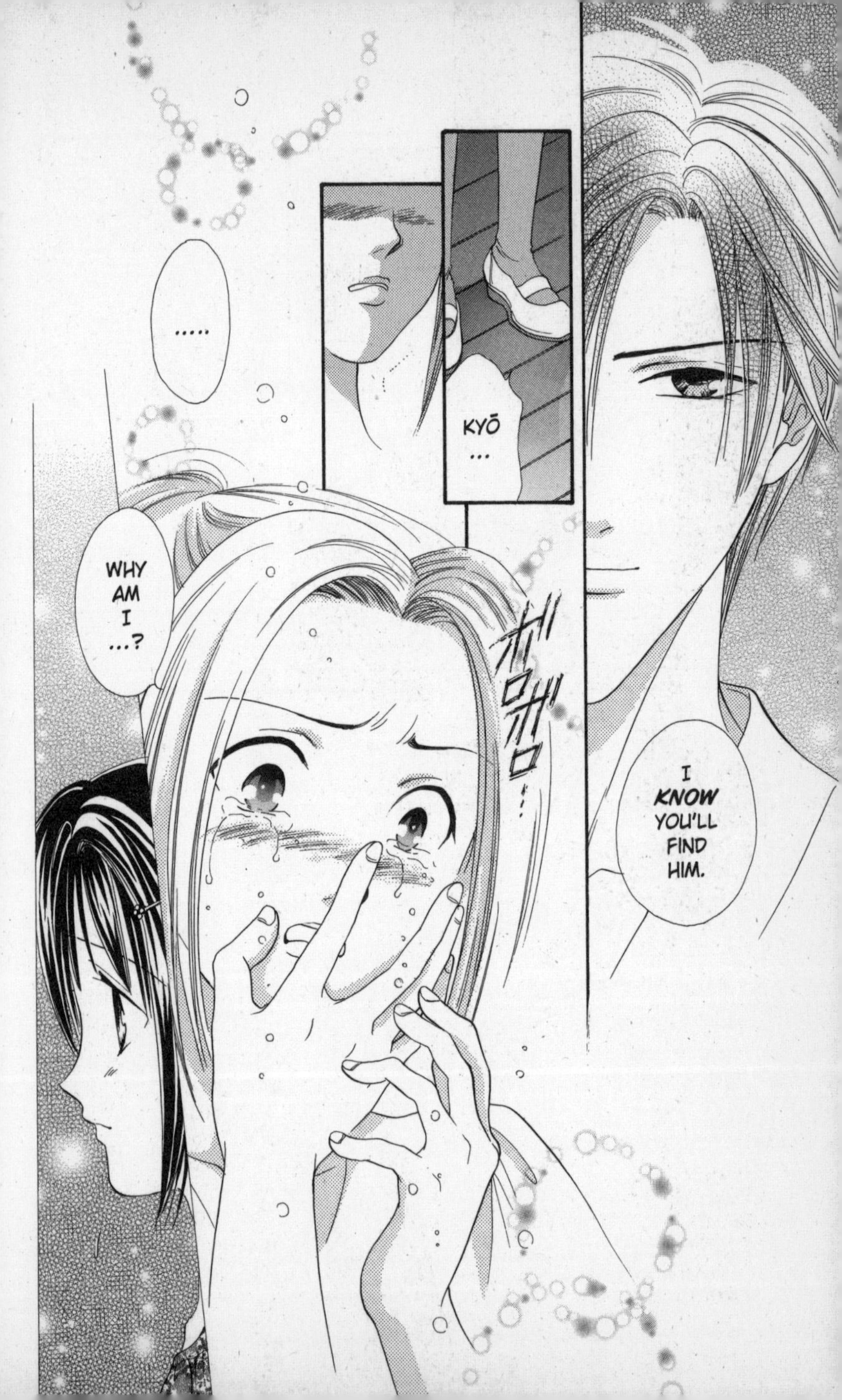

I KNOW YOU'LL FIND HIM.
KYŌ ...
.....
WHY AM I ...?

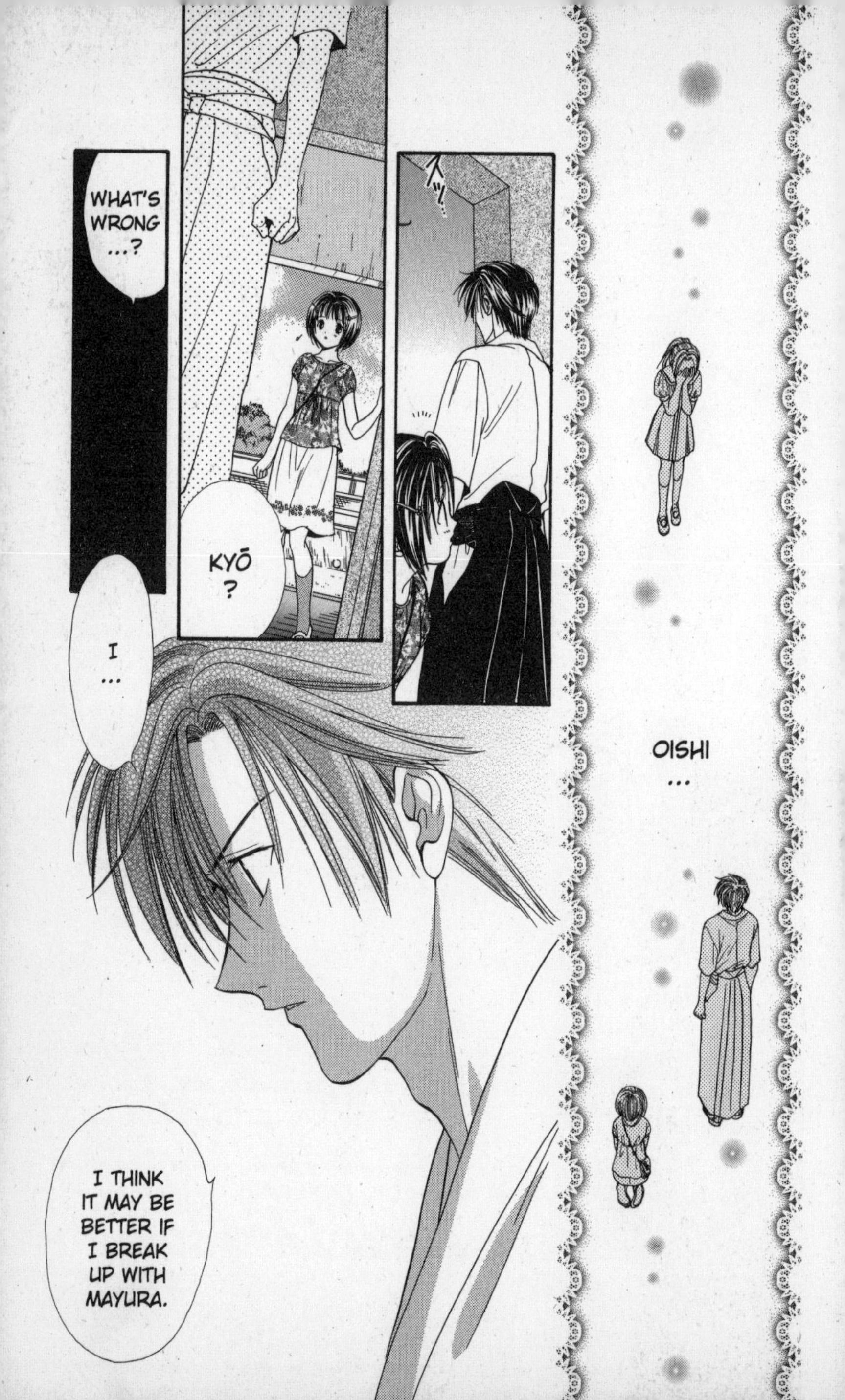
OISHI ...
KYŌ ?
WHAT'S WRONG ...?
I ...
I THINK IT MAY BE BETTER IF I BREAK UP WITH MAYURA.

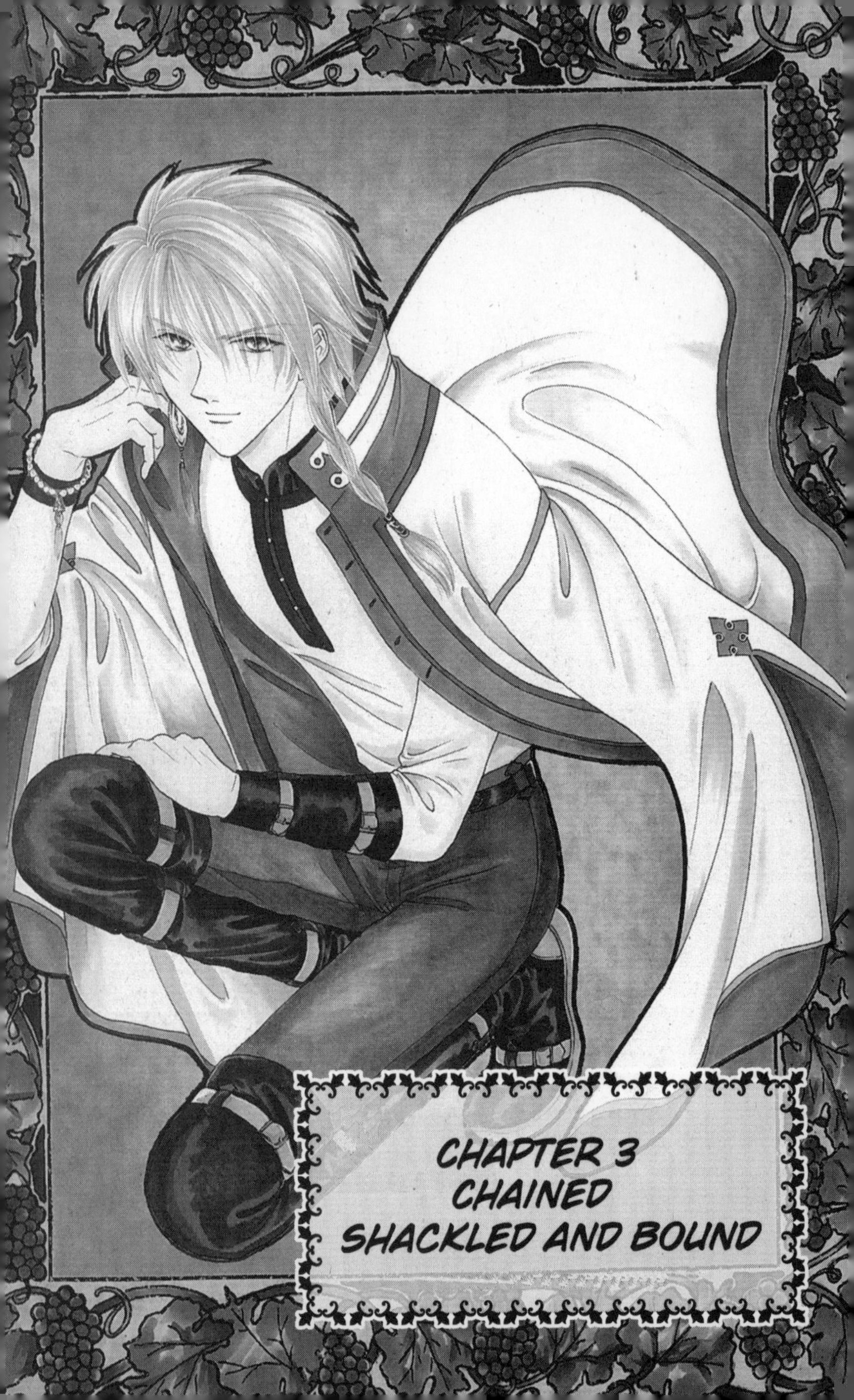
CHAPTER 3
CHAINED
SHACKLED AND BOUND

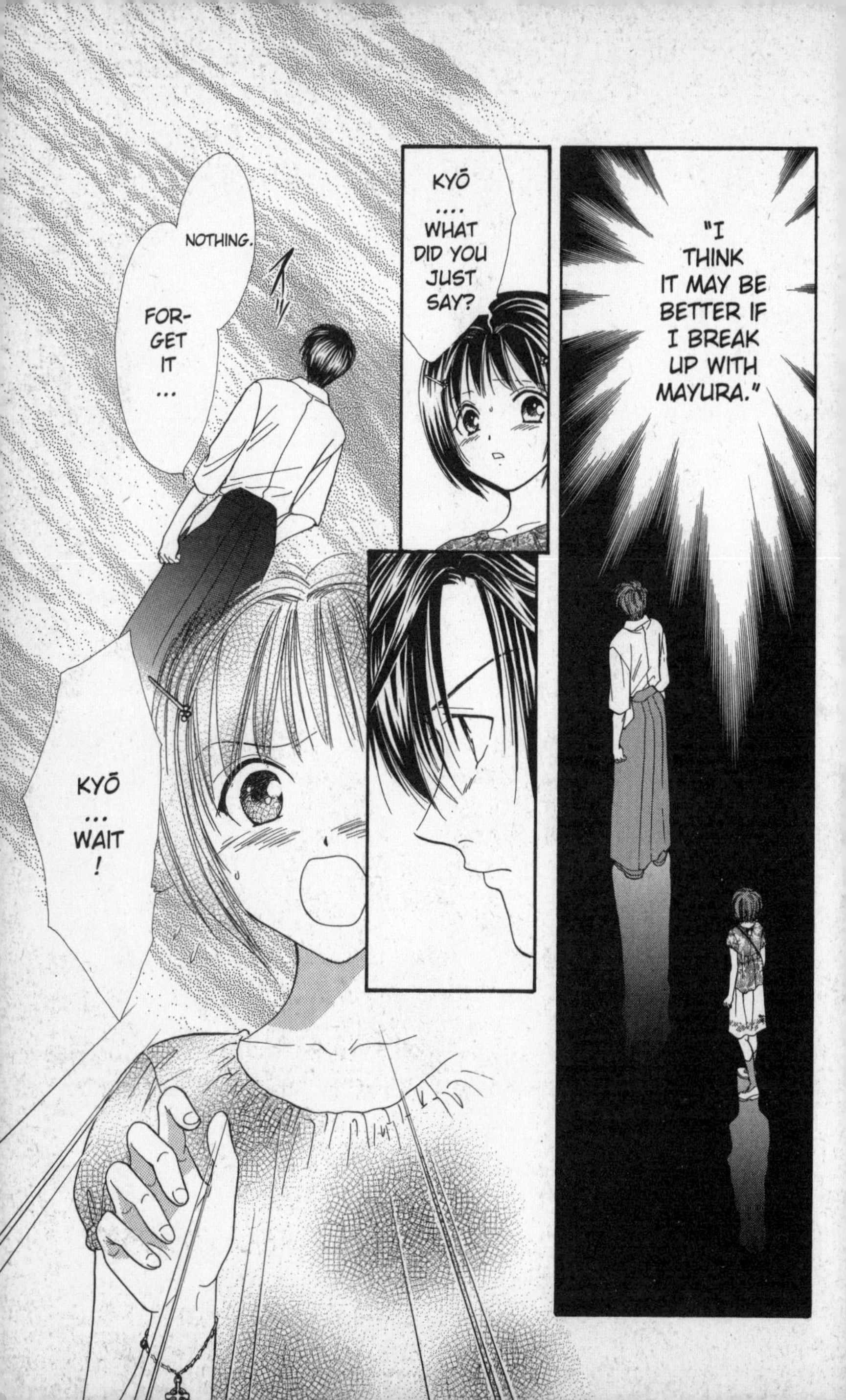
"I THINK IT MAY BE BETTER IF I BREAK UP WITH MAYURA."
KYŌ .... WHAT DID YOU JUST SAY?
NOTHING.
FOR-GET IT ...
KYŌ ... WAIT!

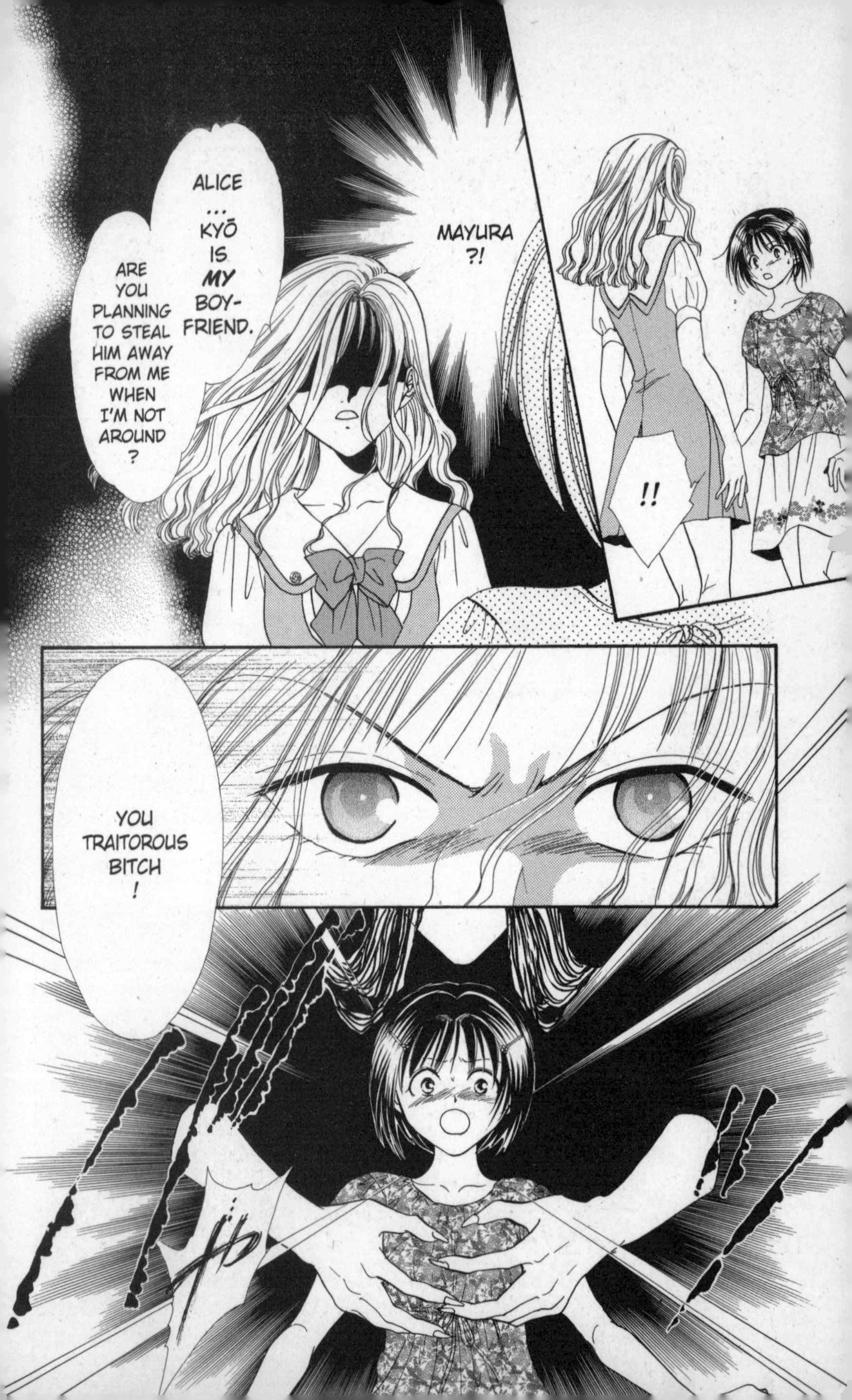
!!
MAYURA ?!
ALICE ... KYŌ IS **MY** BOY-FRIEND.
ARE YOU PLANNING TO STEAL HIM AWAY FROM ME WHEN I'M NOT AROUND ?
YOU TRAITOROUS BITCH !

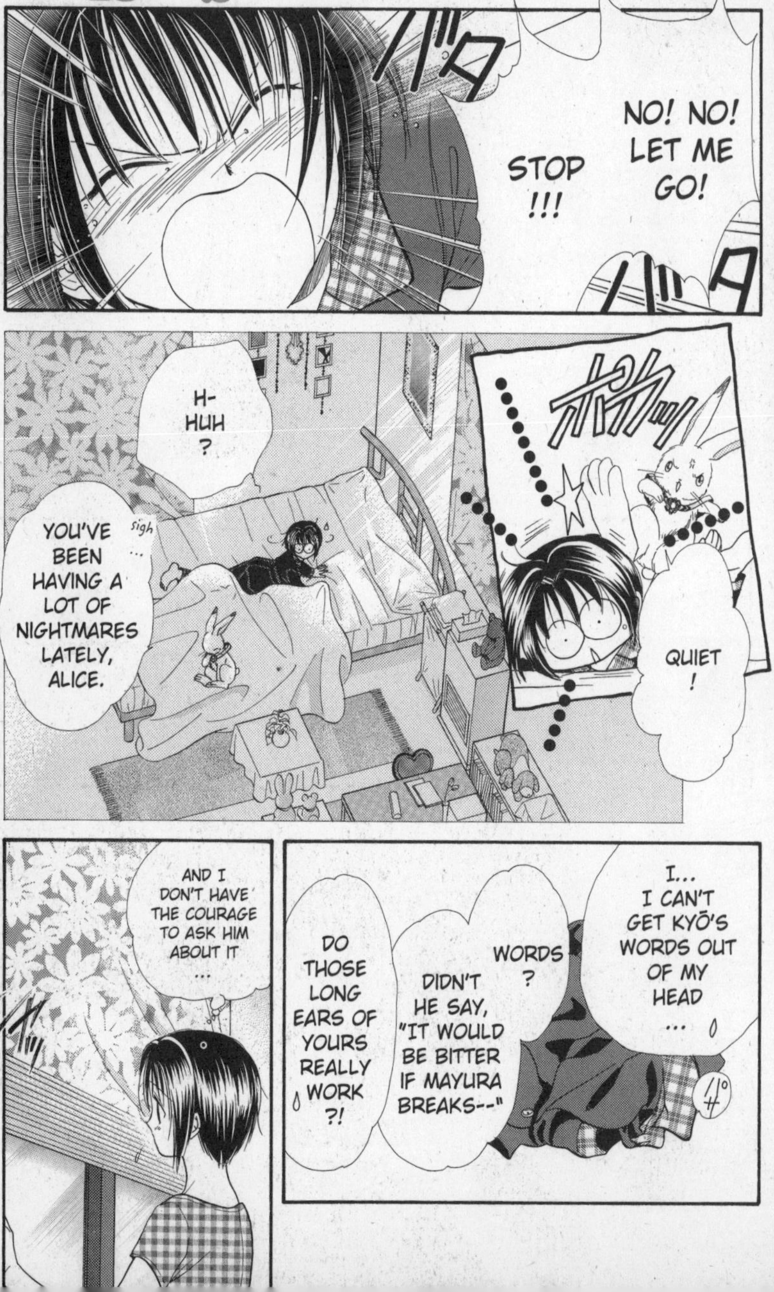
NO! NO! LET ME GO!
STOP!!!
QUIET!
H-HUH?
sigh...
YOU'VE BEEN HAVING A LOT OF NIGHTMARES LATELY, ALICE.
I... I CAN'T GET KYŌ'S WORDS OUT OF MY HEAD...
WORDS?
DIDN'T HE SAY, "IT WOULD BE BITTER IF MAYURA BREAKS--"
DO THOSE LONG EARS OF YOURS REALLY WORK?!
AND I DON'T HAVE THE COURAGE TO ASK HIM ABOUT IT...

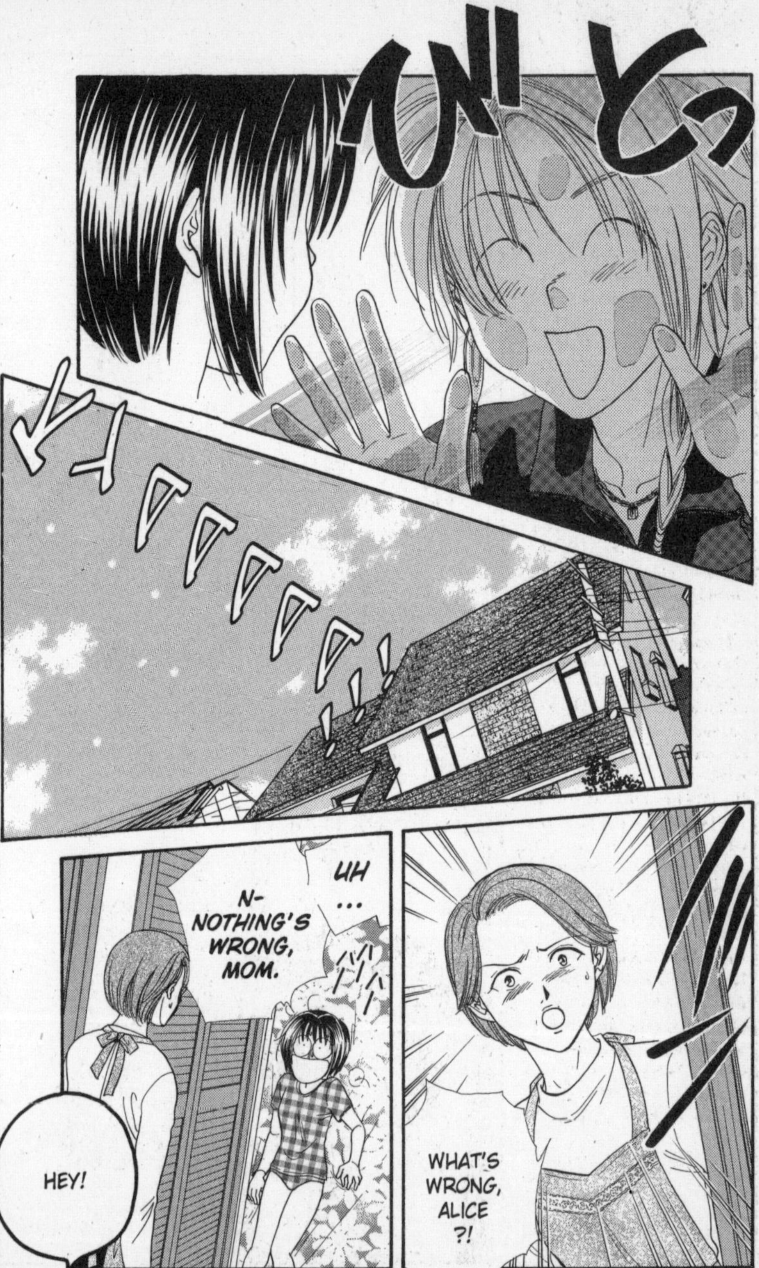
びとっ
キャアアアアア!!!
WHAT'S WRONG, ALICE ?!
UH ...
ハハハ
N- NOTHING'S WRONG, MOM.
HEY!

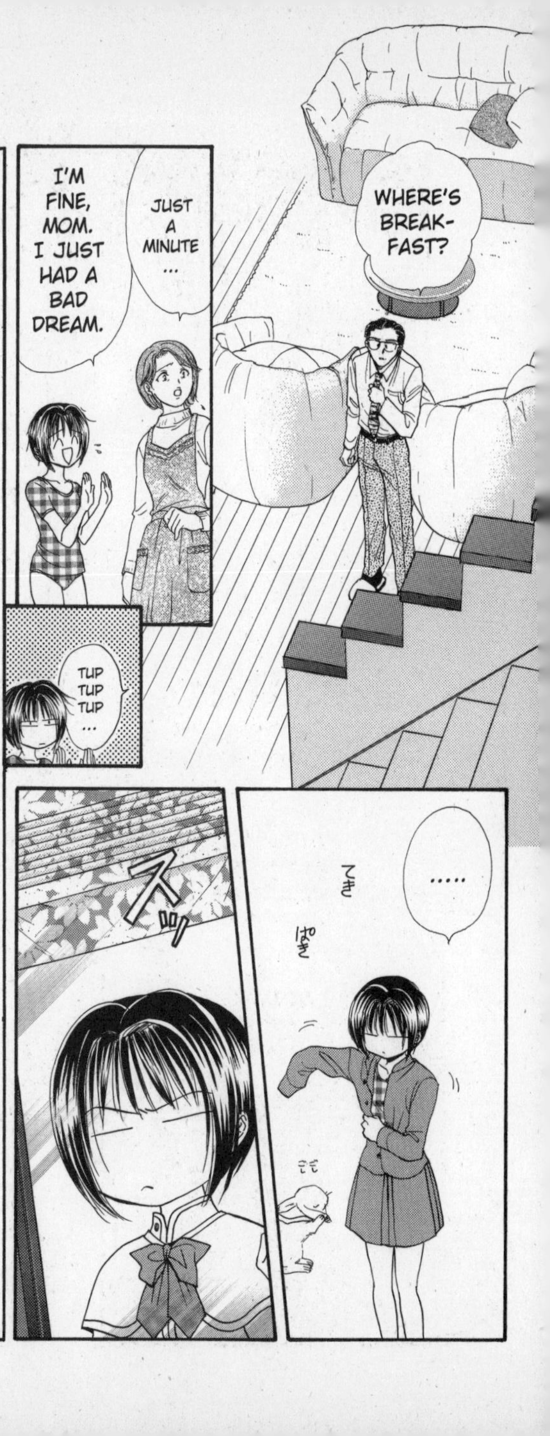
WHERE'S BREAKFAST?
JUST A MINUTE ...
I'M FINE, MOM. I JUST HAD A BAD DREAM.
TUP TUP TUP ...
.....
てき
ぱき

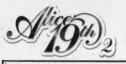

Little details that are difficult... Coming up with ideas for the Inner Heart and thinking of ways that the Lotis words will be used. It's pretty difficult. The Inner Heart is a psychological dimension, so I haven't made it into a complete world. And with the Mara, I try to add humor to the horror. Many of you have probably been wondering exactly what the Lotis is. I used Runes for inspiration, but it's not directly based on them. The words and their meanings have absolutely nothing to do with runes. I also got some inspiration from Sanskrit. There are twenty-four runes, and when I came upon it, it seemed like a good fit.
As for the "19th" in the title, when I was thinking about this story, the number just popped into my head. That's all.
It's unusual that we came up with the title so quickly. My editor asked for something connected to 24. But I couldn't come up with anything, so we decided that "Well, let's make the 19th word the important one for Alice." And that's how we got started. And then there was the issue of readers possibly thinking the title meant "19-year-old Alice." ☺
So the title can be taken to mean "Alice's courage." Please keep up with how the story unfolds. I have many other characters ready to debut, too. See you again in the next volume. There wasn't any time to add character profiles, so next time, okay?

12/12/2001

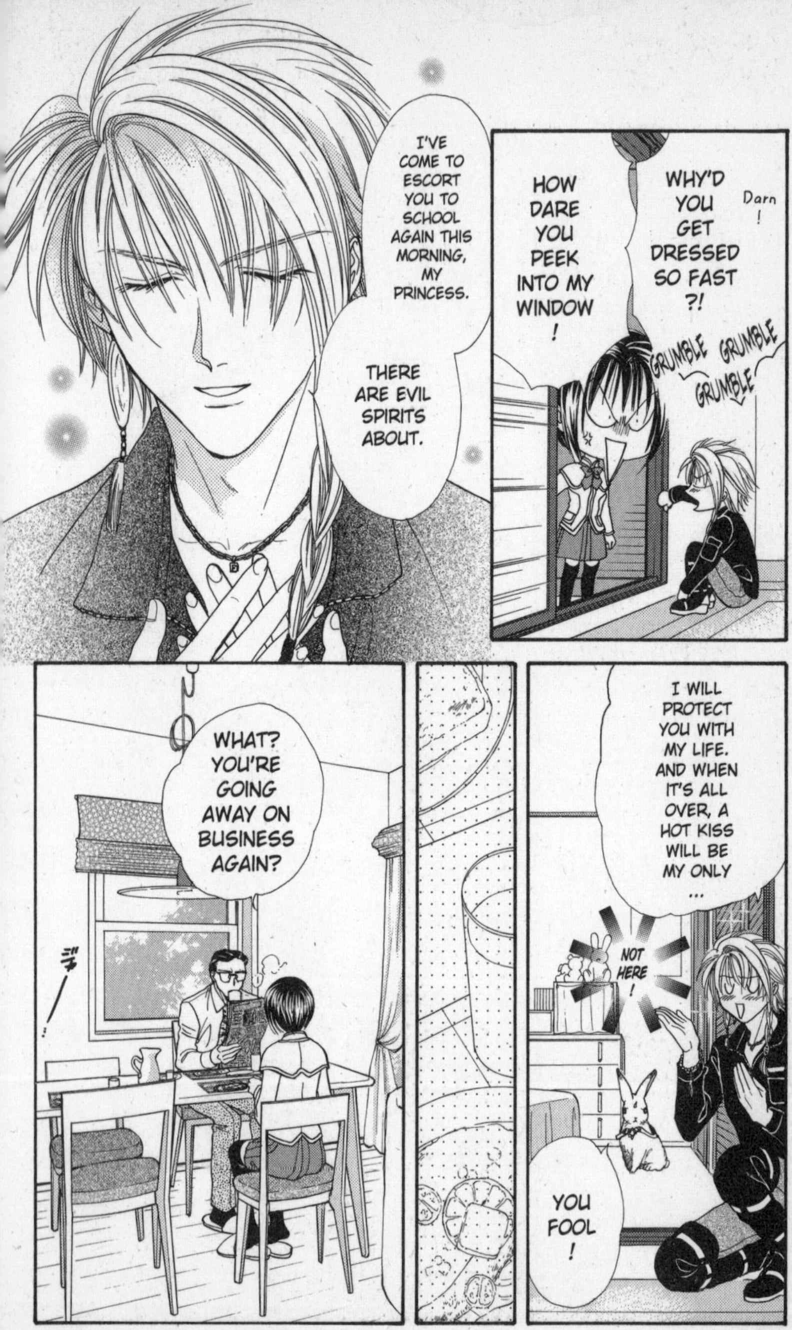
Darn!
WHY'D YOU GET DRESSED SO FAST?!
HOW DARE YOU PEEK INTO MY WINDOW!
GRUMBLE GRUMBLE GRUMBLE
I'VE COME TO ESCORT YOU TO SCHOOL AGAIN THIS MORNING, MY PRINCESS.
THERE ARE EVIL SPIRITS ABOUT.
I WILL PROTECT YOU WITH MY LIFE. AND WHEN IT'S ALL OVER, A HOT KISS WILL BE MY ONLY ...
NOT HERE!
YOU FOOL!
WHAT? YOU'RE GOING AWAY ON BUSINESS AGAIN?

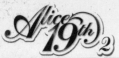

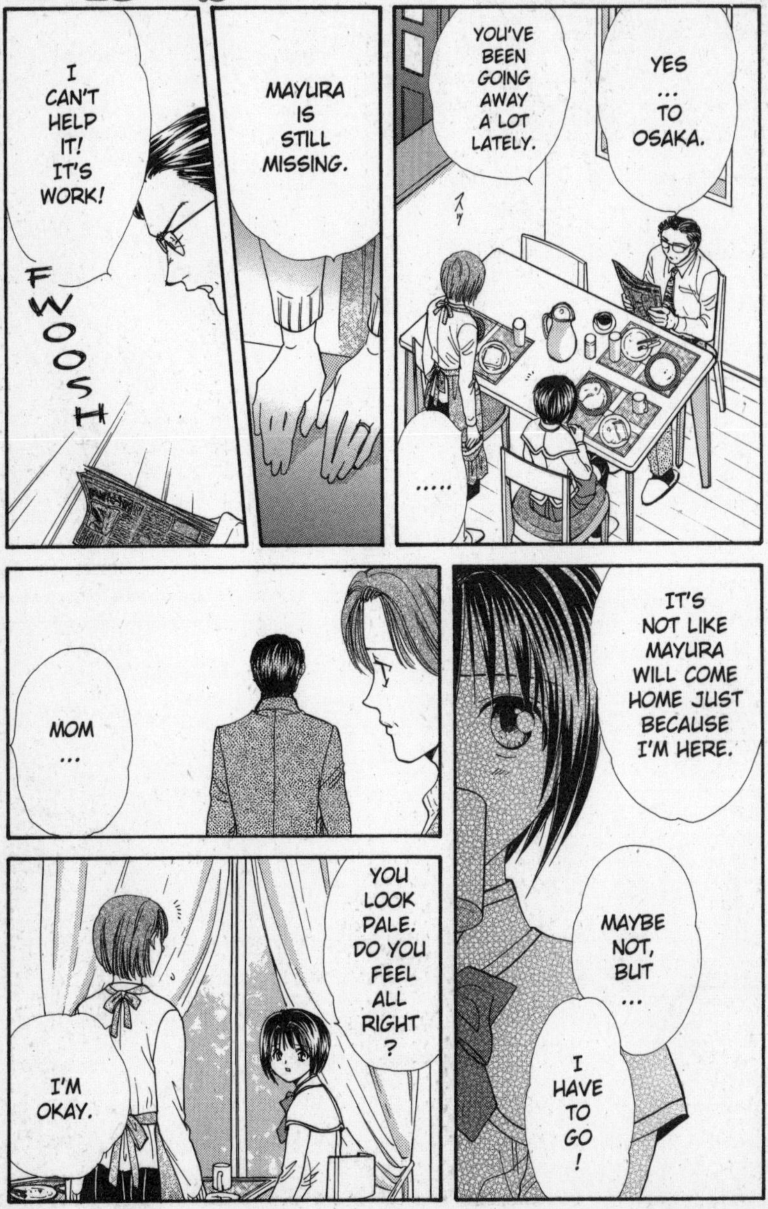
YES ... TO OSAKA.
YOU'VE BEEN GOING AWAY A LOT LATELY.
.....
MAYURA IS STILL MISSING.
I CAN'T HELP IT! IT'S WORK!
FWOOSH
IT'S NOT LIKE MAYURA WILL COME HOME JUST BECAUSE I'M HERE.
MAYBE NOT, BUT ...
I HAVE TO GO!
MOM ...
YOU LOOK PALE. DO YOU FEEL ALL RIGHT ?
I'M OKAY.

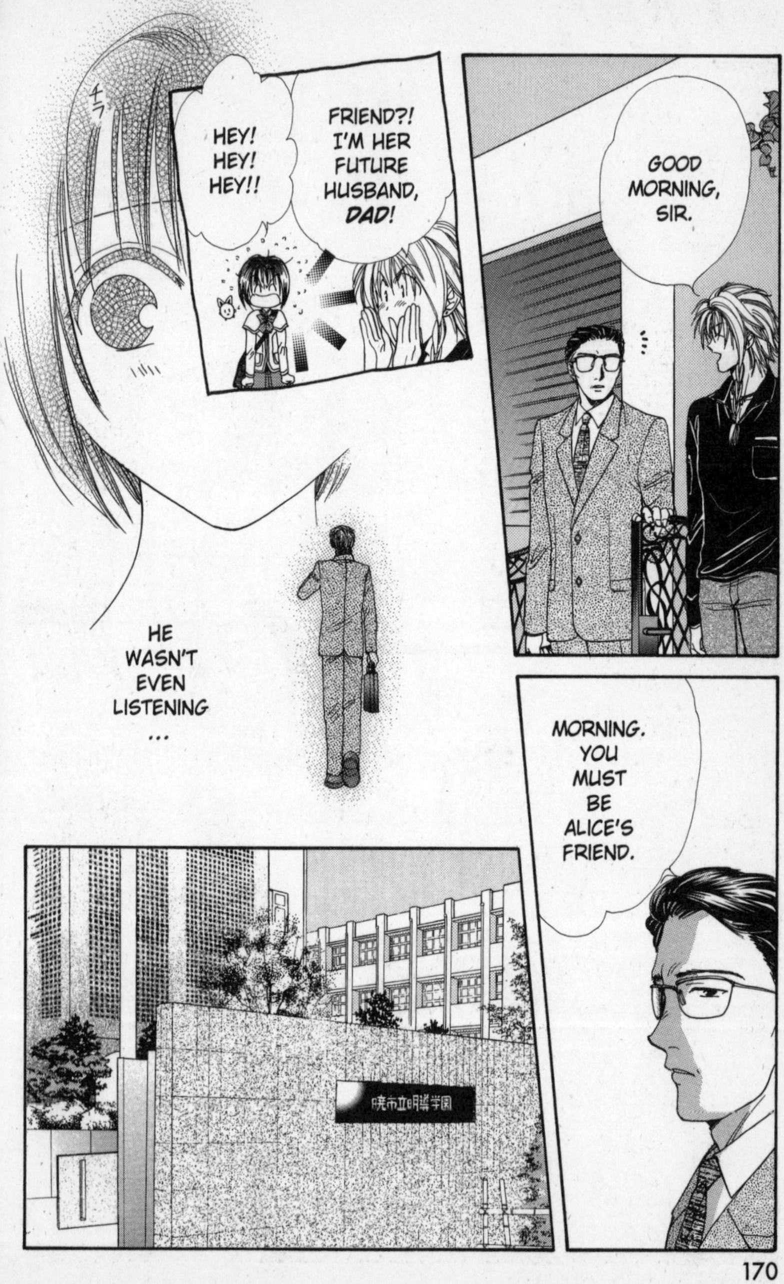
GOOD MORNING, SIR.
FRIEND?! I'M HER FUTURE HUSBAND, DAD!
HEY! HEY! HEY!!
チラ
MORNING. YOU MUST BE ALICE'S FRIEND.
HE WASN'T EVEN LISTENING...
暁市立明導学園

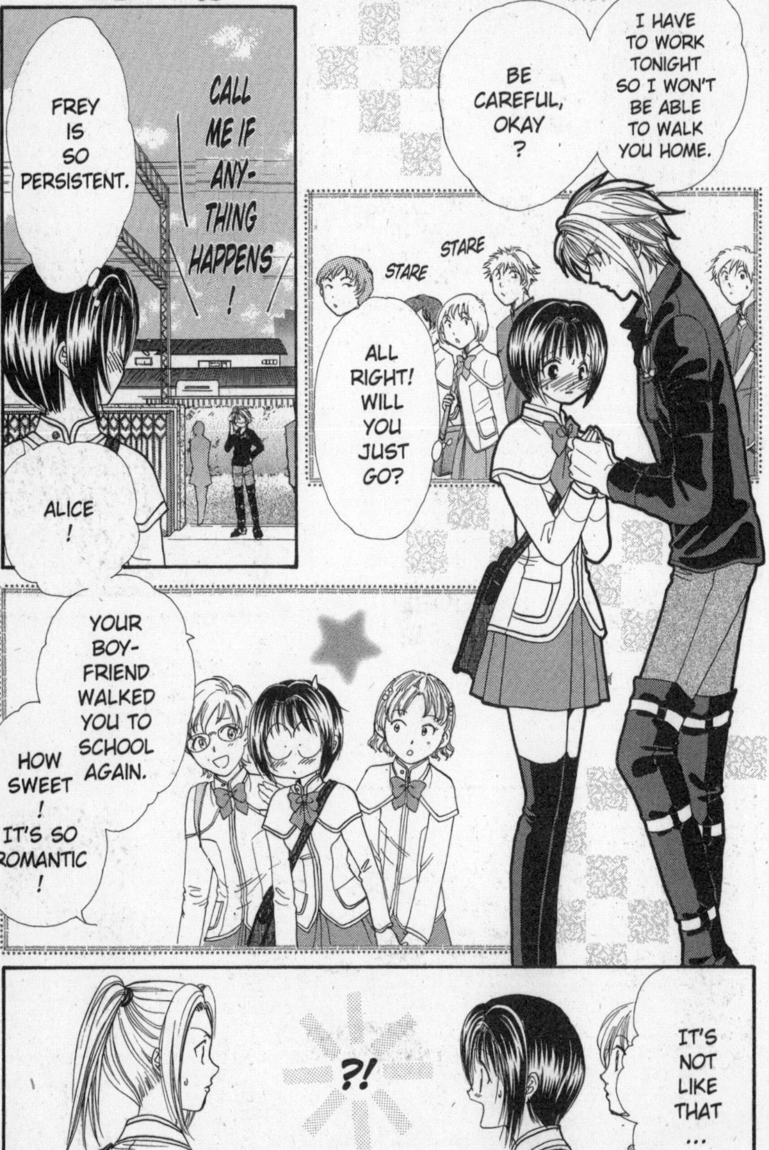
I HAVE TO WORK TONIGHT SO I WON'T BE ABLE TO WALK YOU HOME.
BE CAREFUL, OKAY?
STARE
STARE
ALL RIGHT! WILL YOU JUST GO?
CALL ME IF ANYTHING HAPPENS!
FREY IS SO PERSISTENT.
ALICE!
YOUR BOYFRIEND WALKED YOU TO SCHOOL AGAIN.
HOW SWEET! IT'S SO ROMANTIC!
IT'S NOT LIKE THAT...
?!

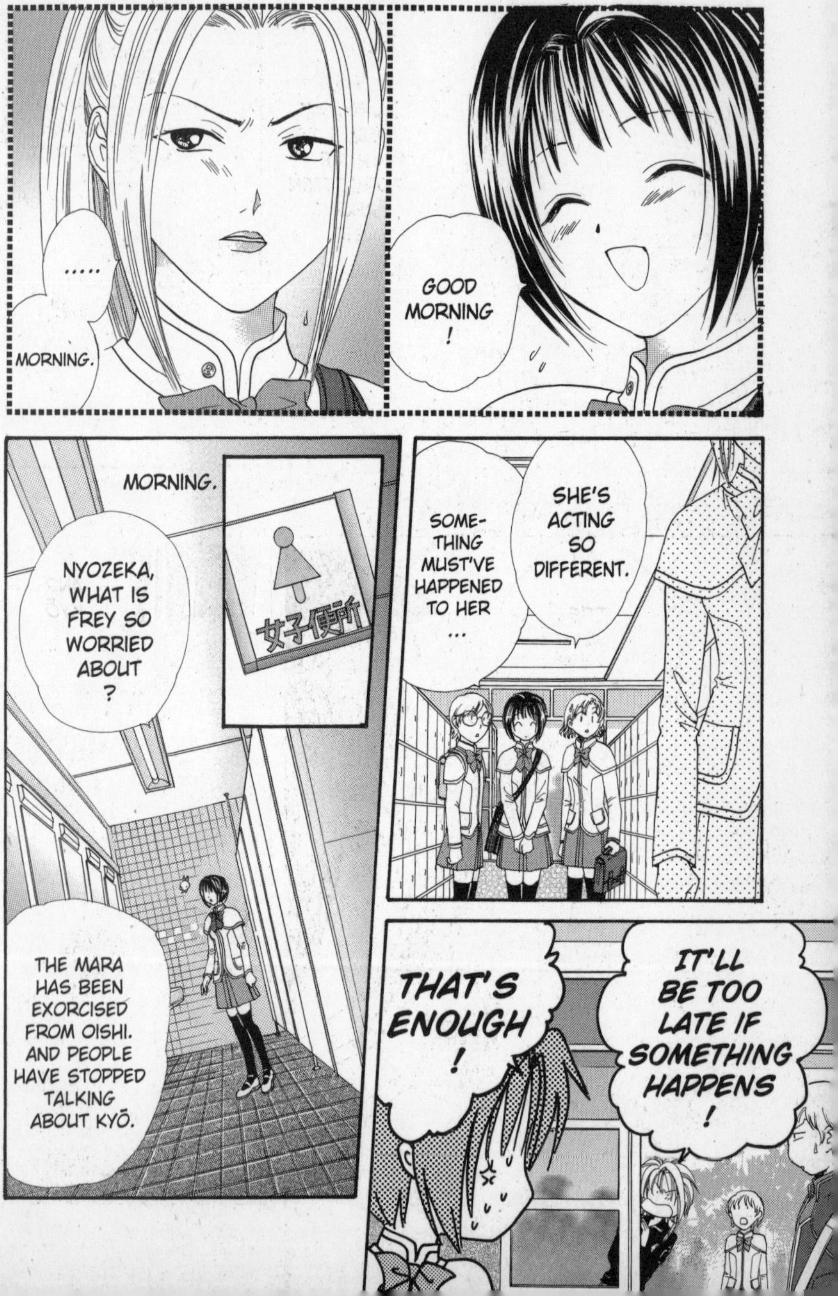
GOOD MORNING!
.....
MORNING.
SHE'S ACTING SO DIFFERENT.
SOMETHING MUST'VE HAPPENED TO HER ...
IT'LL BE TOO LATE IF SOMETHING HAPPENS!
THAT'S ENOUGH!
MORNING.
女子便所
NYOZEKA, WHAT IS FREY SO WORRIED ABOUT?
THE MARA HAS BEEN EXORCISED FROM OISHI. AND PEOPLE HAVE STOPPED TALKING ABOUT KYŌ.

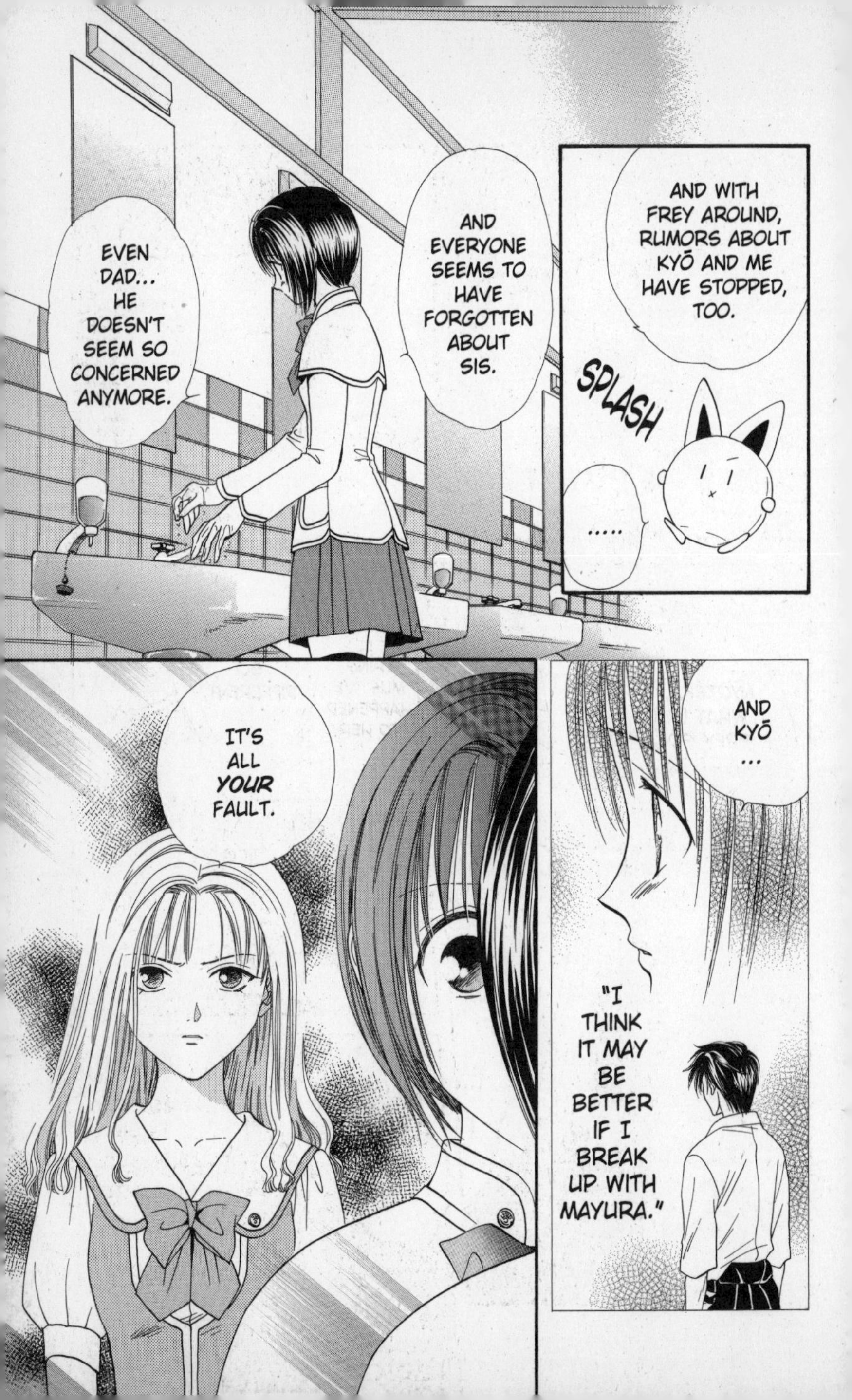
AND WITH FREY AROUND, RUMORS ABOUT KYŌ AND ME HAVE STOPPED, TOO.
SPLASH
.....
AND EVERYONE SEEMS TO HAVE FORGOTTEN ABOUT SIS.
EVEN DAD... HE DOESN'T SEEM SO CONCERNED ANYMORE.
AND KYŌ ...
"I THINK IT MAY BE BETTER IF I BREAK UP WITH MAYURA."
IT'S ALL *YOUR* FAULT.

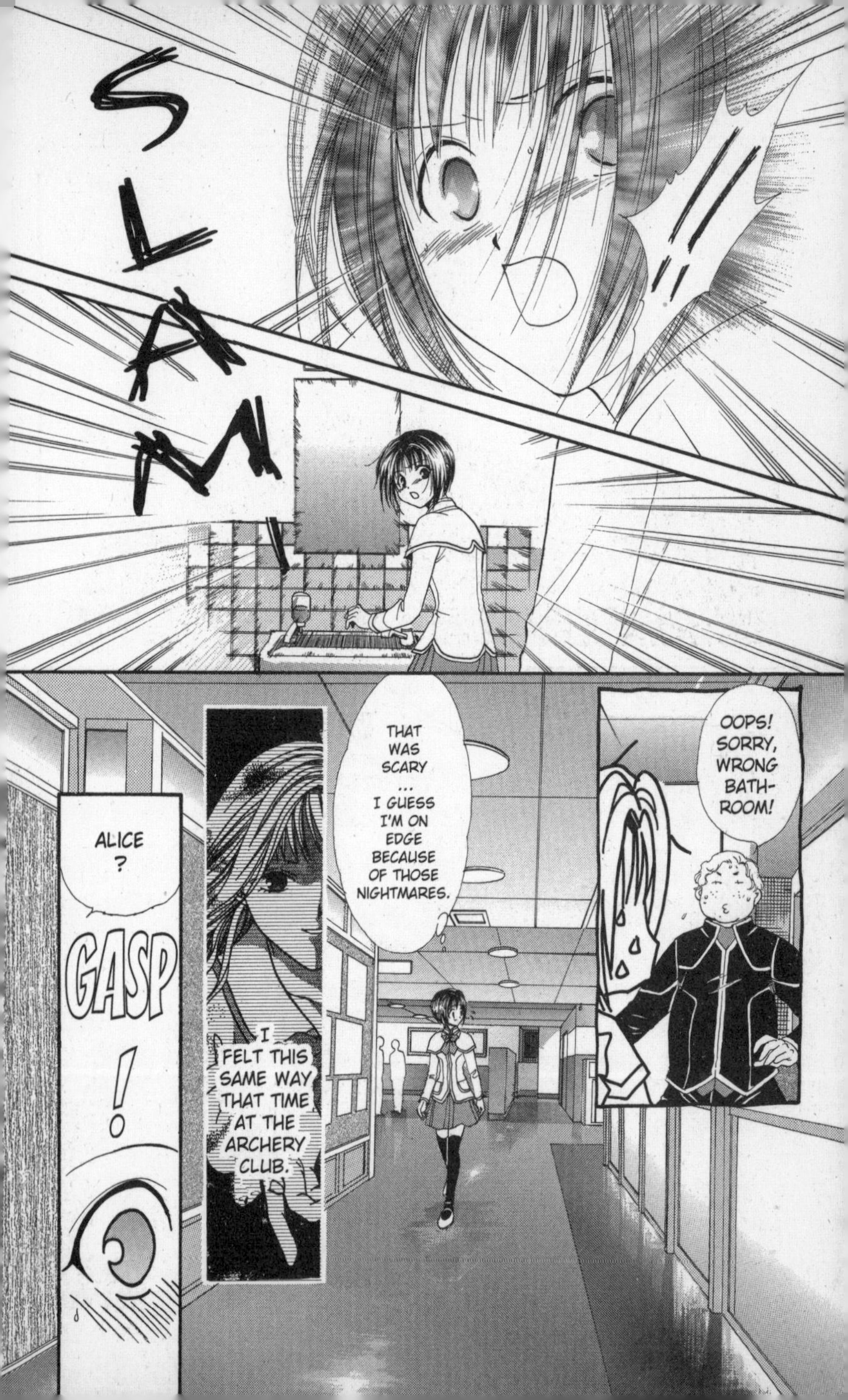
SLAM
!!
OOPS! SORRY, WRONG BATH-ROOM!
THAT WAS SCARY ... I GUESS I'M ON EDGE BECAUSE OF THOSE NIGHTMARES.
I FELT THIS SAME WAY THAT TIME AT THE ARCHERY CLUB.
ALICE ?
GASP
!

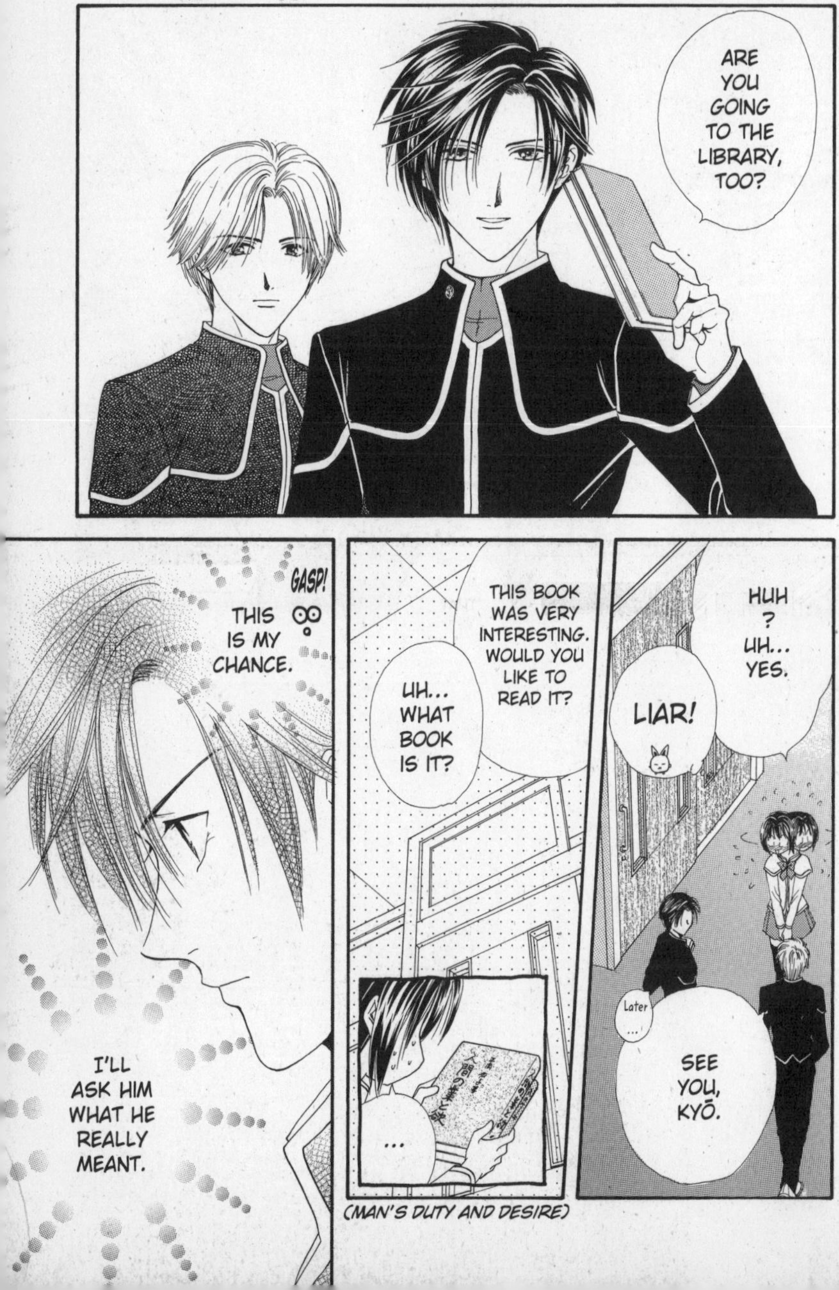
ARE YOU GOING TO THE LIBRARY, TOO?
HUH? UH... YES.
LIAR!
SEE YOU, KYŌ.
Later...
THIS BOOK WAS VERY INTERESTING. WOULD YOU LIKE TO READ IT?
UH... WHAT BOOK IS IT?
...
(MAN'S DUTY AND DESIRE)
GASP!
THIS IS MY CHANCE.
I'LL ASK HIM WHAT HE REALLY MEANT.

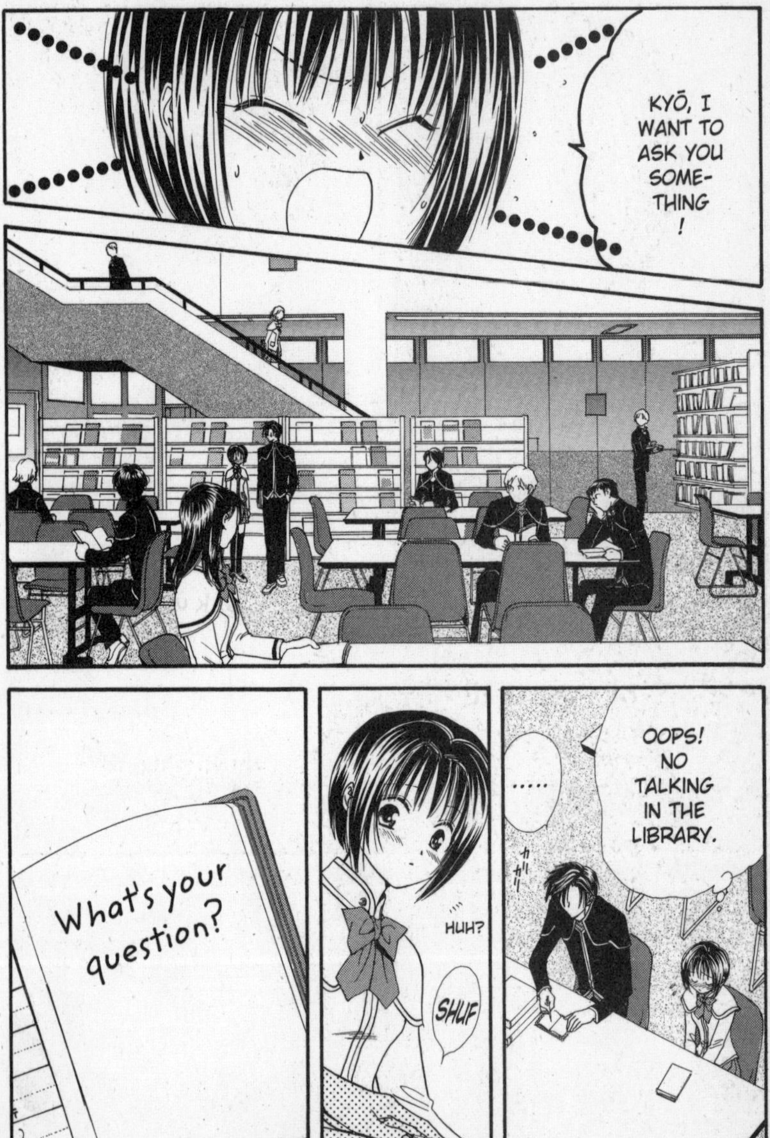
KYŌ, I WANT TO ASK YOU SOME-THING !
OOPS! NO TALKING IN THE LIBRARY.
.....
HUH?
SHUF
What's your question?

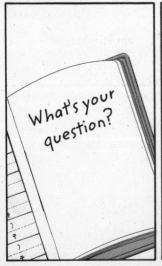

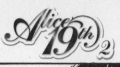

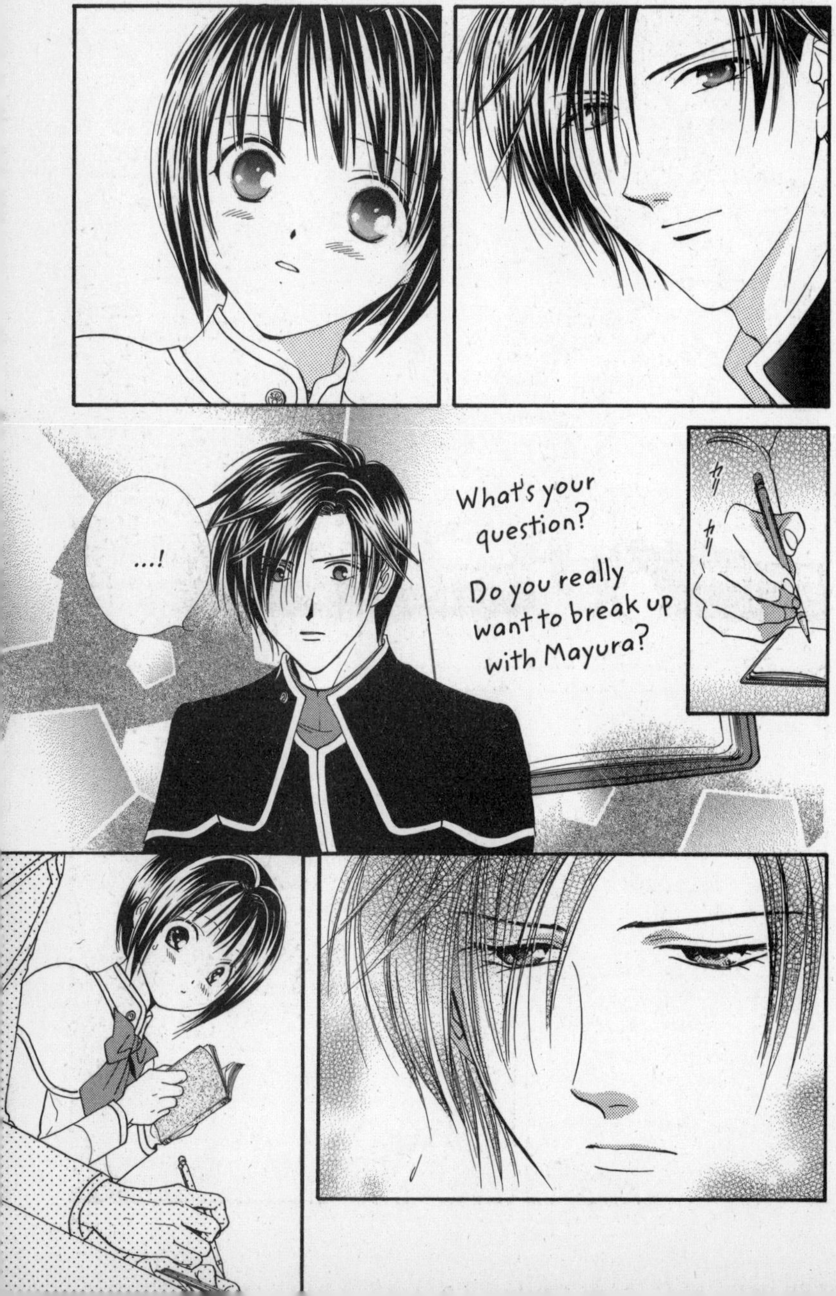
What's your question?
Do you really want to break up with Mayura?
...!

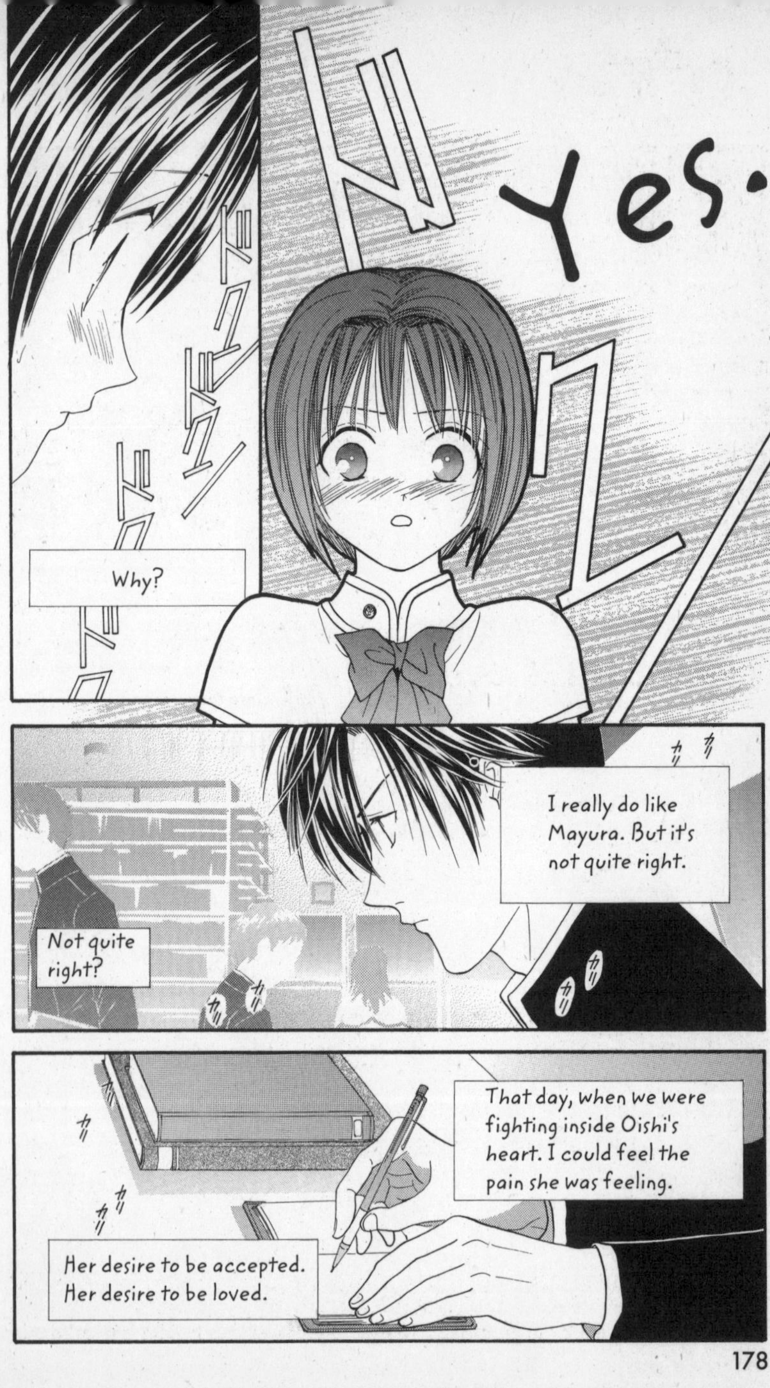
Yes.
Why?
I really do like Mayura. But it's not quite right.
Not quite right?
That day, when we were fighting inside Oishi's heart. I could feel the pain she was feeling.
Her desire to be accepted. Her desire to be loved.

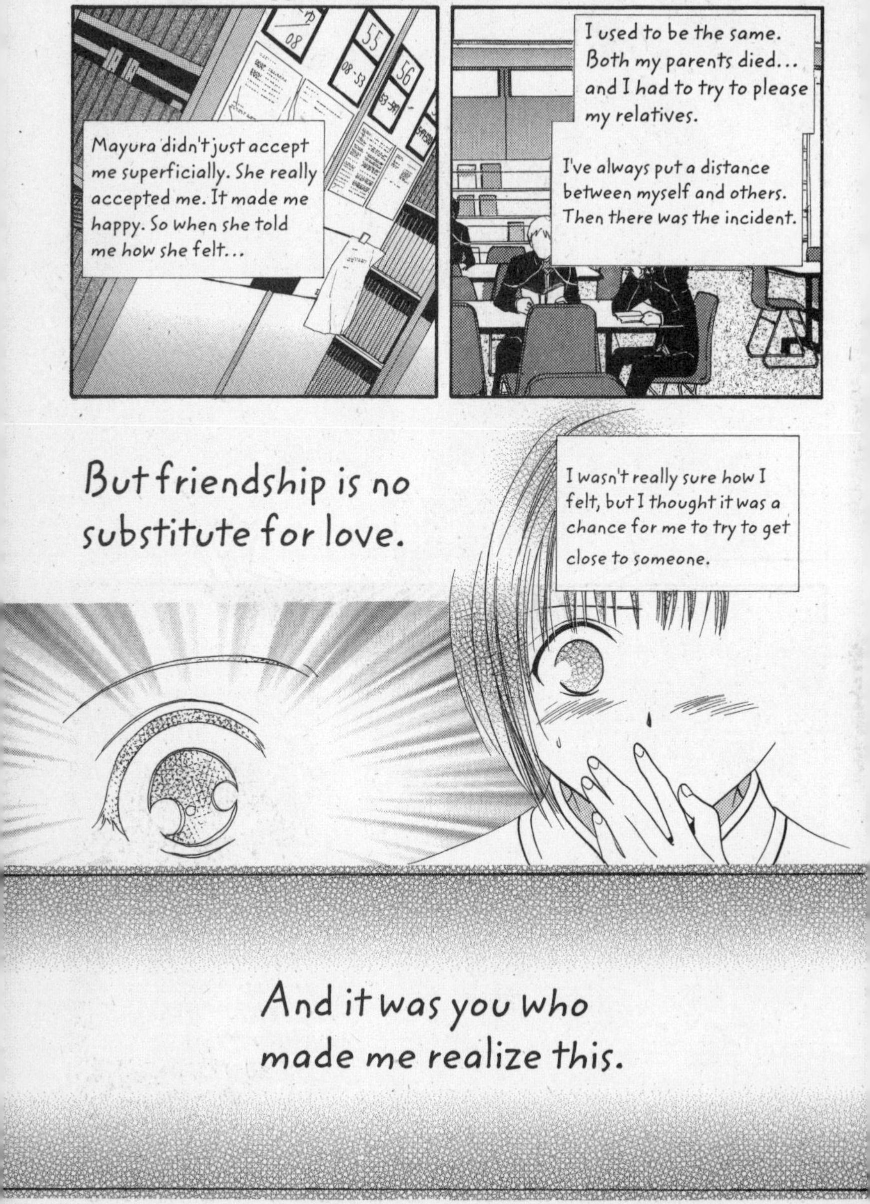
I used to be the same. Both my parents died... and I had to try to please my relatives.
I've always put a distance between myself and others. Then there was the incident.
Mayura didn't just accept me superficially. She really accepted me. It made me happy. So when she told me how she felt...
I wasn't really sure how I felt, but I thought it was a chance for me to try to get close to someone.
But friendship is no substitute for love.
And it was you who made me realize this.

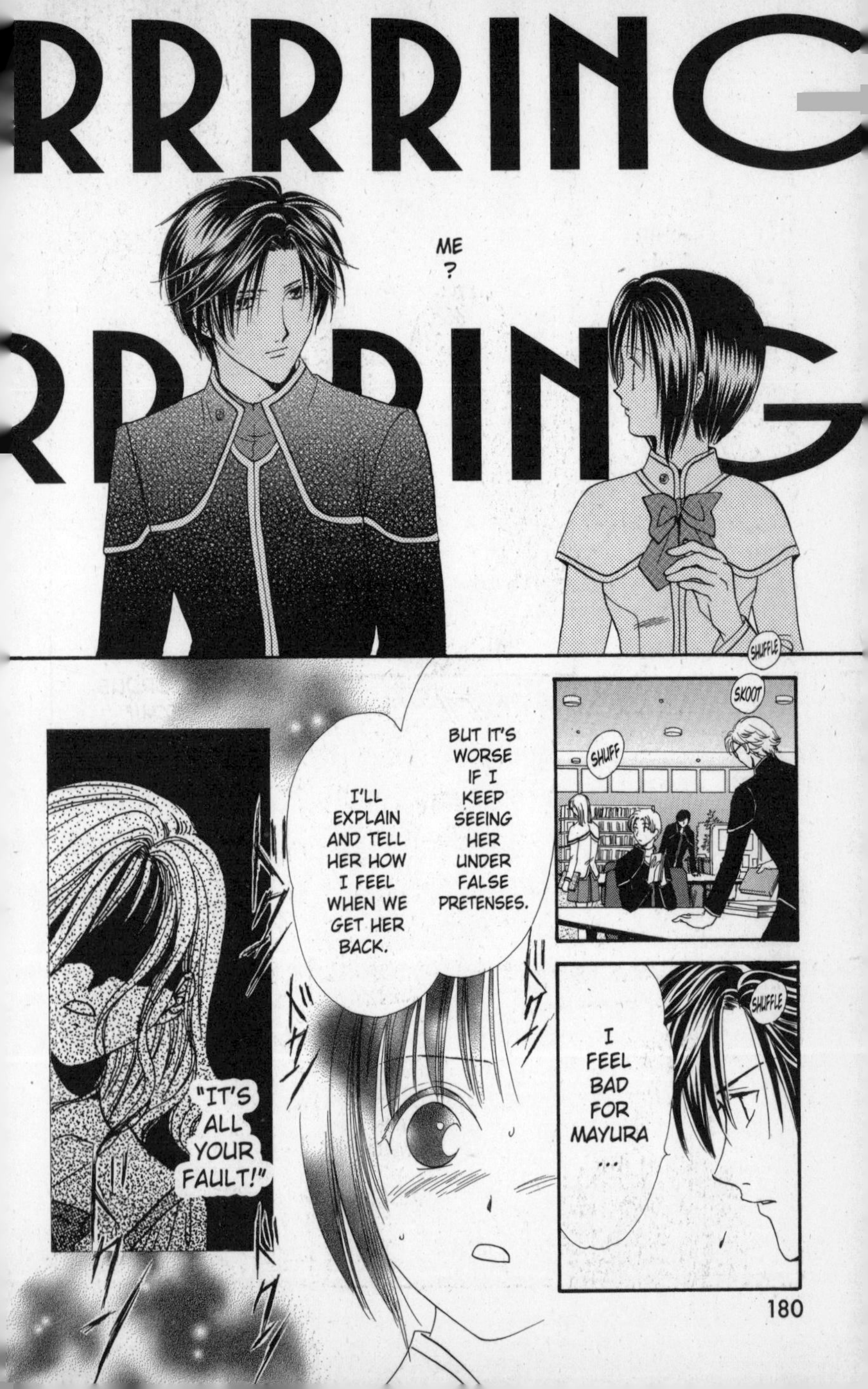
RRRRING
RRRRING
ME ?
SHUFFLE
SKOOT
SHUFF
SHUFFLE
I FEEL BAD FOR MAYURA ...
BUT IT'S WORSE IF I KEEP SEEING HER UNDER FALSE PRETENSES.
I'LL EXPLAIN AND TELL HER HOW I FEEL WHEN WE GET HER BACK.
"IT'S ALL YOUR FAULT!"

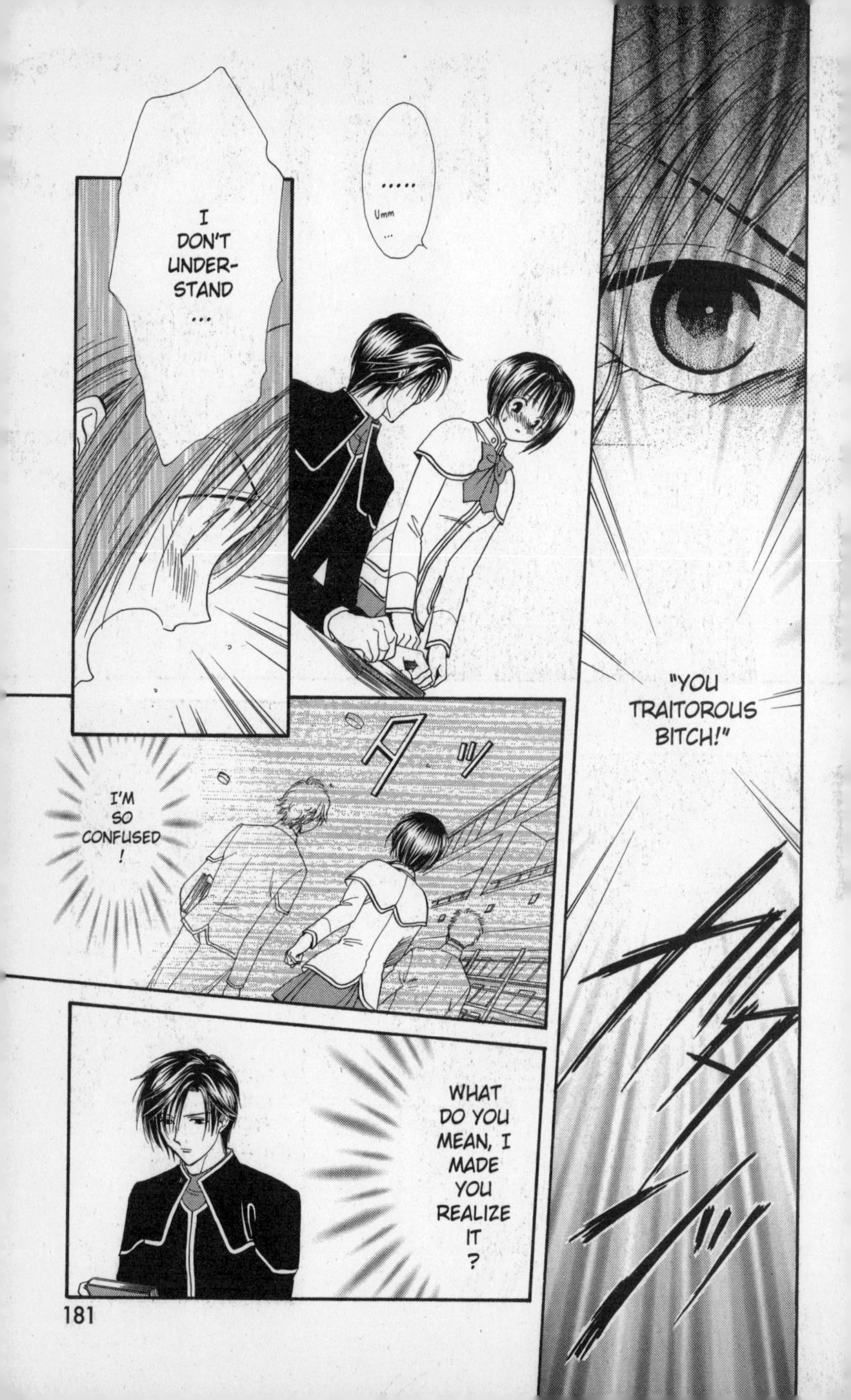
"YOU TRAITOROUS BITCH!"
...... Umm ...
I DON'T UNDER-STAND ...
I'M SO CONFUSED!
WHAT DO YOU MEAN, I MADE YOU REALIZE IT?

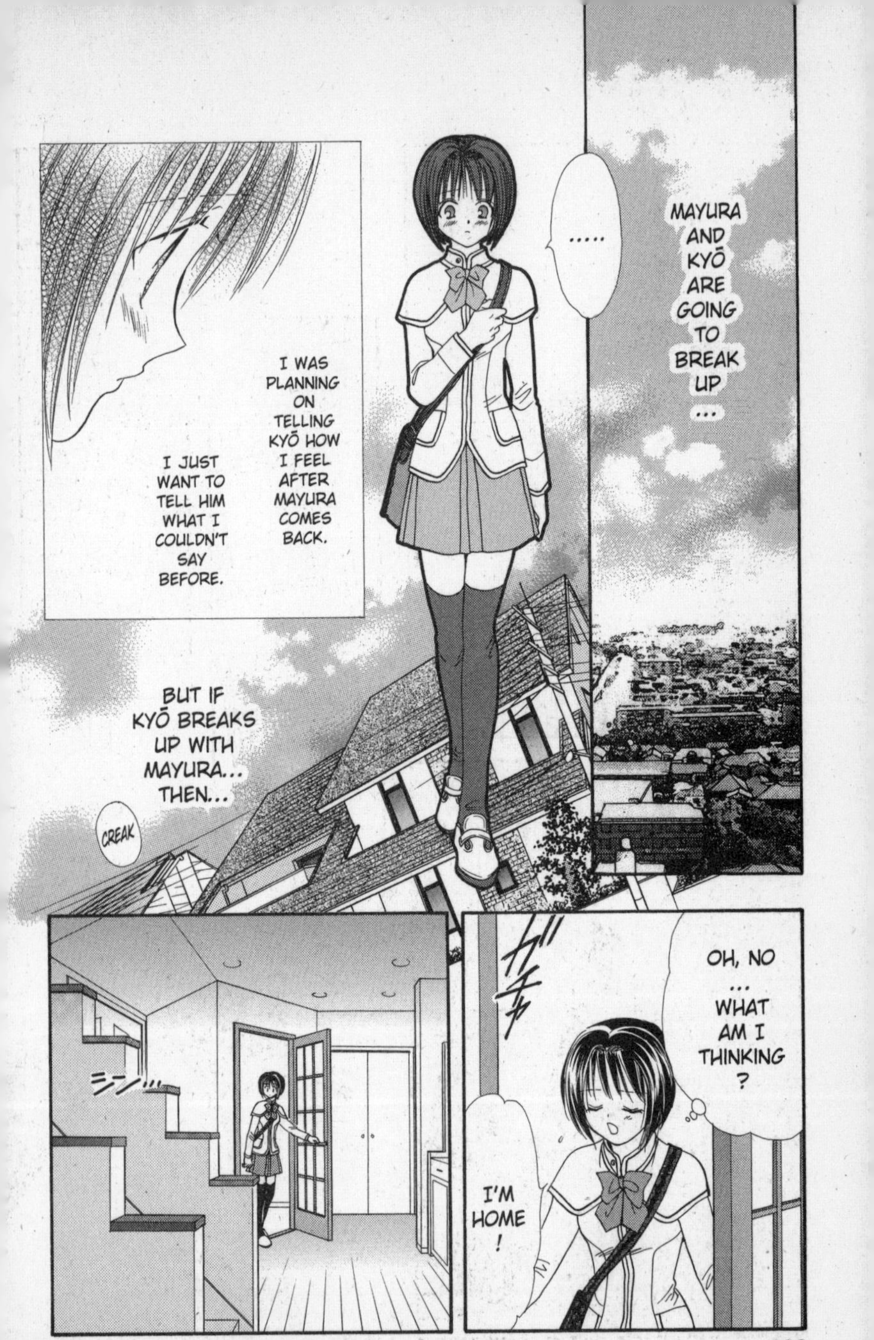
MAYURA AND KYŌ ARE GOING TO BREAK UP ...
.....
I WAS PLANNING ON TELLING KYŌ HOW I FEEL AFTER MAYURA COMES BACK.
I JUST WANT TO TELL HIM WHAT I COULDN'T SAY BEFORE.
BUT IF KYŌ BREAKS UP WITH MAYURA... THEN...
CREAK
ガチャ
OH, NO ... WHAT AM I THINKING ?
I'M HOME !
シーン…

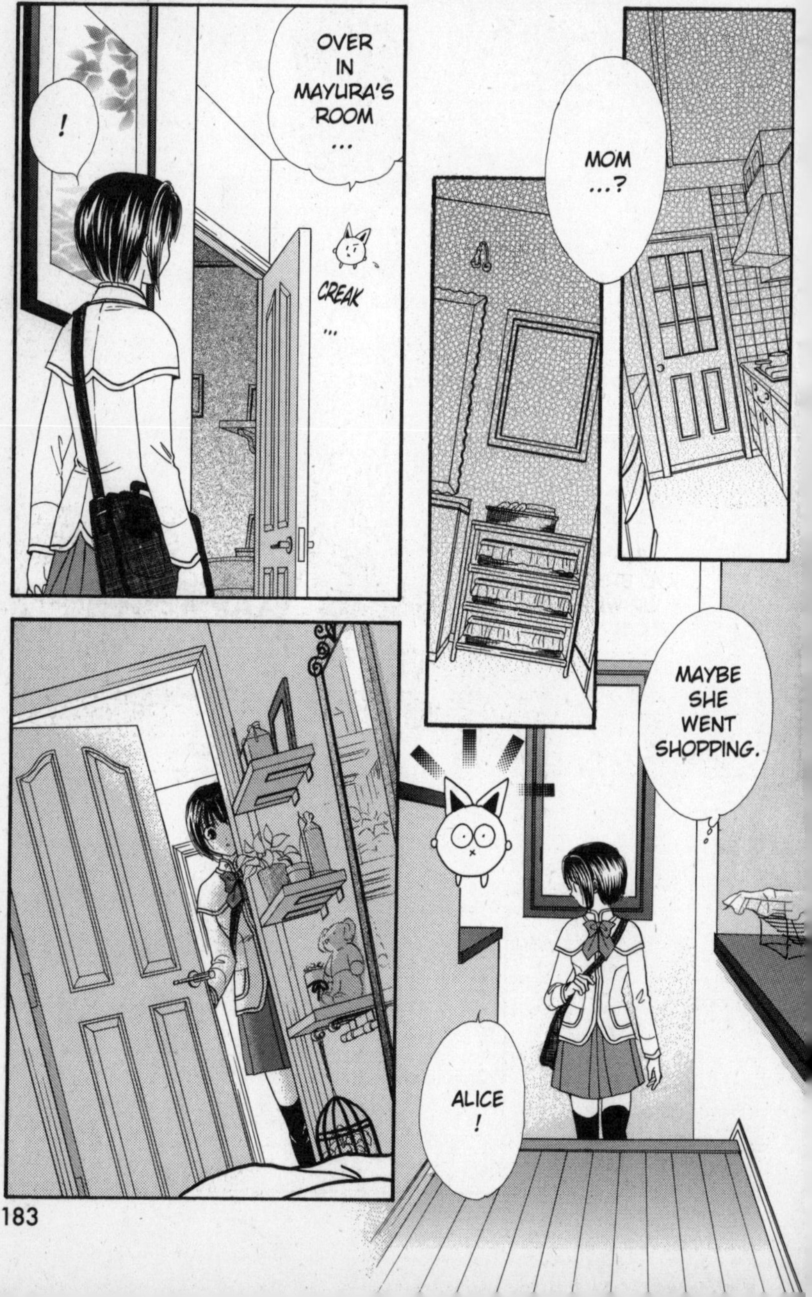
MOM ...?
MAYBE SHE WENT SHOPPING.
ALICE !
OVER IN MAYURA'S ROOM ...
!
CREAK ...

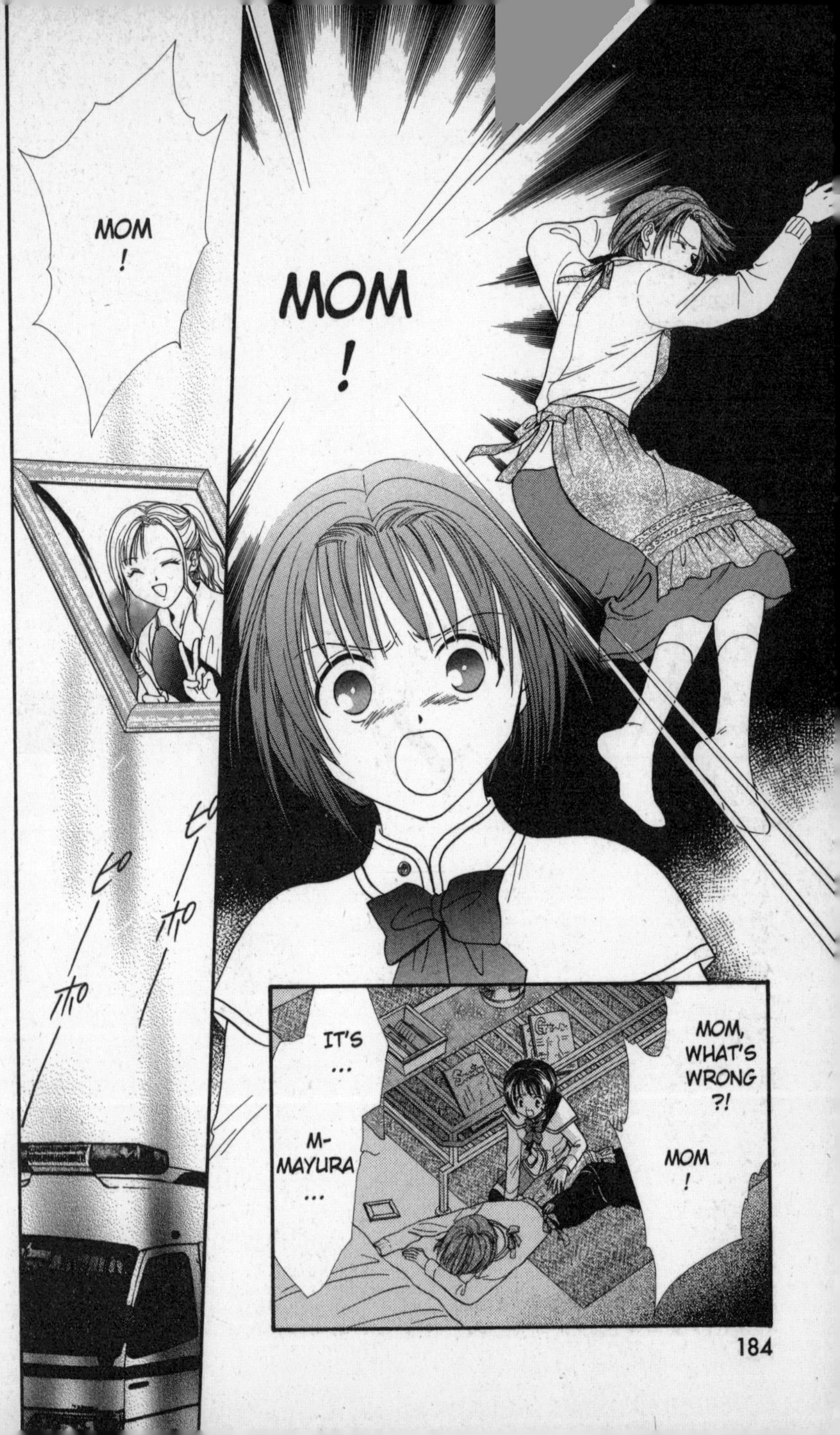
MOM !
MOM, WHAT'S WRONG ?!
MOM !
IT'S ...
M-MAYURA ...
MOM !

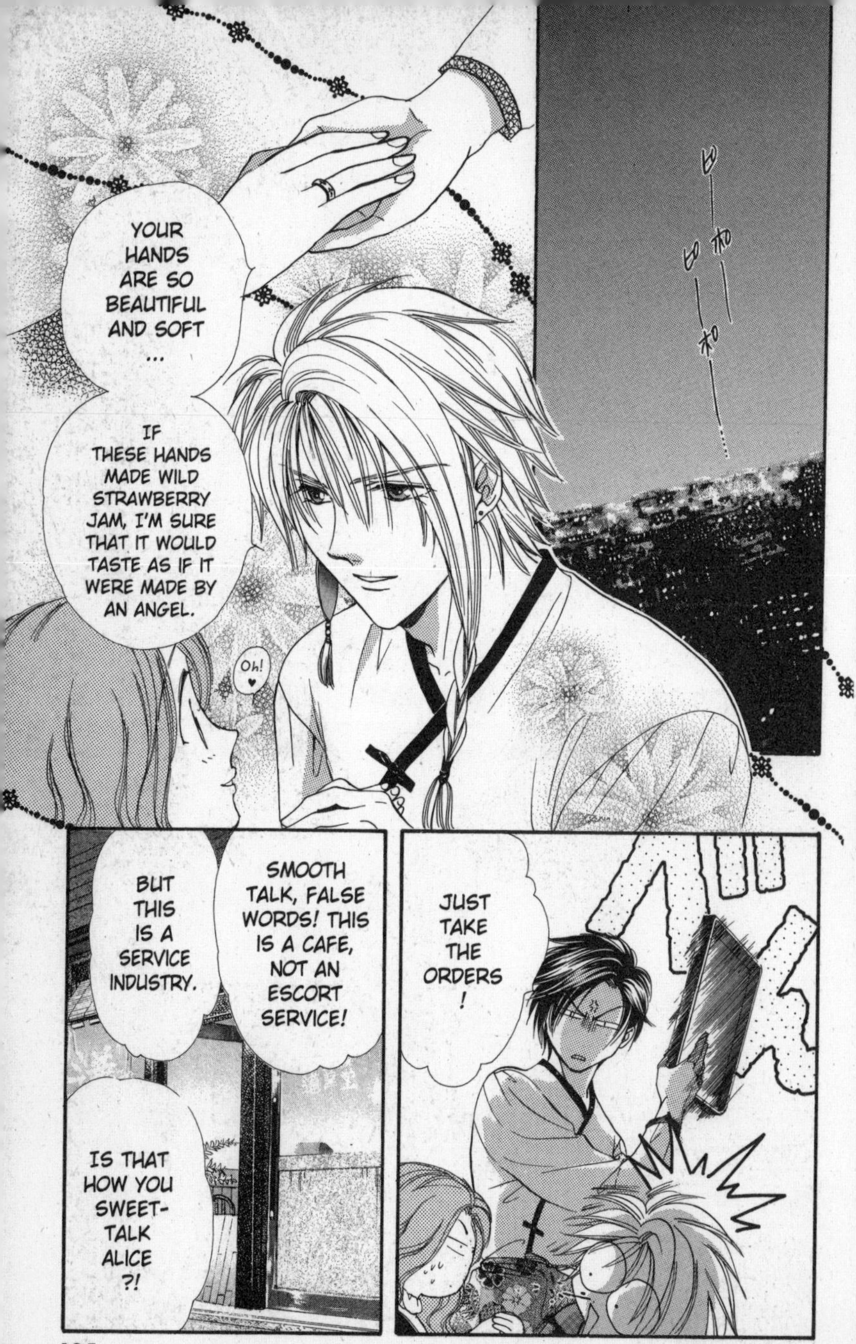
YOUR HANDS ARE SO BEAUTIFUL AND SOFT ...
IF THESE HANDS MADE WILD STRAWBERRY JAM, I'M SURE THAT IT WOULD TASTE AS IF IT WERE MADE BY AN ANGEL.
Oh! ♥
JUST TAKE THE ORDERS!
SMOOTH TALK, FALSE WORDS! THIS IS A CAFE, NOT AN ESCORT SERVICE!
BUT THIS IS A SERVICE INDUSTRY.
IS THAT HOW YOU SWEET-TALK ALICE?!

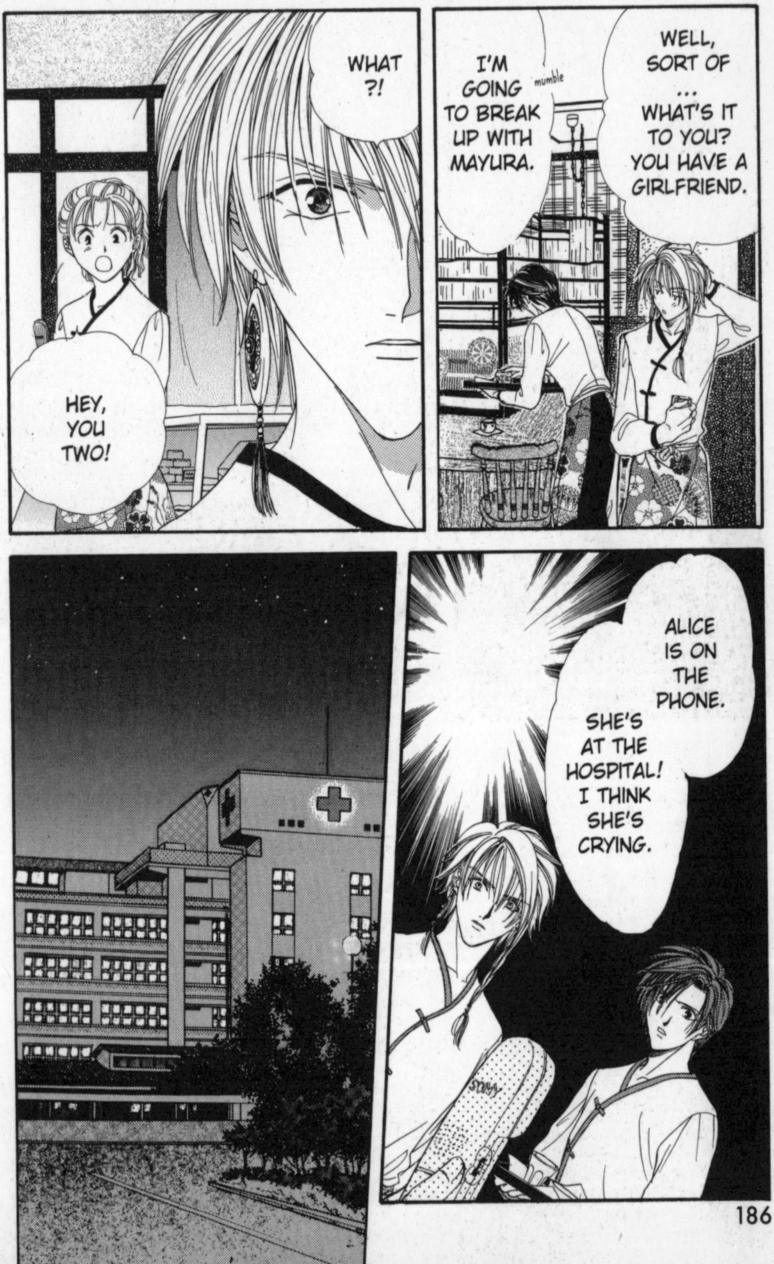
WELL, SORT OF ... WHAT'S IT TO YOU? YOU HAVE A GIRLFRIEND.
mumble
I'M GOING TO BREAK UP WITH MAYURA.
WHAT ?!
HEY, YOU TWO!
ALICE IS ON THE PHONE.
SHE'S AT THE HOSPITAL! I THINK SHE'S CRYING.

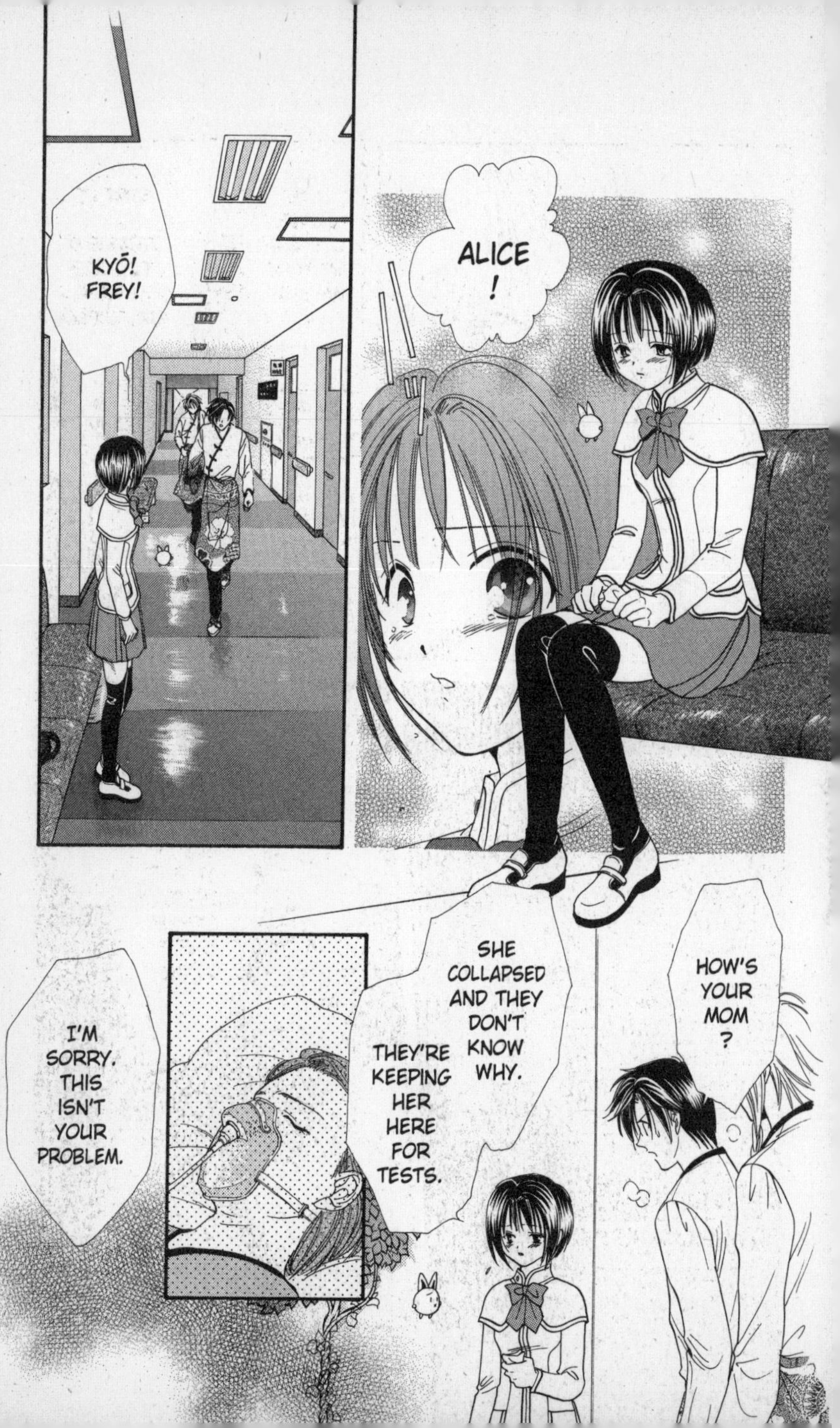
ALICE!
KYŌ! FREY!
HOW'S YOUR MOM?
SHE COLLAPSED AND THEY DON'T KNOW WHY.
THEY'RE KEEPING HER HERE FOR TESTS.
I'M SORRY. THIS ISN'T YOUR PROBLEM.

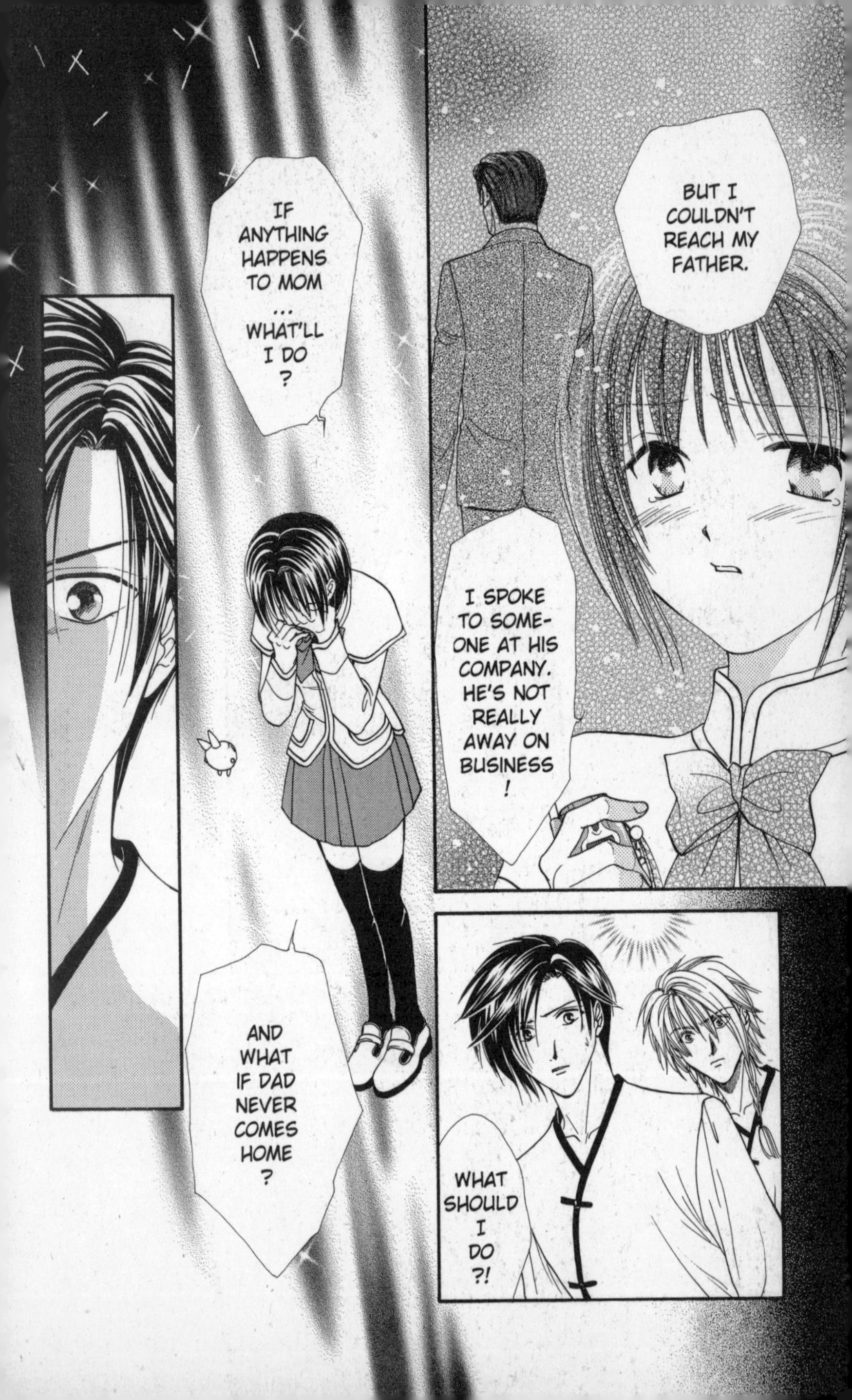
BUT I COULDN'T REACH MY FATHER.
I SPOKE TO SOME-ONE AT HIS COMPANY. HE'S NOT REALLY AWAY ON BUSINESS!
WHAT SHOULD I DO?!
IF ANYTHING HAPPENS TO MOM ... WHAT'LL I DO?
AND WHAT IF DAD NEVER COMES HOME?

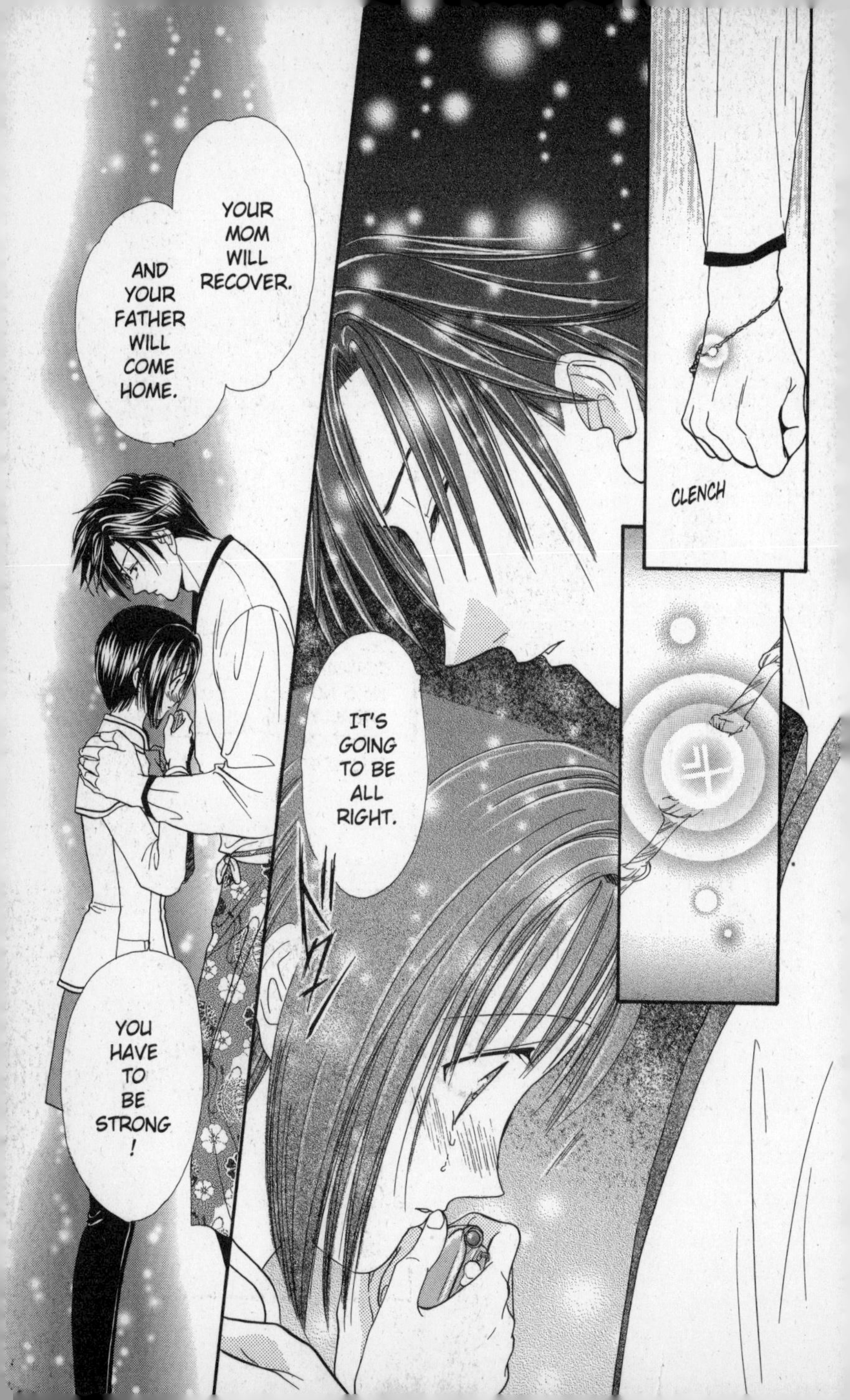
CLENCH
IT'S GOING TO BE ALL RIGHT.
YOUR MOM WILL RECOVER.
AND YOUR FATHER WILL COME HOME.
YOU HAVE TO BE STRONG!

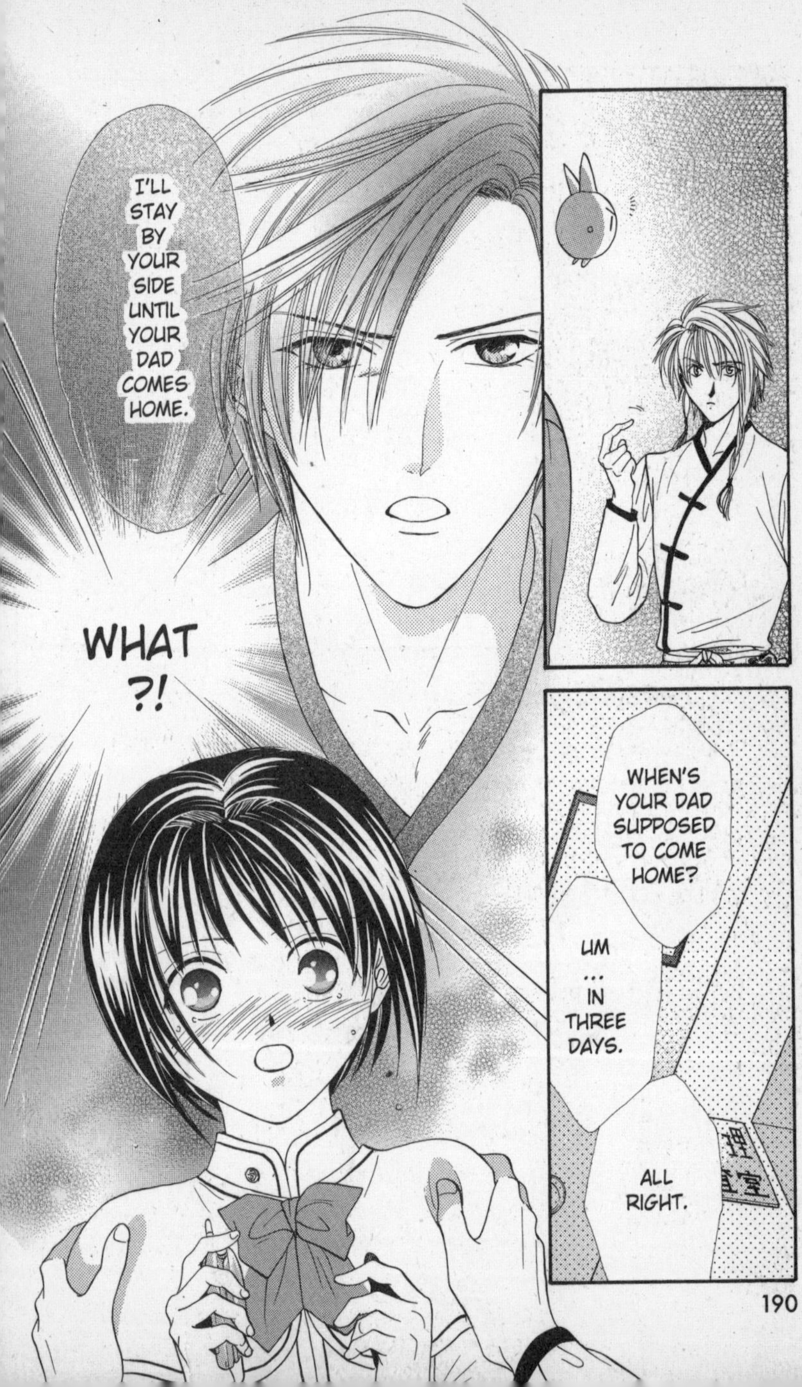
WHEN'S YOUR DAD SUPPOSED TO COME HOME?
UM ... IN THREE DAYS.
ALL RIGHT.
I'LL STAY BY YOUR SIDE UNTIL YOUR DAD COMES HOME.
WHAT ?!

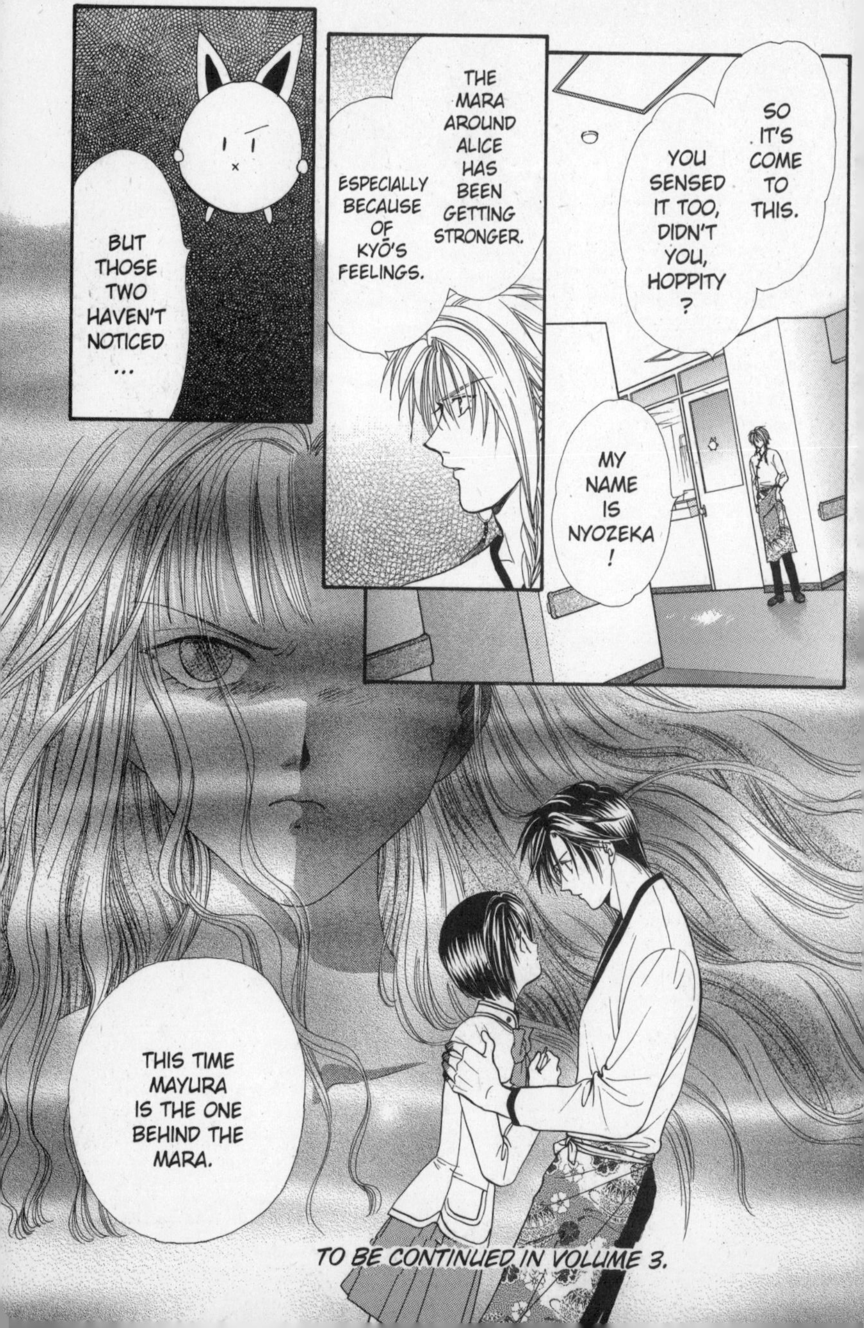
SO IT'S COME TO THIS.
YOU SENSED IT TOO, DIDN'T YOU, HOPPITY?
MY NAME IS NYOZEKA!
THE MARA AROUND ALICE HAS BEEN GETTING STRONGER.
ESPECIALLY BECAUSE OF KYŌ'S FEELINGS.
BUT THOSE TWO HAVEN'T NOTICED...
THIS TIME MAYURA IS THE ONE BEHIND THE MARA.
TO BE CONTINUED IN VOLUME 3.

About the Author:

Yuu Watase was born on March 5 in a town near Osaka, and she was raised there before moving to Tokyo to follow her dream of creating manga. In the decade since her debut short story, *PAJAMA DE OJAMA* ("An Intrusion in Pajamas"), she has produced more than 50 compiled volumes of short stories and continuing series. Perhaps most well known for her smash-hit fantasy/romance stories *FUSHIGI YÛGI: THE MYSTERIOUS PLAY* and *CERES CELESTIAL LEGEND*, her latest work, *APPARE JIPANGU*, is set in the Edo Period and is about a girl who cures people of their sadness. It is currently being serialized in SHÔJO COMIC.

If you enjoyed this manga, then you won't want to miss these other titles by the same author!

Fushigi Yûgi: A girl from modern times is magically transported to the Universe of the Four Gods—a mag-

©1992 Yuu WATASE / Shogakukan Inc.

ical world based on ancient Chinese legend. Another fantasy love triangle extravaganza brought to you by Yuu Watase! More hunky male characters, more of Yuu Watase's great artwork, and another intense story-line!

Ceres Celestial Legend: Aya Mikage thinks she's

©1997 Yuu WATASE / Shogakukan Inc.

just a normal girl in high school until she discovers that she can transform into a vastly powerful "celestial maiden" named Ceres.... But Ceres has a vendetta against Aya's family and is out for revenge! And because of the manifestation of Ceres, Aya's own family is out to kill her!

Glossary of Sound Effects, Signs, and other Miscellaneous Notes

Each entry includes: the location, indicated by page number and panel number (so 3.1 means page 3, panel number 1); the phonetic romanization of the original Japanese; and our English "translation"–we offer as close an English equivalent as we can.

3.4——FX: Don! (bash!)

5.1——FX: Zuka zuka (clomp clomp)

5.3——FX: Jii (stare)

5.4——FX: Gashi! (grab!)

5.5——FX: Hyoi (swoop!)

6.1——FX: Da! (zoom!)

6.3——FX: Ban! (slam!)

6.4——sign: Toyo Kotsu (Toyo Transport Co.)

8.3——FX: Za (change of scene)

8.5——FX: Pin (looking aside)

8.6——FX: Kuru (turning around)

9.1——FX: Pa! (pop!)

9.3——FX: Pote (landing on head)

10.1——FX: Jita bata (struggling)

10.2——FX: Gyu (squeeze)

10.2——FX: Wa! (ahh!)

10.3——FX: Paniku (panic)

12.1——FX: Gan! (crash! shock)

12.4——FX: Gah! (shove!)

12.2——FX: Kah! (anger)

14.1——FX: Kuru (turn)

16.2——FX: Go! (wham!)

17.4——FX: Hyuo! (fwoom! suddenly appears)

17.5——FX: Kaaa... (vwoosh)

18.4——FX: Doki doki doki! (ba-bump ba-bump)

20.5——FX: Kiri (hard look)

22.3——FX: Zun! (shock!)

23.1——FX: Yoro (wobble)

23.3——FX: Za! (voom!)

23.1——FX: Ka! (flash)

24.1——FX: Fu (unh)

25.1——FX: Zo zo (bloop bloop)

25.2——FX: Za! (shock!)

26.1——FX: Don! (blam!)

26.3——FX: Go! (roar)

27.1——FX: Bohyu! (ba-blam!)

27.2——FX: Chira (glance)

27.4——FX: Fuon! (fwoom!)

28.1——FX: Hyu! (whoosh)

28.2——FX: Fuwa (softly enclosed)

29.4——FX: Ha! (gasp!)

32.5——FX: Ni (grin)

34.3——FX: Saa (whoosh)

41.2——FX: Chu! (smak! kiss)

43.3—FX: Don! (gah! boom)

43.5—FX: Gacha (door opening)

44.1—FX: Ban! (slam!)

44.4—FX: Sha (spray)

47.4—FX: Pan pan (clap clap)

47.5—Sign: Akatsuki Shiritsu Meido Gakuen (name of high school)

49.2—FX: Ta! (turn)

51.3—FX: Assari (just like that!)

53.3—FX: Kin kon kan kon (school bell)

54.1—FX: Basa! (whap!)

54.3—FX: Basa (rustle, book falls)

55.5—FX: Bashi! (whap!)

57.2—FX: Pita (stop)

57.3—FX: Funya (whooah!)

58.5—FX: Nugi! (whisk)

62.1—FX: Kan kon (school bell)

63.1—FX: Pisha (click, door shuts)

63.5—FX: Su! (moving in closer)

65.2—FX: Ha (gasp)

65.3—FX: Ba! (push!)

67.2—FX: Zawa! (mood change)

71.1—FX: Zawa zawa (crowd chatter)

72.1—FX: Ku! (step)

72.5—FX: Su (pass by)

73.3—FX: Kan kon (school bell)

73.4—FX: Zun! (gloom)

75.1—FX: Ki! (hard stare)

76.5—FX: Gyumumu (wrench)

79.4—FX: Koso (sneak)

80.6—FX: Su (pass)

83.4—FX: Ha (small gasp)

86.2—FX: Supan! (thok!)

86.3—FX: Kiri kiri kiri... (bowstring stretching)

88.2—FX: Gah! (grab!)

88.3—FX: Baki! (crack!)

88.4—FX: Ga! Dosu! (pow! bash!)

89.1—FX: Yoro (feeling unsteady)

89.2—FX: Gya ha ha ha (ha ha ha)

89.3—FX: Ga! (trip!)

90.4—FX: Doka! (kick)

90.4—FX: Ga! (kick)

91.1—FX: Ga! (wham)

92.1—sign: Akatsuki Shiritsu Meido Gakuen (name of high school)

92.4—sign: Kyudojo (archery Club)

92.5—FX: Doka! (thud)

100.2—FX: Ha! (shock)

101.5—FX: Su (soft light touch)

102.1—FX: Bwa (darkness enveloping)

103.4—FX: Ha! (surprise)

130.3 —FX: Dokin Dokin Dokin (heartbeats)

131.1 —FX: Dokin Dokin (heartbeats)

131.2 —FX: Dokin Dokin (heartbeats)

134.2 —FX: Zawa! (rustle of branches)

135.1 —FX: Go! (loud roar)

136.1 —FX: Zuzuzu… (slide)

136.3 —FX: Gui! (grab)

136.4 —FX: Ba! (fwoosh)

137.2 —FX: Doki-doki-doki (rapid heartbeat)

139.1 —FX: Kuru! (quick turn)

140.3 —FX: Gacha (door opening)

140.4 —FX: Batan! (slam)

141.3 —FX: Batan! (door slamming)

142.1 —FX: Fuwa (fwom)

142.1 —FX: Ha (surprise)

142.4 —FX: Su (fading away)

146.1 —FX: Gacha! (door opening)

146.1 —FX: Wan! (whoosh)

148.2 —FX: Su! (quick turnaround)

148.3 —FX: Su! (hand on wall)

149.2 —FX: Ka! (sparkle)

149.4 —FX: Don! (smash)

150.1 —FX: Gara! (crumble)

150.2 —FX: Zu-zu-zu! (swoosh)

152.1 —FX: Go! (loud roar)

104.1 —FX: Zuzu (pulling)

104.2 —FX: Ba! (pulling away)

105.1 —FX: Shururu (swishing sound)

105.2 —FX: Giri
(strapping sound, like being restrained)

105.3 —FX: Giri Giri (restraints tightening)

105.4 —FX: Giri Giri (tightening)

106.1 —FX: Ba (fwoosh)

106.3 —FX: Ga (flash)

107.3 —FX: Shin (silence)

107.5 —FX: Kuru! (turning around)

109.2 —FX: Biku! (surprise)

109.3 —FX: Da (dash)

110.5 —sign: Kyudojo (archery club)

112.4 —FX: Go (roar)

113.2 —FX: Pa! (quick transformation)

118.1 —FX: Za (footsteps in sand)

118.2 —FX: Ka (sharp, dry sound)

118.3 —FX: Ka (sharp, dry sound)

118.4 —FX: Ka (sharp, dry sound)

119.2 —FX: Go (roar)

122.4 —FX: Kaa (sigh)

126.2 —FX: Doki! (heartbeat)

128.2 —FX: Za! (shuf)

129.1 —FX: Za Za (shuf shuf)

129.2 —FX: Za (shuf)

177.3—FX: Kari kari (scribbling)

178.1—FX: Doku! (heartbeat)

178.2—FX: Doku-Doku-Doku (heartbeat)

178.3—FX: Kari-kari (scribbling)

178.4—FX: Kari-kari (scribbling)

180.4—FX: Dokun dokun dokun dokun (heartbeats)

181.4—FX: Ta (walking away)

182.6—FX: Shiin! (silence)

184.3—FX: Piipo-piipo! (siren)

185.1—FX: Piipo-piipo! (siren)

187.1—FX: Ha (gasp)

189.3—FX: Dokun (heartbeat)

153.1—FX: Go (roar)

153.2—FX: Don! (roar)

155.3—FX: Zuzuzu (enveloping)

156.1—FX: Ka! (sheen!)

158.2—FX: Suuu (swoosh of bracelet)

159.3—FX: Piku (looking up)

160.4—FX: Boro-boro (tears)

161.2—FX: Su (turn)

163.4—FX: Su (walking away)

164.4—FX: Ba! (vwoosh)

165.1—FX: Bata! Bata! (struggling)

165.2—FX: Poka! (boot)

165.4—FX: Pasa! (throwing off clothes)

165.5—FX: Sha (raising blinds)

166.1—FX: Bito! (face on glass)

166.3—FX: Ban (slam)

166.4—FX: Ha-ha-ha (breathing hard)

167.4—FX: Teki-paki (briskly putting on clothes)

167.4—FX: Goshi-goshi (rubbing fur)

167.5—FX: Su! (turning quickly)

168.5—FX: Jaaa (water faucet)

169.1—FX: Su (quietly coming to table)

170.1—sign: Akatsuki Shiritsu Myodo Gakuen (name of high school)

172.5—sign: Joshi benjo (women's restroom)

176.3—FX: Kari-kari (scribbling)

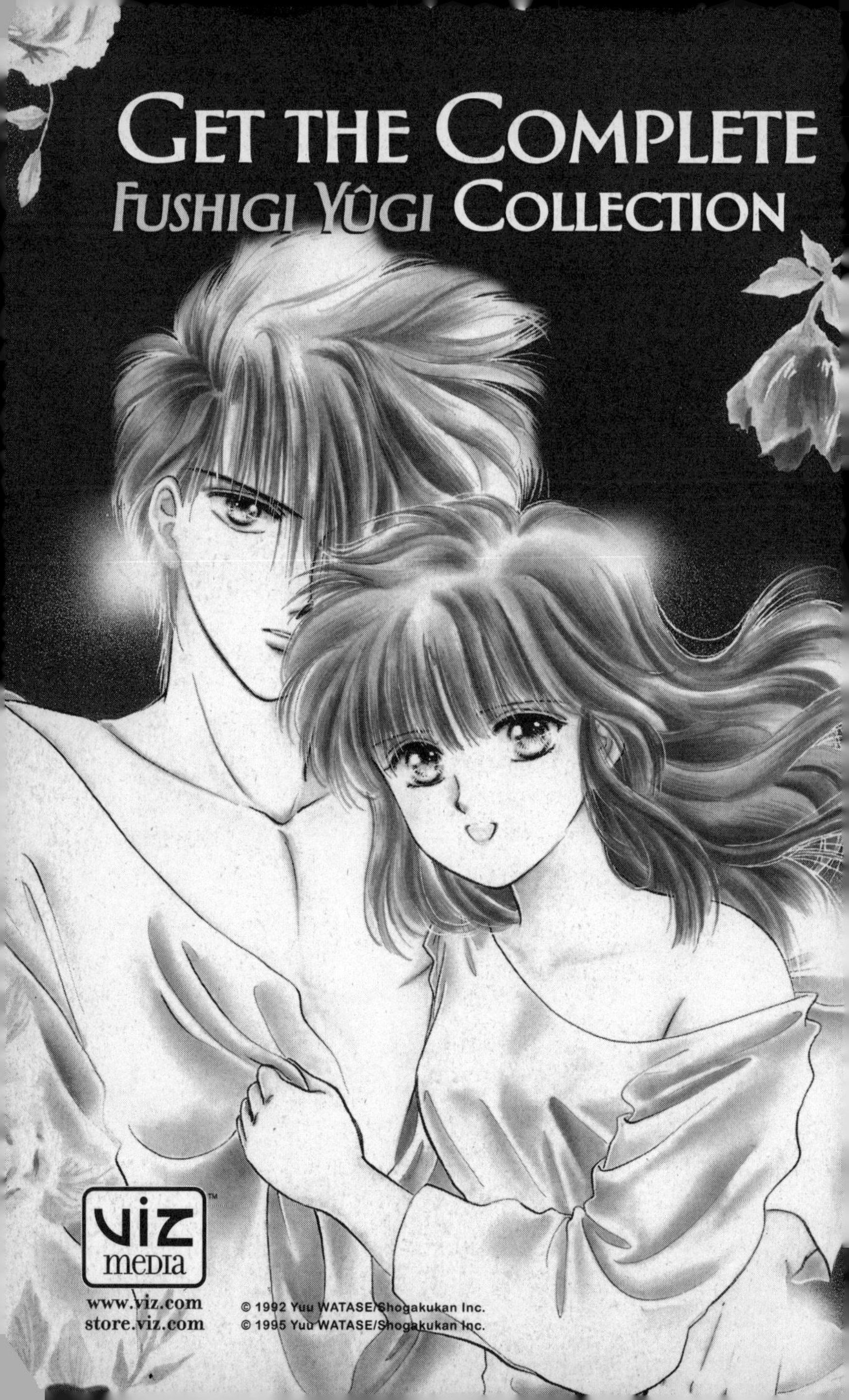
GET THE COMPLETE
FUSHIGI YÛGI COLLECTION
viz media
www.viz.com
store.viz.com
© 1992 Yuu WATASE/Shogakukan Inc.
© 1995 Yuu WATASE/Shogakukan Inc.

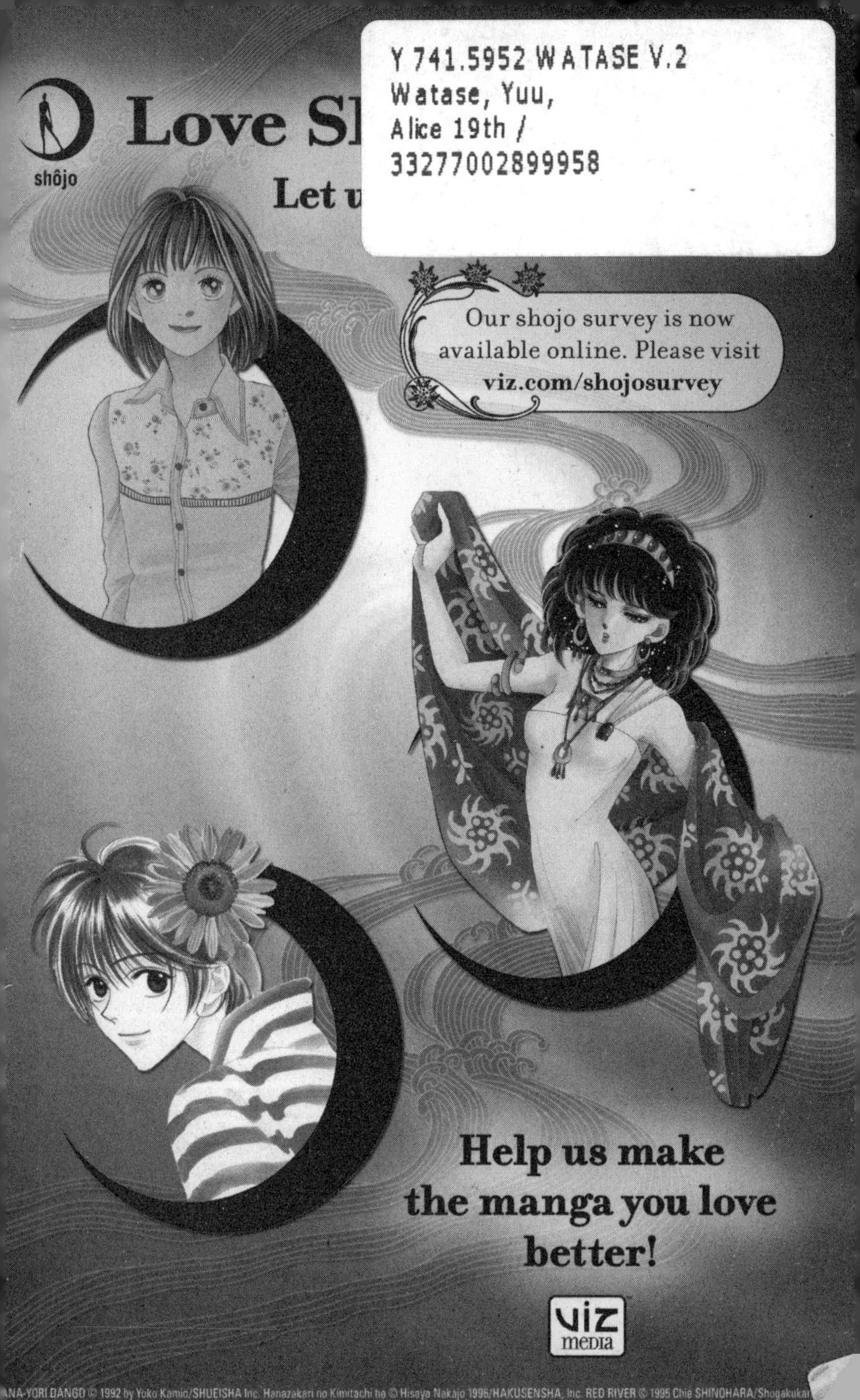
shôjo
Love Sh
Let u
Our shojo survey is now available online. Please visit viz.com/shojosurvey
Help us make the manga you love better!
VIZ media